MW00559762

Joseph Smith III

Joseph Smith III

PRAGMATIC PROPHET

Roger D. Launius

University of Illinois Press
Urbana and Chicago

This book is printed on acid-free paper.

Library of Congress Cataloging-in-Publication Data

Launius, Roger D.
  Joseph Smith III : pragmatic prophet.

  Bibliography: p.
  Includes index.
  1. Smith, Joseph, 1832–1914.   2. Mormons—United
States—Biography.   3. Reorganized Church of Jesus
Christ of Latter Day Saints—History.   4. Mormon
Church—History.   I. Title.
BX8678.S6L38   1988   289.3'33'0924   [B]   87-35724
ISBN 0-252-01514-2 (alk. paper)

to my parents

Contents

Preface

Joseph Smith III, the son of the founder of Mormonism, was one of the most interesting figures to follow the Latter Day Saint faith in the last half of the nineteenth century. Born in late 1832, as a boy Smith was taught the Mormon religion by his parents and experienced firsthand the hardships and triumphs as the movement founded a succession of settlements at Kirtland, Ohio; Independence and Far West, Missouri; and Nauvoo, Illinois. After the death of his father at the hands of a mob in Carthage, Illinois, in June 1844, Joseph Smith III witnessed the splintering of the church as several would-be prophets claimed leadership over a portion of the membership.

Brigham Young gained the presidency of the largest single element of the church and led an epic trek to the Great Basin, where it founded a powerful religious kingdom. Other factional leaders arose and flourished for a time, but in 1851 remnants from several sects coalesced to form what would become the Reorganized Church of Jesus Christ of Latter Day Saints. After repeated overtures from Reorganized Church officials and a series of experiences during the 1850s that Smith believed were divinely inspired, Joseph Smith III became prophet-president of the Reorganization on 6 April 1860.

During his fifty-four-year tenure as president, Smith built the Reorganized Church into a major Mormon faction, second only to the organization built by Brigham Young. Throughout his long presidency Smith sought to recover the lost Saints who had ventured with other leaders at the time of his father's death, to purify the church's doctrine and public image of what he considered errors in the movement, and to erect a strong organization that would be capable of guiding the Saints toward the Christianization of the world and the establishment of the kingdom of God on earth. By the time of his death in December 1914 Smith was satisfied that he had set the movement on the proper course toward the accomplishment of these objectives, ever mindful that the journey had only begun. It would be years, perhaps centuries, before the movement would attain these lofty ideals, Smith noted, but if the Saints persisted, victory would be assured. In beginning this epic trek, Smith had assisted in the antipolygamy struggle, overseen the conversion of hundreds of Utah Mormons to his church, and erected a bureaucracy that would continue to provide effective leadership to the Saints after his death.

Joseph Smith III has enjoyed a positive public image since his death. Considered a great religious teacher, prophet, and lawgiver, Joseph has been accorded a veneration and respect few others within the Latter Day Saint movement have enjoyed. Smith was indeed a man of many admirable qualities—personal integrity, genuine honesty, tolerance of others, and spiritual conviction. Certainly he conducted himself in a manner that brought dignity and respectability both to himself and to the Reorganized Church. During the more than seventy years since his death, Reorganization members have emphasized these qualities until for many Saints Smith has achieved the status of a human idol. He has been presented as a remarkably gifted prophet who foresaw all options in questions affecting the church and directed the Saints without conflict and with a dynamism equal to that of his illustrious father. Essentially, Joseph Smith III's career has been interpreted in a consensus framework—a model that emphasizes unity and commonality, steadfastness of purpose, and rightness of action.

This, however, was certainly not the whole of Joseph Smith III's character, for he was no marble man, no two-dimensional icon, no religious totem. He was a human being who lived and breathed, who fought desperately for what he believed was the truth yet recognized the necessity of practical compromise. On all too many occasions he had tremendous doubts about the choices before him, but he tried always to do what he perceived was right and just. He largely created the moderate Mormonism of the Reorganized Church during the latter decades of the nineteenth century and with his style of leadership left a legacy to the church that has survived to the present.

While accomplishing these goals Joseph Smith III had to contend with his share of difficulties; he dealt with hard issues of church theology, procedure, and personality. He experienced crises of conscience and periods of self-doubt. Yet throughout his tenure as president Smith functioned admirably as a practical politician, balancing elements within and without the movement, managing strikingly different types of individuals with tact and compassion, and all the while building a relatively harmonious organization out of a diverse set of personalities and attitudes that could have destroyed the movement had it been under lesser men. Indeed, the creation of a viable movement and the building of a fragile consensus out of a variety of elements associated within the Reorganization was Joseph's great lasting contribution to the Restoration Movement. In the following chapters I have emphasized this aspect of Smith's career, and consequently the image that emerges is largely that of a man of affairs—a manager, a planner, a promoter, a master politician, and a superb organizer. Thus this is in large part a study of the uses and limits of power within an organization.

With no intention of questioning his integrity and belief in the principles of the movement, I contend that Joseph Smith III was essentially a pragmatist. Since Joseph was a second-generation Saint, he was not as overcome by the awe of the spiritual vision as those who had gone before; he was able to take aspects of the grandiose dreams of his father, separate the logical from the impractical, and build on them. Therefore, he took what he considered the most important parts of that sacred vision and put them into operation in a secular world. The rest of his father's vision Joseph either rejected outright by noting that his father had never instituted it— plural marriage, for example—or deferred until the Saints were prepared to accept it by virtue of greater spiritual commitment—for instance, the Zionic ideal and the orientation toward community-building. At some future date the membership could be led forward to greater spiritual heights, Smith believed, but the process should not be forced too quickly or the result could destroy the church's organization, as happened at the death of his father in 1844. A man of principle and a man of conviction, Joseph Smith III was also a man of practicality who recognized above all the nature and uses of power to accomplish worthy goals and saw the necessity of patience and compromise. In the Reorganized Church's history, his course was the supreme example of the union of principle and pragmatism; he moved as swiftly toward his goals as his followers and the world at large would allow.

I am grateful to many for assistance given during the preparation of this book. I extend my appreciation to the staffs of the Library–Archives of the Reorganized Church of Jesus Christ of Latter Day Saints, the Historical Department of the Church of Jesus Christ of Latter-day Saints, the Utah State Historical Society, the J. Willard Marriott Library at the University of Utah, the Harold B. Lee Library at Brigham Young University, the Frederick Madison Smith Library at Graceland College, the Chicago Historical Society, the Lovejoy Library at Southern Illinois University–Edwardsville, the Troy H. Middleton Library at Louisiana State University, and the Beinecke Library at Yale University. Particular thanks are due to James B. Allen, Leonard J. Arrington, Alma R. Blair, Paul M. Edwards, Charles J. Gross, Richard P. Howard, Perry D. Jamieson, William E. Juhnke, Richard H. Kohn, Walter L. Kraus, F. Mark McKiernan, D. Michael Quinn, William D. Russell, Richard C. Roberts, Richard W. Sadler, Clare D. Vlahos, and Ronald W. Walker. The staff at the University of Illinois Press, especially Richard L. Wentworth, Elizabeth Dulany, and Cynthia Mitchell, deserve particular acknowledgment for their support, expertise, and good humor during the lengthy publication of this book. Additionally, I would like to extend my appreciation to John L. Loos, Willian J. Cooper, Jr., Robert A. Becker, Karl A. Roider, Jr., and Sam B. Hilliard, under whose direction this project began at Louisiana State University as a doctoral dissertation. This book is better for the efforts of all these people. Finally, portions of the material in this book previously appeared in *Restoration Studies II* and *III*, the *John Whitmer Historical Association Journal*, *Western Illinois Regional Studies*, the *Annals of Iowa*, *Dialogue*, and the *Restoration Trail Forum*. I wish to thank the various editors of these publications for permission to include this material.

Joseph Smith III

1

A Mormon Heritage

On the evening of 6 November 1832 snow was falling lightly over the counties making up the Western Reserve section of northern Ohio. As the snow fell Emma Smith, twenty-eight-year-old wife of Joseph Smith, Jr., the Mormon prophet, gave birth to a sturdy, healthy son whom she named after her husband.[1] Joseph Smith III's birth took place unobtrusively in the upper room of Newel K. Whitney's store, the Smiths' home much of the time since coming to Kirtland, Ohio, in February 1831.

By the time of young Joseph's birth, his father was already a living legend. Born of poor farm stock in Sharon, Vermont, on 23 December 1805, the young Mormon prophet experienced several religious manifestations during his adolescence in western New York; eventually published the Book of Mormon, a purported religious history of a group of Hebrews that migrated to America in the fifth century B.C. and reared a powerful civilization in the new world; and in 1830 organized what would later be named the Church of Jesus Christ of Latter Day Saints.[2]

Gathering a small group of stalwart followers in upstate New York, Smith sent missionaries into outlying areas, proselytizing any who would listen. Their message was eloquent in its simplicity and powerful in its attraction. They spoke of the boy prophet who had received divine guidance to correct the errors of the Christian churches by calling the world to repentance and baptism into the pure church of Jesus Christ. They appealed to the adolescent republic's natural curiosity about the ancient inhabitants of America with the story told in the Book of Mormon. They propounded the doctrine of divine revelation—not just as experienced in Biblical times but for their own day as well—and asserted that Joseph Smith, Jr., was a prophet like Ezekiel, Isaiah, and Elijah. And finally, they adopted a popular ideal of the time concerning the imminent advent of Christ and the beginning of the millennial reign. The themes of millennialism, current divine revelation, the Book of Mormon, and the restoration of Christianity to its ancient purity—the bases upon which Smith built early Mormonism—were exciting and meaningful to many Americans of the 1830s and 1840s, a period when the religious ferment of antebellum America spawned many religious movements, several adopting one or more of the basic themes of Mormonism.[3]

What made Smith's movement so unique was its blend of themes and the energy and vitality of both its leadership and membership, which guaranteed the survival of the Mormon religion when many of its counterparts failed. Mormonism survived largely because of a second generation of leaders who took the vision of the prophet, cut it loose from the more sublime and unacceptable concepts of the early church organization, and put it more in concert with a practical reality. Joseph Smith III was one of these leaders.[4]

Joseph and Emma Smith came to Kirtland, Ohio, after one of the church's missionary teams had converted a dynamic Reformed Baptist preacher named Sidney Rigdon early in the church's history. A minister of the Disciples of Christ, which was led by Alexander Campbell, Rigdon had been the pastor of a very successful church in the Kirtland area. One of his parishioners became a Mormon and told his old pastor about the church and its mission. As a result of his efforts Rigdon was baptized in the fall of 1830, leading many of his more than 100 followers into the Latter Day Saint fold. Following his conversion Rigdon mounted a sustained campaign to convince the young prophet that, instead of languishing in New York, he and his small band of followers should emigrate westward to Kirtland, where they could join with a large and successful congregation of believers.[5]

Kirtland in 1831 was certainly no Garden of Eden. It was a little frontier village—only a few stores and shops, a grist mill, a post office, one hotel, and a few community buildings.[6] The Mormons, however, made their headquarters there and turned the town into something more than it might have been otherwise. Smith carried out an ambitious missionary program that brought hundreds of loyal church members into the Kirtland area. He also prosecuted an elaborate construction program, reshaping Kirtland along the lines that he envisioned for the holy city of God that would arise during the millennial reign. As a result he completely reorganized Kirtland's road system, laying out the town on a strict compass setting with broad streets, huge city lots, and a masterful complex of church administration and worship buildings. Under his direction the church built houses—some of them exceptional by frontier standards—a printing office, a church store, a bank, several ancillary buildings, and, as a crowning achievement, a magnificent house of worship.[7]

Although the senior Joseph was killed by a mob in 1844, his son grew to manhood under the shadow of his famous and sometimes infamous father. Relying on his mother's teachings that his father had been a good man and his own murky recollections, which substantiated that belief, Joseph Smith III eventually tried to reconcile the person he had known as a child with the legend that surrounded the Mormon prophet after his death. In time this son became a proponent of his father's religious vision, taking what he considered the essence of the Mormon religion and transforming it into a rational institutional system that he closely related to orthodox Protestantism.[8]

In most ways Joseph Smith III was like his father. Young Joseph had his father's broad face, high forehead, lantern jaw, and Roman nose. But the Mormon prophet was tall, more than six feet according to contemporary sources, and considered a fine physical specimen in the best athletic condition. Young Joseph was only five feet eight inches tall, from early manhood until the end of his long life over 200 pounds, and had the appearance of a barrel with a head, two skinny arms, and two spindly legs attached. Young Joseph also thought somewhat like his father. He accepted the teachings of Mormonism early in life and clung to what he considered the essential parts of them until his death. He could not forsake them, he said, for they were a part of his culture, his subconscious, his life-style.

If Joseph Smith III was very much like his father in most respects, he was also quite different from him in others. The founder of Mormonism, like the founders of very nearly everything of worth in the world, was a dreamer and a visionary. Joseph Smith, Jr., had a sacred experience as a young boy and his entire life was an attempt to recapture that moment in a secular world. The Mormon prophet was remarkably perceptive in reading the social, economic, and cultural world around him and, trying to weave it into a meaningful life-style, created the fabric of Mormonism with its religious meetings, its style of leadership, its doctrine, its unique social and political relationships, and its communities built throughout the nation.[9]

Joseph Smith III, on the other hand, was neither a dreamer nor a visionary. Unlike his father, he dealt in the secular, not the sacred, and was much more concerned with the practical workings of an organization, the administration of mundane affairs, and the details of a particular policy than with the grand design. As president of the Reorganized Church of Jesus Christ of Latter Day Saints, from 1860 until his death in 1914, Joseph Smith III demonstrated repeatedly his concern over the means of, rather than the reasons for, accomplishing goals.[10] In contrast to his father's oftentimes disastrous impracticality, Joseph III's striking pragmatism seems very much a part of frontier America. Frederick Jackson Turner, in a remarkable essay first published in 1893, suggested that the frontier helped shape tendencies in Americans that became a part of the national character—a rugged individualism, a sense of equality and fair play, a fervent belief in democracy, and, most importantly, a pragmatism that induced Americans to adopt workable solutions, make compromises when necessary, and deemphasize impractical ideals. While Turner's thesis has been significantly revised since its first appearance, that quality of pragmatism he described remains a viable descriptor of the frontier. Joseph Smith III displayed this pragmatism throughout his life with regards to the Mormon movement. He was fiercely loyal to his father's legacy but almost never let his loyalty stand in the way of pragmatic solutions.[11]

Throughout his life Joseph Smith III held strong to four basic conceptions of Mormonism, rejecting or denying others that did not meet his tests of divinity, practicality, or acceptability. The first was his belief in the divine nature of the Book of Mormon. For the younger Smith the book was exactly what his father had claimed it to be—the record of a Hebraic people who migrated to the Western hemisphere before the time of Christ and left a religious history of their civilization. The second was his belief in divine revelation throughout the ages. He accepted as prophets those men and women of the Bible who recorded their experiences with God, but he also placed himself and his father in the ranks of the prophets of the living God. Third, he believed that Jesus Christ would return to earth and usher in the millennial reign and that the Latter Day Saints must work to make the world ready for that second coming. Finally, Joseph Smith III sought to remain true to his father as the founder of the Latter Day Saint movement, as a man called from among the human race to perform a special task commanded by God. He believed he had a special mission to consolidate and present to the world the essence of his father's work and to correct misconceptions held and even practiced by some concerning it. All else, Smith asserted, was subservient to these central conceptions and was therefore subject to emphasis or deemphasis as expedient.[12]

Although these became the guiding concepts of Joseph Smith III's life, he adopted them gradually as he grew to adulthood and formed his opinions about life. His earliest learning experiences, central to the development of these conceptions, began at Kirtland. Young Joseph was well-liked in the community and, as the son of the prophet, was expected to act the fine minister's son. One instance of the importance of the boy at Kirtland was a special blessing bestowed upon him by his grandfather, Joseph Smith, Sr., in December 1836. As later recalled by Joseph's grandmother, the blessing alluded to some future responsibilities the lad would have within the leadership of the church:

> I lay my hand upon your head to bless you Your name is after the name of your father   you are Joseph the third   you shall live long upon the earth And after you are grown you shall [have] wisdom knowledge and understanding And shall search into the mysteries of the Kingdom of God   Your heart shall be open to all men   And your hand shall be open to relieve the wants of the poor. You shall be admired by all who shall behold you   you shall be an honor to your Father and Mother—And a comfort to your mother   you shall have power to carry out all that your Father shall leave undone when you become of age   And you shall have power to wield the Sword of Laban.[13]

Although there was no evidence prior to the death of Joseph Smith, Jr., in 1844 that this blessing had special significance, some concluded during the crisis of leadership in 1844 and 1845 that the statement "you shall have power to carry out all that your Father shall leave undone" could well be interpreted as a designation of the boy as his father's successor, and the younger Smith recognized it as such later.

Joseph Smith III, as a mere child of five years old at Kirtland, did not understand the difficulties that forced his family and most of the other Mormons out of the community in early 1838. He was aware only that his father was a good man whom he loved and that the church members in the area were good people whom he trusted. Consequently, he concluded that those nonmembers from the surrounding countryside persecuting the Saints were acting wrongfully. As a result of this persecution, his father and his close associate Sidney Rigdon left the little Mormon community on the evening of 12 January 1838, bound for a new church settlement in northwestern Missouri, known as Far West. They rode to the little town of Norton, Ohio, about sixty miles southwest of Kirtland, and stayed with some church members until their families could join them. Two days later Emma Smith and Phoebe Rigdon arrived with their children in hurriedly packed wagons to begin the trek to Far West. They set out the next day, reaching the new Mormon headquarters on 14 March 1838. There the Smith family established a new home.[14]

Far West, Missouri, had been created in 1836 by the Saints expelled from Jackson County, on the Missouri-Kansas border, and by the time of the Smiths' arrival it had grown into a town of over 1,000 people. Soon after the arrival of the prophet and his family, other Latter Day Saints from the Kirtland area began moving into the community and the church began a massive building program to house all the new residents in the Mormon-controlled area. As the community's population swelled and the Saints bought land and settled in the surrounding areas, difficulties again arose between the church members and those not associated with the movement. The non-Mormons decried the clannishness, fanaticism, and smugness of the Saints, while the Mormons grew to distrust and even hate the non-Mormons in the area. The difficulties between the groups erupted violently in the fall of 1838 with the so-called Mormon War.[15]

It began on 6 August 1838, voting day at the thriving town of Gallatin, county seat of Daviess County, in northwestern Missouri and did not end until November 1838 after over forty people had been killed, thousands of dollars in property had been destroyed, the Mormon prophet and his closest advisors were jailed on charges ranging from rioting to treason, and the Mormon church was officially expelled from the state.[16] While in jail, Joseph Smith, Jr., wrote a touching and sentimental letter to his wife and family. Joseph Smith III was deeply moved by this letter, claiming that it showed the "inward life and feelings of the man" and was evidence of his innocence of all wrongdoing. Written on 24 November 1838, the letter read in part:

> We are prisoners in chains and under strong guard for Christ's sake and for no other cause; although there have been things that might seem to the mob to be a pretext for them to persecute us; but on examination I think that the authorities will discover our innocence and set us free; but if this blessing cannot be obtained, I have this consolation, that I am an innocent man, let what will befall me. . . .
>
> Oh, God grant that I may have the privilege of seeing once more my lovely family in the enjoyment of the sweets of liberty and sociable life; to press them to my bosom, and kissing their lovely cheeks would fill my heart with unspeakable gratitude. Tell the children that I am alive, and trust I shall come and see them before long. Comfort their hearts all you can, and try to be comforted yourself all you can. . . .
>
> Tell little Joseph he must be a good boy. Father loves him with a perfect love; he is the eldest—must not hurt those who are smaller than he, but comfort them. Tell little Frederick [born in 1836 at Kirtland] Father loves him with all his heart; he is a lovely boy. Julia [an adopted daughter born in 1831] is a lovely little girl; I love her also. She is a promising child. Tell her Father wants her to remember him and be a good girl. Tell all the rest that I think of them and pray for them all. . . . O, my affectionate Emma, I want you to remember that I am a true and faithful friend to you and the children forever. O, may God bless you all.[17]

On 13 November 1838 Joseph Smith, Jr., and his associates went before a state judge for arraignment. At the end of a thirteen-day session most of the Mormon leaders were released because of insufficient evidence for prosecution, but Joseph Smith and four others were sent to jail at Liberty, Clay County, Missouri, to await trial for treason. Emma Smith visited her husband at least twice while he was in this jail, taking the six-year-old Joseph III with her each time. The first visit occurred on 8 December 1838 Smith later recalled, the jailors allowing Emma Smith and her son to stay overnight in the cell. Emma Smith and the boy also visited the prophet in his jail cell on the night of 20 December, the boy especially enjoying this experience because of the festive activities there that night. On one of these two visits, according to Joseph Smith III, the Mormon prophet "with another, laid his hands upon my head and blessed me, as his eldest son, to the blessings which had come down to him through the blessings of the progenitors."[18] Lyman Wight, one of the men held in the jail with Joseph Smith, Jr., recounted the story of this blessing in a letter to a newspaper editor in 1855. He said he had seen the prophet "lay hands on the head of a youth and heard him cry aloud 'You are my successor when I depart.'" In later years this blessing became very significant to both Joseph Smith III and the Reorganized Church in establishing the legitimacy of the Mormon group.[19]

During their visits in the jail, Emma and Joseph decided that she should take the children and move with many of the other Saints to Quincy, Illinois, a town that had offered asylum to the battered church. Accordingly, toward the end of January 1839 Emma and the children packed their belongings and prepared to leave Far West. Jonathon Holmes and Stephen Markham, friends of the family, offered to drive the Smiths to Quincy during the harsh winter. They loaded the wagon, hitched it to a pair of beautiful, matched black horses, and left the ruined town of Far West for a better life in Illinois. Moving slowly over the frozen earth, the Smith wagon made the 150-mile trip to Quincy in two weeks. One of the horses, young Joseph recollected, died during the journey, but otherwise they reached the Mississippi River without mishap.

The Smith family crossed the frozen Mississippi River on 15 February 1839. Since there was a chance that the ice over the river would not hold the weight of the wagon, the family, and the horses, Markham and Holmes told Emma to take her children and carefully walk across the ice behind the wagon. Joseph III described the crossing: "Carrying in her arms my brothers, Frederick and Alexander [the latter born at Far West in June 1838], with my sister, Julia, and myself holding onto her dress at either side, my mother walked across the frozen river and reached the Illinois shore in safety. This, then, was the manner of our passing out of the jurisdiction of a hostile State into the friendlier shelter of the State of Illinois, early in 1839." At half past ten that night the Smith wagon rolled up in front of a house outside Quincy, the home of George Cleveland, a friend of the Mormons and the Smith family although not a member of the sect. Before making the trip from Far West, Emma had written asking them for lodging until they could secure a home of their own. Emma and her children stayed with the Clevelands for the rest of the winter, awaiting Joseph's eventual release from prison and the establishment of another home for the Mormons somewhere in the state.[20]

The Smiths were certainly not the only Mormons to come into Quincy during the winter of 1838–39. Since the exodus from Missouri, the town had become a Mormon commonwealth, some 3,000 Saints arriving there by the first blooms of spring. Among those who arrived in Quincy were Joseph Smith and his fellow prisoners, to the great joy of the Mormons. They reached the city on 22 April 1839, after they had been allowed to escape. By April 1839 the local judge, the sheriff, and the guards at the Liberty Jail had realized that Smith and his party were an embarrassment to the state, so they turned their backs on the Mormon prisoners long enough to ensure their safe departure, thus avoiding a lengthy, vindictive, and unpopular trial.[21]

As soon as he was free, Joseph Smith prepared to build another city and to lead his followers toward economic and social independence. The site chosen for the new Mormon stronghold was on a great bend in the Mississippi River, about fifty miles north of Quincy, where a limestone jetty forced the river westward around flatland. Overlooking it from the east were jagged cliffs which had long served Indian and white navigators alike as landmarks. When Joseph Smith, Jr., and his family finally arrived at the new townsite, the prophet found that most of the acreage was a wilderness thick with trees and underbrush. Some of it was also marshy and would have to be drained before building would be feasible. Nonetheless, overtaken with the scenic majesty of the area, Smith decided to build the new Mormon citadel there. He chose to call the new city Nauvoo, which he said was a transliteration of the Hebrew phrase meaning "beautiful place."[22]

The Saints began settling in Nauvoo during the hot summer

of 1839, the Smith family moving into a two-story blockhouse that had been built thirty-five years earlier as a trading post and home for a Sauk and Fox Indian agent named William Ewing. The swamps had yet to be drained, however, and many more settlers suffered from malaria during the hot summer. Joseph Smith III, only six years old at the time, contracted the fever as well. Emma Smith tried several home remedies and some of the most advanced store-bought drugs—including Sappington's Pills, a fine wood fiber molded into a round pill and coated with a bitter covering, and a patent medicine called Dover's powder, whose principal ingredient was opium—but nothing seemed to help young Joseph. Finally, a recently converted physician, John M. Bernhisel, arrived in the town and treated young Smith; his prescription of bed rest and a careful diet aided the boy's recovery. Like all malaria victims, the lad suffered intermittent attacks of fever and chills for the next several years, but Dr. Bernhisel warned Emma of this inevitability and prepared her for proper nursing when it occurred.[23] In part as a result of his help in curing her children, the doctor became a lifelong friend of Emma Smith.

In time the Saints built an impressive city on the limestone flat by the Mississippi. In 1840 it received a charter from the Illinois legislature granting virtual autonomy to the city and providing for a large militia to be called the Nauvoo Legion. The legion became one of the great status symbols of Nauvoo, representing the security and power of a once persecuted and downtrodden people. With the legion the Saints signaled that the church would not allow the tragedy that had occurred in Missouri to take place again. Joseph Smith, Jr., became heavily involved in the legion's operation, gaining the appointment from the Illinois legislature of lieutenant general in the militia and commander of the Nauvoo Legion. The Saints in general and the prophet in particular enjoyed the pomp and ceremony of the military parades and reviews. After 1840, at very nearly every public occasion the legion marched and drilled for the city's residents.[24]

The adults had no sooner created the Nauvoo Legion than the Mormon boys formed a 500-man military unit of their own. Joseph Smith III took part in this unit for a time, enjoying the drilling and thrill of conquest. Armed with wooden swords and a banner that read, "Our Fathers we respect; our mothers we'll protect," the boys took a prominent part in the city's military festivities. The prophet encouraged his son's participation and helped organize activities for the boys.[25]

On one occasion this boys' troop staged a mock attack on the legion as it marched through the Nauvoo streets. By moving across an open field and intercepting the unit while making as much racket as possible, banging "tin pans, pails, sticks, and whatever other noisemakers they could muster," the boys hoped to scare the horses and scatter the legionnaires. To disperse the boys Joseph Smith ordered a cavalry charge. As the horsemen approached the boys, wrote Joseph Smith III, "all of a sudden the young company with a shout sent up a lively beating upon drums and pans and such a vigorous waving of branches and poles that the horses refused to charge them. Their riders became very much disconcerted. The Commanding General ordered another troop to try it, but they had no better success." Finally, Joseph Smith, Jr., spurred his almost deaf horse, Charley, toward the column of boys, and since his horse was not frightened by the racket, he easily scattered the boys' troop and ended the afternoon's fun.[26]

Nauvoo, despite the militaristic leanings brought on by a fear of further persecution, was not Sparta or even Prussia. While the Saints generally perceived the Nauvoo Legion as a defensive force, a vocal minority within the city during the 1840s was deeply troubled by the apparent love of war evidenced by those in the legion, and some refused to join the militia. Emma Smith, for one, opposed the legion and asked young Joseph to leave the boys' troop soon after the mock battle. The boy did so, but not without mixed feelings, for many of his friends were part of the unit. In later years, however, he came to understand his mother's concern. "Looking back along the pathway," he wrote, "I feel it was a pity that such a [martial] spirit crept in among them, however, and a still greater one that the leading minds of the church partook of it."[27]

The Mormons began construction of the city of Nauvoo during the summer of 1839 and continued a massive building program until the church abandoned the site in early 1846.[28] By the end of the Saints' first year, Nauvoo was essentially an overgrown wilderness community of log homes, a few shops, and an infant mercantile and manufacturing economy. Building seemed to be taking place on every side. George Miller, later a bishop in the church, captured the vitality of Nauvoo in the summer of 1840, enthusing that the community "was growing like a mushroom (as it were, by magic)."[29] Joseph Smith, Jr., remarked in 1841 that "the number of inhabitants is nearly three thousand, and is fast increasing. If we are suffered to remain, there is every prospect of its becoming one of the largest cities on the river, if not the western world. Numbers have moved in from the seaboard, and a few from the islands of the sea."[30] The city continued to grow rapidly thereafter. According to newspaper editor Thomas Gregg of Warsaw, Illinois, during the heyday of Nauvoo the Saints built about "1,200 hand-hewn log cabins, most of them white-washed inside, 200 to 300 good substantial brick houses and 300 to 500 frame houses."[31]

Nauvoo's population grew rapidly during the first years of the 1840s. At its peak in 1845 there were 11,057 residents within the corporate limits and about another 3,000 Saints in the surrounding areas.[32] This population base brought with it the necessity of manufacturing, mercantile, and other business undertakings by investors. Joseph Smith, Jr., built only one of an estimated thirty-five general stores that were operating in Nauvoo during its heyday. The prophet's store, however, was unique. Housed in a two-story brick building erected in 1842 on Water Street not far from the Smith home, the Red Brick Store, as it was called, served not only as a general merchandise store but also contained a number of civic and church offices. Smith maintained an office and research room on the second floor, and the bishopric had an office where tithes could be paid and property transactions could be recorded. The construction committee for the Nauvoo Temple, a religious edifice to be erected on the bluff overlooking the city, held its meetings and kept offices in the building; various members of the church's leading priesthood quorums used the building for meetings; and several of the civic offices were located there as well. Moreover, the second floor contained a large council room used for both religious and secular meetings.[33]

Young Joseph III had many pleasant experiences in his father's store. He remembered one particular incident when he went to the store to escape, in typical boyish fashion, some chores assigned by his mother and found that his father had spent most of the afternoon wrestling with customers. The grassy turf outside the store had been dug up and stomped down by the wrestlers and the excited spectators. As the boy entered the shop, he heard the men gossiping about the wrestling matches and learned that his father had thrown, in turn, everyone in the store. Young Smith remembered that not long after his arrival Cornelius P. Lott came in to buy supplies for his family. Although rather old, Lott was still strong and muscular and was usually willing to demonstrate his strength. Indeed, the older man carried a threatening-looking blacksnake whip that seemed to challenge all comers. The prophet's eyes lit up as Lott walked in, and he exclaimed, "Here! I have thrown down pretty nearly everybody about the place except Brother Lott, and I believe I can throw him down, too!" The older man, accepting the challenge, cackled in a high voice, "Well, my boy, if you'll take it catch-as-catch-can you can't throw old man Lott!" Smith took off his coat and vest and Lott discarded his whip, and the two headed outside to the wrestling area followed by the other people in the store. The prophet and Lott began the match, but neither could best the other. In fact, Joseph could only manage to bring the older man to his knees. After a few minutes the prophet conceded to Lott and received a fine ribbing from the onlookers about being unable to throw "an old man." "In the midst of the jibes," young Joseph recalled, "I heard the old man pipe out again, 'I told you, my boy, that you couldn't throw old man Lott!' "[34]

To Joseph Smith III, by far the most important event in the Red Brick Store was a special blessing he received from his father in the second-floor council room. According to reminiscences many years later, many of the local church officials and a few of the general authorities in the city were asked to attend. Among those present, according to some accounts, were Joseph and Hyrum Smith, John Taylor, Willard Richards, Newel K. Whitney, Reynolds Cahoon, Alpheus Cutler, Ebenezer Robinson, George J. Adams, W. W. Phelps, and John M. Bernhisel, all important individuals in the church's complex hierarchy. The prophet seated his son in a chair in the assembly room, and Newel K. Whitney anointed his head with oil in a solemn assembly. Then Joseph Smith pronounced a special blessing which suggested that young Joseph should succeed his father in the leadership of the church. Apparently concerned about trials within the church and pressure from without, Joseph Smith, Jr., might have speculated that he would not live much longer and needed to bless his son to carry on after him. The recollections of this blessing became increasingly important to Joseph III as he matured and took the leadership of the Reorganized Church.[35]

Apparently, on several occasions Smith publicly stated his opinion that his son should succeed him as president of the church. For instance, on Sunday, 21 January 1844, Joseph Smith, Jr., gave a public address on "sealing the hearts of the fathers to the children and the hearts of the children to the fathers" and made an offhand reference to this blessing.[36] Thus, although there was never a clear path of succession announced and at times the church's law on the subject is a labyrinth, Smith seemed to intend that his son would succeed him. Later, on 6 April 1860 Joseph Smith III accepted the position that his father had foreordained, becoming president of the Reorganized Church of Jesus Christ of Latter Day Saints.

As a lad Joseph III was much like the other youths of Nauvoo. He attended the local school his father had founded on the southern edge of the town, worked at chores around the house and farm, and enjoyed the standard boyish pursuits of the time. He loved horseback-riding and fishing in the Mississippi River. He also took part in boyhood groups and clubs. For instance, following the example of the prophet and other men in the community who had formed a chapter of the Masonic Lodge in 1842, Joseph and some of his friends organized an exclusive society of their own. As Smith later recalled, this club provided them "a good deal of fun, as fun was rated among us." Although starting as a simple organization, it soon developed elaborate initiation ceremonies that included in some cases malicious hazing. On one occasion Jack Allred, a big hulking boy who was something of a bully, asked to be accepted into the group. The members hesitated, but were intimidated into allowing him to join. They determined, however, to teach Allred a lesson and appointed a committee to devise a humbling induction ceremony. Joseph, who proposed the demeaning plan, said: "The plan was to lead him into the schoolhouse blindfolded, take up the trap door, and four boys hold a sheet over the opening into the cellar. Then as he approached the spot another boy, armed with a pillow borrowed surreptitiously from some mother's supply, was to strike him down into the hole. We would clamp the door shut and then all engage in a wild Indian dance and hullabaloo over his head!" But the plan miscarried. When the boy struck him with the pillow and Allred fell into the cellar, he struck his head on a beam and cut a deep gash in his scalp. Allred sat screaming in the dank cellar for some time until the boys upstairs worked up courage enough to let him out. Amends were later made when the boys asked Allred to be the principal performer in a talent show held for their parents.[37]

Most of the time, however, young Joseph was not engaged in such recreational endeavors, either working around the homestead or attending school. By all accounts the lad was a good student, at least as good as the majority of the other children of that frontier community. He excelled in spelling, by his own recollection winning nearly every spell-down in the tiny school he attended. He also did well in geography, history, and literature. He later boasted that he "could commit to memory the Sunday school lessons and lengthy declamations, and had something of a taste for phrases, and could spell any word I ever saw to read it." He was notoriously weak in mathematics, however, failing to master basic arithmetic and having much difficulty with geometry, algebra, and theoretical mathematics. He freely admitted, "The intricacies of figures bewildered me."[38]

During the time that young Smith was growing up in Nauvoo, a cloud hung over his family, and it greatly affected the lad. Ever after Joseph sought to understand the legal problems of his father while they lived in Nauvoo, but he never progressed beyond the simplistic belief that his father the prophet had been persecuted by vindictive men. As a result Smith grew to appreciate the need for understanding between those who called themselves Latter Day Saints and the non-Mormon communities in which they resided. The troubles rested, at least in part, with the escape of the prophet and his associates from the Liberty Jail during the spring of 1839. While some officials in Missouri had allowed Smith to escape to avoid an unpopular trial, others still believed that Missouri should bring him back from Illinois to stand trial so that the state's honor could be vindicated. Escape, they claimed, should never be construed as a pardon, especially for one so prominent as Joseph Smith, Jr. During the early 1840s the Missouri attorney general made several attempts to extradite Smith in order to try him on the charge of "open rebellion against the state."[39]

To hide from these Missouri officials when they came to Nauvoo, the prophet had secret compartments built into his homes. The log blockhouse, the Smith family's first home, contained a secret door in the cellar which led to "a vaulted place, with a dry floor of brick and bricked walls, . . . large enough for a couple of people to occupy, either sitting or lying down, affording a degree of comfort for a stay of long or short duration as was necessary." When Smith built the Nauvoo mansion, the name given to a large, two-story dwelling completed for his family in 1843, the northeast upstairs bedroom contained a secret ladder to a compartment in the attic large enough to house several men for an extended period. Young Joseph and his brothers played in these hideouts from time to time, pretending they were hiding from the Missourians. So general did the knowledge of these compartments become that they were not really secret after a while. Still, all the Mormons thought they were necessary to foil the "so-called officials from Missouri seeking to arrest [the prophet] on trumped-up charges and from whom he had reason to expect harsh and unfair treatment." [40]

Although every extradition attempt ultimately failed, Joseph Smith, Jr., came close to capture by Missouri law enforcement officials on several occasions. On 5 June 1841 the Adams County, Illinois, sheriff arrested the prophet on a warrant from Missouri in a small town south of Nauvoo. He was brought before federal district judge Stephen A. Douglas at Monmouth, Illinois, a few days later for the processing of the extradition, but Judge Douglas dismissed the case on procedural grounds. [41] Smith was also arrested during the summer of 1843 while he and his family were visiting relatives at Dixon, Illinois, about 130 miles northeast of Nauvoo. After a dramatic rescue attempt by the Nauvoo Legion, the prophet was returned to Nauvoo for the preferring of charges and was immediately released by the Mormon judge on a writ of habeas corpus. Both the evidence of the hideouts in the Smith homes and these two arrests of his father convinced young Joseph that his father and the church were being persecuted. It also convinced him that the wisest course for the Saints was to do everything possible to maintain proper and peaceful relations with those outside the movement. Later, as president of the Reorganized Church he tried to avoid misunderstandings between members of the movement and the non-Mormon community. [42]

One final difficulty between Joseph Smith, Jr., and government officials deeply influenced the prophet's son and most directly the course of the church. It arose within the ranks of the Mormon church itself in 1844 and eventually led to the prophet's death. A number of important Latter Day Saints, led by William Law, a counselor to Joseph Smith in the First Presidency since 1841, left the movement because they were convinced that the organization had departed from the true principles of the gospel. The dissenters included Wilson Law, William's brother and a brigadier general in the Nauvoo Legion; Austin Cowles, a member of the Nauvoo Stake's High Council; James Blakeslee, a leading missionary; and Robert D. Foster, Chauncey Higbee, and Charles Ivins, all prominent Nauvoo residents.[43]

These dissidents worked to expose what they considered the evils of the church in a newspaper called the *Nauvoo Expositor*. On 7 June 1844 they issued their only number. In it the editors affirmed that they "know of a surety, that the religion of the Latter Day Saints as originally taught by Joseph Smith, which is contained in the Old and New Testament, Book of Covenants, and Book of Mormon, is true; and that the pure principles set forth in those books, are the immutable and eternal principles of Heaven, and speaks a language which, when spoken in truth and virtue, sinks deep into the heart of every honest man." Although accepting the purity of the movement at the beginning, these Saints asked Smith to function more democratically within the church. They claimed he had become a tyrant who did as he pleased without the regard for others that a man of God must have. They added that he was mixing religion with politics, even to the extent of declaring himself a candidate for the presidency of the United States in the 1844 election. Furthermore, they complained that Smith had started teaching doctrines contrary to the will of God and particularly that he was espousing and practicing reformation of the church along more orthodox lines.[44]

The publication of the *Expositor* raised a furor among most of the Mormons, who took it as a personal affront against their beloved leader and the religion that they had adopted. Smith shared their indignation and as mayor of Nauvoo used his civil authority to have the press destroyed. William Law and his supporters fled to Carthage, the county seat, and swore out a complaint against the prophet and his lieutenants for the unlawful destruction of private property. News of this controversy soon spread throughout the outlying areas of the county and Mormons and non-Mormons began to support publicly one side of the issue or the other. The *Warsaw Signal*, a vehemently anti-Mormon newspaper published a few miles south of Nauvoo, sounded a clear battle call for those who disliked Joseph Smith: "We have only to state that this is sufficient! War and extermination is inevitable! CITIZENS ARISE, ONE AND ALL!!! Can you *stand* by, and suffer such INFERNAL DEVILS! to ROB men of their property rights, without avenging them. We have no time for comment! Everyman will make his own. LET IT BE WITH POWDER AND BALL!" Because of the explosive situation in Hancock County caused by the *Expositor* affair, Governor Thomas Ford moved quickly to bring in a militia force from outside the area to see that order was preserved in the county.[45]

Although unwilling to do so at first, after promises of protection from the governor against anti-Mormon mobs that might be lurking in Carthage, the prophet surrendered to state authorities on 23 June 1844 and promised to stand trial for the destruction of the press. The fear that Joseph Smith, Jr., would never return alive filled the thoughts of his family as he left for the county seat to turn himself in to the governor. Emma Smith recalled in 1856 that, when he left for Carthage, "I felt the worst I ever did in my life, and from that time I looked for him to be killed." The premonition of impending disaster also overtook the prophet. John Taylor's official account of this episode recorded that Smith's last public statement to his followers had been, "I am going like a lamb to the slaughter; but I am calm as a summer's morning; I have a conscience void of offense toward God, and toward all men—I shall die innocent, and it shall yet be said of me, he was murdered in cold blood." Although young Joseph did not understand the full impact of the events on that summer day, he remembered that everyone was uneasy about his father's future.[46]

Joseph Smith, Jr., of course, did not return from Carthage alive. On the afternoon of 27 June 1844 a mob stormed the jail where the prophet was being held, overpowered the token force placed there, and murdered Joseph and his brother Hyrum. Early the next morning a courier arrived in Nauvoo with news of the death of the Smith brothers. Anson Call heard of the murders from Porter Rockwell, who announced the tragic news as he galloped through the city shouting, "Joseph is killed—they have killed him! Goddamn them! They have killed him!" During the course of the morning further details of the murders came out and the brutality of the affair infuriated the Saints.[47]

During the afternoon of 28 June the bodies of the prophet and his brother were returned to Nauvoo, and young Joseph remembered watching his father's loyal followers carrying the bullet-riddled corpses into a huge room at the Nauvoo mansion, where they were prepared for burial and were to lie in state. The Smith family bore up surprisingly well under the difficult circumstances. Young Joseph's mother went in to view the bodies soon after they had been readied. "After leaning over the coffin [of her husband]," Smith later recalled, "she placed her hand upon the cheek of my father, and in grief-stricken accents said, 'Oh, Joseph, Joseph! My husband, my husband! Have they taken you from me at last?'" After that, young Joseph went over to the coffin with his mother and the other children. When he saw his dead father, Joseph exclaimed, "Oh, my father, my father!" Then he ran from the room, refusing to return to view the bodies a second time.[48]

The next morning, thirty-nine hours after their martyrdom, the house was opened to allow the Saints a last look at their fallen leaders. The people "commenced assembling at an early hour," reported Dr. B. W. Richmond, "and the surrounding country swarmed with men and women during the whole day." As Richmond described it:

The scene around the bodies of the dead men was too horrible to witness. Hyrum was shot in the brain, and bled none, but by noon his face was so swollen—neck and face forming one bloated mass—that no one could recognize it. Joseph's blood continued to pour out of his wounds, which had been filled with cotton, the muscles relaxed and the gory fluid trickled down on the floor and formed puddles across the room. Tar, vinegar and sugar were kept burning on the stove to enable persons to stay in the apartment. In order to see the bodies, thousands came in at one door and out another, from morning till night they came and went, and in the house for the livelong day the lament of sorrow was heard.[49]

The next day the Saints held an elaborate funeral for the Smith brothers. They were ostensibly buried in the town cemetery on the bluff overlooking the river, but because of a fear of vandalism these caskets contained only stones. Instead, the bodies were secretly buried in the basement of the unfinished Nauvoo House, a large, four-story structure that had been intended as a giant hotel. The Mormon people lost their prophet on 27 June 1844, but Joseph Smith III lost even more. The importance of Smith's death to the life of his son cannot be over-emphasized. It changed the direction of the youth's life and thus, to a very real extent, the direction of Mormonism. It was, in essence, the end of the beginning.[50]

NOTES

1. Several recent biographical studies concerning Joseph and Emma Smith provide much valuable information about their lives. The best are the companion volumes, Donna Hill, *Joseph Smith: The First Mormon* (Garden City, N.Y.: Doubleday and Co., 1977), and Linda King Newell and Valeen Tippetts Avery, *Mormon Enigma: Emma Smith, Prophet's Wife, "Elect Lady," Polygamy's Foe* (Garden City, N.Y.: Doubleday and Co., 1984).

2. *Book of Mormon: An Account Written by the Hand of Mormon, Upon Plates Taken from the Plates of Nephi* (Palmyra, N.Y.: E. B. Grandin, 1830). The literature concerning the Book of Mormon is expansive. Valuable introductions to the subject can be found in Gary P. Gillum and John W. Welch, *Comprehensive Bibliography of the Book of Mormon* (Provo, Utah: Foundation for Ancient Research and Mormon Studies, 1982); David J. Whittaker, "The Mormon Scriptures: A Bibliography of Their History and Textual Development, Part III, the Book of Mormon," *Mormon History Association Newsletter*, June 1983, pp. 14–16; David J. Whittaker, "The Book of Mormon—Attack and Defense, A Bibliographical Essay," Part I, *Mormon History Association Newsletter*, November 1984, pp. 8–10. Analyses of the Book of Mormon include the following representative publications: B. H. Roberts, *Studies of the Book of Mormon*, ed. Brigham D. Madsen (Urbana: University of Illinois Press, 1985); Richard P. Howard, *Restoration Scriptures: A Study of Their Textual Development* (Independence, Mo.: Herald Publishing House, 1969), pp. 24–69; John L. Sorenson, *An Ancient Setting for the Book of Mormon* (Salt Lake City, Utah: Deseret Book Co., 1985); Hugh Nibley, *Since Cumorah: The Book of Mormon in the Modern World* (Salt Lake City: Deseret Book Co., 1967); Wayne Ham, "Problems in Interpreting the Book of Mormon as History," *Courage: A Journal of History, Thought, and Action* 1 (September 1970): 15–22; Susan Curtis, "Palmyra Revisited: A Look at Early Nineteenth-Century Thought and the Book of Mormon," *John Whitmer Historical Association Journal* 2 (1982): 30–37; David Persuitte, *Joseph Smith and the Origins of the*

Book of Mormon (Jefferson, N.C.: McFarland and Co., 1985); Noel B. Reynolds, *Book of Mormon Authorship: New Light on Ancient Origins* (Provo, Utah: B.Y.U. Religious Studies Center, 1982); Timothy L. Smith, "The Book of Mormon in Biblical Culture," *Journal of Mormon History* 7 (1980): 3–21.

3. The unique attraction of Mormonism in the early nineteenth century has been best described in Richard L. Bushman, *Joseph Smith and the Beginnings of Mormonism* (Urbana: University of Illinois Press, 1984), passim; Leonard J. Arrington and Davis Bitton, *The Mormon Experience: A History of the Latter-day Saints* (New York: Alfred A. Knopf, 1979), pp. 20–43; Larry Porter, "The Church in New York and Pennsylvania, 1816–1831," in *The Restoration Movement: Essays in Mormon History*, ed. F. Mark McKiernan, Alma R. Blair, and Paul M. Edwards (Lawrence, Kan.: Coronado Press, 1973), pp. 27–62; Melodie Moench, "Nineteenth Century Mormons: The New Israel," *Dialogue: A Journal of Mormon Thought* 12 (Spring 1979): 42–45; Roger Yarrington, "Context of the Restoration," in *Restoration Studies III*, ed. Maurice L. Draper (Independence, Mo.: Herald Publishing House, 1986), pp. 116–22; Gordon Wood, "Evangelical America and Early Mormonism," *New York History* 61 (October 1980): 359–86.

4. The dichotomy between the administrative and charismatic leadership within Mormonism has been discussed in Jan Shipps, *Mormonism: The Story of a New Religious Tradition* (Urbana: University of Illinois Press, 1985), pp. 33–34; Paul M. Edwards, "The Secular Smiths," *Journal of Mormon History* 4 (1977): 3–17; Jan Shipps, "The Prophet Puzzle: Suggestions Leading toward an Understanding of Joseph Smith," *Journal of Mormon History* 1 (1974): 3–20; Leonard J. Arrington, *Brigham Young: American Moses* (New York: Alfred A. Knopf, 1985), pp. 403–9; D. Michael Quinn, "The Evolution of the Presiding Quorums of the LDS Church," *Journal of Mormon History* 1 (1974): 21–38.

5. The best account of church settlement in Kirtland, Ohio, is Milton V. Backman, Jr., *The Heavens Resound: A History of the Latter-day Saints in Ohio, 1830–1838* (Salt Lake City: Deseret Book Co., 1983). See also Max H. Parkin, "Kirtland: A Stronghold for the Kingdom," in McKiernan, Blair, and Edwards, *The Restoration Movement*, pp. 63–98, and, on Rigdon, F. Mark McKiernan, *The Voice of One Crying in the Wilderness: Sidney Rigdon, Religious Reformer, 1793–1876* (Lawrence, Kan.: Coronado Press, 1971).

6. Warren Jenkins, *Ohio Gazetteer and Traveler's Guide* (Columbus, Ohio: n.p., 1837), p. 248; Backman, *The Heavens Resound*, pp. 33–39; Robert L. Layton, "A Perspective on Time and Place," *Brigham Young University Studies* 11 (Summer 1971): 423–38.

7. Backman, *The Heavens Resound*, pp. 125–41, 311–13, passim; Roger D. Launius, *The Kirtland Temple: A Narrative History* (Independence, Mo.: Herald Publishing House, 1986); Laurel B. Andrew, *The Early Temples of the Mormons: The Architecture of the Millennial Kingdom of God in the American West* (Albany: State University of New York Press, 1977), pp. 36–47.

8. Joseph Smith, "The Memoirs of President Joseph Smith (1832–1914)," *Saints' Herald* 81 (6 November 1934): 1413; Joseph Smith, Jr., *The History of the Church of Jesus Christ of Latter-day Saints*, ed. B. H. Roberts, 7 vols. (Salt Lake City: Deseret Book Co., 1976), 1:260, 295; Joseph Smith, Jr., to Emma Smith, 13 October 1832, Joseph Smith, Jr., Papers, Reorganized Church of Jesus Christ of Latter Day Saints Library–Archives, Independence, Mo.; Hill, *Joseph Smith*, pp. 61–69, 81. Those who use Smith's *History of the Church* should be aware of certain difficulties concerning its compilation. For an able discussion of these see Dean C. Jessee, "The Writing of Joseph Smith's History," *Brigham Young University Studies* 11 (Spring 1971): 439–73; Dean C. Jessee, "The Reliability of Joseph Smith's History," *Journal of Mormon History* 3 (1976): 34–39; Howard C. Searle, "Authorship of the History of Joseph Smith: A Review Essay," *Brigham Young University Studies* 21 (Winter 1981): 101–22.

9. Roger D. Launius, "Probing Joseph Smith III: Reorganized Church Prophet," unpublished address presented at the annual meeting of the Mormon History Association, Omaha, Neb., 5 May 1983; Howard Booth, "An Image of Joseph Smith, Jr.: A Personality Study," *Courage: A Journal of History, Thought, and Action* 1 (September 1970): 1–11; Charles W. Turner, "Joseph Smith III and the Mormons of Utah," pp. 492–503 (Ph.D. diss., Graduate Theological Union, 1985).

10. The Reorganized Church of Jesus Christ of Latter Day Saints emerged as the second largest of some fifteen Mormon factions that arose soon after the death of Joseph Smith, Jr. Founded in the 1850s by dissenters from other Mormon sects, its viability as a major movement was virtually ensured when Joseph Smith III became its president on 6 April 1860. By 1980 the Reorganized Church's membership had grown to some 225,000 members spread throughout the world.

11. Frederick Jackson Turner's "Frontier Thesis" was first stated in his "Significance of the Frontier in American History," presented at the annual meeting of the American Historical Association in 1893 but conveniently printed in Turner, *The Frontier in American History* (New York: Holt, Rinehart, and Winston, 1962), pp. 1–38. The following quote, from page 38 of this essay, describes Joseph Smith III well: "That coarseness and strength combined with acuteness and inquisitiveness; that practical,

inventive turn of mind, quick to find expedients; that masterful grasp of material things, lacking in the artistic but powerful to effect great ends; that restless, nervous energy; that dominant individualism, working for good and for evil, and withal that buoyancy and exuberance which comes with freedom—these are traits of the frontier, or traits called out elsewhere because of the existence of the frontier." A slight revision of Turner's thesis, although still with these characteristics intact, is Ray Allan Billington, *America's Frontier Heritage* (New York: Holt, Rinehart, and Winston, 1967), passim. Examples of Smith's basic pragmatism can be found in Clare D. Vlahos, "Moderation as a Theological Principle in the Thought of Joseph Smith III," *John Whitmer Historical Association Journal* 1 (1981): 3–11; Roger D. Launius, "Joseph Smith III and the Quest for a Centralized Organization, 1860–1873," in *Restoration Studies II*, ed. Maurice L. Draper (Independence, Mo.: Herald Publishing House, 1983), pp. 104–20.

12. Vlahos, "Moderation as a Theological Principle," pp. 3–11; Alma R. Blair, "Joseph Smith III: Prophetic Son of a Prophet," in *Joseph Smith, Sr., Family Reunion Souvenir Program* (Salt Lake City: Joseph Smith, Sr., Family Reunion Association, 1975), pp. 6–12; Alma R. Blair, "The Reorganized Church of Jesus Christ of Latter Day Saints: Moderate Mormons," in McKiernan, Blair, and Edwards, *The Restoration Movement*, pp. 218–26; Launius, "Probing a Prophet," n.p.; Launius, "Joseph Smith III and Quest for Centralized Organization," pp. 104–20.

13. Joseph Smith, Sr., Blessing of Joseph Smith III, remembered by Lucy Mack Smith, Summer 1845, Latter-day Saints Historical Department; also printed in *Saints' Herald* 51 (8 June 1904): 526, 56 (29 July 1909): 702. On the traditions associated with this and other blessings of Joseph Smith III for the Reorganized Church see W. Grant McMurray, " 'True Son of a True Father:' Joseph Smith III and the Succession Question," in *Restoration Studies I*, ed. Maurice L. Draper (Independence, Mo.: Herald Publishing House, 1980), pp. 131–45.

14. This episode is best analysed in Backman, *The Heavens Resound*, pp. 342–67.

15. The best works dealing with this subject are F. Mark McKiernan, "Mormonism on the Defensive: Far West," in *The Restoration Movement*, pp. 121–40; Leland H. Gentry, "A History of the Latter-day Saints in Northern Missouri from 1836 to 1839" (Ph.D. diss., Brigham Young University, 1965); Max H. Parkin, "A History of the Latter-day Saints in Clay County, Missouri, from 1833–1837" (Ph.D. diss., Brigham Young University, 1976).

16. On the Mormon War see, in addition to the above, Reed C. Durham, Jr., "The Election Day Battle at Gallatin," *Brigham Young University*

Studies 13 (Autumn 1972): 36–61; Stephen LaSueur, *The 1838 Mormon War in Missouri* (Columbia: University of Missouri Press, 1987).

17. Joseph Smith, Jr., to Emma Smith, 12 November 1838, Emma Smith Bidamon Papers, Reorganized Church Library Archives; Joseph Smith and Heman C. Smith, *The History of the Reorganized Church of Jesus Christ of Latter Day Saints* (Independence, Mo.: Herald Publishing House, 1973), 2:290–91.

18. Joseph Smith, "Pleasant Chat," *True Latter Day Saints' Herald* 14 (October 1868): 105.

19. Lyman Wight to Editor, *Northern Islander,* July 1855, Lyman Wight Letterbook, Reorganized Church Library–Archives.

20. Smith, "Memoirs," *Saints' Herald* 81 (6 November 1934): 1416; Ann Davis, "Spiritual Experiences," *Autumn Leaves* 4 (January 1892): 18.

21. Smith, *History of the Church* 3:260–71; A. L. Fulwider, *History of Stephenson County, Illinois* (Chicago: n.p., 1910), pp. 88–90; James B. Allen and Glen M. Leonard, *The Story of the Latter-day Saints* (Salt Lake City: Deseret Book Co., 1976), pp. 130–33; Dean L. May, "A Demographic Portrait of the Mormons, 1830–1980," in *After 150 Years: The Latter-day Saints in Historical Perspective,* ed. Thomas G. Alexander and Jessie L. Embry (Provo, Utah: Charles Redd Center for Western Studies, 1983), pp. 42–43.

22. Smith, *History of the Church* 3:375. The best introductions to the Mormon experience in Nauvoo are Robert Bruce Flanders, *Nauvoo: Kingdom on the Mississippi* (Urbana: University of Illinois Press, 1965); David E. Miller and Della S. Miller, *Nauvoo: The City of Joseph* (Santa Barbara, Calif.: Peregrine Smith, 1974). For a perceptive review of the literature on Mormon Nauvoo see Richard D. Poll, "Nauvoo and the New Mormon History: A Bibliographical Survey," *Journal of Mormon History* 5 (1978): 105–23.

23. Smith, "Memoirs," *Saints' Herald* 81 (13 November 1934): 1453–54, 81 (20 November 1934): 1479; Ronald K. Esplin, ed., "Sickness and Faith: Nauvoo Letters," *Brigham Young University Studies* 15 (Summer 1974): 425–34; John D. Lee, *Mormonism Unveiled: Including the Remarkable Life and Confessions of the Late Mormon Bishop, John D. Lee* (St. Louis: Bryan, Brand, and Co., 1877), pp. 108–11.

24. James L. Kimball, "The Nauvoo Charter: A Reinterpretation," *Journal of the Illinois State Historical Society* 64 (Spring 1971): 66–78; *Sangamo Journal* (Springfield, Ill.), 21 January 1842; Smith, *History of the Church* 4:309–10; John C. Bennett, *The History of the Saints; or, An Expose of Joe Smith and the Mormons* (Boston: Leland and Whiting, 1842), pp. 194–99.

25. Hill, *Joseph Smith,* pp. 284–85; Jesse Nathaniel Smith, *Six Decades*

in the Early West: The Journal of Nathaniel Smith, Diaries and Papers of a Mormon Pioneer, 1834–1906, ed. Oliver R. Smith (Provo, Utah: Jesse N. Smith Family Association, 1970), p. 8.

26. Smith, "Memoirs," *Saints' Herald* 82 (1 January 1935): 15–16.

27. Ibid.; Ebenezer Robinson, "Items of Personal History," *The Return* (Davis City, Iowa), February 1890.

28. Flanders, *Nauvoo,* pp. 27–39; Lyndon W. Cook, "Isaac Galland —Mormon Benefactor," *Brigham Young University Studies* 19 (Spring 1979): 261–84; Robert Bruce Flanders, "Dream and Nightmare: Nauvoo Revisited," in *The Restoration Movement,* pp. 144–45; Esplin, "Sickness and Faith," pp. 425–34; Smith, "Memoirs," *Saints' Herald* 81 (13 November 1934): 1453–54, 81 (20 November 1934): 1479; Richard H. Jackson, "The Mormon Village: Genesis and Antecedents of the City of Zion Plan," *Brigham Young University Studies* 17 (Winter 1977): 223–40; Donald L. Enders, "Platting the City Beautiful: A Historical and Archaeological Glimpse of Nauvoo Streets," *Brigham Young University Studies* 19 (Spring 1979): 409–15.

29. George Miller, *Correspondence of Bishop George Miller with the Northern Islander from his First Acquaintance with Mormonism Up to Near the End of his Life, 1855,* Wingfield Watson, comp. (n.p., 1916), p. 117.

30. Smith, *History of the Church* 4:177–78; *Times and Seasons* 3 (1 April 1842): 750.

31. Thomas Gregg, *The History of Hancock County, Illinois* (Chicago: C. S. Griggs and Co., 1880), pp. 296–98.

32. May, "Demographic Portrait," pp. 43–44; James E. Smith, "Frontier Nauvoo: Building a Picture from Statistics," *Ensign,* September 1979, pp. 17–18.

33. Joseph Smith, Jr., "History of Joseph Smith," *Latter-day Saints' Millennial Star* (Liverpool, England) 19 (10 January 1857): 20–21, 19 (20 June 1857): 391; Gregg, *History of Hancock County,* pp. 296–98; Roger D. Launius and F. Mark McKiernan, *Joseph Smith, Jr.'s, Red Brick Store* (Macomb: Western Illinois University Monograph Series, 1985).

34. Smith, "Memoirs," *Saints' Herald* 81 (18 December 1934): 1614.

35. Remembrances of this blessing are in "Testimony of James Whitehead," in *Complainant's Abstract of Pleading and Evidence in the Circuit Court of the United States, Western District of Missouri, Western Division, at Kansas City, Missouri* (Lamoni, Iowa: Herald Publishing House, 1893), pp. 27–28, 32; *Autumn Leaves* 1 (May 1888): 202; W. W. Blair, Diary, 17 June 1874, Reorganized Church Library–Archives; Alexander H. Smith, Diary, 14 May 1864, Reorganized Church Library–Archives.

36. Joseph Smith, Jr., Journal, 21 January 1844; Wilford Woodruff,

Journal, 21 January 1844, both in Church of Jesus Christ of Latter-day Saints Historical Department, Salt Lake City, Utah; Andred F. Ehat and Lyndon W. Cook, eds., *The Words of Joseph Smith, The Contemporary Accounts of the Nauvoo Discourses of the Prophet* (Provo, Utah: Brigham Young University Religious Studies Center, 1980), pp. 317–19. A discussion about the authority, meaning, and nature of his blessing can be found in D. Michael Quinn, "Joseph Smith III's 1844 Blessing and the Mormons of Utah," *Dialogue: A Journal of Mormon Thought* 15 (Summer 1982): 69–90; McMurray, " 'True Son of a True Father,' " pp. 131–45.

37. Smith, "Memoirs," *Saints' Herald* 81 (27 November 1934): 1511.

38. Ibid. 81 (20 November 1934): 1480, 81 (27 November 1934): 1511–14, 81 (4 December 1934): 1543.

39. Smith, *History of the Church* 5:57; George R. Gaylor, "The Attempts of the State of Missouri to Extradite Joseph Smith," *Northwest Missouri State College Studies* 19 (June 1955): 1–15.

40. Smith, "Memoirs," *Saints' Herald* 81 (18 December 1934): 1611–12.

41. Ibid. 82 (23 April 1935): 530; *Sangamo Journal*, 10 June 1842; Robert W. Johannson, *Stephen A. Douglas* (New York: Oxford University Press, 1973), pp. 105–7.

42. Smith, *History of the Church* 5:440–98; Joseph Smith, "What Do I Remember of Nauvoo?" *Journal of History* 3 (July 1910): 334–35.

43. Joseph Fielding, Diary 5:25–26, Church of Jesus Christ of Latter-day Saints Historical Department, Salt Lake City, Utah; Flanders, *Nauvoo*, pp. 305–10; Sarah Scott to Father and Mother, 16 June 1844, in Scott H. Partridge, ed., "The Death of a Mormon Dictator: Letters of Massachusetts Mormons, 1843–1848," *New England Quarterly* 9 (December 1936): 595; Lyndon W. Cook, "William Law, Nauvoo Dissenter," *Brigham Young University Studies* 22 (Winter 1982): 47–62.

44. *Nauvoo* (Ill.) *Expositor*, 7 June 1844.

45. Smith, *History of the Church* 6:432–48; Dallin H. Oaks, "The Suppression of the *Nauvoo Expositor*," *Utah Law Review* 9 (Winter 1966): 862–903; *Warsaw* (Ill.) *Signal*, 12 June 1844.

46. Joseph Smith, Jr., to Emma Smith, 23 June 1844, Joseph Smith, Jr., Papers, Reorganized Church Library–Archives; Vilate Kimball to Heber C. Kimball, 9–24 June 1844, Heber C. Kimball Collection, Latter-day Saints Historical Department; Edmund C. Briggs, "A Visit to Nauvoo in 1856," *Journal of History* 9 (October 1916): 454; Book of Doctrine and Covenants (Independence, Mo.: Herald Publishing House, 1970), Section 113:4; Smith, "What Do I Remember of Nauvoo?" p. 335.

47. Anson Call, "Life and Record of Anson Call," p. 27, Special Collections, Harold B. Lee Library, Brigham Young University, Provo, Utah;

William M. Daniels, "Narrative [of the Murders of Joseph and Hyrum Smith]," *Journal of History* 11 (October 1919): 406; Dallin H. Oaks and Marvin S. Hill, *Carthage Conspiracy: The Trial of the Accused Assassins of Joseph Smith* (Urbana: University of Illinois Press, 1975), pp. 6–29.

48. Lucy Mack Smith, *Biographical Sketches of Joseph Smith the Prophet, and His Progenitors, for Many Generations* (Lamoni, Iowa: Herald Publishing House, 1912), p. 354; Smith, "What Do I Remember of Nauvoo?" pp. 336–41.

49. *Deseret Evening News* (Salt Lake City), 27 November 1857.

50. Dean C. Jessee, "Return to Carthage: Writing the History of Joseph Smith's Martyrdom," *Journal of Mormon History* 8 (1981): 3–21; Richard Van Wagoner and Steven C. Walker, "The Joseph/Hyrum Smith Funeral Sermon," *Brigham Young University Studies* 23 (Winter 1983): 3–18; Newell and Avery, *Mormon Enigma*, pp. 196–97.

2

The Formative Years, 1844–46

At the time of his father's death young Joseph Smith was almost twelve years old. It changed his life: within a space of a few weeks, he had to become an adult. Those who saw him the first few weeks after the prophet's burial remarked that he seemed to take on the manner of a man for the first time, as if his childhood ways had suddenly been stripped from him. He stood tall and straight like the slender reeds that grew along the banks of the Mississippi by the Smiths' Nauvoo home. His long dark hair, broad face, Roman nose, and penetrating eyes bespoke Joseph's new existence as the man within the Smith family. Yet, at the same time, young Smith still had much of the child within him. The days following his father's death had numbed the boy's senses, for it still seemed quite impossible that the man he most loved was dead. It only seemed as if the prophet had left for an extended trip and would return any time to his family and his beloved Nauvoo. Some of the Saints in the city even circulated such rumors, naively suggesting that Joseph the Prophet would arise, Christlike, on the third day, descend from heaven "attended by a celestial army, coursing the air on a great horse," and lead the church on to Zion.[1]

When the various church officials outside of Nauvoo heard of the prophet's murder, they immediately returned to the church to plan for the future, and their ultimate course affected young Joseph greatly. The most important of these officials—the sole surviving member of the First Presidency, Sidney Rigdon, and the members of the Quorum of Twelve Apostles—began arriving in July. Parley P. Pratt, one of the apostles, was the first official of consequence to return to Nauvoo. He found all manner of speculation over the future of the church, especially over who should assume responsibility for its affairs. He counseled caution in both private and public statements to residents of the city, telling the Saints that the Lord would provide an answer to their problems after the return of the rest of the Twelve.[2]

Pratt's counsel was timely, for Latter Day Saints of both small and large stature made claims to the presidential office. Indeed, the question of presidential succession as well as the corollary question of a new leader's policy were the most important items of both idle chatter among the residents and serious meetings between church officials throughout the summer. All Mormons missed their prophet and they worried about the future, but they recognized the necessity of choosing another leader in his stead and each possessed certain ideas about the qualities inherent in such a successor. They wanted someone who was capable, who they could trust, of whom Joseph Smith would have approved, and who could succeed to the office within the confines of the legally defined church government. Unfortunately, a number of candidates were available, for Smith had not established a firm policy regarding presidential succession in the event of his death. Church doctrine, Smith's public and private statements, official church correspondence and records, and common sense provided at least eight different methodologies for succession, many pointing to different successors and all valid to some degree.[3]

On 8 August 1844 the Mormons met in a church conference at Nauvoo to decide the course of the organization and voted to accept Brigham Young, president of the Quorum of Twelve Apostles, as interim leader of the movement. Young was not without challengers, however, for Sidney Rigdon, a member of the First Presidency under the prophet, and a charismatic James J. Strang as well as other would-be leaders asserted claims to the prophetic office. Although these men were not recognized by the Nauvoo church government, each founded rival organizations and thrived for a time.[4]

One who could have made legitimate claims to the prophetic office but did not do so was young Joseph Smith. Numerous hints had been dropped from 1836 on that the prophet wished the lad to succeed him. The prayer of young Joseph's grandfather in the Kirtland Temple and the blessings given by his father in the Liberty Jail in late 1838 and in the Red Brick Store in Nauvoo each attested to this desire. Moreover, in 1841 the prophet revealed that the Lord had spoken to him and said, "In thee, and in thy seed, shall the kindreds of the earth be blessed." So common did this interpretation of Mormon leadership become that when Henry Brown, a non-Mormon, published his history of Illinois in 1844 he addressed this possibility. He announced that the Mormon "Prophet, it is said, has left a will or revelation, appointing a successor; and among other things, it is stated that his son, a lad of twelve years, is named as his successor."[5]

In spite of the evidence indicating that the Mormon prophet wished his son to succeed him, the youth was not in a position to do so for two central reasons. The first was the general ambiguity of the church's law regarding succession. In spite of some evidence supporting lineal succession in church practice—that is, succession within the Smith family much like a monarch's ascension to a throne—as well as for the prophet's appointment of his son to the office before his death, several other means existed that could justifiably serve as routes to the ordination of the president. As in all ecclesiastical matters, these various methods of succession had to be defined and interpreted by church officials, but the supreme voice in this process was dead and no one could readily take his place. The second factor was that young Smith was not yet twelve years old in 1844, and the church could not, in all practicality, choose such a young boy for the key position as president. Many reasoned, probably correctly, that the movement needed strong, able leadership rather than something that would be at best a weak regency.[6]

Brigham Young, the man who assumed the leadership of the majority of the Mormons, provided the organization with just such a strong and able government. He proposed, at first, that the church accept a caretaker administration that would oversee the procedural and governmental concerns of the movement. Young did not claim at the time to be Joseph Smith, Jr.'s successor; he repeatedly stated that no one could take the beloved prophet's place, and this may have been a deciding factor in the acceptance of his administration by many of the Saints in Nauvoo.[7] Young was a remarkable man. Solidly built, with a broad face and long brown hair, he had a powerful magnetism that impressed and in some cases impelled most people he met. Able, ambitious, and sometimes arrogant, Young was as capable as any man in the church.[8]

Young wanted, above all else in 1844, to preserve the religion that he had first joined twelve years earlier. His goal was to continue what he believed had been the prophet's policies and goals for the movement and to create unity among the membership. He revealed much about his concern for the church in his diary entry on the day he was chosen by the Nauvoo conference to assume control of the church's organization. He wrote: "This day is long to be remembered by me, it is the first time I have met with the Church at Nauvoo since Bro Joseph and Hyrum was kild—and the occasion on which the Church caule [called] was somewhat painful to me, . . . now Joseph is gon and it seed [seemed] as though manny wanted to draw off a party and be leaders, but this cannot be, the church must be one or they are not the Lords."[9] Following his accession to the church's leadership Young tried to rule efficiently and benevolently, but always with a sense of urgency and the belief that the church was in crisis and needed a strong and resolute captain at the helm. As a result problems developed between Young and a few church members who did not always agree with his stringent policies. Among those dissidents prominent in the city was the widow of Joseph Smith. These strained relations in Nauvoo ever after colored the manner in which Joseph Smith III perceived Brigham Young and the organization he led.[10]

It was natural that the Nauvoo Saints should have supported Young and the Apostles in this succession crisis. First, it had long been a routine practice at every church conference to sustain the various officials in their posts. When Brigham Young asked, as he did at the 8 August meeting, that the church support the Twelve in their office and calling, all should have been willing to do so. Second, church members distrusted many of the other individuals who aspired to the presidency: they were either older officials who had been out of favor with the prophet just previous to his death, as in the case of Sidney Rigdon, or relatively unknown men who tried to force their ways into the presidency, as in James J. Strang's peculiar instance. Third, over 4,000 members of the Nauvoo church population were immigrants from Great Britain. The British mission had been under the direction of the Twelve since its inception in 1837, and at one time or another virtually all of the Apostles had served there. Many of these immigrants had been converted to Mormonism by a member of the Twelve, and they certainly trusted the members of the quorum. Therefore, the English converts in Nauvoo naturally supported men whom they knew and trusted. This core support, moreover, was certainly large enough to ensure the general acceptance of Brigham Young and the Twelve. Finally, Young and the Quorum of Twelve embraced and perpetuated the development of unique theological conceptions introduced by Joseph Smith a few years before his death—especially the religious ceremonies wrapped up in the Nauvoo Temple.[11]

Although not technically president of the church after this meeting, Young still held operational control of the church administration and did not wait long before exercising this authority. On the day after the meeting, acting as head of the Apostles, he issued a series of executive orders that firmly placed the machinery of church government in his hands.[12] His firm authority assured that Nauvoo civic and church business functioned smoothly, and most residents of the city were pleased with how he handled the crisis. Affairs seemed to be returning to normal under Young—a welcome change from the church's earlier crisis and confusion. There was, however, the very large gap of prophetic leadership that Young did not try to fill. Young did not even consider the question of succession in the presidency at that time. He was content to manage a caretaker government and to let this question of future prophetic guidance rest for the time being.[13]

Had the situation presented itself, Brigham Young might have given up his control over the church after this crisis in favor of a mature Joseph Smith III.[14] Young acted very coyly regarding the promises and blessings that had been made to young Smith by his father. Although he never clearly stated his policy regarding young Joseph's future presidency, his actions in Nauvoo immediately after the prophet's death and later in Utah suggested that he would have considered Joseph Smith III's candidacy for the presidency of the church very strongly if young Smith would accept the theological and administrative direction Young gave the church following his father's death. According to John D. Lee, whose testimony was admittedly biased because of later developments in Utah but who was, nevertheless, a Nauvoo and Utah Mormon leader, when Lucy Mack Smith, Joseph III's grandmother, visited Brigham Young early in 1845 he indicated that he had no designs on the prophetic office. He claimed that the church was in a time of crisis and that enemies wanted to kill the prophet's successor. He explained that his goals were only to maintain the movement's unity and to shield the successor until the troubles had been dealt with. "If it is known that he is the rightful successor of his father, the enemy of the Priesthood will seek his life," Young supposedly told the old woman. Pragmatically, he added, "he is too young to lead this people now, but when he arrives at a mature age he shall have his place. No one shall rob him of it."[15]

Ample evidence documents the sincerity of Brigham Young's statement regarding the future presidency of Joseph Smith III.[16] Even so, because of a number of circumstances in Nauvoo during the last years of the Mormon headquarters there, the Smith family, and Joseph Smith III especially, could not accept the direction Young gave to the church. Each of these conflicts not only increased the distrust and dislike between Emma Smith and Brigham Young but, more importantly, affected young Joseph III's attitude and eventual behavior toward Mormonism.[17]

The most important difficulty between Emma Smith and Brigham Young arose over the open and increasingly widespread practice of plural marriage and the linking of its beginnings to Joseph Smith, Jr. It sparked much of the Smith family's ill-will toward the church and Young, and led to Emma's conviction that the head of the Twelve was leading the movement into total apostasy. She certainly came to believe the doctrine an evil concept and refused to accept any connection of the practice with either the Smith family or her dead husband. As far as she was concerned, it was based solely upon the lust of Young and his retainers, and she taught her children that their father had neither taught nor practiced such a concept.[18]

Young claimed, on the other hand, that Joseph Smith, Jr., had begun teaching the doctrine as early as 1831 and had become one of its foremost practitioners by the time of his death. The prophet had tried to make his wife understand the religious significance of the plural marriage principle, Young asserted, but she was generally resistant. At times she had been understanding and compliant, even standing as a witness in some of the prophet's polygamous wedding ceremonies, Young argued, but at others she was a fiery banshee, seething with discontent and rebellion, who fought the doctrine with all her might. But whatever vacillation toward polygamy Emma Smith may have exhibited during her husband's lifetime quickly changed to stouthearted defiance after his death. After 1844 Emma adamantly denied her husband's involvement in the practice and proved a very difficult opponent of Young's attempts to expand the practice in Nauvoo between late 1844 and the exodus of most of the Saints in early 1846.[19] The two individuals' differences over this issue created terrific distrust, which later turned to hatred. On one occasion in Utah, for instance, Young remarked to his followers about Emma, "Joseph used to say that he would have her in the hereafter, if he had to go to hell for her, and he will have to go to hell for her as sure as he ever gets her."[20]

After the disagreements over plural marriage, other difficulties between the Smith family and the church administration seemed to increase in both number and severity. These problems affected young Joseph Smith greatly. The exposure to such difficult trials at a relatively young age hardened his perceptions and made him more stoical and cautious in the manner in which he wished to conduct his affairs. No longer could he act as a child; he felt it necessary to act more like an adult and shoulder responsibility for the family. It also caused him to develop a very uncomplimentary view of Young. In writing of this period in his memoirs many years later, Joseph Smith labeled the section dealing with the trials in Nauvoo "Oppression." He claimed that in 1844 and 1845 Brigham Young became a ruthless man who "had assumed control of church affairs, and seemed inclined to dominate and make everything and everybody bend to his will." He added, "This did not suit my mother; and besides she could not fellowship some other things that were occurring." As a result a contest developed between Emma Smith and Brigham Young, each seeking to gain the advantage over the other. The two jousted over seemingly little things, each doling out to the other what young Joseph later called a "good many petty annoyances and also some things that were much more serious." Brigham Young, however, dealing from his position of authority, was capable of giving much the worse to the Smith family during the confrontation.[21] To his credit, there is very little evidence of overt malevolence toward the Smith family. What there was present, however, was exacerbated by perceptions on the part of the Smiths.

One difficulty between the two, in addition to the plural marriage controversy, was the settlement of Joseph Smith, Jr.'s estate. Smith had died intestate, presenting the Hancock County, Illinois, Probate Court with a complex legal problem. Smith's personal property was inextricably tied up with the property of the church; therefore, Young thought that church officials should handle the settlement of the estate. On the other hand, Emma Smith was concerned about providing for herself and their five children, and did not want to lose control of any property that might be hers for an instant, especially since the church made no promises about providing for the family's welfare. Therefore, she treated all of it as her husband's personal property. Three weeks after the prophet's murder Emma went to Carthage and obtained appointment as administratrix for Joseph Smith's estate and legal guardian of their children. In spite of the fact that this act occurred before the 6 August conference, Young was furious that Emma had gone ahead without approval by a recognized official and especially that she intended to handle the estate herself. He did all in his power to have the order rescinded but failed to do so during the summer of 1844.[22]

He finally succeeded on 19 September 1844, when the presiding judge appointed a prominent Mormon, Joseph W. Coolidge, as administrator of the prophet's estate in her place. Emma protested, but there was little she could do, for she had failed to raise a bond demanded by the court, and Young persuaded the judge to appoint Coolidge. Coolidge served as administrator for four years, obtaining few favorable decisions for the family while selling off approximately $1,000 worth of the Smiths' property to pay funeral expenses and administrative costs. Young Smith bitterly remembered that Coolidge's administration of the estate had been particularly cruel for the family. He allowed them, for instance, to retain only their household goods, two horses, two cows, Emma's spinning wheels, and $124 per year in income from rental property.[23]

Young Joseph believed that the Twelve forced Coolidge to impose this harsh settlement on the family in order to make Emma accept Brigham Young's authority. He wrote in his memoirs that he "formed the impression that while Joseph Coolidge was, under ordinary circumstances, an honest man, in this matter he was under

the domination of others." He continued: "Our family was subjected to a series of injustices at his hands and disagreeable experiences which became almost unbearable. Whether or not Coolidge
lent himself willingly to the efforts made by others to distress and
annoy mother and her family, I do not know, but conditions, as
they developed, seem to warrant that conclusion." To make the
serious affair worse, Coolidge was a very poor administrator who
even left the state without completing the duties assigned him by
the court, taking with him some of the estate's money. Had not
Joseph and Emma Smith deeded various pieces of Nauvoo property
to their minor children during bankruptcy proceedings in 1842,
the Smith family would have ended up with much less than they
actually received after the Coolidge administration.[24]

As part of the controversy over the estate, Emma Smith angered
Brigham Young over the matter of the control of her husband's
papers. Smith had a large collection of papers at the time of his
death, but they were scattered about Nauvoo in various offices and
church officials' homes. Emma Smith gathered up some of them before Young returned to Nauvoo and tried to obtain others but was
unsuccessful. After his arrival in Nauvoo in August, Young learned
of her action and tried to regain those papers she had been successful in collecting. Claiming the papers were church property, Young
sent messengers to the Smith home to retrieve these manuscripts,
but Emma refused to part with them. She claimed she would never
give them up. Fortunately, Young was not too concerned about
most of the papers Emma had, since the items of greatest importance to the church—the bulk of the prophet's official correspondence, his autobiography, the official record and minute books, and
ledgers of church business transactions—were still in the hands of
church members loyal to the new administration. The document
that Young wanted to obtain most, however, was a manuscript of
part of the Bible, known to the Saints as the New Translation,
which was an "inspired revision" of the King James version that
had been prepared by Joseph Smith and his assistants. Emma refused to let the church take the manuscript because, as she later
explained to her son, "she felt the grave responsibility of safely
keeping it until such time as the Lord would permit or direct its
publication."[25]

To assure the New Translation's safety, Emma hid it in a trunk
for which she had a false bottom built. Apparently, only one person

outside the Smith family was allowed to use this document between 1844 and 1846, for fear that Young would somehow confiscate the manuscript. Emma did permit John M. Bernhisel, her good friend for many years, to borrow and copy a portion of the manuscript, but even with him she was cautious. She distrusted Brigham Young so greatly by this time that she always maintained her guard. She made a telling indictment of Young and his lieutenants concerning this incident in 1867. "It is true that every L.D.S. cannot be trusted to copy them [the manuscript pages], and I did not trust many of them with the reading of them," she wrote to her son, "and I am of the opinion that if I had trusted all that wished the privilege you would not have them in your possession now."[26]

Another conflict between Young and Emma Smith apparently arose over the bodies of Joseph and Hyrum Smith. A few months after the prophet's death, in the early fall of 1844, Emma Smith, heavily pregnant with the prophet's last child and assisted by a small group of men she trusted, removed the bodies from their burial sites in the Nauvoo House basement in the dark of night and reburied them beneath the brick floor of a spring house near the old Smith Homestead. Apparently, young Smith was present at this clandestine burial, although in later years he did not recall the location, and snipped off a lock of his father's light-colored hair as a last momento.[27] Perhaps it was Emma's ultimate harrassment of Brigham Young, or maybe it was the result of other factors, but she swore her assistants to secrecy and told no one of the second burial's exact location until 1879, when she lay dying in Nauvoo.

According to Joseph III, after all these incidents the conflicts between Young and his mother increased dramatically. He wrote that Young had men watch the Smith home and spy on their activities. Evidence indicates that Young may have been merely providing for the family's protection in a city increasingly overcome in 1845 and 1846 with violent rabble, but if so the Smiths did not think it warranted. Joseph later wrote, "In 1845 and 1846 no person was allowed to come to the house without passing a cordon of police." The guards reported to Young all comings and goings in the neighborhood and took the opportunity to observe the Smiths' visitors' subsequent movements in the city. Smith believed the guarding of the home amounted to nothing less than a house arrest for the family.[28]

That Brigham Young did not intend the sentry organization as purely protective seems to be confirmed by an incident Joseph Smith III recalled involving him and Orrin Porter Rockwell. Rockwell, a rough, loyal follower and distant cousin of the dead prophet, had been a long-time friend of the Smith family. After the prophet's death he had been torn by the loyalty he felt for the Smiths and the desire he felt to cast his lot with Brigham Young and the Twelve. Young soon won Rockwell's allegiance, and he became a vocal advocate for the prerogatives of the Apostles. Even so, Rockwell was not exempt from surveillance by guards when he tried to maintain his relationship with the Smith family. Young Joseph reported that one day he saw his old friend walking down the street. He ran out of the house, jumped his picket fence, and bounded down the road to talk with Rockwell. They spoke for only a couple of moments, but Rockwell seemed strangely distant, and all too quickly he pushed Joseph away. As he did so, he tenderly told him: "You had best go back. I am glad you came to meet me, but it is best that you are not seen with me. It can do me no good and it may bring harm to you." That fleeting moment always remained with Smith. It influenced him the rest of his life, leading him one step closer to his eventual rejection of what he called the "Mormon Tyranny." "I climbed back over the fence, to wonder, in my boyish way," he recalled, "how it was possible for men to be so wicked and cruel to good men."[29]

All of these controversies steeled the Smith family to greater opposition to Young and his administration. The family perceived Young's hand in several additional incidents, probably not all of his instigation, but by this time the Smiths attributed any presumed villainy to Young. Joseph Smith remembered that ruffians attacked several of the family's friends when they attempted to visit the Nauvoo Mansion. When Young's guards, who were on duty to handle just such difficulties, failed to intervene, the Smiths concluded that the attacks were sanctioned by church officials. For instance, Joseph Smith III wrote that one such visitor to the Smith home was assaulted near the house by a thug armed with a bowie knife. He fought him off with a huge, ebony cane as the guards watched.[30] Whether Smith's perceptions were correct or not is a moot point; he believed that these actions had been countenanced by Young, and this colored his perception of both the church official and the institution he led.

His perceptions, certainly, had some basis in fact. Some of the

assaults were undoubtedly official acts designed to persuade un-
desirable visitors from remaining in town. During this period a few
youths, known as the Nauvoo "Whistling and Whittling Brigade,"
were organized to intimidate strangers into making hasty depar-
tures from town. Young Smith witnessed this group in action on at
least one occasion. Austin Cowles, a former member of the Nauvoo
High Council who had publicly broken with the church over the
issue of plural marriage, visited the city in 1845, only to be roughly
treated by those of the Whistling and Whittling Brigade gathered
near the Smith home. These youths followed Cowles about, according to Smith's recollection, "urging him with wicked knives, saying
nothing to him, except to tell him to move on when he stopped to
speak to anyone." Smith wrote that he tried to speak to him, but
the "escort struck up their din of whistling and whittling, hustling
the poor man with the ends of broken boards and the sticks they
were whittling."[31]

By the summer of 1845 Brigham Young, while in control of the
church bureaucracy at Nauvoo and firmly administering the programs of the movement, still had not gained the allegiance of the
Smith family. Whenever he and Emma Smith met, they disagreed;
apparently the two could never reconcile. This was most exasperat-
ing for Young; that such a powerful figure as Emma Smith should
remain at odds with the church was a figurative slap in the face.
Emma Smith of all people, he reasoned, should have remained true
to the Mormon faith, yet she rejected the church as it existed under
Young.[32]

As the chasm between the Smith family and the church's administration widened, another point of contention directly affecting
Joseph Smith III rode into Nauvoo in the person of William B.
Smith, the hyperbolic, erratic, and contentious younger brother of
the slain prophet.[33] Arriving in the Mormon stronghold on 4 May
1845, William was initially accepted by the church administration
as the presiding patriarch, a very significant ecclesiastical office
but one without great administrative authority.[34] Within a month
of his arrival, however, William Smith was vocally in opposition
to Brigham Young and the Twelve and openly courting dissenters,
trying to create a movement that would give him an authoritative
position. Joseph Smith III played a prominent part in his efforts to
gain such a following.

For a time William apparently tried to push Joseph III for president of the church with Emma Smith and himself as coregents until Joseph came of age.[35] Although Emma never publicly embraced his position, she evidently lent him some support at first. According to James Monroe, the Smith children's schoolteacher, Emma told him that William "seemed to have correct principles" concerning the succession and direction of the church.[36] On 23 May 1845 William Clayton wrote that "William Smith is coming out in opposition to the Twelve in favor of [George J.] Adams. The latter has organized a church in Augusta, Iowa Territory with young Joseph Smith for President, William Smith for Patriarch. . . . there is more danger from William Smith than from any other source, and I fear his course will bring us much trouble."[37] This effort with Adams was unsuccessful, however, and William dropped it during the summer of 1845. In fact, none of William Smith's schemes came to anything, and since he had demonstrated his disloyalty to Young and the Twelve on several occasions, at the October 1845 conference he was shorn of both his apostleship and his office of presiding patriarch. However, his activities in Nauvoo in 1845 apparently did establish very firmly in the minds of the Smith family the concept of lineal priesthood, the passing on from father to son the rights and duties of the religion.[38]

Evidently, all of these contentions prompted some of Young's followers to take it upon themselves to rid Nauvoo of the Smith family. According to Joseph III, these renegades sent Emma an ultimatum demanding that she pack up and leave town within three days or her house "would be burned over her head." Emma flatly refused to be intimidated and went about her business as if nothing had happened. On the third day after the threat, however, she took precautions. Emma prepared pallets on the floor near the door so that her children could easily escape should fire break out, but she slept in her second-story bedroom in a forthright defiance of the threat. The children, aware of the threat, were a bit fearful, but said their prayers and laid down to sleep. Joseph remembered the event: "We lay down in the quietness and finally went to sleep. In the morning the house was found to be still over our heads and intact, but on the north side were discovered the remains of some fire material piles against the wall. A fire had been started and a portion of the siding was scorched, but it had not caught sufficiently to set the house on fire; hence we escaped."[39] Joseph thought at the time that the family had been very lucky. Emma, however, had been reasonably sure that the house would not burn. Years later she explained why. "I have often thought," she wrote to Joseph Smith in 1867, "the reason that our house did not burn down when it was so often on fire was because of them [the 'New Translation' papers hidden in the house] and I still feel there is a sacredness attached to them." [40]

The battle waged between Emma Smith and Brigham Young from 1844 to 1846 affected Joseph Smith III deeply. He had an interest in its outcome and naturally sided with his mother at every point. As a result he developed an abiding hatred of all for which Young stood. He distrusted the man and believed that he had duped the thousands of Latter-day Saints who followed him to the Great Basin. Although Joseph Smith recognized that he was much too young to have led the church in 1844, he believed that Young, who may have acted rightly at first, went far beyond his initial grant of authority in charting the course of the church along lines that the Smith family disapproved. Joseph adopted his mother's view of plural marriage, fighting his entire life to prove that his father had never been involved in the practice. He repeatedly announced, as he did in a letter in 1895, that "Father had *no wife* but my mother, Emma Hale, to the knowledge of either my mother or myself, and I was twelve years old, nearly, when he was killed." [41] Brigham Young, therefore, was the great villain, according to Smith. He had instituted polygamy and had tried to place the burden of its origination on the prophet. Consequently, Joseph never took part in any Mormon movement that Young led. He could never bring himself to accept this variety of Mormonism and thus forsook his call as the successor to the main body of the Saints, eventually accepting leadership of a Mormon group better suited to his particular religious conceptions. [42]

Two documents which young Joseph wrote in January and February 1845 illustrate how the stress of his family's life in Nauvoo affected him. The first, entitled "Rules of Behavior for Youth," contained Joseph's assessment of proper conduct. In it he listed not only standard etiquette of the day, but also rules that seem to reflect the unhappy Nauvoo experience: "Speak not when you should hold your piece. Many questions, remarks and sarcasms may be better answered by silence than by words—by silent contempt. Turn not your back to others. . . . Show not yourself glad at the misfortune of others, though it be your enemy. . . . Be not hasty to believe flying reports to the disparagement of any one. Associate with men of Good character and remember it is better to be alone than in bad company." The most important rule, which impressed young Joseph at this time and which he tried to observe throughout the rest of his life, may also have been prompted by the difficulties between his family and the church hierarchy: "Never attempt anything but what you can do openly; free from fear of consequences."[43]

The second document was an account of "A Thrilling Dream." In this dream the adolescent Smith, armed with pistols and a sabre, was admiring a magnificent garden. While captivated by the garden's size and beauty, he heard a scream and rushed toward the sound, finding a "savage monster" assaulting a beautiful lady. She was clad in a white, flowing robe and was obviously very pure. Drawing his sabre, Smith defended her and "laid him dead with a single blow." Other enemies soon appeared to attack the lady, but Smith fought them off. In the midst of one last, desperate struggle with a particularly powerful enemy, he suddenly awoke in a terrified state. One is tempted to surmise that this dream was prompted by Smith's subconscious reaction to the harsh realities of life in Nauvoo and to conclude that he was defending his mother against her enemies, the last of whom was particularly powerful and resourceful.[44]

In the midst of these events within Nauvoo, external anti-Mormon activity increased during the fall of 1845. Brigham Young made a hasty agreement with the non-Mormon officials directing the removal of the Saints from Nauvoo during the spring of 1846 in return for peace. Consequently, Young spent the winter mobilizing the church members for the move, locating a new gathering spot in the West, acquiring necessary resources for the migration, and making travel arrangements. By the end of January 1846 about 2000 Mormons were ready to leave the city, and the first companies departed during February. Most of those left in Nauvoo had departed by May 1846, and the city became a virtual ghost town.[45]

The decision not to go west with Brigham Young's faction of the church had been easy for the Smith family. After all that had happened between Emma Smith and Brigham Young, she could never submit to his authority. More important, however, Emma understood that going west would mean that she would have to give up her property, her home, and her means of livelihood. She would have to rely upon the church for everything, and since Brigham Young controlled the church, she would have to rely directly upon him. When the main body of Saints left Nauvoo, therefore, she remained behind to raise her children in a city past its heyday.[46]

As the Mormons withdrew from Nauvoo, a power vacuum developed in which lawlessness reigned as never before. Friends, among them Dr. Bernhisel, persuaded Emma Smith to take her children away from the town until order could be restored. Consequently, she rented the Nauvoo Mansion to a recent settler, a Mr. Van Tuyl, and booked passage upriver on a tramp steamer. The Smiths boarded the *Uncle Tobey* on 12 September 1846 and proceeded to Fulton City, Illinois, 120 miles to the north. There they settled with a growing band of Mormon dissenters, including William Marks, Loren Walker, and Jared Carter, all prominent Mormons, to await the restoration of law and order in Nauvoo.[47]

No matter what importance one may assign to this chapter of Mormon history, the time between 1844 and 1846 were years of trial for the church, the Smith family generally, and Joseph Smith III in particular. All were changed, marked by the events following the death of Joseph the Prophet—young Smith perhaps most of all. He was forced during a very short period to cast off his childhood and assume many adult responsibilities. That, of course, is a common experience for youths who lose a stable family environment because of death or divorce of the parents. Smith's experiences, however, colored by the very difficult circumstances of the feud between his family and Young and the church, shaped many of his lifelong beliefs about certain church leaders, church doctrine, and administrative practices. Smith's memoirs often betray his perception that Brigham Young was a negative role model and the institution he headed the opposite of what he believed the church should become in the world. Although these conceptions would not be realized for many years, they were already forming in the mind of Joseph Smith III as he stood on the deck of the *Uncle Tobey* enroute to Fulton City on that autumn day of 1846. Thus Smith's experiences between 1844 and 1846 served as a crucible for most of the concerns, fears, and ideals expressed in later life. The intolerance, pettiness, and promulgation of esoteric doctrine that he perceived within the church during this period made him all the more tolerant, magnanimous, and cautious in the explanation of doctrine once he became president of the Reorganized Church. Later these ideals would be seasoned with a basic pragmatism that also incorporated principles in the governing of his own church.[48]

NOTES

1. Thomas Ford, *The History of Illinois from Its Commencement as a State in 1818 to 1848* (Chicago: C. S. Griggs and Co., 1854), p. 357; Oliver Huntington, Journal, pp. 54–55, Church of Jesus Christ of Latter-day Saints Historical Department, Salt Lake City, Utah.

2. Parley P. Pratt, *Autobiography of Parley Parker Pratt* (Salt Lake City: Deseret Book Co., 1976), p. 333.

3. These methods of succession have been brilliantly analyzed in D. Michael Quinn, "The Mormon Succession Crisis of 1844," *Brigham Young University Studies* 16 (Winter 1976): 187–233. Quinn asserted that the eight methods included succession (1) by a Counselor in the First Presidency (Sidney Rigdon); (2) by special or secret appointment (James J. Strang, Lyman Wight, Alpheus Cutler, Joseph Smith III); (3) through the office of associate president (the disfellowshipped Oliver Cowdery and the deceased Hyrum Smith); (4) by the presiding patriarch (the deceased Hyrum Smith and William B. Smith); (5) by appointment through the Council of Fifty (Lyman Wight, Alpheus Cutler, Peter Haws, George J. Adams, George Miller, John E. Page); (6) by Quorum of Twelve Apostles (Brigham Young); (7) by the Priesthood Councils of the Seventy, the High Council, and the Twelve Apostles (William Marks); (8) and by a member of the prophet's family (the deceased Hyrum Smith, William B. Smith, and Joseph Smith III).

4. For discussions of the rise of splinter groups in 1844, see Steven L. Shields, *Divergent Paths of the Restoration: A History of the Latter Day Saints* (Bountiful, Utah: Restoration Research, Inc., 1982).

5. The prophecy is in the Book of Doctrine and Covenants (Independence, Mo.: Herald Publishing House, 1970), Section 107:18c. Additional information on Smith's possible succession can be found in D. Michael Quinn, "Organizational Development and Social Origins of the Mormon Hierarchy, 1832–1932" (M.A. thesis, University of Utah, 1973), pp. 125–45; Quinn, "Mormon Succession Crisis," pp. 214–33; W. Grant McMurray, " 'True Son of a True Father': Joseph Smith III and the Succession Question," in *Restoration Studies I,* ed. Maurice L. Draper (Independence, Mo.: Herald Publishing House, 1980), pp. 131–45. The quotation from the secular history is from Henry Brown, *History of Illinois* (New York: J. Winchester, 1844), p. 489.

6. This issue is raised in Quinn, "Mormon Succession Crisis," pp. 187–233, and Ronald K. Esplin, "Joseph, Brigham, and the Twelve: A Succession of Continuity," *Brigham Young University Studies* 21 (Summer 1981): 301–41.

7. James M. Monroe, Diary, 24 April 1845, Mormon Collection, Beinecke Library, Yale University, New Haven, Conn.; T. Edgar Lyon, "Nauvoo and the Council of Twelve," in *The Restoration Movement: Essays in Mormon History,* ed. F. Mark McKiernan, Alma R. Blair, and Paul M. Edwards (Lawrence, Kan.: Coronado Press, 1973), pp. 191–98.

8. For an excellent biography of Brigham Young, see Leonard J. Arrington, *Brigham Young: American Moses* (New York: Alfred A. Knopf, 1985). See also Newell G. Bringhurst, *Brigham Young and the Expanding American Frontier* (Boston: Little, Brown and Co., 1986), and Stanley P. Hirshson, *The Lion of the Lord: A Biography of Brigham Young* (New York: Alfred A. Knopf, 1969).

9. Brigham Young, Journal, 8 August 1844, Latter-day Saints Historical Department.

10. Joseph Smith, "The Memoirs of President Joseph Smith (1832–1914)," *Saints' Herald* 82 (8 January 1935): 47–49; Roger D. Launius, "William Marks and the Restoration," *Saints' Herald* 126 (1 May 1979): 7–8, 126 (1 June 1979): 6–7; Linda King Newell and Valeen Tippetts Avery, *Mormon Enigma: Emma Smith, Prophet's Wife, "Elect Lady," Polygamy's Foe* (Garden City, N.Y.: Doubleday and Co., 1984), pp. 210–20.

11. Personal trust is a basic ingredient in loyalty. For discussions of this issue see Harry O. Reiken et al., *When Prophecy Fails* (Minneapolis: University of Minnesota Press, 1956); James McGregor Burns, *Leadership* (New York: Random House, 1980); Eric Hoffer, *The True Believer* (New York: Alfred A. Knopf, 1958). Statistical information concerning Nauvoo inhabitants is computed from Dean L. May, "A Demographic Portrait of the Mormons, 1830–1980," in *After 150 Years: The Latter-day Saints in Historical Perspective,* ed. Thomas G. Alexander and Jessie L. Embry (Provo, Utah: Charles Redd Center for Western Studies, 1983), pp. 43–44; James E. Smith, "Frontier Nauvoo: Building a Picture from Statistics," *Ensign,* September 1979, pp. 17–18. Theological pronouncements taught by the Twelve have been discussed in Lyon, "Nauvoo and the Council of Twelve," pp. 190–91; T. Edgar Lyon, "Doctrinal Development During the Nauvoo Sojourn, 1839–1846," *Brigham Young University Studies* 15 (Summer 1975): 935–46; Lisle G. Brown, "The Sacred Departments of Temple Work: The Assembly Room and the Council Chamber," *Brigham Young University Studies* 19 (Spring 1979): 360–74; Andrew E. Ehat, "Joseph Smith's Introduction of Temple Ordinances and the 1844

Mormon Succession Question" (M.A. thesis, Brigham Young University, 1983).

12. Joseph Smith, Jr., *The History of the Church of Jesus Christ of Latter-day Saints*, ed. B. H. Roberts (Salt Lake City: Deseret Book Co., 1976), 7:247–52; Robert Bruce Flanders, *Nauvoo: Kingdom on the Mississippi* (Urbana: University of Illinois Press, 1965), p. 320.

13. Heber C. Kimball to William B. Smith, 9 January 1845, William B. Smith Collection, Latter-day Saints Historical Department.

14. This opinion is reinforced by the analysis of Esplin, "Joseph, Brigham, and the Twelve," pp. 333–41.

15. John D. Lee, *Mormonism Unveiled: Including the Remarkable Life and Confession of the Late Mormon Bishop, John D. Lee* (St. Louis: Bryan, Brand, and Co., 1877), p. 161. At the time Lee prepared this memoir, he was under indictment for his role in the Mountain Meadows Massacre and certainly no friend of Brigham Young. Even if his account is not entirely accurate, however, such an exchange was possible, given Young's basic reverence for the Smith family and his later statements about welcoming the Smith sons into the fold in Utah as discussed in Esplin, "Joseph, Brigham, and the Twelve," pp. 333–41. This issue will be discussed in greater detail in chapter 10, "The Utah Mission."

16. Two of these favorable statements toward Joseph Smith III can be found in *Journal of Discourses* (Salt Lake City), 8:69, and *Latter-day Saints' Millennial Star* (Liverpool, England), 16:442. Edward W. Tullidge, a Utah Saint who joined the Reorganization, suggested that Young held great respect for the promises made about Joseph Smith III concerning succession in the church's presidency and would have welcomed him into the Utah hierarchy. But because of his animosity to Young and the doctrines of his church, Smith could never in good conscience have become a part of that movement. See Tullidge, *The Life of Joseph the Prophet* (Plano, Ill.: Herald Publishing House, 1880), pp. 614–15.

17. For a detailed discussion of the distrust between these two individuals, see Linda King Newell and Valeen Tippetts Avery, "The Lion and the Lady: Brigham Young and Emma Smith," *Utah Historical Quarterly* 48 (Winter 1980): 81–97.

18. Smith, "Memoirs," *Saints' Herald* 82 (2 April 1935): 432; Newell and Avery, *Mormon Enigma*, pp. 95–220, passim; Joseph Smith, "The Last Testimony of Sister Emma," *Saints' Herald* 26 (1 October 1879): 289–90.

19. *Journal of Discourses* 3:266, 17:159; Andrew Jenson, "Plural Marriage," *Historical Record* 6 (July 1887): 205–36. The controversy over plural marriage has prompted voluminous studies in recent years. A valuable survey of the literature of this subject is Davis Bitton, "Mor-

mon Polygamy: A Review Article," *Journal of Mormon History* 4 (1977): 101–18. The most extensive studies of the origins of plural marriage are Lawrence Foster, *Religion and Sexuality: Three American Communal Experiments of the Nineteenth Century* (New York: Oxford University Press, 1981); Danel W. Bachman, "A Study of the Mormon Practice of Plural Marriage before the Death of Joseph Smith" (M.A. thesis, Purdue University, 1975); Donna Hill, *Joseph Smith: The First Mormon* (Garden City, N.Y.: Doubleday and Co., 1977), pp. 335–61. On the possible early origins of the doctrine see Danel W. Bachman, "New Light on an Old Hypothesis: The Ohio Origins of the Revelation on Eternal Marriage," *Journal of Mormon History* 5 (1978): 19–31. For a different approach to the subject see Richard P. Howard, "The Changing RLDS Response to Mormon Polygamy: A Preliminary Analysis," *John Whitmer Historical Association Journal* 3 (1983): 14–29.

20. *Journal of Discourses* 17:159. See also *New York Tribune,* 16 December 1871; *New York Herald,* 17 November 1868; William Hall, *The Abominations of Mormonism Exposed, Containing Many Facts and Doctrines Concerning That Singular People during Seven Years Membership with Them; from 1840 and 1847* (Cincinnati, Ohio: I. Hart, 1852), pp. 43–44; *New York World,* 2 October 1870; *Springfield* (Ill.) *Weekly Republican,* 1 December 1866.

21. Smith, "Memoirs," *Saints' Herald* 82 (29 January 1935): 144.

22. Probate Records, Book A (1840–1846), pp. 341–42, Hancock County Courthouse, Carthage, Ill.; State of Illinois, Hancock County to Emma Smith, 17 July 1844, Lewis Crum Bidamon Papers, Reorganized Church of Jesus Christ of Latter Day Saints Library–Archives, Independence, Mo.

23. Probate Records, Book A (1840–1846), pp. 354–55; Probate Records, Book C (1844–1849), pp. 28, 43, Hancock County Courthouse; Smith, "Memoirs," *Saints' Herald* 82 (29 January 1935): 144; Chancery Records, Book A, p. 490, Hancock County Courthouse.

24. Smith, "Memoirs," *Saints' Herald* 82 (29 January 1935): 144; Probate Records, Book A (1840–1846), pp. 412, 421; Probate Records, Book E (1842–1849), pp. 191, 212; Claims Records, Book C, p. 242, all in Hancock County Courthouse; M. Hamlin Cannon, ed., "Bankruptcy Proceedings Against Joseph Smith in Illinois," *Pacific Historical Review* 14 (December 1945): 423–33, 14 (June 1946): 214–15; Dallin H. Oaks and Joseph I. Bentley, "Joseph Smith and Legal Process: In the Wake of the Steamboat *Nauvoo,*" *Brigham Young University Studies* 19 (Winter 1979): 167–99.

25. Smith, "Memoirs," *Saints' Herald* 82 (29 January 1935): 144. On the "Inspired Version" see Richard P. Howard, *Restoration Scrip-*

tures: A Study of their Textual Development (Independence, Mo.: Herald Publishing House, 1969), pp. 70–193; Robert L. Matthews, *"A Plainer Translation": Joseph Smith's Translation of the Bible, A History and Commentary* (Provo, Utah: Brigham Young University Press, 1975).

26. L. John Nuttall, Diary, p. 335, Special Collections, Harold B. Lee Library, Brigham Young University, Provo, Utah; Emma Smith Bidamon to Joseph Smith, 20 January 1867, Emma Smith Bidamon Papers, Reorganized Church Library–Archives.

27. Smith, "What Do I Remember of Nauvoo?" *Journal of History* 3 (July 1910): 336–41; Smith, "Last Testimony of Sister Emma," pp. 289–90; Newell and Avery, *Mormon Enigma*, pp. 212–13.

28. Joseph Smith, "Autobiography," in Tullidge, *Life of Joseph*, pp. 746–48.

29. Smith, "Memoirs," *Saints' Herald* 82 (22 January 1935): 111.

30. Joseph Smith, "What Do I Remember of Nauvoo?": 338.

31. The best discussion of this tactic to control dissidents in Nauvoo can be found in Thurman Dean Moody, "Nauvoo's Whistling and Whittling Brigade," *Brigham Young University Studies* 15 (Summer 1975): 480–90. Smith's remembrance of the Austin Cowles incident is contained in Smith, "Autobiography," in Tullidge, *Life of Joseph*, p. 749.

32. Numerous rumors that Emma Smith no longer believed in Mormonism were published in newspapers in the region. See the discussion of these in Newell and Avery, *Mormon Enigma*, pp. 213, 221–26; Linda King Newell and Valeena Tippetts Avery, "New Light on the *Sun:* Emma Smith and the *New York Sun* Letter," *Journal of Mormon History* 6 (1979): 23–35. Some of these were motivated by maliciousness, but other rumors were based on the fact that she was adamantly opposed to the Mormonism of Brigham Young. In these latter instances, depending upon one's viewpoint, the statements could be construed as true.

33. Several studies that highlight the life and interesting career of William B. Smith have appeared recently. See Irene M. Bates, "William Smith, 1811–1893: Problematic Patriarch," *Dialogue: A Journal of Mormon Thought* 16 (Summer 1983): 11–23; Paul M. Edward, "William B. Smith: The Persistent Pretender," *Dialogue: A Journal of Mormon Thought* 18 (Summer 1985): 128–39.

34. For a discussion of the Smith crisis in Nauvoo in 1845, see E. Gary Smith, "The Patriarchal Crisis of 1845," *Dialogue: A Journal of Mormon Thought* 16 (Summer 1983): 24–39.

35. Alma R. Blair, "The Reorganized Church of Jesus Christ of Latter Day Saints: Moderate Mormons," in *The Restoration Movement: Essays in Mormon History*, ed. F. Mark McKiernan, Alma R. Blair, and Paul M. Edwards (Lawrence, Kan.: Coronado Press, 1973), p. 213.

36. Monroe, Diary, 24 April 1845.

37. William Clayton, Journal, 23 May 1845, as quoted in Edwards, "William B. Smith," p. 129. The first scholarly biography of Clayton has recently appeared. Serious students should review the seminal work, James B. Allen, *Trials of Discipleship: The Story of William Clayton, A Mormon* (Urbana: University of Illinois Press, 1987).

38. *Times and Seasons* 6 (1 November 1845): 1008–9.

39. Smith, "Memoirs," *Saints' Herald* 82 (29 January 1935): 144.

40. Emma Smith Bidamon to Joseph Smith, 2 December 1867, Joseph Smith III Papers, Reorganized Church Library–Archives.

41. Joseph Smith to Caleb Parker, 14 August 1895, Joseph Smith III Letterbook #6, Reorganized Church Library–Archives.

42. Smith, "Memoirs," *Saints' Herald* 82 (8 January 1935): 47–49.

43. Joseph Smith, "Rules of Behavior for Youth," January 1845, Special Collections, Harold B. Lee Library, Brigham Young University, Provo, Utah.

44. Joseph Smith, "A Thrilling Dream," 14 February 1845, Special Collections, Harold B. Lee Library, Brigham Young University, Provo, Utah.

45. Flanders, *Nauvoo*, pp. 337–41; Arrington, *Brigham Young*, pp. 126–29; Lewis Clark Christianson, "Mormon Foreknowledge of the West," *Brigham Young University Studies* 21 (Fall 1981): 403–15; Susan W. Easton, "Suffering and Death on the Plains of Iowa," *Brigham Young University Studies* 21 (Fall 1981): 431–39.

46. Newell and Avery, *Mormon Enigma*, pp. 227–41.

47. Smith, "Memoirs," *Saints' Herald* 82 (8 January 1935): 48–49, 82 (29 January 1935): 145; Hubert Howe Bancroft, *The History of Utah* (San Francisco: The History Co., 1889), pp. 226–33.

48. A basic theme of this study is the development of Joseph Smith III's tolerance, caution, and pragmatism tempered by principle. This will be discussed especially as Smith reaches maturity and enters the presidency of the Reorganized Church. Examples of Smith's basic pragmatism can be found in Clare D. Vlahos, "Moderation as a Theological Principle in the Thought of Joseph Smith III," *John Whitmer Historical Association Journal* 1 (1981): 3–11; Roger D. Launius, "Joseph Smith III and the Quest for a Centralized Organization, 1860–1873," in *Restoration Studies II*, ed. Maurice L. Draper (Independence, Mo.: Herald Publishing House, 1983), pp. 104–20. For an exciting comparative study of the leadership styles demonstrated by Smith's father and his uncle, see Paul M. Edwards, "The Secular Smiths," *Journal of Mormon History* 4 (1977): 3–17.

CHAPTER

3

Maturity, 1846–56

The Smith family arrived at Fulton City a few days after leaving Nauvoo. Tiny Fulton City was a very different environment from what young Joseph had been used to in the Mormon stronghold. Nauvoo had been constantly in motion and always exciting, while this new community was sleepy and predictable. Emma Smith, however, loved Fulton City for just these reasons. She rented a cottage near the edge of town and set up housekeeping for her family, sharing rooms with several other individuals from Nauvoo. Additionally, William Marks and a few other Mormon dissidents from Nauvoo also settled in the community, many of them becoming frequent visitors to the Smith home throughout the winter of 1846–47. They discussed the affairs of the movement with dissatisfaction, causing serious questions in the mind of young Joseph about the Latter Day Saint religion and prompting him to ponder seriously for the first time the sect and its perceived mission in the world.[1]

In contrast to Joseph's youthful questioning about the Mormon religion, Emma tried to create an environment that was Christian but relatively un-Mormon. The manners and morals she taught her children were very close to those taught in other Christian homes of the era. She was probably quite bitter toward the organized Mormon religion, and numerous reports circulated about her purported rejection of Mormon institutions. In November 1844 a Rock Island, Illinois, newspaper reported that the prophet's widow "has lost all confidence (if she ever had any) in the Mormon Faith."[2] This was certainly an overstatement, but she definitely refrained from any formal affiliation within Mormonism. William Smith, Emma's brother-in-law, wrote on 25 December 1846 to James J. Strang, the founder of one of the many Mormon splinter groups arising after the prophet's death, about Emma's lack of interest in Mormonism, suggesting that she would not allow Joseph Smith III to have any association with the church because of her bitterness. He wrote that she "would not let him have anything to do with Mormonism at present."[3]

Emma Smith's intransigence toward Brigham Young's brand of Mormonism prompted Strang to visit Fulton City and attempt to convince Emma of her error in disassociating herself from the church. He wanted to convert the entire Smith family and particularly Emma Smith and her oldest son to his faction, at least in part because of the prestige the family's name would bring him. Joseph Smith was attending a party at a local hotel when Strang, whom he did not know, came in with William Marks. They turned toward the ballroom and began looking for Joseph among the crowd of teenagers assembled. When Marks spotted him, he called the fourteen-year-old over and introduced him to Strang.[4] Strang explained that he was presently leading a large contingent of Saints who had chosen to reject Brigham Young's authority and would very much like to enlist Joseph's support.[5] Strang and Joseph talked for several minutes, but the erstwhile prophet could not persuade the boy to have anything to do with the movement without his mother's permission. Strang proposed to visit her at their house in the town, but when he did, he found out quickly that Emma Smith had no intention of affiliating with any so-called Mormon church and would not allow her children to do so.

Although the meetings with the Smith family turned out badly for Strang, he did win some followers in Fulton City, notably William Marks and his family, and decided to hold a preaching series with the intention of gaining more. Strang invited Joseph to attend this series, to be held in the Marks home, but the young man declined the offer because of a "severe earache" brought on by the cold weather. Strang succeeded in establishing a small congregation of followers at Fulton City because of his preaching efforts, but he failed to bring in the prized Smith family. During 1847 Emma continued to hold herself and her family aloof from all connection with Mormonism.[6]

In mid-February 1847 the Smiths' stay in Fulton City was interrupted by disturbing news from Nauvoo. When Emma had left the troubled city, she had rented the Nauvoo Mansion to a businessman named Abram Van Tuyl, who agreed to maintain the house in good order during her absence while running it as a hotel. At this time, however, Emma received word from Dr. John M. Bernhisel that Van Tuyl planned to build a flatboat on the Mississippi River, take all the furniture and valuable goods from the mansion, and head downriver before the Smiths returned to Nauvoo. Emma quickly packed the children into a wagon and set out for the old Mormon stronghold in late February, determined to reach home before Van Tuyl could carry out his plan. Her early return thoroughly shocked the would-be thief, who could not complete his plan until the spring thaw on the Mississippi. With the aid of the county sheriff she literally threw him out of the house and reopened the mansion under her own management.[7]

The Nauvoo to which the Smiths returned was far different from the Mormon community of which they had been a part since 1839. Most of the Saints had already gone and had been replaced by new citizens who had neither the religious convictions nor, in many cases, the uprightness of the old Latter Day Saints. Joseph III, remembering these new settlers, did not appreciate their lifestyles. He described them as "a mob of rough, lawless 'river element' [who] came into the city, ransacking, pillaging and destroying. . . . The people who came in were of varying classes, but all were moved by somewhat similar impulses—to obtain cheaply the property being sold by the departing Saints, most of whom were glad to get any price others were willing to pay."[8] Almost overnight Nauvoo became a rowdy river town infested with single men on the make. The stable social institutions that had flourished under the Saints —law and order, religion, and schools—almost completely broke down after the Mormon exodus. A visiting Philadelphia lawyer, Thomas L. Kane, expressed the feelings of most observers when he described Nauvoo in 1848 as a mere shadow of its former majestic past.[9]

In this rough river town between 1847 and 1856 young Joseph Smith became a man. His mother took in boarders at the mansion to earn a living, and Joseph, as the eldest son, served as her bill collector, hired hand, and assistant manager of the family business. Thus Smith learned much about dealing with people and gained valuable experience in practical affairs. Moreover, he quickly discovered the realities of the secular world and learned how to plan for possible contingencies and manipulate situations to best advantage. It was during this period that Smith's basic pragmatism was first expressed in a serious way. This made him deal carefully with what was possible and accept what he could have no control over. At the same time, Smith demonstrated ably his basic principled character, refusing to compromise seriously his beliefs in right and wrong to achieve an end. He adopted a style, demonstrated repeatedly in his church life, in which he defined a goal based on his understanding of what was fair and just and then worked to achieve that goal using whatever methods his basic pragmatism suggested. Many times his methods required lengthy periods of time to even partially achieve his goal, but that was acceptable if the wait calmed confrontational situations and eased feelings. At other times Smith would press ahead, confronting the issue and the people supporting it head on if he was assured that he had authority sufficient to achieve victory. In virtually every instance he sized up the issue carefully before making a nonretreatable stand.

One incident that demonstrated young Smith's grasp of practical affairs as well as his concern for principle occurred in 1847 when a boarder, known only as Dr. Stark, moved from the mansion leaving a $14 hotel bill unpaid. When Emma Smith learned that Stark planned to move from the city in the near future, she was afraid that he might "forget" his debt and sent Joseph to collect it before Stark left. Young Smith confronted the doctor in his office in Nauvoo and asked politely that he settle the account. Stark, busy with a patient at the moment, told Joseph to wait until he was free. After Joseph had waited patiently for an hour, Stark finally turned to him and asked what he wanted. He said nothing but handed Stark a written bill, which the doctor refused to settle. He said that he would be moving soon and had no cash on hand, that the bill should have been collected months ago if the Smiths had intended that it be paid at all, and that Joseph's mother had been unfair in sending a mere boy to play on his sympathies.

With these excuses Joseph left the doctor's office but then thought better of it and returned, determined not to leave without the money. When asked why he had come back, Smith told Stark he was staying until he got the money. It was a matter of principle that his mother be paid for services rendered in good faith, he told the doctor, and a matter of practice that he use whatever reasonable means available to obtain a settlement. Therefore, Smith said, he would stay with Stark until he decided to pay. "I cannot pay it," Stark shouted at the boy. "Just tell your mother to go down in that old stocking of hers and get out some of the coin that is rusting away there and use that, if she needs any, and not come bothering me!" True to his pledge, however, young Smith refused to leave and sat in the doctor's office the rest of the afternoon. Finally, toward the end of the day Dr. Stark gave in. Turning to the boy he said, "Well, I suppose if I must, I must!" He gave the youth the fourteen dollars he owed and swore he would never be in debt to the Smith family again. Joseph happily trotted home to his mother, who thanked him for collecting the money, never knowing what he had gone through to get it.[10]

His manner in collecting this debt suggested a theme that ran throughout his life: a belief in right and wrong, a grasp of what must be done to correct injustice, and a determination to achieve the goal through pragmatic methods. In this instance Smith recognized several important factors that brought him to act as he did. First, Dr. Stark was wrong to leave his debts unpaid, especially since the debt was owed to Joseph's mother. Second, Smith found very quickly that Stark would not pay the debt without some coercion. At this point Smith could easily have returned home, informed his mother that Stark refused to pay, and let her handle it from there. His decision to return to the doctor's office pointed up his basic responsibility in the matter. Finally, Smith decided upon a course of action that essentially badgered Stark into paying off his Nauvoo Mansion bill, a reasonable and totally pragmatic approach. He was forced to prompt action because of Stark's imminent departure from Nauvoo. Although he had the weight of all law and justice to back him—there was apparently no question about the legitimacy of the debt—he handled the issue informally without bringing in other parties who might have complicated the issue considerably, especially if legal action had been undertaken. The incident suggested quite well Smith's basic approach to dealing with issues— the conducting of principled action using pragmatic methods.

One of the new citizens, a middle-aged businessman named Lewis Crum Bidamon, had a tremendous impact on the entire Smith

family and, of course, on young Joseph Smith. Bidamon had originally met the Smiths while delivering to the mansion a carriage ordered by the prophet from his Canton, Illinois, shop in 1844. After
Smith's death Bidamon dealt with Emma several times and came to
respect her cool business head.[11] Later, after the Mormons decided
to leave Nauvoo during the winter of 1845–46, he came to Nauvoo
with the intention of buying their property. While there Bidamon
continued his business relationship with the prophet's widow, and
the two became friends. While in Nauvoo in the summer of 1846,
he used his office as major in the Illinois militia to aid the Smiths in
keeping their Nauvoo property safe from looters during the chaos
of the exodus.[12] In early 1847, while Emma was still in Fulton City,
Bidamon wrote to her, asking if he might rent the mansion from
her, and although she already had a renter, Emma responded that
they could perhaps work something out in the future.[13]

After her return to Nauvoo in February 1847, Emma Smith and
Lewis Bidamon worked out something far more lasting than a business relationship. Already friends, they began to court. "A fine
looking man," young Joseph contended, Bidamon was "six feet tall,
with high forehead and splendid bearing, usually dressed very well,
and always wore, a 'citizens' hat,' as the high-crowned, somewhat
formal ones of the period were called." The widow was attracted by
Bidamon's dashing and debonnaire manner, and the town buzzed
with the exciting news that Emma Smith was having a middle-aged
romance with the prosperous businessman who had recently moved
to town.[14] Within the year the courtship led to marriage: the wedding took place on what would have been the prophet's birthday,
23 December 1847. The Methodist minister in Nauvoo, William
Hana, performed the simple ceremony, with only a few people be-
side the family present.[15] Sarah M. Kimball, a Mormon still in the
town at the time, gossiped about the marriage to a friend in Council Bluffs, Iowa. "The Bride," Kimball wrote, "was dressed in plum
collored [*sic*] satin, a lace tuck handkerchief, gold watch and chain,
no cap, hair plain. We were not honored guests but were told things
passed off very genteely." [16]

The word of Emma's marriage to Bidamon soon reached Brigham
Young. John S. Fullmer, a Mormon leader still in the Midwest, told
him: "I suppose you know by this time that there was a certain
widow in this place, who was lately given . . . 'in holy matrimony'

to one of his Satanic Majesty's high priests, to wit, one Lewis Bidamon. Now these twain being one flesh concocted a grand scheme by which to enrich themselves." [17] Almon Babbitt, the Mormon leader remaining in Nauvoo to see to the sale of the church's property, was so incensed over the marriage that he even went to Emma and told her she had no right to marry the major and in so doing had forsaken her commitment to the Mormon faith. Young, Fullmer, and Babbitt all realized that Emma's marriage to Lewis Bidamon assured that the prophet's family would never go west and that the heirs of Joseph Smith, Jr., would probably be in opposition to Young's administration.[18]

Young Joseph Smith immediately began to compare his natural father with his new stepfather. He recorded his impressions in his memoirs many years later: "He was a man of strong likes and dislikes, passionate, easily moved to anger, but withal ordinarily affable in manner, decidedly hospitable, and generous in disposition. He made friends quite easily, but, unfortunately for him, lost them quite as easily. His love for intoxicating liquors and his lack of religious convictions were the two most serious drawbacks to the happiness of our home, and tended to color materially the after-events of our lives." [19] While young Smith may not have fully approved of his stepfather's habits when compared to his perception of his natural father, the two developed an amiable rapport, if not a genuine affection, over the years.[20] At the same time, the memory of his dead father became stronger following Bidamon's entry into the family. He perceived both positive and negative points in Bidamon's character, but only the idyllic memory of his natural father remained. The marriage probably solidified for Smith some of his central conceptions about Joseph the Prophet's basic character. He never saw him as anything less than exceptional. Although he never expressed this comparison explicitly, Smith may have concluded that his natural father was as exceptional as Bidamon was ordinary.

After he and Emma married, Bidamon determined to see that his stepchildren were given a fair start in business careers, and thus Bidamon was directly responsible for Joseph Smith's first halting entrance as a young man into the business world. When he married Emma Smith, Bidamon had been the partner of a Mr. Hartwell in a dry-goods business in Nauvoo. They subsequently dissolved this partnership, but Bidamon used his influence to get fifteen-year-old

Joseph a job as clerk in Hartwell's store. Smith, by this time a teenager of average height, striking dark eyes, an unruly mass of dark hair, and the beginnings of a scraggly beard, began clerking for Hartwell in early 1848 and remained there learning the trade until the summer.[21]

After Joseph had mastered the art of storekeeping sufficiently to operate without supervision, the major proposed that he and Emma reopen the Red Brick Store with young Smith as manager. The parents each invested $1,000, renovated the store, bought a fresh supply of stock, and established Joseph as the proprietor. Bidamon thought at the time that it would be a fine contribution to the youth's start in the business world, but, unfortunately, the venture failed. Crucial to its success was Smith's ability to enter the grain trade on the Mississippi, and although Joseph was involved in the local grain trade, acting as an agent for a few St. Louis brokers, he was unable to break into the market in any significant way because of a cartel that controlled the majority of the trade on the river around Nauvoo.[22]

A second difficulty that made the store unprofitable was the exodus of the majority of the Mormons. The main business district of Nauvoo had moved away from the limestone flat, where the Red Brick Store stood, onto the bluffs overlooking the river, where the majority of the non-Mormons had lived. Hence, the store only attracted those persons who were looking for goods more cheaply than could be had elsewhere. When these bargain-hunters appeared, Joseph was unwilling to dicker over the price. While Bidamon did not hesitate to mark down a commodity to move it off the shelf, Joseph would insist upon receiving the original price. Soon Joseph had few customers and simply could not compete effectively.[23]

After several months Joseph and his supporters realized that the Red Brick Store would not be profitable. When Joseph finally closed its doors in 1849, he did so sadly but with the determination to move into business in other areas. He was, some Nauvooans thought, over optimistic about his prospects. Joseph took a number of menial jobs to accumulate some working capital for new ventures. He worked as a barkeep for a short time and as a farmhand for his stepfather and others. As soon as he was financially able, however, Smith worked out an agreement with the Warsaw and Rockford Railroad Company to build twenty-six miles of road for it. Acting as contractor, foreman, and oftentimes laborer, Smith began the construction project and had actually completed a few miles of roadbed before the company went into receivership and the project was scrapped. Smith was discouraged but not defeated by this event. He next went into land development and managed to acquire several acres of prime residential property in the center of Nauvoo. He also purchased fifteen acres of farmland outside of town, for which he paid a total of $2.00. At one point in his modest business career Smith even bought the rights to a thirty-foot barge that had come loose from its moorings in Nauvoo and floated downstream. Smith recovered the barge and sold it at a substantial profit.[24]

Joseph Smith, along with his stepfather, developed one other venture during the late 1840s in Nauvoo that proved to be most lucrative—tourism. After the exodus of most of the Saints in 1846, thousands of visitors came to see where the Mormons had once lived. They visited the Smith home (where many of them took pride in renting rooms); the homes of other leaders, especially Brigham Young's; the unfinished Nauvoo House; and, most importantly, the majestic Nauvoo Temple. Bidamon and his stepsons capitalized on this interest by establishing an informal guide service based at the mansion, where they maintained a team and buggy for showing tourists about the town. Joseph often acted as driver and guide, earning fares and tips that financed his other business deals.[25]

Some of the visitors Joseph showed about Nauvoo were impressive public figures. On one occasion in 1848 Owen Lovejoy, antislavery congressman from Illinois, visited the city to deliver a speech and meet constituents. Smith drove him through the town, showing him the sites and telling him the story of Nauvoo's Mormon past. Smith could not resist telling Lovejoy how much he admired his rigorous opposition to slavery in Congress and the respect he had for his slain brother, Elijah Lovejoy, the antislavery editor of a newspaper in Alton, Illinois, who had been lynched in 1837.[26] Nauvoo had long been a hotbed of antislavery sentiment, had been a major stop on the underground railroad, and consequently Smith had grown to sympathize with the abolitionist crusade.[27]

The most impressive tourist attraction was lost on the night of 8–9 October 1848 when an arsonist set fire to the three-story Nauvoo

Temple. Joseph III remembered that he was sleeping in the upper room of the store, trying to protect the closed building from burglars, when he awoke to the sounds of fire bells and confused voices on the street below. He staggered out of bed and ran to the north window, where he saw a colossal fire on the cliffs above the Nauvoo flats. Smith opened the store's window and called to John Mason, a neighbor whom he saw running toward the fire, asking what had happened. Mason told him that the temple was burning and that the townspeople were assembling bucket brigades to fight the fire. Smith dressed and ran to his mother's home, only to find that his stepfather was already on the hill organizing bucket brigades. Since the Smith property would be easy prey for thieves or arsonists during the fire, Joseph decided that under the circumstances he should stay in the area, just in case the fire had been set as a diversion. The firefighters worked throughout the night, and although they prevented the fire from spreading to other buildings in the main business section, the temple was all but destroyed.[28]

The gutting of the Nauvoo Temple in this fire meant much more to Joseph Smith than just the loss of an impressive tourist attraction; he viewed its demise with mixed feelings. Indeed, he had a very intriguing love-hate relationship with the building and the ideals for which it stood. On the one hand it had been the grandest vision of his father, embodying all that was good and noble and exciting in Mormonism. And Joseph respected his father and his desires for the church. On the other hand, it symbolized the radical Mormon religion embraced by Brigham Young and his followers. This Mormonism had rejected the Smith family's leadership, had accepted plural marriage and other "despicable doctrines," and had established a virtually independent commonwealth in the Great Basin. While continuing to revere his father, Joseph Smith began to look upon the temple fire as a cleansing of evil, a divine retribution to a once righteous and worthy people. The temple fire may have been a catalyst for a radical shift in the religious convictions of young Smith, for certainly his perspective changed as he matured between 1847 and 1850. He did not affiliate with any formal religions during this period and may have subscribed, at least to a certain extent, to his stepfather's creed: "I believe in one God who has neither partners nor clerks!"[29]

Joseph's mother apparently tried to keep him associated with some type of Christianity during this period, and as a result she began to attend the Methodist church. Bidamon accepted this practice to keep peace in the family, supporting her efforts to maintain contact between their children and organized religion. Emma and the children became so active in the Methodist church in Nauvoo that Almon Babbitt, watching affairs in the city with interest, reported to Brigham Young that "Emma had joined the Methodist Church; they took her on trial. It is to be hoped that she will suit them." Obviously, the statement confirmed Young's worst suspicions about Emma Smith Bidamon, for denial of the church after having accepted it is the greatest sin in Mormon theology and considered "unforgivable." Emma had not, however, actually joined the Methodist church; she merely wanted to see that her children experienced regularly Christian worship and fellowship.[30]

With the relatively loose religious atmosphere of the Bidamon household to encourage him during his teen years, Joseph Smith explored several different religions, some of which were quite eccentric. For instance, he studied phrenology and astrology but quickly found them unsatisfactory. He also scrutinized the cult of Spiritualism and found it more enticing than anything he had experienced before. Arising in the 1840s, the cult spread rapidly throughout the nation. Joseph Smith first heard of it in 1850 from a farmer named James Chadsey, who moved to Nauvoo from the East in the spring of the year. Chadsey claimed to be a medium, a sensitive person who had the power to receive communications from the dead, and held a number of seances for the local citizenry. Smith took part in a few of these meetings and became thoroughly convinced that supernatural events were taking place. Consequently, he studied the theory and practice of Spiritualism with enthusiasm, all the while participating in the seances, admitting later, "we would experience a species of occult manifestations between us."[31]

Smith took part in the seances in Nauvoo for some time, but by at least the summer of 1852 his interest in Spiritualism began to wane. Two significant events turned him against the cult and, in so doing, may have paved the way for his eventual return to a form of Mormonism. The first involved an attempt by a traveling medium to use his father's name to drum up interest. The lecturer claimed that the eternal power of Joseph Smith, Jr., was present everywhere in Nauvoo and that the prophet's spirit wished to tell the community something of great importance. The lecturer advertised that she would speak under the influence of Smith's spirit at a public meeting, and because the dead prophet had such an important message, the price of admission would be only 25 cents. Joseph Smith was incensed at this petty theatrical exhibition and irate that the medium would use his father to make money. Very nearly the whole town turned out to see the presentation, but Smith boycotted the seance. Later, however, he asked several of the people who attended, "Do you really think this woman was actuated by the spirit of Joseph Smith, the Prophet, as she advertised?" In every case Smith heard the medium had failed to conjure up the ghost of the dead prophet. This huckstering made Smith seriously question the legitimacy of the cult.

The second incident leading to Smith's rejection of Spiritualism took place during a seance in 1852 at the home of a local medium who claimed to have received a message from a spirit stating that one of Smith's childhood friends, Oliver B. Huntington, had recently died of cholera at Watertown, New York. Smith was shocked by this information—the two had been corresponding for several years—and refused to believe it until it could be confirmed. He wrote to the Huntington family, explaining that he had heard that Oliver had recently died and asking for verification. A few weeks later Smith received word that Huntington was alive and well and traveling as a missionary for the church.[32]

These incidents convinced Smith that Spiritualism was a bankrupt system, not worthy of further investigation. By 1852 he had completely abandoned the cult. Later he condemned the cult, stating that he was "utterly disgusted with the so-called spiritual manifestations as displayed by those declared to be mediums. I had seen table-tipping and witnessed several times the pencil-writing performances, but came to the conclusion that, so far, my experience had proved there was absolutely no good in it or any part of it. . . . Thenceforward I let it alone regarding it as a matter of mental speculation unworthy of the attention and investigation of an honest man who was not actually willing to be humbugged—a result which I certainly did not wish to invite."[33] Smith assessed the concept with these words in 1855: "I feel it is not a part of the divine plan to allow spirits to communicate with mortals, and I can scarcely see how we can have tangible intercourse with departed spirits."[34] From the perspective he established in the Reorganized Church, Smith criticized Spiritualism mercilessly. He wrote in his memoirs: "Indulgence in weird seances and mysterious contacts will finally wear out the firm texture of the true and higher nature of the individual, and leave him, a pitiful and darkened wreck, upon the shores of the spirit world."[35]

While Joseph Smith was involved with Spiritualism, he showed little interest in any variety of Mormonism. Mormonism, on the other hand, showed considerable interest in him. Many of the scattered Saints thought him a successor to his father, and all wished to redeem the presumably damned Smith family from a hell that they believed the Smiths were sure to inherit because of their waywardness. A few of the old Saints, notably officials in the organization headed by Brigham Young, tried to prod Smith toward accepting the movement. At every opportunity they invited Joseph to join them in the Great Basin. Smith's cousin, George A. Smith, wrote him in the spring of 1849 from Council Bluffs, Iowa, about the possibility of his migrating to Utah. He told Joseph: "It is my present calculation to move with my family, to the Mountains this summer. I should be happy if you could find it convenient to accompany us. . . . Consult your mother on this subject, and do as wisdom shall direct. But if you should conclude to make the journey, I should be much pleased to enjoy your company, as will many of your friends in this region who are going on."[36] Joseph undoubtedly considered this offer and others like it, but ultimately rejected it. His mother was opposed to his going to Utah and asked Joseph to stay in Nauvoo to watch over the Smith property while Bidamon went to California in the Gold Rush. Smith, in spite of what he may have actually wanted to do, did as his mother asked.[37]

Representatives of other Mormon factions also visited Joseph Smith during this period, each trying to lure him into their movements. In 1850 Dr. Joseph Younger, an official of one of these sects—Jehovah's Presbytery of Zion, under the charismatic but erratic leadership of Charles B. Thompson—paid a visit to Smith in Nauvoo, trying to get him to affiliate with his group. Thompson, who went by what he said was the sacred name of Baneemy, had established a communalistic society at the town of Preparation, located in western Iowa, and was in desperate need of hardy followers who could make the town prosper.[38] He had dispatched

Younger to enlist the support of the Smiths in the hope that the family's prestige would attract other converts. Younger took an aggressive approach in his meeting with Joseph and gained the unending dislike of the youth for his trouble. Joseph lashed out at Younger without mercy. Smith later wrote: "He tried to argue me into Baneemyism, and finally, raised his hand to pronounce a curse on me; I stopped him, and reminded him that 'cursings were like chickens; coming home to roost.' And when he got mad and railed against me; I told him what he had been doing, and pre-dicted (prophesied) that if he did not settle down with his family, stop wandering, dragging them about with him, he would waste his money." Smith's "prophecy," coming as it did from the son of the Mormon prophet, frightened Dr. Younger and he left town almost immediately, never to return.[39]

Subsequent visits by the members of various Mormon factions met with a similar lack of success. Joseph Smith seemed to have little interest in the work being done by any of them, although he apparently had a healthy appreciation for his father's religious commitment and vision. For example, when Frederick W. Piercy, a Mormon immigrant from Great Britain, passed through Nauvoo on his way to Utah in 1853, he visited Smith. Their meeting was cordial, Joseph even sitting for a crayon sketch, but he refused to discuss religion. Likewise, when William Walker, an official of the Utah Mormon church, visited Joseph during the fall of 1853, the meeting was civil but Smith limited conversation to secular affairs. Much the same held true when an immigrant company from England stopped in Nauvoo in August 1853 to see the sights before beginning the trek to Utah and a few members of the group met with Joseph one afternoon.[40]

An incident in the late autumn of 1853, however, seems to have begun a metamorphasis of Smith's attitude toward the Mormon religion. Smith was aware of the blessings and promises that had been given him when a small boy and of the belief on the part of some Latter Day Saints that he would one day lead them. He appar-ently had chosen to ignore them until this point. While walking on a street in Nauvoo, however, Smith was stopped by a visitor to the city, an English convert to Brigham Young's organization. The man knew who Joseph was without introduction and had apparently been waiting for the right moment to speak to him. He told Joseph that God had given him a duty to unify and purify the church. He also said that Joseph was "possibly doing a great wrong in allowing the years to go by unimproved" and suggested that Smith prepare himself through study and prayer for the work of the Lord. Smith was ready to push past the Englishman and continue on his way when he thought better of it and replied that he stood "ready to do any work that might fall my lot, or that I might be called to do." He was quick to add, however, that no man was going to force him into committing to a religious work in which he did not believe. He would listen to the dictates of God when they were made known to him, but he would not act prematurely.[41]

As a result of this incident Smith began to study seriously the doctrines and practices of Mormonism. He bought or borrowed everything he could find on the subject during the next two years, studying its history and theology, its current factions and the strange attractions they held for certain types of individuals, its political system and the relationships of the members to the leaders, the secular government, and the world. He read with renewed interest the Book of Mormon and the Doctrine and Covenants. Especially, Smith explored the religious system that had emerged in Nauvoo out of the early Mormon conceptions of the 1830s. This study, intermittant but intensive, led Smith to the conviction that his father's Mormon religion had been theologically sound and worthy of acceptance. But he considered it somehow changed during the 1840s and in need of reformation.[42]

Having determined that he believed a primitive form of Mormonism, Smith began to consider which of the many factions of the church adhered to the necessities of his belief system. At this time Smith did not rule out of hand any of the many schismatic groups on his own, but asked God for direction about the many Mormon factions soliciting his allegiance. While studying and pondering this question Smith said that he had a spiritual experience that eased his concern about which faction he should ally with. He asserted that, while he was studying in his home,

> the room suddenly expanded and passed away. I saw stretched out before me towns, cities, busy marts, court houses, courts and assemblies of men, all busy and all marked by those characteristics that are found in the world, where men win place and renown. This stayed before my vision till I had noted clearly that the choice of preferment

was offered to him who would enter in, but who did so must go into the busy whirl and be submerged by its din, bustle and confusion. In the subtle transition of a dream I was gazing over a wide expanse of country in a prairie land; no mountains were to be seen, but as far as the eye could reach, hill and dale, hamlet and village, farm and farm house, pleasant cot and homelike place, everywhere betokening thrift, industry and the pursuits of a happy peace were open to the view. I remarked to him standing by me, but whose presence I had not before noticed, "This must be the country of a happy people." To this he replied, "Which would you prefer, life, success and renown among the busy scenes that you first saw; or a place among these people, without honor or renown? Think of it well, for the choice will be offered to you sooner or later, and you must be prepared to decide. Your decision once made you can not recall it, and must abide the result.

Believing in this vision and confident that he would one day be offered a clear choice about his life, Smith decided not to continue looking for the proper Mormon faction. He still studied Mormonism and left himself open to new religious experiences for the most part, but he concluded that God would intervene to point him in the right direction.[43] Again, Smith's decision demonstrated his basic patience and practicality in considering his future in organized religion.

As a result of this vision, Smith's emphasis shifted to secular learning and a career in the law. He had long been interested in legal matters, and he began to study law formally in 1853. Joseph came to believe, perhaps rightly, that when he chose his religious career at some future date a knowledge of the law would be helpful. His stepfather enthusiastically encouraged Joseph to enter legal studies full time; however, Bidamon saw it only as a means to fame, wealth, and social status, not as skill useful for a preacher. His mother, on the other hand, harbored doubts about Joseph becoming a lawyer. She distrusted attorneys and as late as 1866 wrote Joseph about her concern. "I know very well if your father had been acquainted with the laws of the country he might have avoided a great deal of trouble," she told her son, "and yet I have a horror of one of my children being entirely dependent upon being a lawyer for a living." Notwithstanding Emma's misgivings, Joseph began reading law in the Nauvoo office of William McLennon during the winter of 1853–54.[44]

The next year Lewis Bidamon arranged for his stepson to go to Canton, Illinois, and study law under William Kellogg. Kellogg took on the would-be attorney and put him to work on a strict six-day-a-week, ten-hour-a-day schedule. Kellogg had been born in Ohio in 1814 but had moved to Canton in 1837 and built up a superb practice, especially in clearing disputed land titles. Kellogg also won acclaim as an outstanding defense attorney in western Illinois and served in the Illinois legislature between 1849 and 1850. Between 1852 and 1855, a part of the time that Smith read law in his office, Kellogg was a judge in the Illinois Circuit Court. No doubt Smith was delighted to be working under such a stellar performer. Writing from his room in Canton in early 1855, Smith told his family, "I am studying as hard as I can, and will try to acquire the mysteries of the Law." [45]

Kellogg harbored political ambitions in Canton and became intensely involved in what would become the Republican party. He was elected to Congress for three successive terms as a member of the House of Representatives beginning in 1856; President Lincoln appointed him minister to Guatemala in 1864, but he declined the appointment; and the next year President Andrew Johnson appointed him chief justice of the Nebraska Territory, where he served until it became a state in 1867. Later he went to Mississippi and undertook a political career as a Republican during the Reconstruction era, but his efforts there failed and in 1870 he returned to Peoria, Illinois, where he practiced law until his death in 1872. Kellogg apparently liked Joseph Smith, using his political connections in the city to gain his hard-working student appointment as a clerk for the city council and deputy postmaster. Smith could do these jobs during his days off and in the evenings and made enough money to pay his room and board and have some spending money left over. [46]

Although Joseph Smith worked hard for William Kellogg, he became, almost overnight, one of the town's more adventurous young men. Twenty-three years old and away from home for the first time, Joseph Smith drank deeply of the waters of frivolity. The smell of his cheap cigars and liquor and his less than proper manner were unleashed at every opportunity. [47] He wrote to his brother Alexander in September 1855, explaining that he had been reprimanded for horseplay in front of a store in downtown Canton. The deputy

Joseph Smith, Jr. (1805–44) and
Emma Hale Smith Bidamon
(1804–79), the father and mother
of Joseph Smith III. These are
portraits supposedly executed in
Nauvoo, Illinois, during the early
1840s. The artist is anonymous.
The originals are the property of
the Reorganized Church of Jesus
Christ of Latter Day Saints,
Independence, Mo. Courtesy
Library–Archives of the
Reorganized Church

The restored Nauvoo "Homestead," home of Joseph Smith, Jr., from 1839 to 1843, and of Joseph Smith III from 1858 to 1866. In the foreground is the log cabin summer kitchen of the house. Courtesy F. Mark McKiernan

The restored Nauvoo "Mansion," home of Joseph Smith, Jr., from 1843 until his death. After his father's death, Joseph Smith III lived here with his mother until his marriage in 1856. Photograph by author

Joseph Smith III as a youth about 1846, while a resident of Nauvoo, Illinois. Courtesy of Library–Archives of the Reorganized Church

Nauvoo, Illinois, about 1846, looking northeast toward the Mormon Temple on the bluff above the main part of the city. Courtesy Library–Archives of the Reorganized Church

Lewis C. Bidamon, stepfather, and the four sons of Joseph Smith, Jr., circa 1860. Standing (l–r): David Hyrum Smith (1844–1904); Alexander Hale Smith (1838–1909). Seated (l–r): Lewis Crum Bidamon (1806–91); Frederick Granger William Smith (1836–63); Joseph Smith III (1832–1914). Courtesy Library–Archives of the Reorganized Church

Joseph Smith III as sketched by Frederick H. Piercy in 1853. Piercy, a British convert to Mormonism enroute to Utah, passed through Nauvoo, where he met Smith and made this sketch, originally published in Piercy's guidebook, *The Route to Great Salt Lake Valley* (Liverpool, England: n.p., 1855). Courtesy Library–Archives of the Reorganized Church sheriff felt compelled to stop his antics and ask him if he was "in fun or in liquor—I told him neither only just in sport."[48] Smith complained not long thereafter that "*Canton* seems to small to hold me!" His activities there were much too wild for Emma Bidamon to accept.[49]

Early in 1856, partly because of a lack of funds but also because of his wildness, the Bidamons made their son give up reading law in the Kellogg office and return to Nauvoo before completing his studies. Regardless of whether or not Joseph Smith III could have completed his legal training, his experiences in those two law offices were critical to the development of his leadership style in the Reorganized Church. He adopted a legalistic framework that informed virtually every issue he dealt with as president of the Reorganization. He believed that all things within nature were governed by law, a natural law created by God which was every person's duty to discover and obey. Smith reasoned that such law was reasonable, consistent, and universal. While Smith never fully developed his legalistic model of understanding the world about him—both the temporal and spiritual aspects of it—he certainly applied it. In some cases his applications were implicit, as in his basic understanding of what constituted right and wrong beliefs and actions. At other times he explicitly applied his legalistic model to explain the Reorganized Church's view of authority, presidential succession, and polygamy.[50] Smith even presented a definition of church authority based on the constitutional analogy: "It is a principle well known in civil law, and ought to be in ecclesiastical circles, that whenever a church is founded, its principles of faith formulated, its traditions fulminated from the forum, pulpit, and press, those declarations become the constitution of its corporate and legal existence." Such a stance, for Smith, served to deny conflicting doctrines that emerged as the church progressed. He used this approach zealously in debating the legitimacy of the Reorganized Church over the Utah Latter-day Saint movement.[51]

All of the groundwork in McLennon's and Kellogg's law offices aside, Smith returned to Nauvoo in 1856 without much thought to his future religious work. Instead, he began to court the woman he eventually married—Emmeline Griswold. Tall, slender, dainty, and dark featured, Emmeline, usually called Emma, reminded Joseph of his own mother. She also possessed a keen and sometimes bit-ing wit, a strong will, good business sense, and a certain winsome sensuality. But most of all, she made him laugh, and that was what finally convinced Smith to court and marry her.[52]

Joseph Smith first met Emmeline in a Nauvoo candy store a short time before he went to Canton to study law. Nothing passed between them at this meeting, but Smith was immediately attracted to her. Several months later, as he and his brother Frederick were driving a buggy down a muddy street in Nauvoo, they saw her picking her way on foot toward her house. At that instant Smith thought of a way to make a date with her. He told Fred, "If you will allow me to use the buggy I will pick her up and take her to her house—and some day I will marry her if I can!" Fred just shook his head and slid out of the buggy. Joseph began courting Emma thereafter and "became her faithful attendent, escorting her to and from all our gatherings and paying continuous court to her, with no other companion or sweetheart."[53] A fervid romance blossomed, but Smith tried to hide some of his most intense feelings about Emmeline until he was sure she shared them. Early in 1856 Joseph wrote to her that he had difficulty expressing emotions, adding, "I loved you and you know what a long time I let pass before I told that and how I told it. . . . You know Emma that I am your most faithful . . . and love you with all my heart."[54]

Joseph proposed to Emmeline in the spring of 1856, making it clear to her, since she had never been a member of the Mormon church and her family was antagonistic toward the sect, that he must be free to respond to any future call to enter religious work. If she agreed to this precondition, Smith promised to be a true and faithful husband for her. Emmeline accepted this proposal with its odd stipulation, and the two set the marriage date for 22 October 1856. The Griswold family objected to the marriage on religious grounds and disowned Emma for the moment, but she preferred Joseph Smith to her family and the marriage took place as planned, a Presbyterian minister performing the ceremony. Soon after the wedding, however, Emmeline made up with her parents.[55]

Without anything approaching a real honeymoon, the couple moved into the old Smith blockhouse in Nauvoo and set up housekeeping. They appeared happy. Years later, in remembering the first months of marriage, Joseph Smith concluded, "The world was before us, clothed in roseate hues of youthful hope and fancy, and we faced it together happily."[56]

NOTES

1. Joseph Smith, "The Memoirs of President Joseph Smith (1832–1914)," *Saints' Herald* 82 (29 January 1935): 145.

2. *Upper Mississippian* (Rock Island, Ill.), 2 November 1844. Numerous rumors that Emma Smith no longer believed in Mormonism were published in newspapers in the region. See the discussion of these in Linda King Newell and Valeen Tippetts Avery, *Mormon Enigma: Emma Smith, Prophet's Wife, "Elect Lady," Polygamy's Foe* (Garden City, N.Y.: Doubleday and Co., 1984), pp. 213, 221–26; Linda King Newell and Valeena Tippetts Avery, "New Light on the *Sun:* Emma Smith and the *New York Sun* Letter," *Journal of Mormon History* 6 (1979): 23–35.

3. William B. Smith to James J. Strang, 25 December 1846, James J. Strang Manuscripts, Coe Collection of Western Americana, Beinecke Library, Yale University, New Haven, Conn.

4. Joseph Smith, "What Do I Remember of Nauvoo?" *Journal of History* 3 (July 1910): 343.

5. The career of James J. Strang will be discussed further in chapter four, as his followers played an important part in the origins of the Reorganized Church of Jesus Christ of Latter Day Saints. Accounts of his life can be found in Milo M. Quaife, *The Kingdom of Saint James: A Narrative of James J. Strang, the Beaver Island Mormon King* (New Haven, Conn.: Yale University Press, 1930); Klaus J. Hansen, "The Making of King Strang: A Reexamination," *Michigan History* 46 (September 1962): 209–29; William D. Russell, "King James Strang: Joseph Smith's Successor?" in *The Restoration Movement: Essays in Mormon History*, ed. F. Mark McKiernan, Alma R. Blair, and Paul M. Edwards (Lawrence, Kan.: Coronado Press, 1973), pp. 231–56; David Rich Lewis, " 'For Life, the Resurrection, and the Life Everlasting': James J. Strang and Strangite Mormon Polygamy, 1849–1856," *Wisconsin Magazine of History* 66 (Summer 1983): 274–91; *Latter-day Saints' Millennial Star* (Liverpool, England) 8 (15 October 1846): 93; Lawrence Foster, "James J. Strang: The Prophet Who Failed," *Church History* 50 (June 1981): 182–92. Strang's commitment to young Smith was demonstrated as late as 1849, when his followers affirmed the youth's future prophetic calling. The annual conference passed "on motion, unanimously, that we give our prayers daily for Joseph, the son of Joseph, that he may be raised up for God to fill the station to which he had been called by prophecy." See *Gospel Herald* (Voree, Wisc.) 4 (April 1849): 16.

6. Joseph Smith, "Autobiography," in Edward W. Tullidge, *The Life of Joseph the Prophet* (Plano, Ill.: Herald Publishing House, 1880), p. 754.

7. Ibid., pp. 748, 752; Smith, "Memoirs," *Saints' Herald* 82 (29

January 1935): 145; Valeen Tippetts Avery and Linda King Newell, "The Lion and the Lady: Brigham Young and Emma Smith," *Utah Historical Quarterly* 48 (Winter 1980): 92.

8. Smith, "Memoirs," *Saints' Herald* 82 (29 January 1935): 145.

9. Thomas L. Kane, "The Mormons," an address delivered to the Pennsylvania Historical Society, 1848. On Kane's career as a friend of the Saints see Leonard J. Arrington, "In Honorable Remembrance: Thomas L. Kane's Service to the Mormons," *Brigham Young University Studies* 21 (Summer 1981): 150–70.

10. Smith, "Memoirs," *Saints' Herald* 82 (29 January 1935): 145–46, 82 (5 February 1935): 175.

11. Deed of Emma Smith to Loren Walker, 21 December 1847; Lewis C. Bidamon to Emma Smith, 11 January 1847, both in Lewis Crum Bidamon Papers, Reorganized Church of Jesus Christ of Latter Day Saints Library–Archives, Independence, Mo.; Valeen Tippetts Avery and Linda King Newell, "Lewis C. Bidamon: Stepchild of Mormondom," *Brigham Young University Studies* 19 (Spring 1979): 377–78.

12. John M. Ferris to Hiram G. Ferris, 3 September 1846, Mormon Collection, H. H. Bancroft Library, University of California, Berkeley, Calif.; Avery and Newell, "Lewis C. Bidamon," p. 378.

13. Lewis C. Bidamon to Emma Smith, 11 January 1847, Lewis Crum Bidamon Papers. Emma Smith's answer was written on the back of this letter.

14. Smith, "Memoirs," *Saints' Herald* 82 (5 February 1935): 176.

15. Marriage Record, Book 1A, 1829–1849, p. 105, Hancock County Courthouse, Carthage, Ill.

16. Sarah M. Kimball to Miranda Hyde, 2 January 1848, Orson Hyde Collection, Church of Jesus Christ of Latter-day Saints Historical Department, Salt Lake City, Utah.

17. John S. Fullmer to Brigham Young, 26 January 1848, Brigham Young Papers, Latter-day Saints Historical Department.

18. Almon W. Babbitt to Heber C. Kimball, 31 January 1848; Almon W. Babbitt to Brigham Young, 31 January 1848, both in Journal History of the Church of Jesus Christ of Latter-day Saints, Latter-day Saints Historical Department; Emma Bidamon to Lewis C. Bidamon, 7 January 1850, Emma Smith Bidamon Papers, Reorganized Church Library–Archives.

19. Smith, "Memoirs," *Saints' Herald* 82 (5 February 1935): 176.

20. Joseph Smith to Emma Bidamon, 8 March 1863, Emma Smith Bidamon Papers; Joseph Smith to Thomas Revell, 2 July 1880, Joseph Smith III Papers, Reorganized Church Library–Archives; Joseph Smith to Lewis C. Bidamon, 4 September 1875, Lewis Crum Bidamon Papers.

21. Smith, "Autobiography," in Tullidge, *Life of Joseph*, p. 755.

22. Smith, "Memoirs," *Saints' Herald* 82 (5 February 1935): 176. A study of the importance of the grain trade and how businessmen tried to control it can be found in John G. Clark, *The Grain Trade of the Old Northwest* (Urbana: University of Illinois Press, 1966).

23. Smith, "Autobiography," in Tullidge, *Life of Joseph*, pp. 755–56; *Nauvoo Neighbor*, December 1842–January 1844; Journal History of the Church of Jesus Christ of Latter-day Saints, 27 June 1842, Latter-day Saints Historical Department; Leonard J. Arrington, *From Quaker to Latter-day Saint: Bishop Edwin D. Wooley* (Salt Lake City, Utah: Deseret Book Co., 1976), pp. 114–17; Roger D. Launius and F. Mark McKiernan, *Joseph Smith, Jr.'s, Red Brick Store* (Macomb: Western Illinois University Monograph Series, 1985), pp. 34–35.

24. Smith, "Autobiography," in Tullidge, *Life of Joseph*, pp. 755–56; Smith, "Memoirs," *Saints' Herald* 82 (12 February 1935): 209–10, 82 (19 February 1935): 239–40; Joseph Smith to Mary B. Smith, 4 December 1876, Joseph Smith III Letterbook #1, Reorganized Church Library–Archives; Sixth United States Census, 1850, Population Schedules, Hancock County, Dwelling 1818, Family 1821, National Archives and Records Administration, Washington, D.C.; Legal Transactions between Julia M. Dixon, Elisha Dixon, and Joseph Smith, 28 July 1851, 4 October 1851; Legal Transaction between Hugh Rhodes and Joseph Smith, 1 May 1852; Legal Transaction between Adolphus Allen and Joseph Smith and Frederick G. W. Smith, 2 July 1853, all in Lewis Crum Bidamon Papers.

25. Avery and Newell, "Lewis C. Bidamon," p. 382.

26. Smith, "Memoirs," *Saints' Herald* 82 (12 February 1935): 207–8. On Owen Lovejoy see Edward Magdol, *Owen Lovejoy: Abolitionist in Congress* (New Brunswick, N.J.: Rutgers University Press, 1967).

27. Smith, "Memoirs," *Saints' Herald* 82 (23 April 1935): 529–30, 82 (30 April 1935): 559–62, 82 (7 May 1935): 589–90.

28. Ibid., 82 (5 February 1935): 176–78, 82 (12 February 1935): 207.

29. Ibid., 82 (5 February 1935): 176–78.

30. Almon W. Babbitt to Brigham Young, 31 January 1848, in Journal History of the Church; Book of Doctrine and Covenants (Independence, Mo.: Herald Publishing House, 1970), Section 76:4; Journal History of the Church of Jesus Christ of Latter-day Saints, 10 September 1849, Latter-day Saints Historical Department.

31. Spiritualism was particularly attractive to Mormons who did not accept any of the factions during this period, in part because it, like Mormonism, placed emphasis upon revelation. A fine explanation of this development can be found in Davis Bitton, "Mormonism's Encounter with

Spiritualism," *Journal of Mormon History* 1 (1974): 39–50. The quote is from Smith, "Memoirs," *Saints' Herald* 82 (19 March 1935): 368.

32. The dates of these incidents are not given in any of Joseph Smith III's writings but can be established from external sources. A key part of his disillusionment with Spiritualism was the information he had received about Oliver B. Huntington's death. He wrote to the Huntington family expressing concern about this rumor. Smith's letter caught up with Oliver while on his way to Utah, and he sent a reply from Fort Laramie, Wyoming, stating that he was alive and well. Oliver B. Huntington and his family reached Utah with the 20th Company of emigrants in the late summer of 1852; consequently, Smith's encounter with Spiritualism must be dated at around this time. See *Deseret News* (Salt Lake City, Utah), 5 September 1852, for a list of families in the 20th Company.

In the Journal History of the Church, 25 November 1855 entry, there is an account of Enoch B. Tripp, a Latter-day Saint missionary, transiting Nauvoo on his way back to Utah. He recorded that Joseph Smith "is a very strong spiritual medium and claims that he through writing (by placing his hands with a pencil on paper) can converse with his father. I informed him that God, angels and the servants of God never have, and never will, converse with the children of men in that way, but that that was the way the powers from beneath communicated with men." Tripp reported that he told Smith to forsake Spiritualism because it was a satanic cult. This account is not credible. Joseph Smith III was in Canton, Illinois, studying law at that time; he was giving anti-Spiritualism advice to Emma Knight; and he had definitely become disillusioned with Spiritualism following the Huntington incident of 1852. In view of this, it appears that Tripp's account was perhaps more a memoir than a journal entry written at the time of the event. He may have remembered some earlier incident after Brigham Young, with real foundation, denounced Joseph Smith III as a Spiritualist.

33. Smith, "Memoirs," *Saints' Herald* 82 (19 March 1935): 368–69, 82 (22 October 1935): 1361.

34. Joseph Smith to Emma Knight, 4 December 1855, Joseph Smith III Papers. See also Joseph Smith to Emma Knight, 4 May 1856, Joseph Smith III Papers.

35. Smith, "Memoirs," *Saints' Herald* 82 (4 December 1935): 1544.

36. George A. Smith to Joseph Smith, 13 March 1849, Miscellaneous Letters and Papers, Reorganized Church Library–Archives.

37. For a description of Bidamon's gold rush activities, see Smith, "Memoirs," *Saints' Herald* 82 (12 February 1935): 207–8; Avery and Newell, "Lewis C. Bidamon," pp. 380–82; Smith, "Autobiography," in Tullidge, *Life of Joseph*, p. 755; Lewis C. Bidamon to Emma Bidamon,

4 May 1849, 5 July 1849, 7 January 1850, 20 April 1850, Lewis Crum Bidamon Papers.

38. Charles B. Thompson's movement was only one of several Mormon factions that arose following the death of Joseph Smith, Jr. For descriptions of his activities see Dale L. Morgan, "A Bibliography of the Churches of the Dispersion," *Western Humanities Review* 7 (Summer 1952): 262–63; Joseph Smith and Heman C. Smith, *The History of the Reorganized Church of Jesus Christ of Latter Day Saints* (Independence, Mo.: Herald Publishing House, 1969), 3:53–61; F. R. Autumn, "A Minor Prophet in Iowa," *Palimpsest* 8 (July 1927): 253–60; Newell G. Bringhurst, "Charles B. Thompson and the Issues of Slavery and Race," *Journal of Mormon History* 8 (1981): 37–47.

39. Joseph Smith to Caroline Case, 27 March 1894, Joseph Smith III Letterbook #5, Reorganized Church Library–Archives.

40. John Kirk to Calvin Smith, 3 April 1853, Mormons in Illinois Microfilm Collection, Lovejoy Library, Southern Illinois University, Edwardsville, Ill.; Frederick Piercy, "A Visit to Nauvoo in 1853," *Journal of History* 3 (April 1910): 244; Joseph Smith to Lyman O. Littlefield, 14 August 1883, Joseph Smith III Letterbook #4, Reorganized Church Library–Archives; Smith, "Memoirs," *Saints' Herald* 82 (19 February 1935): 241.

41. Smith, "Autobiography," in Tullidge, *Life of Joseph*, p. 756; Heman C. Smith, ed., "Official Statements of President Joseph Smith," *Journal of History* 11 (October 1918): 386–87.

42. George A. Smith and John Smith to Joseph Smith, 24 June 1854, Joseph Smith III Papers, remarked on this study. See also Smith, "Memoirs," *Saints' Herald* 82 (2 April 1935): 431–32.

43. Smith, "Autobiography," in Tullidge, *Life of Joseph*, pp. 757–58; Joseph Smith to Cousin John, 28 December 1876, Joseph Smith III Letterbook #1A, Reorganized Church Library–Archives; Joseph Smith to John Henry Smith, 20 January 1886, George Albert Smith Collection, Special Collections, Marriott Library, University of Utah, Salt Lake City.

44. Emma Bidamon to Joseph Smith, 11 October 1866, Emma Smith Bidamon Papers; Audentia Smith Anderson, *Ancestry and Posterity of Joseph Smith* (Independence, Mo.: Herald Publishing House, 1929), p. 656; Smith, "Autobiography," in Tullidge, *Life of Joseph*, p. 757.

45. Joseph Smith to Emma Bidamon, 15 June 1855, Emma Smith Bidamon Papers.

46. Ibid.; Joseph Smith to Frederick G. Mather, 23 December 1879, Joseph Smith III Letterbook #4; Joseph Smith to Israel A. Smith, 21 December 1899, Miscellaneous Letters and Papers; "Editorial," *True Latter Day Saints' Herald* 21 (1 March 1874): 144; *History of Ful-*

ton County, Illinois: Together with Sketches of Its Cities, Villages and Townships, Educational, Religious, Civil, Military, and Political History; Portraits of Prominent Persons and Biographies of Representative Citizens (Peoria: Charles C. Chapman and Co., 1879), p. 404; Jesse Hevlin, *History of Fulton County* (Chicago: Munsell Publishing Co., 1908), p. 493; Charles Lanman, comp., *Dictionary of the United States Congress, Compiled as a Manual of Reference for the Legislator and Statesman* (Washington, D.C.: Government Printing Office, 1864), p. 211.

47. Joseph Smith, Diary, 17 March 1859, Reorganized Church Library–Archives; Smith, "Memoirs, *Saints' Herald* 82 (29 January 1935): 146.

48. Joseph Smith to Alexander H. Smith, 27 September 1855, Joseph Smith III Papers.

49. Joseph Smith to Emmeline Griswold, 20 February 1856, Miscellaneous Letters and Papers.

50. A detailed discussion of Joseph Smith III's legalism can be found in Clare D. Vlahos, "Moderation as a Theological Principle in the Thought of Joseph Smith III," *John Whitmer Historical Association Journal* 1 (1981): 4–6. My discussion of this aspect of Smith's character through this study is based upon the ideas Vlahos emphasized in this article.

51. Joseph Smith III, *The Rejection of the Church* (Lamoni, Iowa: Herald Publishing House, n.d.), pp. 8–10.

52. Ruth Lewis Holman, "Women of Good Works: Emmeline (Emma) Griswold Smith," *Saints' Herald* 104 (9 September 1957): 860–61, 866; Frances Hartman Mullikin, *First Ladies of the Restoration* (Independence, Mo.: Herald Publishing House, 1985), pp. 27–32.

53. Smith, "Memoirs," *Saints' Herald* 82 (19 February 1935): 241.

54. Joseph Smith to Emmeline Griswold, 20 February 1856, Miscellaneous Letters and Papers.

55. Joseph Smith to John Henry Smith, 20 January 1886, George Albert Smith Collection.

56. Smith, "Memoirs," *Saints' Herald* 82 (19 February 1935): 241–42.

4

Origins of the Reorganization

While Joseph Smith III grew into maturity in the rowdy river town of Nauvoo, the church that he eventually came to lead made its first halting steps toward organization, arising largely out of scattered elements of the early Mormon movement. When Smith's father was murdered in Carthage in 1844, total church membership was probably as high as 30,000—more than just a tiny troupe of loyal subjects who followed Joseph Smith, Jr., from state to state and upon his death followed Brigham Young to the sanctuary of the Great Basin.[1] Scattered throughout the nation, particularly in the Northeast and Midwest, were congregations who believed in the prophet's message and, when he died, faced the dilemma of choosing someone to follow.

Immediately after Smith's death Brigham Young and several others vied for control of the ecclesiastical machinery that rested at Nauvoo. While Young captured this central administration, assuring his success as a major factional leader within Mormonism, its control did not ensure his complete victory in the succession struggle. He did not, for instance, command the allegiance of all the important members of the priesthood hierarchy and soon found himself in stiff competition for control over the hinterland congregations not directly under the rule of Nauvoo's theocratic government.[3]

During the first two years after the prophet's death, one man in particular was crucial to the development of the Reorganized

Church. He was James Jesse Strang, a man of elegant charm, entrancing charisma, brilliant dreams, and haunting good looks. Soon after Smith's assassination Strang claimed to be the true successor on the basis of several miraculous experiences curiously similar to those of the youthful Joseph Smith, Jr., during the 1820s. From the time of his meteoric rise in mid-1844 until his murder at the hands of conspirators within his own movement in 1856, Strang was an important force within Mormondom, a man whom Brigham Young could not take lightly.[4]

Because of his claims to divine revelation and his charisma, Strang gained an immediate and enthusiastic following in the areas that would later become the Reorganized Church's strongholds—northern Illinois, eastern Iowa, southern Wisconsin, and the Great Lakes region to the east. Most of the members that he drew into his organization had been living outside of Nauvoo and had felt keenly the vacuum in church leadership left at the death of the prophet. Strang stepped in and filled this void. He made impressive efforts to convert many of the old Saints who had been living in the hinterlands and was astonishingly successful.[5]

Strang even made a few converts from among the Nauvoo disciples of Brigham Young. For instance, when Reuben Miller left Nauvoo and began recruiting a company from among the Saints in Ottawa, Illinois, to emigrate to the West with the main body of the church in early 1846, Strang challenged him to a debate over religious differences between them. Some sixty of Strang's supporters were in the audience, and this cheering section may have helped the force of Strang's argument, but his delivery was so impressive and his reasoning so powerful that he converted Miller to his cause. Miller then returned to Nauvoo to preach the Strangite message to the followers of Young. While there Miller presented the new leadership with an ultimatum that they appear before a Strangite church court to stand trial for apostasy. Neither Young nor his advisors, apparently, even acknowledged Miller's ultimatum.[6]

Later in the spring of 1846 Strang sent one of his chief assistants, Moses Smith, to Nauvoo to seek out converts among the followers of Young. Moses Smith faced official censure when he reached Nauvoo, but because of a general interest in the Strangite message, the local officials allowed Smith to present his organization's claims in the Nauvoo Temple, which was nearing completion.

Undoubtedly he won a few converts, but certainly there could not have been many, and exact numbers have been lost.

More important, however, Moses Smith opened the way for the conversion of a very significant set of church members, individuals who had held high office during the lifetime of Joseph Smith, Jr. Within the next few months after Moses Smith's mission Strang gained the support of John E. Page, a member of the Twelve Apostles; William Smith, brother of the prophet and presiding patriarch until October 1845; William Marks, former stake president of Nauvoo, an administrative post over several congregations; Bishop George Miller, one of the chief financial officers of the movement; Seventy George J. Adams, a member of the church's missionary arm; Lucy Mack Smith, the prophet's mother; and several of Joseph Smith, Jr.'s sisters.[7]

A major disappointment to Strang, however, was his failure to gain the allegiance of Emma Smith and her children. The prestige of the prophet's family would have assured his continued success as a factional leader. Moreover, Strang evidently believed that Joseph Smith III would one day become president of the whole Mormon church. In 1849, for example, a conference of Strang's followers affirmed the youth's future prophetic calling. It passed "on motion, unanimously, that we give our prayers daily for Joseph, the son of Joseph, that he be raised up for God to fill the station to which he has been called by prophecy."[8] As late as 1863, years after Strang's death and long after young Smith had accepted leadership of the Reorganization, a conference of Strangites agreed that the factions of Mormonism must merge together and to that end voted to "sustain young Joseph in the office whereunto God hath called him by our prayers and faith," thus opening the way for the virtual assimilation of Strang's followers into the Reorganized Church.[9]

Nonetheless, during the late 1840s Strang's missionary efforts were nothing short of astounding. He sent teams throughout the Midwest and East, saturating areas that had previously yielded numerous Mormon converts and gathering in whole Mormon congregations that had been largely independent since the death of the prophet. For instance, he incorporated a sizable number of Saints at Kirtland, Ohio, birthplace of Joseph Smith III, into his movement in 1846. Strang himself visited Boston, New York, Washington, Baltimore, and Philadelphia. While Strang pursued an aggressive missionary program, Brigham Young concentrated on organizing the exodus from Nauvoo. This allowed Strang to build a powerful movement from among those Latter Day Saints outside of western Illinois and to create a widespread movement all over the upper Midwest and Northeast. Young did not seriously challenge him in this arena in 1845–46. Instead, he withdrew from the region in favor of building a commonwealth secluded from the rest of the United States.[10]

From its inception Strang's organization was far different from Young's Mormon faction, and these differences explain much of Strang's success. His was essentially a movement filled with dissenters. Strang voiced strong and effective opposition to the rule of Brigham Young and the remaining Twelve Apostles, charging them with usurping control over the church from the rightful successor and perverting the "pure doctrines" of Mormonism. He provided a moderate Mormon organization, at least during his first years of power, opposing the more radical doctrinal teachings of the Young schism, especially the rapidly advancing doctrine of plural marriage. Strang's movement, therefore, served as a rallying point for those who could not accept Young's teachings or administration. It also offered an alternative to Saints who did not want to journey into the deserts of the American West.[11]

Finally, Strang's style of leadership pointed up the striking contrast between the two Mormon leaders. At this time Young was essentially an administrator who did not publicly claim to be a prophet in the sense that Joseph Smith, Jr., had been and offered a very practical "caretaker" government to the Saints, while Strang was a dynamic leader who claimed to have remarkable spiritual manifestations similar to those of the dead prophet. He issued revelations, "translated" sacred documents with the "gift and power of God," and flamboyantly led his followers as had Joseph the Prophet.[12]

The year 1846 marked the zenith of Strang's power as a Mormon leader, for it saw the retreat of Brigham Young's followers from the Midwest and the Strangite capture of many of the Saints remaining in the region. By the close of the year he could claim some 7,000 members, almost all of them coming from the highly successful missionary work among the Saints outside of Nauvoo. But at the time of his greatest apparent successes, James Strang's movement was already beginning to fail.[13]

Essentially three factors led to the demise of the Strangite movement as a viable force in Mormondom. The first was a series of administrative problems that forced Strang to remain at his church's headquarters instead of out where he had enjoyed his greatest successes in the past, winning converts in the missionary field. Second, he short-sightedly ordered his supporters to "gather" together on Beaver Island, Wisconsin, in the middle of Lake Michigan, thus draining the various outlying congregations of his most zealous and capable supporters. Without these individuals to lead the local churches, they began to die, to drift out of Mormonism entirely, or to associate themselves with other claimants to the prophetic mantle. Third, and most important, in the late 1840s a growing schismatic movement arose within the Strangite faction over a diversity of opinion concerning church doctrine. This dissension grew in strength and vocality as it became known that Strang had adopted a form of plural marriage in 1849 and 1850.[14]

As a result of this dissension, a wide assortment of exotic, bizarre, and egocentric movements emerged from Strang's organization during the late 1840s. For the most part these groups were small, loosely organized, highly unstable, and relatively short-lived. They generally centered around one charismatic leader, and their only real importance for the development of the Reorganization was that they filled a void of years. Old Mormons drifted from one group to another searching for what they considered the "true faith" of the original church. Had these factions not existed, the old church members might well have left Mormonism altogether. As it was, however, many of them remained loosely affiliated with Mormonism and receptive to the message of the movement that became the Reorganized Church during the 1850s.

The most important group to arise out of the Strangite movement was led by William B. Smith, the hyperbolic, erratic, and ambitious younger brother of the slain prophet. Smith had been a member of the Twelve Apostles since the quorum's constitution in 1835 and had been granted a measure of respect and power in the early church.[15] After the death of Joseph Smith, Jr., he had tried to assert his influence in Nauvoo, but his caustic manner and unique conceptions about church government and theology forced him out of Young's movement. The Apostles arranged for William's excommunication on 15 October 1845; following this the erstwhile patriarch made a savage newspaper attack on Young and his lieutenants.[16]

After his verbal assault on Young, William Smith moved on to other activities. Apparently, during the winter of 1845–46 Smith served as pastor of a Baptist church in the East, but he left that position in short order after being charged with heresy. By the spring of 1846 Smith had joined James Strang's faction, probably because it offered a legitimate alternative to Young's group, it would accept Smith as presiding patriarch, and it extolled the doctrine of lineal priesthood even to the extent of acknowledging the authority of young Joseph Smith—which William Smith had championed in Nauvoo in 1845—to govern the church at some future time should he choose to do so. However, Smith did not last long as a Strangite; a High Council excommunicated him for rebellion against Strang's leadership in late 1846.[17]

This time William Smith struck out on his own, arguing that he alone should be his brother's successor. He wrote a series of detailed and provocative tracts not only arguing his theological position but also condemning all other Mormon splinter groups as apostates and their leaders as usurpers and charletons. With a handful of followers William Smith undertook a missionary program to gather in a following from among the outlying congregations of the Midwest. Although never as successful as Strang, Smith did gain a modest following.[18]

William Smith's assertions that he had been called to be his brother's successor were extremely attractive to many of the displaced Mormons who had been wandering in the spiritual wilderness since the death of the prophet. Most of these people had been jumping from Mormon faction to Mormon faction and were completely confused over which splinter group represented the "truth" that they had once believed they possessed. He was able to convert, for example, Isaac Sheen, a long-time church member from Cincinnati, Ohio, who had worked in the river city as a printer for many years. Smith coaxed Sheen into editing a newspaper, the *Melchisedec and Aaronic Herald*, on behalf of Smith's claims, and the nine numbers that appeared in 1849 and 1850 violently attacked Brigham Young and his church, serving as a vehicle for presenting Smith's claims to the church's presidency. This publication proved most successful in gaining him converts.[19]

Smith also gained wide recognition by sending a petition to Congress in 1849, opposing the admission of the State of Deseret to the Federal Union. Deseret was the name Brigham Young gave to the Mormon-controlled territory of the Great Basin, encompassing the present areas of Utah and Nevada, southern California and Idaho, western Colorado, and northern Arizona and New Mexico. Young wished to establish a virtually autonomous Mormon state in the West, and the propriety of such a creation was a matter of intense congressional debate. Smith inserted himself and his church in the affair with his petition to the House of Representatives and thereby garnered wide publicity. Congress refused to grant statehood at this time, using the next half-century to carve up Deseret into secularly controlled states.[20]

The movement that became the Reorganized Church of Jesus Christ of Latter Day Saints arose in large part out of a schism within William Smith's faction in 1850. After the death of the prophet, two key church members, Jason W. Briggs and Zenos H. Gurley, Sr., had faced the dilemma of joining one or another of the factions that arose. Their decisions were crucial: both were pastors of congregations, located in northern Illinois and southern Wisconsin respectively, and their decisions would largely be accepted by their congregations. Each independently affiliated with various groups at various times, but was always disappointed by what he considered an apostasy from the pure principles of the restoration, especially the introduction of plural marriage. During the winter of 1845–46 both Briggs and Gurley separately came into contact with James Strang and brought their followers into his organization, but in 1849 they withdrew their support when they learned he was practicing polygamy. Each set out independently, acknowledging no authority greater than that of his congregation.[21]

Early in 1850 Briggs and Gurley came into contact with the movement headed by William Smith and decided to investigate. Briggs, recalling the events of this period during the 1870s, explained how he and others moved toward acceptance of William Smith as president of the church. He said that in the spring of 1850 he attended a conference in Covington, Kentucky, and became excited by the lineal succession doctrine Smith emphasized. This doctrine stipulated that presidential authority passed within family lines in much the same way that secular kingdoms were passed between various members of royal families. Briggs commented that this concept had been "pretty clearly shown in the [scriptures of the Mormon movement but] . . . had been almost entirely overlooked or forgotten by the Saints." Confident of the correctness of the lineal succession doctrine, Briggs asked for admission into the movement, and Gurley soon followed. Briggs and Gurley were instrumental in bringing "many branches and nearly all the Saints in Northern Illinois and Southern Wisconsin" into William Smith's fold.[22]

Six months after a conference in Covington in October 1850, William Smith and an associate, Joseph Woods, traveled to Beloit to visit Briggs and other Saints in the vicinity. During the trip Briggs learned that Smith had become involved in polygamy, as had Strang and Young. Briggs wrote of this discovery: "In the course of their visit it transpired, that they not only believed in the plurality of wives, but were really in the practice of it steathily, and under the strongest vows of secrecy. This created in some minds a terrible conflict between faith and infidelity." Briggs himself was one of those most upset with this development, but since he still had faith in the doctrine of lineal succession to the church's presidency and had no hard evidence that Smith was a polygamist, he decided to wait and see what would happen in the near future.[23]

Accordingly, Briggs agreed to attend a conference of Smith's movement held at Palestine, Illinois, on 6 October 1851. He went with high hopes of correcting what he considered to be errors of doctrine but returned aghast at the services of the conference. The leaders of the faction, Briggs wrote, "threw off the mask, in what they called a priest's lodge, and confessed to the belief and practice of polygamy in the name of the Lord." After this announcement Briggs abandoned his attempts to reconcile his differences with Smith. He immediately took his branch out of fellowship with the Smith movement. Gurley and other pastors soon did the same. The feelings of many were expressed by Israel A. Rogers, who left William Smith's group immediately after this conference and eventually became the first presiding bishop of the Reorganized Church. He wrote: "I . . . did not continue with him long, as I soon discovered he was teaching the spiritual wife doctrine, which I knew was false. Those were dark days."[24]

Jason Briggs grew increasingly depressed after this meeting. One by one he had seen the groups in which he had placed such high expectations fail to meet even minimal goals. As far as he could tell, the entire church that he had loved since the days of the prophet had fallen into apostasy. All the religious choices left were unacceptable in Briggs's mind, so taking a lesson from the experiences of young Joseph Smith, Jr., he began to ask God for direction.

Briggs claimed that the answer to his pleadings came on 18 November 1851. As he knelt in prayer on the prairie near his Beloit, Wisconsin, home, he received a revelation from God and "visions of truth opened to my mind." He said a heavenly messenger visited him and counseled:

> Behold, I have not cast off my people; neither have I changed in regard to Zion. Yea, verily, my people shall be redeemed, and my law shall be kept . . .
>
> And because you have asked me in faith concerning William Smith, this is the answer of the Lord thy God concerning him: I, the Lord have permitted him to represent the rightful heir to the presidency of the high priesthood of my church by reason of the faith of prayers of his father, and his brothers, Joseph and Hyrum Smith, which came up before me in his behalf; and to respect the law of lineage, by which the holy priesthood is transmitted in all generations. . . . And for this reason have I poured out my Spirit through his ministrations, according to the integrity of those who received them.
>
> But as Essau despised his birthright, so had William Smith despised my law, and forfeited that which pertained to him as an apostle and high priest in my church. . . . [he] shall be degraded in [this life], and shall die without regard; for [he] has forsaken my law. . . .
>
> Therefore, let my elders . . . preach my gospel as revealed in the record of the Jews, and the Book of Mormon, and the Book of Doctrine and Covenants; and cry repentance and remission of sins through obedience to the gospel, and I will sustain them and give them my Spirit; and in mine own due time will I call upon the seed of Joseph Smith, and will bring forth one mighty and strong, and he shall preside over the high priesthood of my church; . . . and the pure in heart shall gather, and Zion shall be reinhabited. . . .

Briggs testified that he was told to "write, write, write the revelation and send it unto the Saints at Palestine [Illinois], and at Voree

[Wisconsin], and at Waukesha [Wisconsin], and to all places where this doctrine is taught as my law; and whomsoever will humble themselves before me, and ask of me, shall receive of my Spirit a testimony that these works are of me."[25]

This record was the first genuine document of what would become the Reorganization of the church. It affirmed several essential points for Briggs, confirming his suspicions that William Smith was a false prophet, reinforcing his belief that polygamy was a doctrine contrary to the laws of God, and altering his belief in lineal succession to the presidency to include only those who were direct descendents of Joseph Smith, Jr., of whom the eldest son, Joseph III, was the most likely candidate to accept his father's prophetic mantle. At this time Briggs seemed unaware of the prophet's statements concerning young Joseph's succession to the presidency, which would have reinforced his already strong convictions. However, Briggs and the people who soon came to associate with him based the law of succession completely upon the concept of lineal priesthood. The new church later defended its belief in this law. Writing in 1855, Zenos Gurley told a prospective convert: "This [law] Brother Cutler (tho plainly taught in the revelations of God in the order of the Priesthood) was unknown to us untill revealed through the gift of the ghost to several who were tired and sick of the doctrine of men and of Devils and had by fasting and prayer sought the Lord to know from him the true and right way." Additionally, Briggs became convinced that in time God would influence the chosen successor to accept his rightful place at the head of the church.[26]

A few days after its writing, Briggs read his revelation to a few men within his congregation. They were undeniably wary of such a pronouncement, perhaps fearing the rise of yet another would-be prophet, and seriously challenged Briggs's right to receive such a revelation. They also feared the implications of organizing a new movement. Finally, after lengthy debate, they decided to pray for a testimony of the document's divinity. They prayed independently but after a time came together, and each confirmed, at least for himself, the truthfulness of the record. They then made copies of the vision for distribution to other congregations.[27]

Early in 1852 one of Briggs's messengers, David Powell, brought Zenos Gurley a copy of the revelation; it was the first he had heard of Briggs's experience. Although immediately skeptical, he read the document carefully. After considering the divinity of this revelation for several days, Gurley claimed to have received confirmation of its truthfulness. He wrote:

> About ten or fifteen days after I had heard of the revelation, while sitting by my evening fire, my boys came running into my room, declaring with great earnestness that their little sister was up to Brother [Reuben] Newkirk's, speaking and singing in tongues. For a moment I was overpowered with joy. I exclaimed, "Is it possible that God has remembered my family?" Immediately I went up, and when I was within one or two steps of the house, I paused. I listened, and O thrill of Joy that went through my soul! I knew that it was of God, My Child, my dear child was born of the Holy Spirit. I opened the door and went in. It appeared to me that the entire room was filled with the Holy Spirit. Shortly after I requested them to join with me in asking the Lord to tell who the successor of Joseph Smith was. I felt anxious to know that I might bear a faithful testimony. We spent a few moments in prayer, when the Holy Spirit declared, "The successor of Joseph Smith is Joseph Smith, the son of Joseph Smith the Prophet. It is his right by lineage, saith the Lord your God."

Not long thereafter, Gurley wrote to Briggs, telling him simply, "We have received evidence of your revelation." From that point on, the destinies of Gurley and Briggs and, to some extent, of young Joseph Smith were joined together.[28]

During the first months of 1852 messengers carrying Briggs's revelation visited most of the branches of the Midwest. Many of the Saints living in Waukesa, Voree, Burlington, Yellow Stone, and Beloit, Wisconsin, as well as those in Palestine and Jacksonville, Illinois, accepted the document as a statement of God's divine will. Many within these congregations, accustomed as they had been to the tightly organized ecclesiastical system of early Mormonism, asked for formal organization into a new church. But the leadership was hesitant, doubting this body had the authority to organize. Within a very few months, however, popular pressure forced the various branch presidents to bring their congregations together in Beloit for a June 1852 conference. There the assembled believers attempted a tentative "reorganization," claiming that their work was "based upon the law of God, and justified by the law of the land."[29]

The conference that met in Beloit on 12 and 13 June 1852 was unique in the annals of Mormon history. It had no acknowledged head, no organization for which to transact business, no authority to act, and no business to transact. It was united only in its opposition to other Mormon factions, in its acceptance of the Briggs document as divine revelation, in its belief that Mormonism as set forth in the Scriptures was correct, and in its affirmation that the proper successor to the prophetic office was growing to maturity in Nauvoo and would one day step forth to accept his calling.

Jason Briggs, who served as chairman of the meetings, and Zenos Gurley cautiously managed this first conference. Briggs did not allow the body to implement a formal church organization, but they did pass a series of resolutions that formed a loose creed for the believers. These resolutions could have properly been called the new movement's "Declaration of Independence." They read:

> Resolved, that this conference regard the pretensions of Brigham Young, James J. Strang, James Colin Brewster, and William Smith and Joseph Wood's joint claims to the leadership of the Church of Jesus Christ of Latter Day Saints, as an assumption of power, in violation of the laws of God, and consequently we disclaim all connection and fellowship with them.
>
> Resolved, that the successor of Joseph Smith, Jun., as the Presiding High Priest, in the Melchisedec Priesthood, must of necessity be the seed of Joseph Smith, Jun., in fulfillment of the law and promises of God.
>
> Resolved, that as the office of First President of the Church grows out of the authority of the Presiding High Priest, in the high priesthood, no person can legally lay claim to the office of First President of the Church without a previous ordination to the Presidency of the High Priesthood.
>
> Resolved, that we recognize the validity of all legal ordinations in this Church, and will fellowship all such as have been ordained while acting within the purview of such authority.
>
> Resolved, that we believe that the Church of Christ, organized on the sixth day of April A.D., 1830, exists as on that day wherever six or more saints are organized according to the pattern in the Book of Doctrine and Covenants.
>
> Resolved, that the whole law of the Church of Jesus Christ is contained in the Bible, Book of Mormon, and Book of Doctrine and Covenants.
>
> Resolved, that, in the opinion of this conference, there is no stake

to which the saints on this continent are commanded to gather at the present time, but that the saints on all other lands are commanded to gather to this land preparatory to the reestablishment of the church in Zion, when the scattered saints on this land will also be commanded to gather and return to Zion, . . . and it is the duty of the saints to turn their hearts and their faces toward Zion and supplicate the Lord for such deliverance.

Resolved, that we will, to the extent of our ability and means, communicate to all the scattered saints the sentiments contained in the foregoing statements.

Resolved, that this conference believes it the duty of the elders of the church, who have been legally ordained, to cry repentance and remission of sins to this generation, through obedience to the gospel as revealed in the record of the Jews, the Book of Mormon, and Book of Doctrine and Covenants, and not faint in the discharge of duty.

Following the passage of these resolutions, which were accepted unanimously, the Saints decided to meet again on 6 October 1852.[30]

Jason Briggs remembered that this first conference was successful beyond all expectation. Those assembled found "visible the tokens of divine care, which, like the clouds of the size 'of a man's hand,' to the ancient prophet, confirmed [their redemption], in the due time of the Lord," Briggs noted, "and they were determined to wait and prepare for that 'time.' "[31] But the Saints were not content merely to wait for divine intervention, and they began an informal missionary program during the summer and fall of 1852, with priesthood members traveling throughout the Illinois-Wisconsin area spreading the word of the reorganizing efforts. As a result the Saints had even greater representation at the October 1852 conference, although neither Briggs nor Gurley allowed any substantive organizational developments at this meeting.

By April 1853 many of those associated with the reorganizing movement were vociferously demanding that formal organization take place soon. Briggs remembered that "it had been no part of the expectation of the [leading] brethren from the first to organize other than branches, advise the branches to meet together in Conference capacity for mutual instruction, and await the coming of the successor." But the membership's importunings led Briggs and Gurley to reconsider the propriety of beginning a completely new organization.[32]

Decidedly conservative and legalistic in their religious temperament, the first leaders of the Reorganization were not sure that they possessed the priestly authority to organize further. Not wishing to appear to be placing power and authority in their own hands, these leaders decided to pray about the matter, asking not only for guidance but also for a blueprint for reorganization. On 20 March 1853, after days of prayer, Henry H. Deam, an old, shy fellow who had been a member of the church for many years, visited Gurley and told him he had received a solution to the problem from God. Gurley was pleased that the Lord had favored him with a revelation, he said, and asked the old gentleman to write it down. It said:

> Verily, thus saith the Lord, as I said unto my servant Moses, "See thou do all things according to the pattern," so I say unto you. Behold, the pattern is before you. It is my will that you respect authority in my church; therefore let the greatest among you preside at your conference. Let three men be appointed by the conference to select seven men from among you, who shall compose a majority of the Twelve Apostles; for it is my will that the quorum should not be filled up at present. Let the President of the Conference, assisted by two others, ordain them. (The senior of them shall preside.) Let them select twelve men from among you, and ordain them to compose my High Council. —Behold, ye understand the order of the Bishopric, the Seventy, the Elders, the Priests, Teachers, and Deacons. These organize according to the pattern. Behold, I will be with you unto the end; even so. Amen.[33]

When the conference met in Beloit, Wisconsin, the body asked if the acknowledged leaders of the movement had devised a plan of organization. After some discussion on the matter, Gurley announced that Deam had received a remarkable revelation and asked the conference to consider its merits. The members deliberated for a short time but without much hesitation accepted it as a divinely inspired directive and elected three men to choose the apostles. This committee chose Briggs, Gurley, and Deam, as well as four others to be ordained members of the apostolic office, with Briggs becoming the president of the quorum.[34]

The April 1853 conference might appropriately be called the founding vehicle of the Reorganized Church. Between 1853 and 1856 a reinvigorated organization emerged, began serious missionary operations, and enforced a modest amount of orthodoxy upon

the members. The Reorganization's missionaries went forth thereafter with a threefold message: "to reassert the faith and doctrines
contained in the sacred books, to reclaim the backslider, and to
vindicate the character of the Latter Day Work, which had become
odious through the evil deeds of its professed advocates."[35]

During this founding period the Reorganized Church possessed
several valuable assets that not only made it attractive to others
but also shaped its future in both doctrine and policy. Unlike the
egocentric and autocratic operators of some of the other Mormon
factions, its leaders were very conservative in their moves to bring
about the "new organization." Apparently they never sought the
status and power of leadership that had motivated some of the other
Mormon factional leaders. Moreover, they were, in large measure,
men who had been minor figures in the church while the prophet
lived; they had not been intimate friends with Joseph Smith, Jr.,
and had known little of affairs in Nauvoo. Their understanding of
the Mormon religion rested almost entirely on the written word,
the scriptures of the restoration, and they used them tenaciously as
measuring sticks against which all teachings had to be compared.
This produced in the Reorganized Church a literalism more pronounced than that in the days of the prophet in Nauvoo or within
the faction headed by Brigham Young. Consequently, the Reorganization's leadership had generally not been taught plural marriage
or other exotic concepts by Joseph Smith, Jr., and many did not
have the burning desire to reconcile Smith's heartfelt belief in these
doctrines with contrary scriptures. If the prophet had believed these
conceptions at all, they argued, he had been seduced by some spirit
other than that of God and they were free to reject any prophet
who advocated these teachings. In addition, the new organization's
leadership claimed that the successor should be a literal descendent
of Joseph the Prophet, with the birthright falling to the first-born
son. What these leaders developed, then, was a very moderate and
conservative Mormon movement that respected the rights of individuals and fit loosely into the mainstream of American Protestant
religion.

The years between 1851 and 1856 were fundamental to the development of this peculiar brand of Mormonism. Little of this
slowly coalescing movement's story was known to the young man
who would eventually accept its leadership, although young Joseph

Smith received copies of its missionary tracts and heard bits and snatches about it whenever old friends visited him in Nauvoo. But he made no response either positively or negatively to the Reorganized Church during this period. In 1856, however, the church and the young man converged for their first head-to-head confrontation. The outcome precipitated Smith's ordination as its president on 6 April 1860 and his long reign thereafter.[36]

NOTES

1. Joseph Smith, Jr., estimated church membership in 1844 at approximately 200,000, although few records were kept that could be used to document this figure. This is certainly too large a number. See Joseph Smith, Jr., "The Latter Day Saints," in *He Pasa Eklesia, an Original History of the Religious Denominations at Present Existing in the United States,* ed. Israel Daniel Rupp (Philadelphia: N. Y. Humphreys, 1844), p. 409. The 30,000 membership figure is that estimated in Dean L. May, "A Demographic Portrait of the Mormons, 1830–1980," in *After 150 Years: The Latter-day Saints in Historical Perspective,* ed. Thomas G. Alexander and Jessie L. Embry (Provo, Utah: Charles Redd Center for Western Studies, 1983), pp. 43–45. May confirms the impression that a sizable percentage of Latter Day Saints did not follow Brigham Young to the Great Basin and may have been, therefore, part of the various Mormon factions. His "calculations suggest that the proportions of Mormons migrating west from Nauvoo between 1846 and 1850 may have been substantially less than had been thought and that a very high proportion (38 percent) of the western U.S. Mormons were British born—persons converted under the ministry of the apostles and perhaps feeling a special loyalty to that body" (May, "A Demographic Portrait," p. 50).

2. "New York and Philadelphia District," *Journal of History* 1 (January 1908): 66, 79.

3. Among the major factional leaders were Sidney Rigdon, Lyman Wight, William B. Smith, William McLellin, Charles B. Thompson, James J. Strang, James Colin Brewster, Austin Cowles, David Whitmer, Granville Hedrick, and Alpheus Cutler. Historical information on most of these is scanty, but the best introductions are Steven L. Shields, *Divergent Paths of the Restoration: A History of the Latter Day Saints* (Bountiful, Utah: Restoration Research, Inc., 1982); Joseph Smith and Heman C. Smith, *The History of the Reorganized Church of Jesus Christ of Latter Day Saints* (Independence, Mo.: Herald Publishing House, 1973), 3:29–91, 195–213.

4. Accounts of James J. Strang's life can be found in Milo M. Quaife, *The Kingdom of Saint James: A Narrative of James J. Strang, the Beaver Island Mormon King* (New Haven, Conn.: Yale University Press, 1930); Klaus J. Hansen, "The Making of King Strang: A Reexamination," *Michigan History* 46 (September 1962): 209–29; William D. Russell, "King James Strang: Joseph Smith's Successor?" in *The Restoration Movement: Essays in Mormon History,* ed. F. Mark McKiernan, Alma R. Blair, and Paul M. Edwards (Lawrence, Kan.: Coronado Press, 1973), pp. 231–56; David Rich Lewis, " 'For Life, the Resurrection, and the Life Everlasting': James J. Strang and Strangite Mormon Polygamy, 1849–1856," *Wisconsin Magazine of History* 66 (Summer 1983): 274–91; Lawrence Foster, "James J. Strang: The Prophet Who Failed," *Church History* 50 (June 1981): 182–92.

5. Quaife, *Kingdom of Saint James,* pp. 11–28.

6. Ibid., p. 22.

7. Ibid., pp. 25, 29; Russell, "King James Strang," p. 239. See also the statement written by William Smith, signed by several members of the Smith family, and printed in *Voree* (Wisc.) *Herald,* July 1846. The wife and children of the prophet were not included in the statement, however, and were conspicuous in their absence. In an affidavit drawn up in 1899, some of the surviving Smiths stated that they had never signed the earlier document supporting the claims of Strang. See *Saints' Herald* 46 (26 April 1899): 261.

8. *Gospel Herald* (Voree, Wisc.) 4 (April 1849): 16.

9. Minutes of the Hixton, Mich., Conference, 25 December 1863, Special Collections, Clarke Historical Library, Central Michigan University, Mount Pleasant, Mich.

10. Quaife, *Kingdom of Saint James,* p. 42.

11. Robert Bruce Flanders, "Mormons Who Did Not Go West: A Study of the Emergence of the Reorganized Church of Jesus Christ of Latter Day Saints" (M.A. thesis, University of Wisconsin, 1954), pp. 28–29; Roger D. Launius, "The Bridge—Between 1844 and 1852," *Restoration Trail Forum* 9 (August 1983): 1, 6–7; Alma R. Blair, "The Reorganized Church of Jesus Christ of Latter Day Saints: Moderate Mormons," in McKiernan, Blair, and Edwards, *The Restoration Movement,* pp. 209–15.

12. For an example of Strang's "prophetic" activities, see William D. Russell, " 'Printed by Command of the King': James J. Strang's *Book of the Law of the Lord,*" *Restoration* 3 (April 1984): 19–21.

13. Quaife, *Kingdom of Saint James,* p. 243; Foster, "James J. Strang," pp. 188–92.

14. Flanders, "Mormons Who Did Not Go West," pp. 27–28; Russell,

"King James Strang," pp. 243–53; Lewis, " 'For Life, the Resurrection, and Life Everlasting,' " pp. 274–91.

15. Difficulties in which William B. Smith was involved within the early church have been documented in Wilford Woodruff, Journal, 13 February 1859, Church of Jesus Christ of Latter-day Saints Historical Department, Salt Lake City, Utah; Joseph Smith, Jr., *The History of the Church of Jesus Christ of Latter-day Saints,* ed. B. H. Roberts (Salt Lake City, Utah: Deseret Book Co., 1976), 2:295–96, 334, 338–44, 346–47, 352–55.

16. This episode has been summarized in E. Gary Smith, "The Patriarchal Crisis of 1845," *Dialogue: A Journal of Mormon Thought* 16 (Summer 1983): 24–39. See also Irene M. Bates, "William Smith, 1811–1893: Problematic Patriarch," *Dialogue: A Journal of Mormon Thought* 16 (Summer 1983): 11–23; Paul M. Edwards, "William B. Smith: The Persistent Pretender," *Dialogue: A Journal of Mormon Thought* 18 (Summer 1985): 128–39.

17. Edwards, "William B. Smith," p. 130; Calvin P. Rudd, "William Smith: Brother of the Prophet Joseph Smith" (M.A. thesis, Brigham Young University, 1973), pp. 136–49.

18. See broadsides of William B. Smith, *William Smith, patriarch & prophet of the most high God. Latter Day Saints, Beware of imposition* (Ottawa, Ill.: n.p., 1847); *A revelation given to William Smith in 1847, on the apostacy of the Church and the pruning of the vineyard of the Lord* (Philadelphia: n.p., 1848); *Zion's Standard, a voice from the Smith Family* (Princeton, Ill.: n.p., 1848).

19. Inez Smith Davis, *The Story of the Church* (Independence, Mo.: Herald Publishing House, 1976), p. 436; Dale L. Morgan, "A Bibliography of the Churches of the Dispersion," *Western Humanities Review* 7 (Summer 1952): 111.

20. "Remonstrance of William Smith, *et al.,* of Covington, Kentucky, Against the Admission of Deseret into the Union, December 31, 1849," in *Miscellaneous Documents Printed by Order of the First Session of the Thirty-First Congress Begun and Held at the City of Washington, D.C., December 3, 1849* (Washington, D.C.: William M. Belt, 1850), Document No. 43, 31st Cong., 1st Sess. (Serial Set No. 581).

21. "Testimony of Jason W. Briggs," in *Complainant's Abstract of Pleading and Evidence in the Circuit Court of the United States, Western District of Missouri, Western Division, at Kansas City, Missouri* (Lamoni, Iowa: Herald Publishing House, 1893), pp. 401–3; Richard P. Howard, "The Reorganized Church in Illinois, 1852–1882: Search for Identity," *Dialogue: A Journal of Mormon Thought* 5 (Winter 1970): 64; Blair, "The Reorganized Church of Jesus Christ of Latter Day Saints," p. 214;

Smith and Smith, *History of Reorganized Church*, 3:745. Note that the spelling of Gurley's first name in this study is Zenos, in spite of a common spelling of Zenas used by many Reorganized Church historians. Zenos was the spelling of Gurley's name in his "History of the New Organization of the Church," the first installment of which was published in the *True Latter Day Saints' Herald* in January 1860.

22. Jason W. Briggs, "History of the Reorganized Church," *The Messenger* (Salt Lake City, Utah) 2 (November 1875): 1.

23. Ibid.

24. Israel A. Rogers, quoted in Blair, "The Reorganized Church of Jesus Christ of Latter Day Saints," p. 228.

25. Briggs, "History," *Messenger* 2 (November 1875): 1. See also Smith and Smith, *History of Reorganized Church*, 3:200–201; W. W. Blair, Diary, 1 May 1864, Reorganized Church of Jesus Christ of Latter Day Saints Library–Archives, Independence, Mo.; Jason W. Briggs, "A Condensed Account of the Rise and Progress of the Reorganization of the Church of Latter Day Saints," pp. 146–48, M. H. Forscutt-H. A. Stebbins Letterbook, Reorganized Church Library–Archives.

26. Zenos H. Gurley to Alpheus Cutler, 29 November 1855, Miscellaneous Letters and Papers, Reorganized Church Library–Archives. See also Stephen Post to Warren Post, 7 September 1850, Miscellaneous Letters and Papers.

27. Briggs, "A Condensed Account," pp. 148–49; Briggs, "History," *Messenger* 2 (November 1875): 5.

28. Zenos H. Gurley, Sr., "History of the New Organization of the Church," *True Latter Day Saints' Herald* 1 (January 1860): 18–22; Smith and Smith, *History of Reorganized Church*, 3:209.

29. Briggs, "A Condensed Account," p. 173.

30. "Early Reorganization Minutes," Book A, 13–14 June 1852, Reorganized Church Library–Archives; Smith and Smith, *History of Reorganized Church*, 3:210.

31. Briggs, "History," *Messenger* 2 (December 1875): 9; Briggs, "A Condensed Account," p. 156.

32. Briggs, "A Condensed Account," p. 159.

33. Ibid.; Gurley, "History of the New Organization," *True Latter Day Saints' Herald* 1 (February 1860): 55.

34. Gurley, "History of the New Organization," *True Latter Day Saints' Herald* 1 (February 1860): 55–57; "Early Reorganization Minutes," Book A, 8 April 1853; Briggs, "History," *Messenger* 2 (December 1875): 21–27.

35. Briggs, "A Condensed Account," p. 161; *The Voice of the Captives,*

Assembled at Zerahemla, In Annual Conference April 6, 1854, to their Brethren Scattered Abroad (Janesville, Wisc.: n.p., 1854).

36. Blair, "Reorganized Church of Jesus Christ of Latter Day Saints," pp. 225–31; Davis, *Story of the Church,* p. 454; Flanders, "Mormons Who Did Not Go West," p. 85.

CHAPTER

5

The Search

Even as the Reorganized Church was rising out of the ashes of the various Mormon splinter groups that had existed in the American Midwest following the death of the prophet, young Joseph Smith III was beginning his life with his new wife in Nauvoo, Illinois. In November 1856, soon after his wedding, the stout, bearded Smith moved with his bride to a farm outside of the town and set out to become a gentleman farmer. He worked by day with his brother, Frederick, who had part interest in the farm, and by night he and his wife enjoyed quiet evenings at home. Both were avid readers of the popular magazines and books of the day, especially *Harper's Monthly* and the novels of James Fenimore Cooper. Sometimes Smith went into town to have fun with some of his long-time friends, but usually he stayed home with Emma.[1]

Although relatively happy with this simple life, Joseph Smith III still felt a certain uneasiness, a nagging reminder that he had a destiny yet to fulfill. As this uneasiness continued through the winter of 1856–57 and into the spring, Smith began to take an increasingly active interest in the details of Mormonism. He delved further into the nuances of doctrine, history, and current development of the major factions and became one of the more knowledgeable members of the community about the peculiar religion, although he sometimes modestly claimed to have little genuine understanding. While concerned about his destiny, Smith remained calm, reasoning that God would provide answers to his religious questions in due time.

In 1856 Smith was still convinced that the vision he had received three years earlier would yet come to fruition and that he would be given a choice about service in the secular or religious sphere. His general moderateness as well as his concern about this issue was expressed well in May 1855 in a letter to a friend concerned about religion. He told her to do much as he, and "examine all [doctrines] faithfully and carefully, weighing well the merits and demerits before you commit yourself to any." If individuals did this, Smith contended, they would realize that, by living "uprightly and honestly before the world, having a conscience void of reproach," they were "Christian whether they have joined the tenets of any church or not." Only by taking this approach, he added, can a person fulfill "the destiny for which you were placed on earth."[2]

Unfortunately for Joseph Smith, the choice that he expected was neither clearly delineated nor offered at a single cusp of time. Instead of a clearly marked fork in the road, one path leading to religious fulfillment and the other to status in the secular world, Smith was forced to undergo a torturous series of incidents that gradually nudged him toward the leadership of the Reorganized Church. Later in life Smith remembered these incidents as essentially divine intervention to prompt him to do the will of the Lord. In much the way that God struck down Saul on the road to Damascus to persuade him to do His will, Smith explained, God sent a series of crises into his life between 1856 and 1860, causing him to turn toward the Lord for strength and security and thereby opening the door for the young man's acceptance of leadership within the Reorganization. To a very real extent, Smith noted, the experiences of these years served as the refiner's fire out of which his faith was forged.[3]

The first incident, tremendously important in charting Smith's course into the Reorganization, came in 1856, as Smith began to reconsider his longstanding beliefs concerning Utah Mormonism. Conversations with several Nauvoo friends, particularly with Christopher E. Yates and his son, Putnam, caused Joseph to view the Latter-day Saints in the Great Basin in a startlingly different manner from what he had been taught by his mother and had adopted as a result of his experience in Nauvoo between 1844 and

1846. The Yates family had lived in Hancock County since before the Mormon exodus of 1846 and had often stood up for the
rights of the Saints during the early 1840s. Consequently, mobs in
the country had labeled Christopher Yates a "Jack-Mormon" and
had burned his barn, destroyed his crops, killed his livestock, and
terrorized his family during this period.[4]

Smith and the Yates men often worked together, and invariably
the subject of Mormonism came up in conversation. In one such
discussion, Putnam suggested that Smith seriously consider going
to Utah, where Putnam thought he might be able to accomplish
much good. As a reformer within the movement, Putnam asserted,
Smith could take "the lead away from Brigham; breaking up that
system of things there." Even if he did not wish to reform Mormonism, Yates added, Joseph could go to Utah and adopt "the style of
things there, become a leader, get rich, marry three or four wives
and enjoy yourself." Yates went so far as to suggest that going to
Utah might be his duty to the faith. None of this rested easily with
Smith, however, and he told Putnam that he could never under any
circumstances brook the practice of polygamy.

But Smith began to reconsider his beliefs about Utah Mormonism and to question, albeit without changing, his conception of
plural marriage. As a result, he began to ask himself, "Why not
go to Utah?" He reasoned: "There are the men who were with my
father, or a great many of them. There, a large part of the family;
there, also, seem to be the only ones making a profession of the
belief in Mormonism who appear to be doing anything. Does not
duty demand that I go there and clear my name and the charge of in-
gratitude to my father's character? Is not polygamy, against which
you object, a correct tenet? Is not your objection one of prejudice
only?"[5] For weeks Smith considered these questions somberly but
without arriving at an acceptable answer.

As his pondering continued, Smith began to grow disturbed. The
more he tried to sort out options and establish clear objectives, the
more confused he became. Finally, he decided to pray for answers
to his questioning, and, Smith claimed, his prayers led to a religious experience that aided him immeasurably. He described it in
his 1880 autobiography: "I heard a slight noise like the rush of the
breeze, . . . I turned my gaze slightly upward and saw descending
towards me a sort of cloud; funnel-shaped with the widest part

upwards. It was luminous and of such color and brightness that it was clearly seen, though the sun shone in its summer strength. It descended rapidly and settling upon and over me enveloped me completely so that I stood within its radiance." As he stood in the light, Smith said, he was told to have nothing to do with Utah Mormonism, because "the light in which you stand is greater than theirs." After this statement the vision ended, leaving Smith the full impact of the message. The experience, of course, settled the question of Smith's joining with Brigham Young's group but still left him without an answer to the question of which Mormon faction, if any, he should accept.[6]

A second incident opening the way for Smith to enter the Reorganization took place near the end of November 1856. Two Utah Mormon missionaries, George A. Smith, a relative of Joseph's, and Erastus Snow, both members of the Twelve Apostles since the 1840s, visited him on his farm while enroute to the East.[7] They came to the Smith farm ostensibly to bring Joseph a copy of Frederick Piercy's book, *The Route to Great Salt Lake,* "which contained a detailed account of a trip from Liverpool to Salt Lake, sketches and portraits made on the way," said Smith. Joseph Smith had posed for a crayon sketch while Piercy was in Nauvoo in 1853, working on the book, and the artist-author wanted to thank him for his cooperation by presenting him with a copy of the work. Far more important than the delivery of this gift, however, was the opportunity for Snow and George Smith to determine Joseph's current views toward the church in the Great Basin.[8]

After a friendly greeting, Snow began to ask leading questions of Joseph, seeking an explanation of his beliefs concerning Christianity, the Book of Mormon, his father's work, and the possibility of migrating to Utah. Joseph answered candidly that he believed in the "Bible and the *Book of Mormon,* . . . but not as you people interpret them." He went on to say that he could never "go out there and make my home with you while you are teaching and practicing as you are." The two missionaries quickly realized that he was referring to the doctrine of plural marriage. Accepting the power of young Smith's conviction about this practice, a conviction strengthened by his recent spiritual experience, they concluded that irreconcilable differences would keep the Utah movement and the Smith boy apart, for polygamy was a way of life in Deseret and could not be readily changed. After they left Joseph's home, Snow and George Smith decided to report to Brigham Young that there was little likelihood of the prophet's eldest son joining them.[9]

Had Joseph Smith decided to accept the missionaries' offer and migrate to Utah, he probably would have been accepted with great joy by the Saints, who still considered the Smith family a part of the church and any member of the family's presence among them only natural. But had he gone west, Joseph would have been forced to accept the de facto authority of Brigham Young as well as the practice of plural marriage. He would have been a prodigal son returning home, but with no guarantee as to his future role in the church. Smith, understandably, was not willing to do this, particularly since he considered it degrading, unnecessary, and doctrinally incorrect. When Erastus Snow and George A. Smith walked down the road from the Smith farm, the Utah Mormon flirtation with Joseph Smith ended. At no future time did any Utah church authority officially invite Joseph Smith to enter Brigham Young's movement. Thus, after 1856 not only had Smith rejected the Utah faction of the church as a movement he might join, the factional leaders in the Great Basin had finally rejected him as well.[10]

The third incident directing Smith to move in the direction of the Reorganized Church took place soon after the meeting with the Utah Latter-day Saint missionaries. At the fall conference of 1856 the Reorganization's membership had voted to send two members of the Quorum of Seventy, the church's missionary arm, to visit Joseph Smith and to ask him to join them. They believed that the messengers, Samuel H. Gurley and Edmund C. Briggs, brothers of Zenos H. Gurley, Sr., and Jason Briggs, would have easy success in Nauvoo. Jason Briggs recorded his assessment of this mission, stating that all believed that "the response of the message would be the immediate appearance of Joseph, the eldest son, to take the place of his father; for until now, it had not been fully determined in the minds of some of the brethren which of the four sons would be called to that dignity."[11] The result of this meeting, however, sadly disappointed the membership of the church.

Gurley and Briggs arrived at the Smith farm about four in the afternoon on 5 December 1856. Joseph was not at the house when they knocked at the door, but Emmeline invited them in to await his return. Within a short time Joseph appeared and they sat down to talk. These missionaries said they represented a "new organization" of the church whose tracts had previously been sent to Smith and had a very special message from the Saints that they wished him to read and consider. Joseph accepted a letter, written by Jason Briggs, that Gurley thrust into his hands and started to read. This letter stated in part:

> The God of Abram, Isaac, and Jacob covenanted with him and their seed. So the God of Joseph covenanted with him and his seed, that his word should not depart out of his mouth, not out of the mouth of his seed, nor out of the mouth of his seed's seed, till the end come. A zerubbel in Israel art thou. As a nail fastened in a sure place, so are the promises unto thee to make thee a restorer in Zion: —to set in order the house of God. And the Holy Spirit that searcheth the deep things of God, hath signified to us that the time has come. For through fasting and prayer hath the answer from God come; unto us saying, Communicate with my servant Joseph Smith, son of Joseph the Prophet. Arise, call upon God and be strong, for a deliverer art thou to the Latter Day Saints. And the Holy Spirit is the prompter. The Apostles, Elders and Saints who have assembled with us, have beheld the vacant seed and the seed that is wanting. And like Ezra of old with this brethren, by the direction of the Holy Spirit have we sent faithful messengers to bear this our message to you, trusting that you will by their hands notify us of your readiness to occupy that seat, and answer to the name and duties of that seed. For this have our prayers been offered up without ceasing for the last five years. We are assured that the same Spirit that has testified to us, has signified the same things to you. Many have arisen perverting the work of the Lord. But the good and the true are throughout the land waiting the true successor of Joseph the Prophet. In our publications—sent to you—we have shown the right of successorship to rest in the literal descendent of the chosen seed, to whom the promise was made, and also the manner of ordination thereto. We can not forbear reminding you that the commandments, as well as the promises given to Joseph, your father, were given to him, and to his seed. And in the name of our master, even Jesus Christ, as moved upon by the Holy Ghost we say, Arise in the strength of the Lord and realize those promises by executing those commandments. And we by the grace of God are thy helpers in restoring the exiled sons and daughters of Zion in their inheritances in the kingdom of God and to the faith once delivered to the Saints.[12]

When Joseph had finished with the document, he handed it back without comment, although he was visibly shaken by its contents.

Samuel Gurley asked him for an official response, but Joseph only said, "Gentlemen, I will talk with you on politics or on any other subject, but on religion I will not allow one word spoken in my house." Since both men had expected Joseph's decision to join the Reorganization, this rebuff shocked them, but their reactions were markedly different. Gurley broke down and wept while Briggs became irate. "Mr Smith," Briggs retorted, "while we respect your feelings as a man and do not wish to injure your feelings, yet we will not allow you to hinder us in doing our duty, as we have been sent by the command of God to tell you what we know and most surely believe in relation to your calling as the successor of your father." Smith came very near ordering these missionaries from his house, but his wife intervened and calmed the situation. Joseph still refused to discuss religion, although before Briggs and Gurley left two hours later, they had exacted a promise from Smith to think over the proposition and meet with them the next day at his mother's home in Nauvoo to discuss it further.[13]

The two missionaries returned to Nauvoo and spent a fitful night in the Bidamon boarding house. The next morning, a Sunday, they ate a leisurely breakfast and waited for Joseph to come in from his farm. He soon appeared in the mansion door and asked to speak with them in private. They went upstairs to a deserted bedroom and closed the door. As Smith turned to speak, Briggs noticed that he looked haggard. Apparently he, too, had spent a fitful night. Once in private Smith did not mince words. He told the missionaries he had received no indication that the Reorganization's proposal was the will of God and until such time as he was satisfied that it was divine will he would take no part in the church. He also told them he was convinced that the Lord had a work for him to do, that it would be made known to him without intervention, and that he should be left alone to prepare for that work. When they hesitated in accepting this decision, in a fit of exasperation Smith added, "If you men have been commanded of God to do anything, why can't you do it without reference to me, for I know that no man or the angels from heaven can lead the church in the condition it is now in." He concluded, "I am through and will take responsibility upon myself for my own actions." He then opened the door, walked down the stairs, and out the front door. Briggs and Gurley saw Smith mount his horse and ride away.[14]

A few days after this meeting Samuel Gurley returned to Zerahemla, Wisconsin, to report to the church leaders on the unsuccessful attempts to persuade Smith to join them. He noted that, while Smith declined the initial invitation, he expressed a willingness to listen to the promptings of the Holy Spirit. Edmund Briggs remained in Nauvoo for nearly a year, working as a farmhand—part of the time for Joseph Smith—and preaching whenever and wherever he could find time and an audience. While in Nauvoo Briggs took every opportunity to show Joseph Smith the correctness of the Reorganized Church's teachings, and this tutorial program may have had a significant impact on Joseph Smith's eventual decision to unite with the Reorganization. Briggs reported that he was impressed with Joseph's knowledge of the church, concluding that he was "aware of his calling as the successor of his father, but that human agency would not influence him to take any stand in the church, and that he was unalterably and utterly opposed to polygamy."[15]

In 1855 and 1856 a crisis of the first magnitude completely outside the realm of religion, a truly significant financial problem, goaded Smith, as he later testified, toward a greater reliance upon God as a source of power, direction, and strength. In partnership with his next younger brother, Frederick G. W. Smith, Joseph had gone into business managing several hundred acres of prime Illinois farmland. The farming operation proved successful for a short time, but a series of wet years and recurring infestations of army worms began to limit the farm's production, and early in 1856 the brothers were forced to borrow heavily to continue operating. By the winter of 1858 they were $2,500 in debt and seemed to be sinking further into the quagmire each year. When Frederick died suddenly in 1862, the debts as yet unpaid by the partnership fell solely to Joseph. Many years later he remembered this situation with uneasiness and advised his own children to "keep out of debt. Forty years of paying interest had emphasized this lesson to me and I want my sons to profit by my errors."[16]

This inability to remain financially solvent created the impetus for a fifth crisis in Smith's life, again prodding him toward greater openness toward what he later considered the will of God in accepting the presidency of the Reorganization. His wife's family, none too pleased with Emmeline's marriage to Joseph in the first place, used his financial problems as a wedge to drive the couple apart. One day in 1859, Smith recalled, he took Emmeline to visit the Griswolds for the day while he attended to business in another town. When he returned after a long day's work, he found Emmeline depressed. She appeared to have been crying most of the day. Upon questioning his in-laws, Smith found that he had been the day's principal topic of discussion and Emmeline had been encouraged to leave him and return home. He learned that his relatives had "talked so disparagingly of me, of the work with which I was trying to make a living, and of its successive failures, that my wife had become quite discouraged and embittered towards me."

Smith told the family he would not accept their meddling, and if they did it again, he would neither return nor even allow Emmeline to call on them. Seething with anger, Smith told his wife to gather her things and get into the wagon for the trip home. When she hesitated, Smith completely lost control and gave her an ultimatum: "I told her to just act according to her own pleasure and preference at whatever cost to me. Taking out my watch I gave her five minutes in which to make up her mind what to do—whether she would go with me or stay with her mother. This may have seemed cruel, but it is part and parcel of the story and romance of my life. I was fully determined not to be at warfare with her or her family, and so I left her entirely free to make her own choice, resigned to have her leave me out of the reckoning if she felt inclined so to do. I am glad to say that her love for me triumphed, and before five minutes had expired, she came to my side." After this hard-headed stand the Griswold family began to accept Joseph Smith as an equal. However, less serious marital difficulties between Joseph and Emmeline persisted thereafter.[17]

While these incidents prepared the way for Joseph Smith's affiliation with the Reorganization, he did not dwell on religious concerns. Indeed, he only began to attach religious importance to these crises in hindsight. At the time he took each in stride but with each became less reticent to pray to God for aid and comfort and more willing to accept the verdict exacted by the world. Nonetheless, in later years he thought of them as humbling experiences that gradually but steadily pushed him toward the calling as his father's successor in the prophetic office of a Mormon faction.[18] Once again, this perspective on these incidents suggests a certain pragmatism in Smith's approach to issues. He believed not only that he had a duty to perform as a religious leader but that he had to be called by God in a manner as unmistakable as it was undeniable.

Meantime, during the four years between 1856 and 1860 Joseph Smith developed an intense interest in politics, especially in moral issues. Smith had leaned for several years toward a strong denunciation of slavery. He accepted, for instance, his father's proposed solution to the slavery question, made in 1844, calling for the purchase and manumission of slaves by the federal government. Later, however, he recognized that this plan was impractical, in large measure because of the tremendous costs involved, and opted for the more modest solutions to the slavery questions offered by the prewar Republican party. Consequently, in the presidential election of 1856, Smith cast one of only six votes in the town of Nauvoo for John C. Frémont, the Republican candidate.[19]

He also agreed with the Republican party's opposition to the Dred Scott Decision of 1857, confiding that, when he heard of the Supreme Court's decree that even if a slave was in free territory he was still property and could be treated as such, "my political blood figuratively boiled within." When a slave catcher from Missouri asked him not long thereafter if he had seen a runaway slave pass through Nauvoo, Smith replied, "Well, sir, I haven't seen him, but if I had, I would not tell you, because I am no slave catcher!" Seeing that the Missourian had been properly insulted by this response, Smith decided to go even further and added that had he seen the slave he would have given him money and clothes and wished him luck in his escape attempt. When reminded that the Fugitive Slave Law of 1850 required cooperation in apprehending runaway slaves, Smith replied, "Don't you know that the United States courts and the courts of this State combined could not make laws fast enough or binding enough to make a slave catcher out of me! You need never ask me to help you or any one catch runaway slaves!"[20]

Joseph Smith was also politically active in local affairs throughout this period of the late 1850s. He always attended local political meetings and took part in Nauvoo community activities. Perhaps as a result of this involvement he decided to run for local office.

Consequently, in 1857 he let his name stand during a nominating meeting, and the inhabitants of Nauvoo elected him justice of the peace. Although Smith later disavowed any desire for political office, he remained active in Hancock County politics, possibly continuing the interest sparked during the time he read law in the office of William Kellogg during the winter of 1855–56. In addition to serving in Nauvoo as justice of the peace between 1857 and 1866, when he moved from the community, Smith also served as school director for the first ward during the same period. As late as 1860 he even ran for mayor of Nauvoo, and although he received a substantial minority of the votes cast, especially from the German and French citizens of the community, he lost the election.[21]

While sympathizing with the platform of the Republican party in national politics, Smith did not join the party formally until the hard-fought senatorial campaign of 1858 between Stephen A. Douglas and Abraham Lincoln. On 11 October 1858 Douglas visited Carthage, the Hancock County seat, and delivered one of his many speeches about popular sovereignty. Smith had long admired Douglas—for his principles and for the help he had given his father during the early 1840s, when he had been a judge at Monmouth, Illinois—and fully intended to vote for his supporters in this election. He arrived early for the speech to ensure a good viewing spot and was not disappointed in this decision when some 4000 attended that meeting. Joseph Smith was appalled by the spectacle, however, for Douglas appeared to be drunk. He slurred his words so badly that many could not understand him and those that could found his sentences incomprehensible. Smith returned to Nauvoo completely disillusioned.[22]

Eleven days later the much-less-known Abraham Lincoln visited Carthage, and 5000 turned out to see the challenger speak, Joseph Smith among them. Someone had erected a crude canopy of tree boughs to shade the speaker's platform from the warm autumn sun, but it was so low that Lincoln had to stoop to keep from hitting his head. When he first arose and started to speak, Smith said, Lincoln was unimpressive, but "he had spoken for only a few minutes when he abandoned his stooping posture, stepped a little back from the front of the platform, squared his shoulders and attempted to straighten up. His head came into sudden contact with the boughs above him. A humorous expression aroused his face and, turning his head slightly to one side, with a sudden movement he thrust it upward, entirely through the bowery business above him! There he stood towering, like some queer creature whose head was detached from its body!" The crowd erupted with laughter, but soon several men removed the tree branches and Lincoln continued his speech. Lincoln soon warmed to his audience; Joseph Smith recalled that "by the time the lecture was over, I was completely and altogether a Lincoln man, with a political conscience more firmly fixed than ever in opposition to slavery its evils." Thereafter, Smith remained a staunch Republican until his death in 1914.[23]

All this time members of the Reorganized Church awaited Smith's acceptance of the church's presidency, but no one made another visit to him. W. W. Blair, a very effective young traveling minister, expressed the feelings of most Latter Day Saints when he wrote in his diary in 1859 that he was "looking for young Joseph." Jason Briggs, as pro tem head of the church, commented on the group's official policy concerning Smith's decision. He wrote, "All had been done to this end that had been required, according to the light and ability given, and nothing remained but to wait the full period of that '*due time*' " that the Lord had promised.[24]

The Saints did not have to wait much longer, however, for in 1859 the religious wanderings of Joseph Smith III finally came to an end. The difficulties of the past had been mere prelude to the final crisis that virtually forced young Smith into the Reorganization. During this time Smith's wife was seriously ill and near death on several occasions, but the death of a baby daughter prompted Smith to ask the questions of God that he believed led him to a career with the church. On 25 January 1859 after a difficult pregnancy and delivery, Emmeline gave birth to the Smiths' second child, Evelyn Rebecca. During the summer little Eva, as Smith called the baby, suddenly became ill with convulsions. Smith summoned the doctor, but he was unable to do anything. Smith felt helpless as he watched his baby daughter, "unrelieved of her pain, restlessly moving her head from side to side as she lay in her little crib, and constantly moaning with her suffering." Finally, Eva died on 30 September 1859. Smith recorded his grief in his diary, his anguish apparent in this passage: "At home all day   evening   little Eva dying   Oh! how sorrowful 9 o'clock Eva dead."[25]

Pushed to the brink of despair by his personal and financial problems, Joseph Smith felt as if he were being punished by God, that he was somehow being tested as Job had been in an earlier day. The oppression that Smith felt was captured in the words of a poem he wrote during this time.

> I stood upon a rugged steep, my staff
>   the stay of many a weary mile, had dropped
> from my nervous grasp, just and gained
>   the height wherein I stood. My feet
> were torn and bruised by jagged stones which
>   here and there
> Lay thick upon the path which I passed; . . .
>
> Below I saw but faintly, here and there
>   a portion of the path o'er which I came;—
> A darksome, dreary, tangled, lonesome path—
>   So full of fearful chasms, long wastes between,
> That I had toiled so weary and so sad,—
>   Beset, distressed, perplexed, almost o'erthrown.
> My heart grew heavy with my woes, and faint
>   with hunger unappeased, I stood; while thought
> Dark as the gathering gloom in my brain oppressed.[26]

Out of the depths of this depression Smith received the final answer for which he had "hungered" in the fall of 1859. In an 1880 autobiography Joseph Smith reported that while praying for an explanation of his troubles he received a divine message—that "the Saints reorganizing at Zerahemla and other places, is the only organized portion of the Church accepted by me. I have given them my Spirit and will continue to do so while they remain humble and faithful."[27] A short time thereafter Smith had made the decision to join this faction of his father's church.

During the winter of 1859–1860 Smith discussed this decision with the members of his family, both individually and collectively. He told each of the series of crises that had seemed to thrust him in the direction of the Reorganization and of his unique spiritual experiences that confirmed for him that joining the sect was the will of God. He explained that he knew God had a work for him to do, carrying on that which his father had left undone, and asked that they support him in his difficult decision. His family's reactions were varied. His two middle brothers, Frederick and Alexander, were convinced that Joseph was being foolhardy, but his youngest brother, David, applauded his courage in taking such a stand on behalf of their father's work. Joseph's wife acquiesed in the decision without complaint, remembering a pledge she had made before their marriage not to stand in his way should he ever decide to join a Mormon faction. Joseph's mother expressed her support of his decision and her willingness to consider joining the Reorganization herself. On the other hand, Lewis Bidamon, his stepfather, thought Joseph was sacrificing his opportunity to achieve much that was worthwhile in life by not pursuing his business and political interests. Smith listened to each family member's comments, taking courage from the support of David and his mother without being dissuaded by any contrary arguments.[28]

Having discussed his decision with his family, Smith wrote to the leaders of the Reorganized Church. On 5 March 1860, about one month before the church's annual conference, Smith addressed a letter to William Marks, who had united with the Reorganization in 1859, informing him of his willingness to accept the presidency of the sect:

> I am soon going to take my father's place at the head of the Mormon Church, and I wish that you and some others, those you may consider the most trust-worthy, the nearest to you, to come and see me; that is, if you can and will. I am somewhat undecided as to the best course for me to pursue, and if your views are, upon comparison, in unison with mine, and we can agree as to the best course, I would be pleased to have your cooperation. I would rather you would come previous to the conference in April at Amboy. I do not wish to attend the conference, but I would like to know if they, as a body would endorse my opinions. You will say nothing of this to any but those who may wish to accompany you here.[29]

When Marks received this letter, he was ecstatic; apparently the long-promised successor was close to affiliation with the Reorganization. He immediately wrote to Israel L. Rogers and W. W. Blair, two of his closest associates in the church, asking them to accompany him to Nauvoo to talk with young Smith. On 19 March 1860 Marks visited Rogers at his Sandwich, Illinois, home and they agreed that they would leave for Nauvoo the next day.[30] Since they had received no word from Blair, Rogers decided to take the train to nearby Plano to pick up the other church leader and meet

Marks in Burlington, Iowa, the next day. Rogers traveled excitedly to Blair's home, but when he arrived he found

> Brother Blair at home, attending to his sick nephew. He had failed to receive Brother Marks' letter and therefore was quite unprepared to accompany me. He, however, was not surprised. He had a letter from Z. H. Gurley in Blanchardville, Wisconsin, dated January 29, 1860. It read: "I rejoice in God that the work goes on so finely, and I know if we are united and do what the Lord commands us, the year 1860 will not pass before the Prophet is among us." He consented to go, however, the preparations were hurriedly made, but long before we reached the station, we heard the train whistle. We continued with all speed possible, and though we reached the station fully fifteen minutes late, to our joy we found the train there still apparently waiting for us. This enabled us to meet Brother Marks at Burlington, according to appointment.

At Burlington Marks and his compatriots booked passage on the steamer *Aunt Lettie* and enjoyed a comfortable ride down the Mississippi to Nauvoo.[31]

The *Aunt Lettie* docked at the Nauvoo landing about four o'clock the next afternoon. The men disembarked and quietly walked to the Bidamon boarding house, where they took rooms. Emma received them kindly and sent for Joseph, who had moved across the street to the old Smith blockhouse to facilitate his work as Nauvoo justice of the peace. Soon the stocky, brown-eyed man arrived and met the representatives of the Reorganized Church. Blair commented in his diary that "we expressed our views with regard to the work. On comparison there appeared to be little or no difference of sentiment."[32] During the course of the long conversation, William Marks expressed his concern that Joseph accept the church's presidency only because he believed it divine will. "We have had enough of man-made prophets," he told Smith, "and we don't want any more of that sort. If God has called you, we want to know it. If he has, the Church is ready to sustain you; if not, we want nothing to do with you." With this Smith explained the reasons for his difficult decision, fully satisfying the envoys of his sincerity.[33]

The church representatives stayed overnight in the Bidamon hotel and left for Burlington on the morning of 21 March 1860. Joseph

Smith walked with them to the riverboat landing and told the men that he had decided to attend the conference of the church at Amboy, Illinois, during the first week of April. Marks and company were delighted with this decision. Before they boarded the steamer, each man prayed with Smith for the welfare of the church and guidance for the soon-to-be-ordained president. They welcomed him into the Reorganization, said their goodbyes, and jumped aboard the shallow-draft vessel. As the steamer pulled away from the dock, Joseph Smith waved a cheerful goodbye to his new brethren. He was still quite uncertain of this decision; he was convinced of its correctness but unsure the Reorganization's membership would accept him after his years of procrastination. Would he not be perceived as a "Johnny-come-lately" anxious for prestige? Could he convince the Saints of his very honest sincerity? He would have to await the conference at Amboy to find answers to these and other perplexing questions.[34]

NOTES

1. Joseph Smith III's recreational interests are noted in Frederick M. Smith, "Notes on Joseph Smith III," n.d., Joseph Smith III Papers, Reorganized Church of Jesus Christ of Latter Day Saints Library–Archives, Independence, Mo.; Joseph Smith, "The Memoirs of President Joseph Smith (1832–1914)," *Saints' Herald* 82 (2 April 1935): 431–32; Israel A. Smith, "My Father's Last Years," *Saints' Herald* 81 (6 November 1934): 1409–10, 1426.

2. Joseph Smith to Emma Knight, 24 May 1855, Miscellaneous Letters and Papers, Reorganized Church Library–Archives.

3. Joseph Smith to A. V. Gibbons, 1 June 1893, Joseph Smith III Letterbook #4; Joseph Smith to J. M. Stubbart, 19 May 1896, Joseph Smith III Letterbook #6, both in Reorganized Church Library–Archives.

4. Smith, "Memoirs," *Saints' Herald* 82 (12 March 1935): 336.

5. Joseph Smith, "Autobiography," in Edward W. Tullidge, *The Life of Joseph the Prophet* (Plano, Ill.: Herald Publishing House, 1880), pp. 760–83.

6. Ibid., pp. 761–62.

7. Joseph Smith to Lyman O. Littlefield, 14 August 1883, Joseph Smith III Letterbook #4; George A. Smith to Joseph F. Smith, 17 July 1872, George A. Smith Collection, Church of Jesus Christ of Latter-day Saints Historical Department, Salt Lake City, Utah.

8. Smith, "Memoirs," *Saints' Herald* 82 (15 January 1935): 79.

9. Ibid.; Joseph Smith and Heman C. Smith, *The History of the Reorganized Church of Jesus Christ of Latter Day Saints* (Independence, Mo.: Herald Publishing House, 1973), 3:260; Smith, "Autobiography," in Tullidge, *Life of Joseph*, pp. 764–65.

10. Smith, "Memoirs," *Saints' Herald* 82 (2 April 1935): 431.

11. Jason W. Briggs, "A Condensed Account of the Rise and Progress of the Reorganization of the Church of Latter Day Saints," p. 166, M. H. Forscutt–H. A. Stebbins Letterbook, Reorganized Church Library–Archives.

12. Smith, "Autobiography," in Tullidge, *Life of Joseph*, pp. 765–67.

13. Ibid., pp. 767–68. See also Edmund C. Briggs, "A Visit to Nauvoo in 1856," *Journal of History* 9 (October 1919): 449–51; Alma R. Blair, "Joseph Smith III: Prophetic Son of a Prophet," *Joseph Smith, Sr., Family Reunion Souvenir Program* (Salt Lake City, Utah: Smith Family Association, 1975), p. 8.

14. Briggs, "Visit to Nauvoo": 451–53.

15. Ibid.: 455–58; Smith, "Autobiography," in Tullidge, *Life of Joseph*, pp. 768–69; Smith, "Memoirs," *Saints' Herald* 82 (2 April 1935): 433; Joseph Smith to John Smith, 28 December 1876, Joseph Smith III Letterbook #1A, Reorganized Church Library–Archives.

16. Joseph Smith to Israel A. Smith, 17 February 1898, 26 December 1898, Miscellaneous Letters and Papers; Joseph Smith to Mary B. Smith, 4 December 1877, Joseph Smith III Letterbook #1A.

17. Smith, "Memoirs," *Saints' Herald* 82 (26 February 1935): 272. The date of this incident has been in question; however, the reference to his children during this period places the incident in 1859. His first daughter, Emma Josepha, was born on 28 July 1857. A second daughter, Evelyn Rebecca, was born on 25 January 1859, but she died on 30 September 1859. Only during this eight-month period did Smith have "children" prior to his acceptance of the Reorganized Church's presidency. It was not until the birth of Carrie Lucinda, 15 September 1861, that he again had more than one child at home.

18. Emma Bidamon to Joseph Smith, 27 December 1868, Emma Smith Bidamon Papers, Reorganized Church Library–Archives.

19. Smith, "Memoirs," *Saints' Herald* 82 (23 April 1935): 529–30; *Carthage* (Ill.) *Republican*, 14 November 1856.

20. Smith, "Memoirs," *Saints' Herald* 82 (23 April 1935): 529–30; *Quincy* (Ill.) *Herald*, 7 October 1857.

21. Smith, "Memoirs," *Saints' Herald* 82 (19 March 1935): 370; *True Latter Day Saints' Herald* 26 (17 June 1876): 368–71; Joseph Smith

to Israel A. Smith, 12 March 1909, Miscellaneous Letters and Papers; Horace S. Eldridge, Journal, 12 December 1857, Latter-day Saints Historical Department.

22. *Carthage Republican,* 30 September 1858, 14 October 1858; Smith, "Memoirs," *Saints' Herald* 82 (23 April 1935): 530, 82 (30 April 1935): 559.

23. Smith, "Memoirs," *Saints' Herald* 82 (30 April 1935): 559; *Carthage Republican,* 28 October 1858.

24. W. W. Blair, Diary, 23 June 1859, 28 July 1859, 29 July 1859, 21 September 1859, Reorganized Church Library–Archives; Briggs, "A Condensed Account," p. 167.

25. Joseph Smith, Diary, 26 September 1859, 30 September 1859, 3 November 1859, Reorganized Church Library–Archives; Smith, "Autobiography," in Tullidge, *Life of Joseph,* p. 769; Smith, "Memoirs," *Saints' Herald* 82 (19 February 1935): 242, 82 (26 February 1935): 271–73; Seventh United States Census, 1860, Population Schedules, Hancock County, Dwelling 1953, Family 1874, National Archives and Records Administration, Washington, D.C.

26. Joseph Smith, Poem, [1859], Joseph Smith III Papers, Reorganized Church Library–Archives.

27. Smith, "Autobiography," in Tullidge, *Life of Joseph,* p. 772.

28. Ibid., pp. 773–74.

29. Ibid., p. 773; Smith, "Memoirs," *Saints' Herald* 82 (2 April 1935): 433.

30. Frederick W. Blair, comp., *The Memoirs of President W. W. Blair* (Lamoni, Iowa: Herald Publishing House, 1908), p. 28; Blair, Diary, 19 March 1860.

31. Israel L. Rogers, as quoted in Inez Smith Davis, *The Story of the Church* (Independence, Mo.: Herald Publishing House, 1976), p. 441.

32. Blair, Diary, 20 March 1860.

33. Smith and Smith, *History of Reorganized Church,* 3:264–65; Smith, "Autobiography," in Tullidge, *Life of Joseph,* p. 774; *True Latter Day Saints' Herald* 14 (1 October 1868): 105.

34. Joseph Smith to Charles E. Malstrom, 2 January 1879, Joseph Smith III Letterbook #2, Reorganized Church Library–Archives.

CHAPTER

6

Getting Started

After a fitful sleep Joseph Smith arose early on the morning of 4 April 1860 and prepared to leave for the Amboy conference of the Reorganized Church. He had spent a large part of the last six months pondering his place in the religion of his father and much of the preceding two weeks mulling his decision to unite with the new movement. The fourth of April was the moment of truth. He had to leave for Amboy, a little town in the north-central part of Illinois, on that day or miss the conference and with it, in all likelihood, his opportunity to become president of the sect. If he went, however, he would undertake an entirely different career in an eccentric religious system. No doubt the prospects of church leadership and authority frightened Smith, but his spiritual convictions and the opportunities inherent in the decision excited him as well. He walked outside his Nauvoo home and met his mother, who had decided to accompany him, and the two strolled to a waiting rowboat on the Mississippi River landing, where two friends waited in readiness to take them across to Montrose, Iowa, where they could get a train.

The wind blew and rocked the tiny boat as it departed for Iowa. Emma Bidamon remarked during the crossing that the sudden tempest was probably caused by some evil force seeking to deter them from carrying out their mission. She said that throughout her life whenever she had sought to do the work of God, "the old boy [Devil] seems to be in the elements trying to prevent [it]." So many waves splashed into the boat that Smith had to use his shoes as bailing buckets. But they made the trip safely, and when the couple finally reached the other shore, they proceeded briskly to the railroad station.[1]

The village of Amboy was not unlike other Midwestern towns of the period, and certainly Joseph and Emma were only moderately impressed when they reached it later the same day. Incorporated in 1855 by several ambitious promoters who wanted to create a boom town on the Illinois Central Railroad, Amboy had grown rapidly and boasted an industrious, but less than exciting, atmosphere. By 1860 it had a substantial population of 4,000 people who serviced the railroad line or engaged in manufacturing or trade. The center of the community was its Mechanic's Hall, a trade-union meetinghouse that was the location of the Reorganized Church's conference.[2]

Smith and his mother missed the conference's opening ceremonies, but they did attend evening prayer services on the day they arrived. When they entered the services at a local church member's home just after the meeting started, Zenos H. Gurley, Sr., who was presiding, recognized them immediately but did not announce their arrival to the congregation. Smith sat silently in the back of the room and took in the episode. He was most impressed with the service and later described it as "a definite epoch in my life." After the meeting had progressed for a time, Gurley decided to tell the Saints that Joseph Smith had arrived and that the years of waiting for the prophet's successor were about to end. The congregation as a whole, Smith recalled, "sobbed aloud in their joy and gratefulness" for God's deliverance. "As I listened to the testimonies given in that small, humble room, and heard the statements made by many who had received evidence concerning myself and the work God was calling me to do," Joseph added, "I became fully aware of the fact that the same Influence and Power that had been at work with me, had determined my course of action, and had finally led me into their midst, had also been manifesting itself to many of these faithful, loyal and devoted old-time Saints."[3] After the meeting Smith and his mother returned to their rooms.

The next morning the conference convened at ten o'clock at the Mechanic's Hall. Gurley called the meeting to order and announced to the 300 members present that sermons by Samuel Powers and

Edmund Briggs, both members of the missionary order of Seventy, and himself would follow for the rest of the morning. He added that he and the other leaders had decided to postpone all business until the afternoon session. In their sermons these three speakers discussed the differences between the Reorganization and the other factions of Mormonism, largely directing their comments toward Joseph Smith, possibly hoping to rid the young man of any remaining vestiges of doubt about the propriety of his decision. Concerned about the successor's commitment, they chose to convince him of their desires before he accepted his calling.[4] The correspondent of the *New York Times* commented on this caution concerning Smith's final acceptance of the presidency: "There was a fear that they might experience now, that 'Twixt Cup and lip ther's many a slip.' " But the Saints need not have worried: by study and by prayer, by knowledge and by spiritual experiences, Smith had concluded that his life's work was in the ministry begun by his father.[5]

After lunch the conference reconvened for a business session; everyone knew this was the moment for which they had waited so long. After some preliminary business Gurley arose from his chair on the rostrum, faced the audience, and said with great pride, "I would present to you, my brethren, Joseph Smith." Then Smith stood before the Saints and delivered an address as cautious as it was emphatic, significant as much for what it did not say as for its actual message. He explained briefly his reasons for joining with the Reorganization, studiously commenting on the trials of the past few years and his gradual acceptance of his prophetic calling. "I have come here," he told the congregation, "not to be dictated by any man or set of men. I have come in obedience to a power not my own, and I shall be dictated by the power that sent me."

Smith denounced the practice of plural marriage, declaring that it had never been a part of early Mormonism and was an "abomination in the sight of God." He believed instead "in the doctrine of honesty and truth." He added, "The Bible contains such truth, and so do the Book of Mormon and the Book of covenants, which are auxiliaries to the Bible." None of these books of Mormon scripture sanctioned polygamy, he said, and the Book of Mormon positively denounced it. Smith also acknowledged his allegiance to the secular government of the United States, declaring the church must always support the legal constitution and obey the laws of the nation.

There should be neither antagonisms between church and state nor attempts to supplant civil with religious authority, he said. Commenting on lineal succession in the church's presidency, Smith said that, in spite of what the Reorganization believed about his right to succeed his father, he had done so only because the spirit of God had rested on him and prompted him in that direction.

Smith concluded by admitting that he possessed a number of human deficiencies that would undoubtedly lead to mistakes but promised to serve the church to his best ability. He asked that when the Saints recognized errors they seek to correct them, with understanding. Finally, Smith said, "If the same Spirit which prompts my coming, prompts also my reception, I am with you." With this Smith returned to his seat in the audience.[6]

As soon as Smith had seated himself, Isaac Sheen, the capable editor of the Reorganization's newspaper, the *True Latter Day Saints' Herald,* moved that both Joseph Smith and Emma Bidamon be accepted as members of the church on the strength of their original baptisms during the lifetime of Joseph the Prophet. After the conference passed this resolution, Sheen asked the body to accept and ordain Joseph Smith as prophet-president of the new organization of the Church of Jesus Christ of Latter Day Saints. Jason Briggs and Zenos Gurley then called Smith forward to a special chair in the center of the stage for the ordination. Gurley, president of the Twelve Apostles; William Marks, a high priest since the early days of the church; and Samuel Powers and W. W. Blair, both members of the Twelve, ordained him in a brief, touching ceremony. Upon closing, Gurley said with obvious pleasure, "Brother Joseph, I present this church to you in the name of Jesus Christ." Smith answered solemnly: "May God grant in his infinite mercy that I may never do anything to forfeit the high trust confided to me. I pray that he may grant to us power to recall the scattered ones of Israel, and I ask your prayers."[7]

Joseph Smith III's statements to the Amboy conference encapsulated admirably the central themes of his presidency. In them he explicitly commented on his commitment to legal institutions, both civil and spiritual. This framework of legalism guided Smith in every decision, enabling him to separate, at least in his own mind, right from wrong. It structured his principles, which he believed were inviolate. For example, Smith used scripture to demonstrate why the doctrine of plural marriage was incorrect. As far as he was concerned, the law was clear: "I do not believe," he wrote in 1883, "one thing is heaven's law in 1831 and that another is heaven's law in 1843.[8]

Smith's life-long reliance on legalism, which could have resulted in a very rigid and stilted approach to presidential activities, was tempered with tolerance, patience, moderateness, and gradualism. Although he believed deeply in certain fundamental religious principles, he never assumed to elevate his beliefs into a doctrine, and his opinions bore little, if any, resemblance to what is called ideology today. With problems of all types he carefully considered all ramifications and took actions that could be considered compromises in all too many instances. He was, in the best tradition of American philosophy, a pragmatist: he preferred to see changes come slowly, after due deliberation and with the consent of all affected groups. Almost instinctively, Smith inclined to a middle-of-the-road position on issues. Such a leader was critical to the continued success of what had begun as a loosely organized, extremely heterogeneous movement started by strikingly nonconformist dissenters of the early church.[9]

The spirit of pragmatism Joseph Smith III embodied may be illustrated by comparing Mormonism to a machine. If something goes wrong with the machine, what should one do? The reactionary might say, "Don't fool with it, you'll ruin it." The radical on either side might say, "It's no good, get rid of it and find a new one." The pragmatist would try to fix the machine, to remove the defective part and add a new one, but only after carefully scrutinizing the situation to ensure that his action was correct. As president of the Saints, Smith was willing to take only what he considered appropriate action at what he perceived was the right time. A proposed change had to be both morally, theologically, or politically right and also demonstrably sound in the light of past experience and present realities. And Smith insisted, above all, that while actions were taken and changes made the machine must be kept running. He stressed the necessity of continuous, cooperative action to accomplish the mission of the church as he defined it—to teach the restored gospel and to realize the zionic ideal.[10]

As potentially destructive issues arose, Joseph Smith III was forced to deal with them in ways that affected least the *primary* objectives of the movement. For comparison, consider the examples of several political leaders of the antebellum period. In a study of politics during the Civil War and Reconstruction eras, David Donald found that even if a northern congressman opposed slavery the mandate from his electoral jurisdiction controlled his ability to espouse antislavery ideals. "The more solid his support the more radical he often was," Donald concluded. Consequently, men such as Thaddeus Stevens or Charles Sumner, both of whom had the avid support of their constituents, could dare to be radical. On the other hand, in spite of his personal antipathy toward slavery Lincoln was moderate in his public statements because he could not afford to compromise his questionable popular base of support as president. He recognized that his administration's ability to hold the nation together in the wake of southern secession was dependent upon his walking a narrow path of acceptability to a coalition of factions with sometimes divergent beliefs upon the slavery issue, that without enough support his position as president would be undermined and he would never be able to accomplish anything worthwhile. In spite of personal desires, it was a question for Lincoln of first things first. When the tenor of the nation shifted, then Lincoln was more than willing to act to abolish slavery by executive order. During his presidency Smith faced issues potentially as internally devisive to the Reorganized Latter Day Saints as those Lincoln faced during the Civil War; and except on rare occasions he constantly and pragmatically worked in the middle to achieve a solution at least marginally acceptable to all.[11]

The Saints gathered at this meeting obviously had no clear understanding of how Smith's conceptions expressed in his address would affect the church's development. But they certainly felt gratified that their years of waiting had not been in vain. In 1865 William Marks wrote to others describing his feeling when young Joseph was ordained. He claimed that it "was the hapyest day I think that I ever experienced in my life."[12] Jason Briggs wrote, "These events gave the greatest satisfaction to the church, and to the scattered saints in sympathy with the church in all quarters, and new impetus was given to the work."[13] Perhaps the most moving description of the meaning of Joseph's ordination came from David H. Smith, the new prophet's brilliant younger brother, who wrote this romantic poem about the deaths of his father and uncle, the fate of the church without leadership, and his brother's prophetic calling.

> I came to the spot where the two martyrs lay,
>   And pensively stood by their tomb,
> When in a low whisper I heard something say,
>   "How sweetly we sleep here alone!"
>
> "The tempest may rage and the loud thunders roll,
>   And gathering storms may arise,
> Yet calm are our feelings, at rest are our souls,
>   The tears are all wiped from our eyes."
>
> "We wandered as exiles, and pilgrims below,
>   To publish salvation abroad;
> The trump of the gospel endeavored to blow,
>   Preparing a people for God."
>
> "Go tell our companions and brethren most dear,
>   To weep not for Joseph, though gone,
> Nor Hyrum, for Jesus through scenes dark and drear,
>   Has kindly conducted us home."
>
> I wept for the church, for her prophet was slain,
>   And I felt that deceivers were near,
> Who would lead her from precepts of virtue so plain,
>   Once taught her by Joseph the Seer.
>
> But anguish gives place to a fullness of joy,
>   Revived are the hopes that were slain;
> From th' seed of the Martyr, called by the Most High,
>   Comes a Prophet to lead us again.[14]

The Saints, of course, hailed Smith's ordination as a most important event in the history of the movement; surprisingly, the non-Mormon community agreed. Several secular newspapers covered this conference, and each commented upon the event favorably. A local paper, the *Amboy Times,* for instance, reported just before the opening of the conference, "It is a well-known fact in this and adjoining States there remain a larger number of Latter Day Saints who hold in detestation the polygamous doctrines of Brigham Young, and who are putting forth great efforts for the reorganization of the Mormon Church under head of Joseph Smith." The article described young Smith as "a strong man of good strong sense, opposed to polygamy, and all manner of depredations upon the gentiles." The writer predicted that "under his head undoubtedly the church would be purged of the outrageously bad practices which have brought it such disrepute with all law abiding citizens. To this end it is hoped that young Joseph will feel himself in duty-bound to take the important and powerful position tendered him." [15]

The *Carthage Republican*, the only newspaper published near Nauvoo in 1860, also discussed Joseph Smith's ordination. The report mentioned that Smith was a respected citizen of both Nauvoo and Hancock County, had served in various civic offices, and would undoubtedly continue his upstanding service as head of the church. The writer for the *Republican* predicted that Smith's right to succeed his father "will not be disputed and his mandate will be obeyed, except perhaps by Brigham Young and a few adherents at Salt Lake; but their authority and opposition will be of short duration, it is thought, and the authority of the new leader will soon be universally acknowledged." The writer of this article, like the person who wrote for the Amboy newspaper, suggested that "Mr. Smith, we believe, will soon purify the Church, and do more towards reforming its adherents from their evil practices, than all the troops which the government could send to Salt Lake." [16]

The most important newspaper to report on the Amboy conference was the *New York Times,* which published two major articles in the 11 April issue—a report by a correspondent on the meetings of the conference and an editorial concerning Smith's ordination. The editorial stated that many of the factions into which Mormonism had splintered after the death of Joseph Smith, Jr., had become disgusted "with the proceedings of the Saints in Utah, and have finally taken steps to get rid of the tyranny of Brigham Young." It declared that "the Mormon Church everywhere acknowledges the rightful authority of young Joe Smith, son of the founder of the sect;   —and steps have for some time been in progress to induce him to assume the Presidency. This has at last been accomplished." The editors praised the Reorganization's dissent from the Utah brand of Mormonism and concluded that Smith should be able to reorient the factions of the church and bring them more within the mainstream of American religion. This would necessitate ending the practice of polygamy, the editor predicted, without the government's intervention. "If young SMITH has anything of his father's nerve in dealing with men," the editor concluded, "he may carry this important revolution into effect. The attempt is, in any case, an interesting and important event."[17]

If the Reorganization's membership and many within the non-Mormon community were generally pleased with the ordination of Joseph Smith, the largest faction of the church was not. The leaders of the Utah Mormons had long expected that Joseph Smith's sons would eventually return to assume the leadership of their father's church. In the summer of 1856 Heber C. Kimball, friend and counselor of Brigham Young, predicted that while "at present the Prophet Joseph's boys lay apparently in a state of slumber, everything seems to be perfectly calm with them, but by and by God will wake them up, and they will roar like the thunder of Mount Sinai."[18] The Rocky Mountain Saints were shocked, therefore, when they first learned that the eldest son of the prophet planned to join a rival faction of the church.

Although they had ignored him since 1856, various members of the Utah-based church tried to persuade Joseph Smith not to become a part of the Reorganization. While in Council Bluffs, Iowa, on a mission, his cousin John Smith learned of Joseph's plans. He wrote to Joseph, warning him that he was being used by ambitious promoters who wanted to further their own schemes for prestige and power. In a letter dated 3 April 1860 he said: "While here I have learned something about that matter which we talked about while I was there it is in the mouth of everybody allmost and I have seen some of the parties and by what I can learn it is all speculation and they do not care a d——d for you only want to make a tool of you to carry out thire shceems that they may get gain and I hope you will not take a step in the matter without fully considering the importance of such a step as for my part I cannot sanction any such thing for I fear it will leade us in a difficulty that would bring a stain upon us where in we might suffer loss cousin Joseph there are my sentiments well I wish you would come over here."[19] By the time this letter arrived, Joseph had already left Nauvoo for the Amboy conference, but it is unlikely that it would have swayed him. John Smith's fears proved unfounded, and in hindsight Joseph thought them absurd.[20]

Not long after joining the Reorganized Church Smith received visits from several of his cousins who had gone west, each trying to persuade him to reconsider his actions. Smith was proper and polite with them, but he refused to retreat from his position concerning his religious work. He told his cousin Joseph F. Smith that although he had nothing but the highest regard for the Saints of the Great Basin, "he believed that [they] were in darkness on some things, owing to the teachings they have had, & the influences that surrounded them." Smith added that he had taken the right course and that he was "not afraid but that he will come off right, and that he will take no counsel but from God, for the Lord, if he had a work for him to do—will make his will known to him, before he will to any body els[e]."[21]

The Utah Latter-day Saint officials also bemoaned Joseph's affiliation with the Reorganization. Brigham Young and his advisors still recognized Joseph's right to lead his father's church, but they insisted that to claim that right he repent of his indiscretion by returning to the "true fold," nestled in the Rocky Mountains. Speaking before a congregation in Salt Lake City not long after Smith's ordination, Young said he would accept the young man as successor if he agreed to follow what Young considered legitimate authority. Young told the congregation: "What of Joseph Smith's family? What of the boys? I have prayed from the beginning for sister Emma and for the whole family. There is not a man in this Church that has entertained better feelings towards them. Joseph said to me, 'God will take care of my children when I am taken.' They are in the hands of God, and when they make their appearance before this people, full of his power, there are none but what will say—'Amen! we are ready to receive you.'"[22] Edward Tullidge, the unorthodox nineteenth-century Mormon historian, perhaps best explained Young's feelings on this subject. "There was in Brigham Young's mind," he wrote, "attached an absolute and irrevocable condition, which was that Joseph's seed should come to himself as the Chief Apostle holding the keys of the kingdom." This position demanded, Tullidge remarked, that Smith receive his ordination from Brigham Young himself. This meant that the "prophet in his son must acknowledge on earth what the chief apostle Brigham had done." Joseph, of course, could never have accepted this condition.[23]

Joseph Smith and his mother returned to Nauvoo after the Amboy conference. They made no outward changes in their lives: they held their same beliefs, carried out the same occupations, and pursued the same recreational activities. Joseph carried on his business affairs as farmer, real estate developer, and justice of the peace. These secular activities provided Smith with an income, for he received none from the church at that time.[24]

Only on Sunday and an occasional free evening was Smith really able to enter into outward religious activities. He always reserved the Sabbath for church work and did what he could at other times, constantly crisscrossing Hancock County to visit with the old Saints who had remained and to speak wherever he could find an audience. He invariably preached about the divine origin of the Mormon religion that his father had established and about the Reorganization of the church, and gave his personal testimony concerning his decision to join the movement. On several occasions immediately after his ordination Smith seemed to become depressed about his inability to do more to further the church's mission, but he remained optimistic about the Reorganized Church and his role in it. He told his cousin Joseph F. Smith that he was "sanguine of success & perfectly resigned" to his fate and that "he would do all he could and leave the result with God, and farther he felt *sure* that he would accomplish the work he had begun."[25]

In some ways, perhaps, Smith's lack of satisfaction with church activities in 1860 stemmed from his inability to fit into the mold of a frontier preacher. He found it difficult, for example, to adapt to the peculiar lifestyle and demeanor expected of a religious leader. He was so uncomfortable with this new role that when the census taker came through Nauvoo in the summer of 1860 Smith told him that his profession was justice of the peace rather than minister. In later years, as he grew to accept his position, Smith was not hesitant to announce his religious commitments to the world.[26]

His first efforts as a minister did not foster Smith's confidence either, particularly as others seemed disappointed with his character, actions, and appearance. When Charles Derry first met the new prophet, he remarked that he looked more like "a farmer than a church president."[27] While Derry was pleased with Smith's unpretentious nature, others were not. He disappointed one potential convert when, not long after returning to Nauvoo in 1860, Smith went out early one morning and began fishing in the Mississippi

River. He was busily engaged in this sport when a dusty, tired-looking man appeared, asking if he knew where a traveler could find young Joseph Smith, the new prophet. Smith identified himself, pulled in his line, rowed ashore, and asked the gentleman what he might do for him. John Shippy then introduced himself and told his story: "Mr. Smith, I became a member of the church in 1842, and have preached a good deal in northern Illinois, Michigan, and Canada. When the Saints were scattered at the death of the leader, I became confused. Now I am anxious to be set right. . . . My search for it has led me here, to you, but here I find you, the son of the Prophet, and the leader of the new Reorganization, *fishing!* What am I to think?" Smith explained that he could think whatever he wished but that if he was interested in the Reorganization he should study and pray about its truthfulness rather than pass judgment on it on the basis of something that one member did for sport. Shippy was a little irritated by the way Smith talked to him but agreed to do as he suggested, and he soon joined the movement. During Smith's first months in office incidents of this kind were repeated several times by Saints who were disappointed upon first meeting the young leader.[28]

Joseph Smith fared little better in living up to the preconceptions of prophethood harbored by most outsiders. At the fall 1860 business conference Smith was called from a meeting to greet a local Baptist preacher who wanted to meet a "live prophet of God." Smith met him outside the auditorium and offered his hand, but the minister ignored it, instead surveying him up and down. He walked around Smith, carefully taking in his appearance. Finally the Baptist minister furrowed his brow, frowned slightly, and spoke. "Well," he said to no one in particular, "I confess I am greatly disappointed!" Smith asked him why and he replied, "I have always wanted to see a prophet. I have had particular ideas about them, and have often wished I might have lived in the days they existed and been permitted to talk with them; but now—I must confess I am disappointed!" Smith told the clergyman, "I must say I am sorry, sir, that you are disappointed in me, but I cannot see that I am responsible for that. I am as God made me. It may be a pity that I am not a handsomer man for your especial gratification, sir!" With that, the Baptist minister turned and stalked away, somewhat shaken by Smith's retort.[29]

Many of Smith's early sermons were also less than fully satisfying. He was unaccustomed to speaking before large crowds, and in the early days around Nauvoo some of his audiences were hostile. It took him several years to master public speaking sufficiently to feel comfortable in front of large groups of people. On the other hand, Smith never shirked what he considered his sacred duty, and he held meeting after meeting in Hancock County and other nearby areas during his first year in the church's presidency. The most difficult problem he had to bring under control before becoming an effective preacher was his sense of humor. Smith was anything but solemn and somber, fully enjoying a good joke and seeing the humor in most situations. Although this was an admirable quality that he used throughout his life to defuse tense situations, at times, especially at the beginning of his ministry, it got in the way.[30]

As an example of his difficulties, during the summer of 1860 Smith had arranged to speak to a group of curious nonmembers at a farm outside Nauvoo. It was a hot and humid day, and everybody packed into the tiny room where the service was to be held seemed to swelter. Just before the service began, Smith left his associates for a few minutes of prayer in preparation for the service. As Smith knelt behind the building, a fly buzzed his head and landed on his large nose. As he shooed it away, he remembered a story he had recently read about an eastern minister who had been pestered by a fly that landed on his nose as he read a passage of scripture to his congregation. He brushed it away and began again, but before he could complete the reading it landed a second time. He shooed it away again, but the fly returned once more. Finally, after the minister had gone through this routine four or five times, he reached up, tried to grab the pest, and shouted, *"Damn that fly!"* Smith began to laugh as he remembered this story and completely lost all the soberness he had developed in preparation for the sermon. He walked to his friends chuckling, told them he could not preach, and asked another to take his place. Someone else spoke that afternoon, but the audience was disappointed that it did not hear the young religious leader.

On another occasion about the same time, Smith preached in a schoolhouse across the river at Montrose, Iowa. The house was filled, and almost everyone was listening intently to Smith's message; only two boys seated on the back row seemed unconcerned.

Shortly after Smith began speaking, two young and quite lovely women walked in and sat in the only seats remaining, immediately in front of the boys. One of the ladies had fiery red hair, which she wore in ringlets that fell down her back. Smith described the action thereafter: "Just as I was reaching the climax of my argument, one of these boys reached out with a finger and pushed it lightly into the outer circle of this fiery-hued hair. His eyes were intently fixed upon his action and his whole face and attitude expressing absorption in what he was doing. I could not keep my eyes away from him, and I saw that after holding his finger in the hair for a moment, he laid it on the back of the seat in front of him and proceeded to pound it with his fist, in a very good imitation of a blacksmith pounding a red-hot iron upon his anvil!" This performance made Smith smile, but he knew it had to stop before it distracted the rest of the congregation. He tried to get the boy's attention without letting the lady see, but he failed. By this time he was beginning to snicker and decided to end his sermon before he lost control.[31]

For all his personal difficulties in acceding to the mantle of the frontier preacher during his first year as president of the Reorganized Church, much of what Joseph did was uniquely satisfying. His diligence in working with the old-time Saints around Nauvoo proved fruitful: many of them united with his movement. By gathering together these elements from the past and winning several new converts, Smith was able to establish a congregation in Nauvoo as large as any in the new sect. He served this group as pastor from the outset, at first holding meetings in various members' homes but soon moving into the upper room of the old Red Brick Store. Smith's "Olive Branch," as he called the Nauvoo church, had grown to seventy-five members by 1864 and seemed to be increasing steadily.[32]

When Smith had first told his family that he planned to join the Reorganization, they had reacted in various ways. After his return from Amboy, however, the other Smiths in Nauvoo had to deal with Joseph's new commitment. Eventually each came to terms with the church and many chose to affiliate as well. Besides his mother, the first close relative to demonstrate an active interest in Joseph's church was his youngest brother, David Hyrum.[33] David, born five months after the death of his father in 1844, had never experienced firsthand any of the religious life of Mormon

Nauvoo. His first memories had been of the bitter conflict between his mother and Brigham Young; consequently he had developed a certain skepticism toward the religion. Therefore, Joseph was delighted when David began to attend services at the Olive Branch with their mother during the summer of 1860 and borrowed books and tracts soon thereafter. Finally, after more than a year of study and contemplation, David quietly went to John Shippy, who had moved to a farm near Nauvoo after uniting with the Reorganization, and asked for baptism. Shippy was pleased to perform this sacrament and escorted him to the Mississippi River for the ceremony. Within two years after this incident, David had begun to take a leading role in the church, serving as a traveling minister in the field and as advisor to his brother.[34]

In his reaction to the Reorganization, Joseph Smith's immediate younger brother, Frederick G. W., proved a striking contrast to David. He registered little interest in the movement and never joined. While Frederick acknowledged his older brother's right to lead the church, he had neither the opportunity nor the desire to become involved in the movement. In late 1861, while living on a farm that he and Joseph had farmed jointly since the mid-1850s, he grew severely ill, and his family worried that he might not survive the winter. During this illness Frederick began to show an inkling of interest in religion, perhaps because he feared impending death, and he started discussing Mormonism with Joseph. These discussions sparked Frederick to study the Mormon scriptures and to express belief in the movement's message. Either because he was bedridden and could not be baptized or because he was not yet ready to make a commitment to the church, Frederick did not ask for baptism. To encourage him to do so, David, by this time an active missionary, wrote him a sentimental poem called "An Apeal to my Brother Frederick When on his Sick Bed." Recorded in his diary on 17 February 1862, the poem read:

> Remember Brother Dost thou not
>   What Mother used to say
> Or are her consuls all forgot
>   Her teachings thrown away.
> Remember I how inocent
>   Our early years wer passe

Shall we when Mother's life is spent
  Neglect our God at last.

Remember how she taught us five
  In faithfulness to pray
That God would guard us through the night
  And watch us through the day.
Oh did we think when ere we read
  The Bible! Holy book
In after years that in to it
  We'd be ashamed to look.

O! Shall we stand above her grave
  And in our conscience say
That on life's road we have not walked
  As Mother showed the way.
You know how righteous she has been
  Through all her weary years
Let's turn to her example then
  Lest we repent with tears.

But this plea did not prompt Frederick to be baptized. After being bedridden throughout the winter, he died on 13 April 1862.[35]

The remaining brother, Alexander, had opposed Joseph's affiliation with the Reorganization from the outset and had created ill-will in the family by arguing about the decision. Alexander had never been much interested in religion and had spent most of his time in other, presumably more important and pleasurable, pursuits. His opposition to Joseph's decision, however, was motivated not by atheism but by a fear that it would bring derision on the Smith family from nonmembers in Nauvoo. He was intensely concerned about possible ostracism by his friends. In spite of these concerns, however, when members of the local community began verbal abuse, Alexander defended his brother's actions in public, claiming that Joseph had every right to freedom of religion as guaranteed in the Constitution. This defense and the death of Frederick opened the door for Joseph to discuss the Reorganization with Alexander, and in mid-1862 he baptized him.[36]

After Alexander's baptism, only two of Joseph's immediate relatives in Nauvoo were left outside the Reorganization. Emmeline, his wife, had struggled with her husband's decision to become church president in 1860 but had failed to understand fully his reasons and to accept the change in their lives. Although she had not stood in his way, she had never had any connection with Mormonism and refused to take part in it after 1860. Apparently she resented his religious activities because the accompanying travel and work outside the home took Joseph away from her and their children so much of the time. As a result, the couple seemed to drift apart.

With their marriage none too sound already, Emmeline and Joseph had several difficult years after he began his ministry for the Reorganized Church. Joseph did all in his power to keep the spark of the romance that had accompanied their courtship, but his absenses from home made that difficult. He filled the gap by writing Emmeline at every opportunity, pledging his undying love and devotion. Eventually, Joseph and Emmeline built a measure of respect into their marriage, demonstrated best, perhaps, by Emmeline's decision to join the Reorganization early in 1866, following the death of their young son.[37]

Lewis Crum Bidamon, Joseph's stepfather, was another story entirely. The Major, as he was universally known, had little interest in religion and believed its institutional expression a crutch for the weak. Although he had accepted Joseph's decision to head the Reorganization, he believed that he had thrown away a rich opportunity to gain secular fame and wealth. With the decision made, however, Bidamon said little more about it and even supported Joseph's right to pursue his religious calling publicly among those in Nauvoo who would persecute him. He never united with the church, but he assisted Joseph upon occasion in church business and in time became something of a "Jack-Mormon."

Although Smith's family largely embraced the Reorganization, the non-Mormon community about Nauvoo came to view the church less than favorably during the summer and fall of 1860. Although everyone in the community who had ever dealt with Joseph Smith recognized him as an honest, upstanding citizen, the longtime residents could still remember well the difficulties that had arisen because of the Saints' settlement at Nauvoo during the 1840s. They had seen Smith's father take a frontier area and turn it topsy-turvy in less than five years, and they had no desire to see a second-generation prophet do the same. Most of these people simply waited to see what might happen following the Amboy conference, but a few tried to stir up trouble against Smith. They sparked a significant controversy when they discovered a private letter Smith had written to an old friend, George Edmunds, Jr., on 1 July 1860, stating that he planned to make Nauvoo the church headquarters for at least five years. Non-Mormon spokesmen took this to mean that Smith planned to revive his father's dream of a Mormon commonwealth in the county. Since this would certainly be unacceptable to the non-Mormon residents of the area, a movement arose designed to stop any gathering of the Saints at Nauvoo.[38]

Within a few weeks after discovery of the letter, the misunderstanding reached large proportions. During July rumors circulated, and by the first of August dissident elements in Hancock County began to act against Smith and his followers. On 21 August more than 100 Carthage residents met at the courthouse and passed resolutions prohibiting Smith from practicing his religion anywhere in the region. Other towns soon followed suit, passing their proscriptions on to Smith. Smith completely ignored them.[39]

The most forceful opposition to Smith came from the town of Nauvoo and was led by Mayor Robert W. McKinney. McKinney was apparently motivated in part by his Presbyterian wife's staunch opposition to Mormonism. Under his leadership the townsmen held a rally and passed a series of resolutions prohibiting Smith's religion in Nauvoo, sending a young lawyer in the town, J. Bernard Risse, to deliver the resolutions to Smith at his justice-of-the-peace office. Risse, who knew Smith professionally, gave him the resolutions and stood awaiting a reply. Smith's anchor of legalism showed clearly in the manner in which he dealt head-on with this issue. The young Reorganization president noted immediately that no one had signed the document and it was, therefore, nothing more than an anonymous complaint. More than this, Smith reasoned, quite practically, that the document represented the wishes of only a small percentage of the Nauvoo citizenry and that if the issue grew in importance he would have a substantial backing. After all, Smith was an elected official in the community, possessed a strong following among the residents because of his political and social activities, and was a longtime resident. Many of the older settlers had known him most of their lives and few actually considered him or his religion a threat to their welfare. Moreover, momentum for the anti-Reorganization activity had not built up yet.

All of these factors, as well as others more subtle, prompted Smith to force the issue at that time. He called to Risse's attention the fact that the demands were unsigned, telling him to have the leaders in charge of the meeting sign the resolutions. Risse refused, prompting Smith to ask: "Who is responsible for this move, and for this document? Who authorized it, or who . . . sought in this manner to suppress me in the free expression of any religion? Is this public opinion expressed in this manner? If so, to whom may I look for the enforcement of the interdiction contained therein?" Risse refused to answer these questions and left Smith's office quickly. Smith never heard any more about these resolutions, although he made it clear to anyone who would listen that should they be presented with signatures he would bring suit for violation of freedom of religion.[40]

Smith's instincts were correct in forcing this issue when he did. Throughout the summer and fall of 1860 Smith received a few more demands that he stop practicing Mormonism or leave the county, but he ignored them and nothing more happened. The anti-Mormons were never well organized, and since neither Smith nor his church posed an immediate threat to the community, few people were really concerned about his activities. In addition, some members of the county came to Smith's defense. George Edmunds, a well-known local lawyer and politician, stood up in his behalf, claiming that he had committed no wrong, that he was entitled to basic civil liberties, and that his variety of Mormonism was far different from the type adopted by Brigham Young. Thomas C. Sharp, one of the foremost anti-Mormons of the 1840s, also spoke on Smith's behalf, telling the people of the county that he believed Joseph to be an entirely different type of man from his father, and besides, he had lived through one Mormon war and had no wish to become involved in another. Writers from the *Chicago Journal* and *New York Times* also commented that the opposition to Smith in Hancock County was misguided and that should anyone take direct action against the new Mormon leader he would find that Smith had many supporters, not only in the county but also nationwide.[41]

The mediocre anti-Mormon sentiment in the county during the fall of 1860 was sidetracked during the turbulent political problems of the winter of 1860–61. The Republican party, with a strong presidential candidate in Abraham Lincoln, defeated a splintering

Democratic party headed by Stephen A. Douglas in the North and John C. Breckinridge in the South. Lincoln and the Republicans were antislavery, and their assumption of power at the federal level precipitated the secession of eleven southern states. The crisis of the Union sapped the interest of most citizens of Hancock County in Smith's comparatively insignificant religious issue; the Mormon problem that had seemed so important in August had almost completely disappeared by December 1860.

Like everyone else in the United States during 1860–61, Joseph Smith had to deal with the matter of secession and the likelihood of a war for the Union. But he had to act not only for himself but also as a religious leader who spoke for the entire Reorganized Church. After the outbreak of fighting in April 1861, he was especially troubled by what stand he should take concerning the war. Personally Smith was ardently antislavery, convinced that the institution was both immoral and harmful to everything that was good in the nation. As a result Smith had harnessed his political hope for a better society based on free labor to the fortunes of the Republican party. Viewing the war in a positive light, as a struggle to end slavery not only in the territories but also in the states where it already existed, he felt a strong urge to join the Union army and fight in the emancipation effort. On the other hand, he was the head of a Christian church that condemned violence in any form: "Thou shalt not kill" was a fundamental commandment of his faith. He therefore had to decide whether to follow his personal inclinations or to act in conformity with the basic teachings of the church. Complicating the situation and tending to push Smith toward strong support of the war effort was a prophecy which his father had given in 1832, telling of a forthcoming war between good and evil "beginning at the rebellion of South Carolina, which will eventually terminate in the death and misery of many souls . . . for behold, the Southern states shall be divided against the Northern states, and the Southern states will call upon other nations, even the nation of Great Britain, . . . And it shall come to pass, after many days, slaves shall rise up against their masters, who shall be marshaled and disciplined for war." Thus for Smith this war represented the fulfillment of prophecy and the vindication of his father's prophetic ministry.[42]

During April and May 1861 Smith pondered the situation but

found no easy answers. The church expected his leadership in the matter and would presumably accept whatever he had to say about the war. Other religious leaders in the North felt no hesitation about supporting the war effort both morally and materially, and Smith could easily have taken this approach. Unable to decide what he should do, Smith decided to pray for direction from God. He specifically asked about the propriety of serving in the military and, after weeks of contemplation, received an answer that he said was clear, definite, and unmistakable: "Do not enlist. Enlisting makes your military service an individual and voluntary action, whereby you might shed blood while in the service. Wait; if drafted, the responsibility is lifted. In such case do not hesitate to take your places in the ranks and to do your full duty as good soldiers and citizens, supporting the government to the best of your powers." Smith accepted this direction as the binding policy of the church and cautioned Latter Day Saints to support the war effort as loyal Americans but not to volunteer for military service.[43]

During the period immediately following his ordination as president of the Reorganized Church, Joseph Smith dealt with some important personal problems and made significant advances toward fulfilling his potential as a religious leader. He learned something of the lonely life of a preacher, cultivated his ministerial abilities at the local level, and built a following in the Nauvoo area. In addition, he confronted and effectively defused any potential problems he might have encountered from anti-Mormons in his region, even winning respect and admiration from many Hancock County residents during 1860 and 1861. However, in spite of some tentative steps already made, he had yet to assume full leadership of the Reorganization and make it an organization responsive to central leadership. He wanted to unify the church so that it could more effectively carry out its mission of preaching to the world the virtues of Mormonism and thereby succeed in establishing a zionic community. To do so Smith had to build a solid, effective organization under his direct leadership. Over the course of the next several years he spent much of his time in just such an endeavor, using his broad administrative abilities and his capacity to compromise and develop grand strategies over a lengthy period to forge a viable religious institution.

NOTES

1. Joseph Smith, "Autobiography," in Edward W. Tullidge, *The Life of Joseph the Prophet* (Plano, Ill.: Herald Publishing House, 1880), pp. 774–75; Joseph Smith and Heman C. Smith, *The History of the Reorganized Church of Jesus Christ of Latter Day Saints* (Independence, Mo.: Herald Publishing House, 1973), 3:247.

2. *Lee County Times* (Amboy, Ill.), 7 February 1856, 27 March 1856; John Faivre, "The Mormons in Amboy," *Saints' Herald* 127 (1 January 1980): 21–22.

3. Smith, "Autobiography," in Tullidge, *Life of Joseph,* pp. 774–75. See also Joseph Smith, "The Memoirs of President Joseph Smith (1832–1914)," *Saints' Herald* 82 (9 April 1935): 463; "The Reception of Bro. Joseph Smith, Jr.," *True Latter Day Saints' Herald* 1 (May 1860): 122.

4. The proceedings of the conference were covered in *New York Times,* 11 April 1860; *New York Tribune,* 14 April 1860; *Amboy* (Ill.) *Times,* 12 April 1860.

5. *New York Times,* 11 April 1860.

6. The text of this speech can be found in *New York Times,* 11 April 1860; *Amboy Times,* 12 April 1860; *New York Tribune,* 14 April 1860; "The Mormon Conference," *True Latter Day Saints' Herald* 1 (May 1860): 101–5; Smith, "Memoirs," *Saints' Herald* 82 (9 April 1935): 463–64; Smith and Smith, *History of Reorganized Church,* 3:247–50. Briggs's announcement is quoted from Inez Smith Davis, *The Story of the Church* (Independence, Mo.: Herald Publishing House, 1976), p. 450.

7. Jason W. Briggs, "A Condensed Account of the Rise and Progress of the Reorganization of the Church of Latter Day Saints," p. 169, M. H. Forscutt–H. A. Stebbins Letterbook, Reorganized Church of Jesus Christ of Latter Day Saints Library–Archives, Independence, Mo.; "Early Reorganization Minutes," Book A, 6 April 1860, Reorganized Church Library–Archives; *Amboy Times,* 14 April 1860; W. W. Blair, Diary, 6 April 1860, Reorganized Church Library–Archives.

8. Joseph Smith, "Joseph Smith's Second Reply," *Saints' Herald* 30 (8 September 1883): 579. Smith's legalistic framework as it relates to the plural marriage issue is discussed in chapter 10 of this study.

9. For a general discussion see Clare D. Vlahos, "Moderation as a Theological Principle in the Thought of Joseph Smith III," *John Whitmer Historical Association Journal* 1 (1981): 3–11. Smith may have set the tone for his tolerant, pragmatic style of leadership at the Amboy conference. When a list of candidates for expulsion from the church was presented during the business session that followed his ordination, he persuaded the conference body to table the motion, for such an action, he be-

lieved, would serve no useful purpose. See "Conference Minutes," 6 April 1860, as cited in Clare D. Vlahos, "Images of Orthodoxy: Self-Identity in Reorganization Apologetics," in *Restoration Studies I: Sesquicentennial Edition*, ed. Maurice L. Draper and Clare D. Vlahos (Independence, Mo.: Herald Publishing House, 1980), p. 182.

10. This analogy is related in T. Harry Williams, "Abraham Lincoln: Pragmatic Democrat," in *The Enduring Lincoln: Lincoln Sesquicentennial Lectures at the University of Illinois*, ed. Norman A. Graebner (Urbana: University of Illinois Press, 1959), pp. 26–27.

11. David Donald, *The Politics of Reconstruction, 1863–1867* (Baton Rouge: Louisiana State University Press, 1965), pp. 6–7, 12, 17, 26–28, 82. See also Michael Les Benedict, *A Compromise of Principle: Congressional Republicans and Reconstruction, 1863–1869* (New York: W. W. Norton and Co., 1974), pp. 59–106, passim.

12. William Marks to Hiram Falk and Josiah Butterfield, 1 October 1865, Paul M. Hanson Papers, Reorganized Church Library–Archives.

13. Briggs, "A Condensed Account," p. 169.

14. David H. Smith, "The Two Martyrs," *Saints' Harp* (Plano, Ill.: Herald Publishing House, 1870), no. 1110.

15. *Amboy Times*, 11 April 1860.

16. *Carthage* (Ill.) *Republican*, 12 April 1860.

17. *New York Times*, 11 April 1860.

18. *Journal of Discourses* (Salt Lake City, Utah) 4 (29 June 1856): 6. For a discussion of Brigham Young's apparent willingness to accept Joseph Smith III in Utah, see Ronald K. Esplin, "Joseph, Brigham and the Twelve: A Succession of Continuity," *Brigham Young University Studies* 21 (Summer 1981): 333–41.

19. John Smith to Joseph Smith, 3 April 1860, Miscellaneous Letters and Papers, Reorganized Church Library–Archives; John Smith to Joseph F. Smith, 18 April 1860, Joseph F. Smith Papers, Church of Jesus Christ of Latter-day Saints Historical Department, Salt Lake City, Utah.

20. Smith, "Memoirs," *Saints' Herald* 82 (2 April 1935): 434.

21. Joseph F. Smith to Levira A. Smith, 28 June 1860, Joseph F. Smith Papers. A full account of the visit of his Mormon cousins can be found in Buddy Youngreen, "Sons of the Martyrs' Nauvoo Reunion—1860," *Brigham Young University Studies* 20 (Spring 1980): 351–70.

22. Samuel H. B. Smith to George A. Smith, 11 July 1860, George A. Smith Papers, Latter-day Saints Historical Department; *Journal of Discourses*, 8:69.

23. Tullidge, *Life of Joseph*, pp. 614–15.

24. Smith, "Memoirs," *Saints' Herald* 82 (26 February 1935): 272; Joseph Smith, Journal, 1 January–13 February 1861, 11 February–30

March 1865, Reorganized Church Library–Archives; Thomas Bushnell to Joseph Smith, 4 August 1863, 24 March 1864, 31 May 1864, Mormons in Illinois Microfilm Collection, Lovejoy Library, Southern Illinois University, Edwardsville, Ill.

25. Joseph F. Smith to George A. Smith, 22 August 1860, Joseph F. Smith Papers.

26. Seventh United States Census, 1860, Population Schedules, Hancock County, Dwelling 1953, Family 1874, National Archives and Records Administration, Washington, D.C.

27. Charles Derry, "Autobiography of Charles Derry," *Journal of History* 2 (January 1909): 25.

28. Smith, "Memoirs," *Saints' Herald* 82 (16 April 1935): 495.

29. Ibid. 82 (23 April 1935): 527.

30. For a discussion of Smith's sense of humor see Richard P. Howard, "Images of Joseph Smith Disclosed in His Letters," in *The Memoirs of President Joseph Smith III (1832–1914)*, ed. Richard P. Howard (Independence, Mo.: Herald Publishing House, 1979), pp. 478–79.

31. Smith, "Memoirs," *Saints' Herald* 82 (4 June 1935): 721–22.

32. Smith, "Autobiography," in Tullidge, *Life of Joseph,* pp. 782–83; "Early Reorganization Minutes," Book A, 6 April 1865; Emma Bidamon to Joseph Smith, 22 October 1866, Emma Smith Bidamon Papers, Reorganized Church Library–Archives.

33. The literature concerning David H. Smith (1844–1904) is growing rapidly. David was one of the most intriguing young men in Reorganization history. He was extremely talented in poetry, music, and art, and these talents, coupled with a natural charisma, captured the hearts of the membership. An important early leader of the movement, David Smith eventually was declared insane and lived the last twenty-eight years of his life in an asylum. Paul M. Edwards's sensitive essay, "The Sweet Singer of Israel: David Hyrum Smith," *BYU Studies* 12 (Winter 1972): 171–84, outlined David's life and work and suggested that his creative genius made him susceptible to mental illness. Later in the year F. Mark McKiernan, in "The Tragedy of David H. Smith," *Saints' Herald* 119 (December 1972): 20–22, asserted that David was not mentally ill at all but suffered from acute hypoglycemia, which could not be treated by physicians of the nineteenth century. McKiernan published two other articles on David Smith, discussing his poetry and art: "David H. Smith: A Son of the Prophet," *BYU Studies* 18 (Winter 1978): 233–45, and "David H. Smith—Artist, Poet, Musician," *Saints' Herald* 127 (1 January 1980): 18–20. Finally, Valeen Tippetts Avery has written "Sketches of the Sweet Singer: David Hyrum Smith, 1844–1904," *John Whitmer Historical Association Journal* 5 (1985): 3–15, which is taken from her "Insanity and the Sweet

Singer: A Biography of David Hyrum Smith, 1844–1904" (Ph.D. diss., Northern Arizona University, 1984).

34. *True Latter Day Saints' Herald* 2 (November 1861): 166; E. C. Briggs, Journal, 24 May 1863, Reorganized Church Library–Archives.

35. David H. Smith, Diary, 17 February 1862, Reorganized Church Library–Archives; Smith, "Memoirs," *Saints' Herald* 82 (7 March 1935): 590.

36. Smith, "Memoirs," *Saints' Herald* 82 (12 February 1935): 207–8, 83 (5 September 1936): 1103; Smith and Smith, *History of Reorganized Church*, 4:672–73.

37. Joseph Smith to Emmeline Smith, 20 January 1863, Miscellaneous Letters and Papers; Joseph Smith to Emmeline Smith, 14 October 1863, 14 February 1865, Joseph Smith III Papers, Reorganized Church Library–Archives; Emmeline Smith to Joseph Smith, 16 May 1865, Miscellaneous Letters and Papers; Joseph Smith to Heman C. Smith, 20 January 1908, Miscellaneous Letters and Papers.

38. Joseph Smith to George Edmunds, Jr., 1 July 1860, Joseph Smith III Papers; Smith, "Autobiography," in Tullidge, *Life of Joseph*, p. 777.

39. *Carthage Republican*, 24 May 1860, 23 August 1860; Smith, "Memoirs," *Saints' Herald* 82 (19 March 1935): 370, 82 (26 March 1935): 399–400.

40. *Carthage Republican*, 24 May 1860, 14 June 1860; Smith, "Memoirs," *Saints' Herald* 82 (19 March 1935): 370, 82 (26 March 1935): 399–400.

41. Joseph Smith to D. C. Murdock, 6 January 1894, Joseph Smith III Letterbook #5, Reorganized Church Library–Archives; Joseph Smith to D. A. Alvord, 15 July 1896, Joseph Smith III Letterbook #7, Reorganized Church Library–Archives, *New York Times*, 29 August 1860; *Chicago Journal*, 24 August 1860.

42. Doctrine and Covenants of the Church of Jesus Christ of Latter-day Saints (Salt Lake City, Utah: Deseret Book Co., 1952), Section 87; Joseph Smith to Annie Mack Walker, 25 May 1894, Joseph Smith III Letterbook #5.

43. Smith, "Memoirs," *Saints' Herald* 82 (7 May 1935): 589.

7

Forging an Organization

When Joseph Smith III accepted the leadership of the Reorganized Church, his single most pressing concern was the creation of a central administration that would be capable of accomplishing the goals he envisioned for the church. In the 1850s the Reorganization had functioned under a very loose organizational structure, almost a confederacy of virtually independent congregations that could choose to accept the policies of the general church conference and the Quorum of Twelve Apostles or ignore them completely without fear of punishment. As a consequence the church had been unable to sustain any extended missionary work or forceful policy because of the shifting nature of support from the members.

This had not always been the case: under Joseph Smith, Jr., during the 1830s and 1840s the church had developed a highly structured hierarchy of officers, a reasonably well-defined theology, and a generally workable administrative policy. All of this changed during the years following his death, however, since there was then no accepted head of the church and much of the administrative machinery had disintegrated or been absorbed into other Mormon factions. More than this, the Reorganized Church was a movement made up of dissenters, and the background of the majority of the early membership made it difficult to develop and enforce anything approaching an orthodoxy in either theological or administrative positions. When Joseph Smith III assumed the presidency of the Reorganized Church in 1860, he was an inexperienced young man, not yet twenty-eight years old, who did not understand the intricacies of either the centralized operation of the church under his father or the rather loosely organized confederation within the Reorganization. He quickly realized—his own commitment to the law and legalism mandated this decision—that the Reorganized Church had to reinstitute some form of central direction, come to some understanding of basic doctrine, and work toward the enforcement of orthodoxy if it were ever to grow into anything more than a small faction filled with individualists and cranks.[1]

The building of at least a moderately unified movement between 1860 and the mid-1870s gave Smith's abilities as a pragmatist their first tests. Convinced by his principles that action was required, Smith moved cautiously but deliberately to build a central administration that could accomplish the goals of missionary outreach and Zion building, goals he believed central to the movement's reason for existence. Such an administration with a recognized head could take the actions necessary to expand missionary activity, reconvert the Mormons who had drifted into other factions, and become a force in the reformation of the world into the perfect society promised during the millennial reign in the scriptures.[2]

Centralization of the church's administration took several years of numerous small steps before Smith could begin to claim real authority over the movement. First, he gradually brought the appointment of officers under his control. Then he slowly brought pressure to bear upon these men to act in accordance with his administrative and doctrinal decisions. At the same time, Smith took steps to gain a large measure of authority over the general conference, the chief policy-making body of the church, so that he could use it in the formulation of a coherent administrative stance. While he was carrying out these plans, Smith also worked to define and enforce a rational, logical theology upon the church officers and membership through the power associated with his office. The building of this administrative structure never took a simple path; rather it was a complex juggernaut marked by trial and error. In accomplishing his goals, Smith was rather like the thief walking down the hall of a hotel late at night trying each of the doors to see if one was unlocked. Sooner or later it was likely he would find one. Smith had a goal and he worked toward it relentlessly; if one door that might offer an advancement in his quest was locked, he would try another. Sooner or later he would achieve his ends. Time and circumstances were on his side. By the mid-1870s he had largely succeeded in remaking the church into the type of organization that he believed was required to meet its mission in the world.[3]

Joseph Smith III was no petty dictator. In creating a movement with enough cohesiveness to accomplish its mission, he led the church in a cautious, temperate path. Since his followers as a corporate body were not exactly sure what they believed, direction of the church along certain lines required less coercion and more persuasion from Smith. Perpetually, he groped his way on the edge between latitudinarianism and authoritarianism, at times being chastized by Saints of both stripes. In this effort his basic practicality, shaped by his principles, came into play.[4]

The young prophet moved first to secure the authority of the priesthood quorums of the church. These included the First Presidency, consisting of the prophet and his counselors, an advisory board of twelve high priests called the Standing High Council, the Presiding Bishopric, and the missionary arms of the Quorum of Twelve Apostles and the Seven Quorums of Seventy. As of 1860 there were very few members of these priesthood offices. When the quorums were filled and everyone did his job, the church could run smoothly and efficiently, Smith believed. When these offices were not filled, or when the functionaries were not performing their duties properly, it could be a president's nightmare. That was the case when Smith accepted office in the movement. Needless to say, he was not particularly pleased with the organization of the church, and his displeasure grew with time and experience.[5]

The first attempt Smith made to change the makeup of his administrative machinery was to take the initiative in appointing his officers. Throughout the church's history, members of the ruling ministerial quorums had been considered called of God to function in His ministry, and, therefore, the appointment came through revelation, whether such revelation was canonized or not. However, in the church's past the method of calling these quorum members had varied. In the time of Joseph Smith, Jr., the revelatory appointment could be made by a committee called for the purpose of choosing quorum members, by the prophet in a formal revelation to the church, or by a counselor in the First Presidency.[6] The "new organization," having neither prophet nor First Presidency in the 1850s, early adopted the policy of choosing officers by committee established under the suzerainty of the general conference.[7] This, of course, made the conference the absolute, final authority in appointing general officers.

When Smith accepted the presidency, he acquiesced in this manner of selecting quorum members but soon realized that in order to stabilize the church and assert his legitimate authority he would have to substitute another method. He came to this realization after practical experience—experience in which the general conference challenged his wishes and thwarted his goals. For instance, he wanted to fill the Quorum of Twelve, so when the conference of October 1860 met, he suggested that a committee be appointed to nominate enough men to fill the quorum.[8] This would have called for the ordination of four more men. Three stalwarts were appointed to serve on the committee—W. W. Blair, William Marks, and O. P. Dunham—but they did not believe enough capable men were available in the church and called only three new members.[9] Although this was not acceptable to Smith, the conference had spoken and he accepted this action as the will of the membership with characteristic decorum. However, he was upset when the April 1861 conference took it upon itself to change the minutes of the previous action so that his original recommendation on ordination and the decision of the committee coincided. To Smith's original recommendation in the minutes, "The Quorum of the Twelve should be filled," the 1861 conference added, "as far as practicable."[10]

Although Smith had tremendous popular support among the membership because of his stature as the promised successor to his father, he had been outmaneuvered in the legislative body, where all had equal voice and vote. He had learned a valuable political lesson about the nature of internal administrative machinery, but he used it only on occasions that he thought it warranted. One such time came in 1863, when he felt the driving necessity of appointing a counselor in the First Presidency. In this instance he presented a written revelation to the general conference commanding the ordination of William Marks to the Presidency.[11] Speaking for the Lord, he wrote, "I declare unto you, it is my will that you ordain and set apart my servant William Marks to be a counselor to my servant Joseph, even the president of my church, that the first presidency of my church may be more perfectly filled." [12] In elevating the appointment to the level of a formal revelation written for the church, Smith accomplished two purposes. As God's prophet, he nominated the person to hold the office, and he virtually assured that his recommendation would be accepted by the church body. While the church respected Joseph Smith III, Reorganized Latter Day Saints were independent and might well challenge the nomination enough to overturn it, should it come in any other form. The conference might be open to all types of political workings that could either cause another to be appointed to the office in question or create enough lethargy to delay a decision until some future unspecified meeting. A formal, written revelation of God's perceived will presented an unambiguous choice—either acceptance or rejection. While the members might question the decision of the president at times, they would be unlikely to refuse a message from God through the prophet. The distinctions they saw between the president (who was a man and open to error) and the true prophet of the "Living God" were crucial to Smith's triumph in this matter. In this instance he effectively placed the appointive power in his hands as president, thus centralizing authority in the office.

To Smith's credit, he used this authority, which was built into his presidential office and which his father had used extensively, only when he believed it was necessary—a tool of last resort. Most of the time during the period between 1863 and 1873 Smith relied upon the committee method of appointing general officers for the church.[13] This was, Smith recognized, a stopgap measure at best. He had a vested interest in the appointments made by those committees, and he made his wishes heard, but again the conferences had the right to reject or accept his personal opinions.

By 1873, prompted by the decimation of general officers through death, infirmity, resignation, or defection, Smith had decided that the time had come to reorganize the leading quorums of the church. Smith was operating alone in the Presidency, Rogers was operating alone in the Presiding Bishopric, and less than half of the apostles were functioning. In addition, the Quorum of Seventy had been virtually destroyed as an effective missionary tool.[14] Several attempts to appoint new members to these quorums through the old committee method had met with failure at the conferences, and Smith grew increasingly aware of the necessity of asserting his appointive power in the same manner he had demonstrated so effectively in 1863. At the conference of 1872 he hinted that such a revelatory reorganization could soon be on the agenda and that finally God through His prophet would handle the problem quickly, efficiently, and—more importantly—without political conflict.[15]

Smith finally asserted his appointive power with the declaration of a revelation in March 1873.[16] When he presented it to the conference for consideration at its meeting of 10 April, it was accepted as the word of the Lord through his prophet and passed without heavy debate. It commanded the most comprehensive administrative reorganization in the church to date. Smith's revelation called W. W. Blair, an apostle, and the prophet's brother, David H. Smith, into the First Presidency, filling the quorum for the first time in the Reorganization's history. In addition, seven men were called into the ranks of the Twelve, bringing the total number to ten; the Standing High Council was filled; a number of men were called to serve as seventies; and provision was made for the ordination of counselors in the Presiding Bishopric.[17]

This document established Smith as the supreme power in the church and set the precedent for all subsequent appointments to the general ecclesiastical quorums. It also pointed up the great patience and general pragmatism Smith exhibited throughout his career. During his first years of presidency, Smith moved cautiously, accepting the whims of the general conferences. Finally, he determined that firm action on his part was necessary, and after first setting the stage for such a revelation in earlier conferences, he took control in 1873. But he certainly reviewed the matter carefully beforehand. He had historical and scriptural precedent for his action; he determined that the church as a body had no strong feelings about his taking the lead in this way; and he never abused the authority the prophetic role gave him. Finally, it should be noted that he did not actually fill the Quorum of Twelve in 1873, a decision that seems highly significant because of the Reorganization's longstanding tradition of having only a partially-formed quorum. The lesson of the conferences in 1860 and 1861 were probably in his mind at that time.[18] This action was a continuation of Reorganization policy, even as it was precedent for stronger presidential action.

Very early in his presidential career Smith also found it necessary to curb the democratic excesses that he found rampant in the general conferences. At times he considered the action taken by those bodies as less than wise and timely. Still, according to the belief of the church, the central administration rested upon the members of the movement, who were organized into relatively autonomous congregations. The basically congregationally oriented philosophy of the Reorganization meant that the members diligently guarded prerogatives within the power structure.[19] They accomplished this by carefully monitoring administrative policies at the general conference. The concept known in the church as "common consent" emerged as a fundamental goal of the conference members —a means of ensuring that oligarchy could never take root. Based on the assumption that the people had to endorse freely and openly the acts of the administrative hierarchy, "common consent" meant much more than majority rule, even with minority rights; it meant a consensus arrived at in free and equal debate.[20]

While Smith philosophically accepted this conception, he recognized that in practice it was being implemented very poorly. As each person did exactly as he wished, absolute freedom was closely akin to chaos, and in the early Reorganization conferences democracy more closely approximated pandimonium than reasonable deliberation in which all sides of an issue were democratically considered. Joseph Smith III's pragmatism played an important role in his approach to this issue. He never questioned the right of the church membership to exert a role in policy direction; if anything, he embraced that idea. But he did institute several policies that decreased the role of the individual and brought the conferences more fully under his authority. Such an action, he believed, was fully in keeping with divine law that he as president should direct the church and would contribute to the more efficient prosecution of the church's mission in the world. In this case Smith's actions were probably not thought out carefully in advance—more reactions to situations than part of a master plan for increasing his own control.

Smith's first identifiable role in reigning in the conferences was his own example. As chairman of every conference in which he took part, he always conducted himself in an orderly manner. He never took part in debate, which although common in other policymaking gatherings, had not always been the case in the church's history, and he always put forth a fair image in all debates. Second, Smith subtly guided the discussions along the paths that he believed would be most productive. Third, to check some of the more boistrous members and bring about a standard of order and decorum in the business meetings, he early instituted the use of parliamentary rules of order governing debate. He even went so far as to compile *A Manual of Practice and Rules of Order and Debate for Deliberative Assemblies of the Church of Jesus Christ of Latter Day Saints.* Such an action demonstrated once again the twin themes of pragmatism (which prompted the cautious way in which he approached the issue) and legalism (which informed his desire to establish certain rules of conduct). He clearly stated his reasons in the manual's preface: "The want of understanding how to conduct and preside in various meetings held by the Church; . . . together with the lack of understanding and order in preparing, presenting, and supporting, before the respective assemblies, the several motions and resolutions for which consideration is asked and action demanded, make such a work a necessity. . . . Order promotes peace; hence a uniform understanding how to conduct meetings held for the contemplation, consideration, and decision of matter of importance will greatly aid in preserving the harmony, dignity, and peace of coworkers in Christ; and will in no wise prevent the prevailing of the Spirit of God, which must ever be a spirit of harmony and order."[21] The fears behind this statement are obvious. Dissension was rife in the conferences and chaos seemed to be on the upswing. The measures that Smith adopted in dealing with these problems, however, went far toward achieving a certain stability and centralization of the movement around its prophet.

Even with such vehicles in place, Smith was never able to stage-manage a conference completely, nor did he want to do so; he perceived healthy debate as a positive benefit of the theocratic democracy that he envisioned. But he was able in large measure to achieve a compromise between the cut-and-dried conferences of the Utah Latter-day Saints and the rollicking donnybrooks common among some of the Protestant organizations of the time. He gave a great deal of thought, time, and energy to the general conferences, always looking upon them as challenges.[22] Sometimes, he overprepared for the meetings, draining himself of patience, reason, and general evenmindedness before the session got under way. Recognizing that his brother might be wallowing in the doldrums over the upcoming conference, David H. Smith wrote the prophet in March 1871 from his mission in the Great Lakes region to counsel how best to prepare for the April conference: "Before the coming conference I would council [*sic*] you to rest your mind as much as possible, if you are weary then and worn, the influences will widen if you are fresh and cheerful the same hopeful spirit will pervade. The welfare of the church demands that you shift lesser cares and be strong for the greater. . . . Take Tatty [Smith's horse] and go for a rest and *dont preach preach preach* until your brain is utterly drained."[23] Whether Smith did as his brother suggested cannot be determined, but he was able to enjoy a productive conference.[24] Generally, during the years between 1860 and 1873 he achieved greater direction over the thrust of the general conference with each passing meeting. The result was a steady, albeit plodding, centralization of authority in his presidential office.

Joseph Smith III's bid to tighten the direction of the church under his leadership did not stop with asserting greater control over the appointive power or with the restraining of the general conferences. Concurrent with those developments he moved to coordinate and assume responsibility for the operation of the church's printing concerns. When he took office, the only regular publication was the *True Latter Day Saints' Herald,* a monthly tabloid under the care of Isaac Sheen. The church had no printing plan in the early 1860s, but Sheen solicited manuscripts from the membership, wrote much of the material himself, and jobbed the actual printing out to a commercial house in Cincinnati. Smith and others in the church recognized that the central organization needed control over this most effective of communication tools. They came to consider it the president's prerogative to direct the church's publishing concerns, and an early move arose to place Smith in a direct position to control the *Herald* and any other publications that might be published under church auspices. At the October 1861 conference a resolution was passed, with the full support of the church hierarchy, granting Joseph Smith as president "the examination and supervision of the matter going into the *Herald.*"[25] Smith immediately perceived the power of this mandate to increase the centralization of church authority, to shape theology, broadcast policy statements to the membership, and present a vehicle for unified direction of the movement.[26] As a consequence, he sought to expand the publishing arm of the church. He lobbied with the membership for donations to purchase a printing plant, to expand publication to include tracts, scriptures, and religious books of all types, and to enlarge the size and increase the variety of articles found in the *Herald*.[27]

In 1865 the conference voted to appoint Smith working editor of the *Herald* and general business manager of the printing office. When he assumed this responsibility the following May, he tried to enforce a rational and fair editorial policy for the publication, but everyone in the church bureaucracy knew that finally a central direction would be given to the church through its columns.[28] Smith was a capable writer, and his technical expertise shone through almost from the outset of his editorial career. He demonstrated some selectiveness in the articles he published but nearly always steered down a middle course in theological debate. Most importantly, he guided members away from heated debates concerning any matter of church doctrine, policy, or procedure. His editorship of the *Herald* greatly increased his administrative authority over the church; its gradual centralizing influence was felt before it was realized by the overwhelming majority of the membership. More important for Smith, this effort, coming as it did over a period of years, ensured that no sustained opposition was brought to bear upon his centralizing efforts.[29]

When Smith assumed responsibility for the church publishing office, he found that living in Nauvoo cut him off from mainstream church operations. A church printing office had by that time been located in Plano, Illinois, and logistics prevented efficient operations. He moved to Plano in January 1866 and settled in a home donated for his use by some of the Plano Saints. It was there, among a small congregation of church officials, that the first official church headquarters was established.[30]

Smith relentlessly worked to expand the role of the printing office to more effectively facilitate the prosecution of the church's mission. He also continued to extend his own authority and control over the church's central administration. During this period he moved the offices twice within Plano, each time substantially increasing the size and complexity of the operation. Soon he presided over a printing establishment filled with both paid and volunteer assistants, small rooms overflowing with proof and standing presses, compositors' areas, a modern bindery, numerous storerooms, a well-stocked bookstore, and an efficient steam printing press.[31]

Smith also broadened the variety of materials published throughout the 1860s to meet the needs of the growing church. He under-took the publication of hymnals, devotional and doctrinal books, pamphlets, tracts, stationery, Sunday School curriculum materials (such as certificates, report forms, and classroom supplies), and the scriptures.[32] In mid-1871, for instance, he was able to advertise an inventory of twenty tracts in English, two in German, and one in Danish. In addition, this bookstore stocked fifteen different titles for sale to the Saints, including the scriptures of the church, sev-eral concordances, study materials, biblical history texts, travel ac-counts of explorers in Central America, and even the Koran.[33] Nor did Smith neglect the expansion of periodical publication. In July 1869 he began issuing *Zion's Hope,* a children's newspaper. He wrote in an advertisement, "Every child in Israel should be supplied with the *Hope.* It is designed specifically to qualify them for the great future in which we anticipate their performing so important a part."[34]

Without a doubt Smith's greatest publishing accomplishment during this period was the issuance of a long-awaited Bible revision that his father had undertaken in the 1830s. In December 1830 Joseph Smith, Jr., had begun an inspired revision of the Bible but had not completed it by the time of his death. In 1866 the general conference resolved that the time had come to recover the materi-als used in this revision from Joseph's widow, to prepare them for publication, and to market an edition as soon as practicable. A committee was appointed to wait upon Emma Smith Bidamon, and another, headed by Joseph Smith III, to carry out the actual business of publication.[35] The committee obtained the documents with no difficulty and took them to Plano, where the publishing committee began its work in mid-1866.[36] Smith employed Marietta Hodges Faulconer—a young and vivacious widow who attained fame within the church under her later married name of Marietta Walker—and Mark H. Forscutt, a very capable associate, as scribes to take the document fragments that had been made and assem-ble a coherent printer's copy. Smith's group made decisions about exact wording and doctrinal interpretations when questions arose, as they often did. By the end of the year the manuscript had been virtually completed.[37]

In January 1867 the committee began proofreading the Faul-coner-Forscutt manuscript and negotiating with a number of job printers, for this publishing venture was considered too large for even the expanded *Herald* operation.[38] In order to facilitate rapid publication, Smith concocted a subscription system in which church members reserved copies for a mere $2.50 each.[39] He dispatched trusted aides throughout the country to collect the subscriptions and by the end of the summer of 1867 had gained $5,000 toward publication costs. Next he sent Ebenezer Robinson—one of the committee members with substantial publishing experience, the former editor of Nauvoo's *Times and Seasons*—to contract with a publisher. It was a joyous day for Smith when the Bibles arrived late in 1867. According to the Saints, he had accomplished "a major act of goodness" that significantly aided in the mission of the church. It added to his prestige immeasurably.[40]

Smith's pragmatic centralization program also defined church policy and procedure. When he entered the church, a multiplicity of questions over relatively mundane procedural and administrative problems raged in the movement. Previously, no one had exerted sufficient authority to obtain even a loose concensus of opinion on most of them. He began to exercise influence in the formulation of specific answers and to shove the church along a stable path. At that time, because of the steady and practical way in which he did this, relatively few questioned Smith's right to formulate policy. Later, it would create a major dissenting movement within the church. He used sound judgment in this endeavor, seeking to learn all sides of any argument and offering his suggestions. He never inserted himself into areas that he did not feel his legitimate domain and usually was able to use the conference to buttress his position. As a result, during the 1860s and 1870s he established, at least tentatively, administrative procedures and doctrinal issues for dealing with the form of baptism; the selection of local officers; the correct method of reporting to superiors, of keeping records, and of handling divisions within the headquarters staff; the day of the week regarded by the church as the Sabbath; the determination of the legality of marriages and divorces; the jurisdiction of officers; the acceptance or rejection of secret fraternal societies; the means of serving the Communion; the nature of priesthood authority; and a myriad of other questions that required some resolution.[41] In every case, he demonstrated a tremendous pragmatic ability to enforce his direction upon the church without creating turmoil from those who disagreed.

Smith's program for the delineation of doctrine carried at least

as much weight as his centralizing work. At the time of his ordination, church doctrine had not been well defined. Few agreed on
anything other than lineal succession in the presidency and opposition to polygamy. Smith worked to correct this decidedly indefinite
approach to theology throughout the 1860s and 1870s. He went
along with the relatively ill-defined approach to theology when he
joined the church in 1860, making no doctrinal statements other
than to denounce the Mormon plural marriage practices. Instead he
pledged to uphold Christian virtues and ideals, both rather vague
platitudes that would find no opponents within the Reorganization.

During his early presidency he steered the Reorganization down
a middle path that emulated the church's theology and policy accepted in his boyhood days in Kirtland during the mid-1830s. At
the same time he worked efficiently to reject the baggage that had
become a part of the movement's doctrine during the Nauvoo experience or subsequently—the concepts of plural marriage, secret
temple rituals, plurality of gods, blood atonement, eternal progression, the denial of priesthood to blacks, and the formation of a
theocratically managed, independent nation-state. Over a period of
years, with the skill of a masterful politician, he directed the church
into the adoption of his more moderate beliefs.[42] In his guerrilla
warfare against the doctrines that he loathed, and in his attempt to
bring the Reorganization within even a loosely established set of
beliefs, the young prophet early established his own legalistic bent,
citing the scriptures of the church—the Bible, the Book of Mormon,
and the Doctrine and Covenants—as the standard against which
all doctrine must be measured. If a doctrine ran counter to this set
of scripture as interpreted by the final authority of the church (that
is, the prophet in council with the general conference), it could be
rejected.[43]

Joseph Smith III was an absolute master at handling most controversial doctrinal questions without polarizing individuals on either
side of the issue. Indicative of Smith's skill was his delicate handling
of the nature of God and the Godhead. The *Book of Abraham*, supposedly translated from ancient Egyptian papyri by Joseph Smith,
Jr., was accepted by several influential leaders in the early Reorganization as legitimate in its theological teachings, although it had
no official status in the canon of scripture.[44] The book very clearly
taught the concept of a plurality of gods. According to the record,

these gods formed a council, which was presided over by a supreme Lord. The council organized the universe, placed human beings on the earth, and offered a plan of salvation that allowed them to become gods provided they adhered to the system.[45]

While Smith refused to accept such doctrine as correct, he recognized that it had strong support from several of the church's leading men. In 1865 he was present in a joint council in which church leaders debated the issue and voted that they considered the doctrine scriptural.[46] He succeeded, however, in having inserted into the meeting's minutes the statement that belief in the doctrine could not be considered a test of fellowship within the organization and demanded that it not be taught, except on rare occasions.[47] As time passed, those occasions for preaching the concept grew rarer, while many of its staunchest supporters grew old and began to die off. Rather than inciting a long and heated doctrinal debate, Smith had taken the pragmatic approach of simply waiting out the proponents of the theory. Gradually the church came around to the concept that he proposed—the prevailing Christian view of God and the Godhead. By the late 1870s his victory had been assured. Thereafter Smith began reprimanding the priesthood both more often and more severely for preaching the doctrine publicly.[48]

Joseph Smith III's handling of the ordination of blacks within the Reorganized Church also pointed up his practical leadership style. For years the Mormon movement had worried over the question of what role black Americans should play in the church. Before the Civil War most blacks were slaves, and the church was unwilling to preach to them without the consent of their masters because of the difficult political troubles such a practice could cause. The crisis of the Union, however, significantly affected the manner in which Smith and the Reorganized Church approached the race issue.

Smith took it as a personal success when Abraham Lincoln announced the final Emancipation Proclamation on 1 January 1863, thereby effectively turning the war into a moral crusade to eliminate what the prophet believed was a blot upon the American character. But as the Union's triumphant armies slowly constricted the Confederate States' life during 1863 and 1864, questions of how best to deal with the newly freed slaves became increasingly important. At both the national and local political levels American leaders were forced to decide how the freedmen were to be assimilated into the social, political, economic, and cultural milieu. The considerable argument and opposing legislation that resulted from this consideration made the Reconstruction era one of the most turbulent in American history.[49] For a time during the 1860s and 1870s, at least, blacks within the United States enjoyed a more visible and heightened, although not equal, status as radical Republican legislation mandated social and political change.[50]

The urgency with which national leaders considered the race issue during and immediately following the Civil War was repeated on a much smaller scale within the Reorganized Church. Between 1 and 5 May 1865 a joint council of the church's First Presidency, the Bishopric, and the Quorum of Twelve Apostles, held at the home of Bishop Israel L. Rogers near Sandwich, Illinois, discussed several important issues, including the church's approach to dealing with black converts, particularly the possibility of ordination for men of that race. W. W. Blair, an Apostle present at this council, remembered that this consideration was prompted by discussions among other church members. The general concern about the issue was pointed up well by the statement by Joseph Smith III at a prayer meeting a month earlier, on 2 April 1865, in which he prophesied that "prejudice of race, color, and caste would soon be done away among the Saints."[51] On the evening of 3 May at the joint council meeting, Blair noted, the desirability of ordaining blacks was debated "pro and con, with great warmth and persistency."[52] One of the participants offered the resolution "that the gospel makes provision for the ordination of men of the negro race, who are received into the church by obedience to its ordinances," but when it came time for a vote, Blair reported, "none would vote for it nor against it."[53]

Since the council had reached an impasse, Zenos H. Gurley, Sr., president of the Quorum of Twelve, suggested that Joseph Smith be asked to seek inspiration. The meeting minutes noted what transpired thereafter:

> After much discussion, it was
> *Resolved*, That we refer the above matter to the Lord, and that we come together fasting and praying to God, that He will reveal His will on this point unto His servant Joseph Smith.
> Adjourned until Thursday morning at 8 o'clock.[54]

The participants accepted this resolution "and sought earnest and diligently unto the Lord, and on the following day the Lord was pleased to answer our prayers, . . ."

At 8 o'clock the next morning, 4 May, Smith presented the revelation included as section 116 of the Book of Doctrine and Covenants in which the church was told, "It is expedient in me that you ordain priests unto me, of every race who receive the teachings of my law." The document further commented:

> Be not hasty in ordaining men of the Negro race to offices in my church, for verily I say unto you,
>
> All are not acceptable unto me as servants, nevertheless I will that all may be saved, but every man in his own order, and there are some who are chosen instruments to be ministers to their own race. Be ye content, I the Lord have spoken it.[55]

Although the revelation accepts ordination of blacks, it was very much a pragmatic document addressed to the needs of the era immediately following the Civil War. It cautioned the church leadership not to move too quickly in ordaining black converts, probably because of the recent emergence of the majority of them from slavery (without education and experience in dealing with the vicissitudes of freedom they could be manipulated by white charletons) and also because of fear that some priesthood officers would ordain blacks simply because of the heightened concern for the race manifested in the Reconstruction era. It became a cause célèbre during the period, just as it did during the civil rights movement of the 1950s and 1960s, for individuals and groups to act on behalf of the freedmen without real interest in their welfare. For some it was merely a stepping stone to prestige and authority. The document also noted that the church would accept a segregated ministry, the implication being that it would also accept a segregated church. Once again, this was very much a standard for the era; virtually all churches of the late nineteenth-century were segregated.[56] Since the Reorganization had such a small black membership, in a couple of instances in the South congregations of black and white met together, but this created serious difficulties.[57] Smith's revelation—a document that was forward-looking without being revolutionary—represented an important first step for the church. It was practical and equitable, at least in terms of the time, providing for black ordination in a church without black members but also catering to the beliefs of more traditional members.

Smith's method of destroying belief in temple rituals differed only in degree from the cautious approach previously described. These doctrines had never received the support from the membership mustered for the plurality of gods; the prophet therefore believed he could quickly and efficiently dismantle any bastions of support. He mounted a frontal attack, pointing to the prime practitioners, the Utah Latter-day Saints, and calling the rites one of the finest examples of "priestcraft" he had ever witnessed. He stood at the forefront of those in opposition to the Mormon temple ceremonies of sealings, marriage for eternity, sacred washings and anointings.[58] On one occasion he wrote a friend, confiding that he held few temple rituals worthwhile. He commented, "I would not value going through the temple a dollar's worth. . . . I cannot see anything sacred or divine in it."[59] He was not seriously challenged in his denunciations of the practice of temple endowments, probably because it was inextricably linked with the Saints of the Great Basin, and, of course, that ensured its opposition from a majority of Reorganized Church members.[60]

Only in one instance did Smith refrain from outright denial concerning the temple endowments, in the case of baptism for the dead.[61] Predicated on the double assumption that God loves all people and grants each an opportunity for salvation, and that salvation cannot be granted without baptism on earth, the doctrine provided for the baptism of all persons by proxy. Those who died without accepting the gospel could be taught after death, and others could be baptized on earth in their stead. It was an extremely attractive concept for many Latter Day Saints, because it allowed for the salvation of all and signified the justice of God. Smith also understood that his father had definitely openly preached the doctrine in Nauvoo, and his reverence for his father's actions may have played a role in his attitude toward the concept's acceptance within the Reorganization. Whatever the case, throughout his life Smith recognized the doctrine as possibly legitimate, at least in principle.

At the May 1865 meeting he discussed the idea of baptism for the dead with other leaders of the church and produced the first offical stand on the subject. William Marks, the one man in the Reorganization to have been "in the know" concerning doctrinal ideas of the Nauvoo period, stated at this meeting that the doctrine had originally been taught as a permissive rite, to be practiced under the most restricted conditions in a temple built especially for the purpose.[62] Under the younger Smith's direction the council resolved "that it is proper to teach the doctrine of baptism for the dead when it is necessary to do so in order to show the completeness of the plan of salvation, but wisdom dictates that the way should be prepared by the preaching of the first principles."[63] This stand did not change during his presidency, but with the stipulation that baptisms for the dead had to be carried out in a temple and with no prospect for the building of such an edifice in the immediate future, the doctrine was shunted into a nether land between belief and practice.[64] Gradually the church stopped teaching the doctrine altogether. To ignore, as Alma R. Blair has indicated, was to reject.[65]

Smith also deemphasized the "Word of Wisdom," a series of dietary regulations which the Saints were encouraged to follow. Joseph Smith, Jr., had given them as a revelation in 1833 but had rarely made their practice a test of fellowship. The document recommended that the Saints abstain from alcoholic beverages, tobacco in any form, hot drinks, stimulants and depressants, and excessive amounts of meat. On the other hand, the Saints were admonished to eat grains, vegetables, and fruits and to drink water. If they followed the dictates of the revelation, they would have longer natural lives and better all-around health.[66] The younger Smith, like his father, refused to make the revelation a test of fellowship but also showed a much more accepting side than had the church in an earlier period. In all cases where the Saints violated the "Word of Wisdom," Smith considered temperance the most important factor.[67]

As Smith gained increasing control of the administrative machinery and refined and focused the movement's doctrine and policy during the 1860s and 1870s, he faced some minor opposition. It was never well organized or rationally led, and he easily overcame the dissent. Usually those who disagreed with his policies and pronouncements misunderstood his intentions, and he was able to mend rifts within a short time. Furthermore, he adopted an open, casual stance, welcoming those who disagreed to come to him with their concerns. As Apostle Charles Derry wrote, "No man is questioned or snubbed for thinking and voting contrary to the majority."[68] Even so, once decisions were made, Smith asked that the church membership publicly support the stand. He confided to Derry in 1865, "With a man's private belief we have nothing to do, but when that belief is propagated as a doctrine of the church we can and will put a foot upon it to its extinction."[69] Smith followed this philosophy throughout his career, but he was pragmatic about the enforcement of orthodoxy. Usually he refrained from any action unless clear damage had been done to the movement's stature, morale, or doctrinal standards.[70]

Smith enforced order within the church, when he believed it was necessary, through an ingenious system of missionary operations over which he exercised ultimate control. During the first year of his presidency he asked that all missionaries for the church be appointed in the conference to carry out work in specified areas and to have their expenses paid by the church.[71] All of the administrative officers of the organization were put on this system as well. In order to receive this stipend, all of these men had to submit periodic reports on activities to the church, and the report had to be approved by the president. Thus the church's most important ministers, feeling bound to satisfy Smith's expectations, taught the standard church policy so that the First Presidency would not be displeased. This, of course, was a subtle and pragmatic maneuver that gave the president tremendous power over both church policy and doctrine.[72]

Smith also ensured a general orthodoxy within the church by employing a couple of men who worked directly under his supervision and answered only to his orders. During the 1860s he used them largely as troubleshooters, investigating problems in local congregations, resolving gross doctrinal differences, and generally enforcing the policies that he and the church administration had formulated. Joseph's brothers, Alexander and David Smith, were two of his most trusted aides in this position. They worked throughout the Midwest and made several trips to Utah, all under Joseph's direction.[73] In addition to his brothers, Smith employed two other young men as alter egos in the field—Charles Derry and Mark H. Forscutt, both Englishmen and both converts from Utah Mormonism.[74] Each of these men assumed difficult duties for the prophet and carried out several complicated missions during the 1860s.

The efforts of Joseph Smith III to bring some order to the Reorganization during the 1860s and 1870s were largely successful. He created some semblance of authority in his office, and, equally important for Smith, he accomplished it without anything approaching real controversy. That would come later. Throughout this experience Smith seemed to take as his watchwords, "I will cause them to walk by the waters in a straight way, wherein they shall not stumble."[75] However, two of the stickiest issues of his career—the church's position concerning zionic community and the movement's relationship to the Utah Latter-day Saints—still needed to be settled.

NOTES

1. In spite of the fact that administrative history is fascinating and rewarding, few have explored this theme in much detail. Much of the background of this chapter has been surveyed in Alma R. Blair, "The Reorganized Church of Jesus Christ of Latter Day Saints: Moderate Mormons," in *The Restoration Movement: Essays in Mormon History*, ed. F. Mark McKiernan, Alma R. Blair, and Paul M. Edwards (Lawrence, Kan.: Coronado Press, 1973), pp. 207–30.

2. Joseph Smith III's efforts to create an organization with a central head could be compared to his son's efforts as president of the church in the 1910s and 1920s in a similar direction, but to a much greater degree. This led to what has been referred to as the Supreme Directional Control controversy. On this subject see Larry E. Hunt, *F. M. Smith: Saint as Reformer, 1874–1946* (Independence, Mo.: Herald Publishing House, 1982), pp. 233–386 passim; Paul M. Edwards, "Theocratic-Democracy: Philosopher-King in the Reorganization," in McKiernan, Blair, and Edwards, *The Restoration Movement*, pp. 341–57.

3. Concerns about Smith's control of church government led to an important revolt of two church officials in the 1880s, discussed in chapter 12. See also Clare D. Vlahos, "The Challenge to Centralized Power: Zenos H. Gurley, Jr., and the Prophetic Office," *Courage: A Journal of History, Thought, and Action* 1 (March 1971): 141–58; Robert D. Hutchins, "Joseph Smith III: Moderate Mormon" (M.A. thesis, Brigham Young University, 1977), pp. 88–91; Alma R. Blair, "The Tradition of Dissent—Jason W. Briggs," in *Restoration Studies I: Sesquicentennial Edition*, ed. Maurice L. Draper and Clare D. Vlahos (Independence, Mo.: Herald Publishing House, 1980), pp. 146–61.

4. Smith expressed his basic democratic tendencies in these essays: "The Voice of the People Should Rule," *True Latter Day Saints' Herald* 20

(15 October 1873): 650; "Authority—Its Use and Abuse," *Saints' Herald* 42 (20 March 1895): 179; "Supreme Authority," *Saints' Herald* 52 (16 April 1905): 416. See also Hunt, F. M. *Smith,* pp. 238–43; Clare D. Vlahos, "Moderation as a Theological Principle in the Thought of Joseph Smith III," *John Whitmer Historical Association Journal* 1 (1981): 3–11.

5. The organizational details of the church are described in several revelations to the movement collected in Book of Doctrine and Covenants (Independence, Mo.: Herald Publishing House, 1970), Sections 13, 16, 17, 41, 42, 43, 48, 58, 64, 68, 72, 99, 104, 105. The administration is more rationally explained in William H. Kelley, *Presidency and Priesthood: The Apostacy, Reformation, and Restoration* (Lamoni, Iowa: Herald Publishing House, 1908), pp. 292–97; First Presidency, *Handbook of Church Organization and Administrative Policies and Procedures* (Independence, Mo.: Herald Publishing House, 1975), pp. 11–28; Peter A. Judd and A. Bruce Lindgren, *An Introduction to the Saints Church* (Independence, Mo.: Herald Publishing House, 1976), pp. 115–31.

6. Methods of appointing quorum members are discussed by Richard P. Howard, "Selection of Apostles, 1835–1873: A Tradition Emerges," *Saints' Herald* 118 (April 1971): 48. See also Joseph Smith and Heman C. Smith, *The History of the Reorganized Church of Jesus Christ of Latter Day Saints* (Independence, Mo.: Herald Publishing House, 1967), 2:116; *Latter-day Saints Millennial Star* (Liverpool, England) 17 (15 March 1855): 168; *Times and Seasons* (Nauvoo, Ill.) 2 (1 April 1841): 387.

7. Early Reorganization Minutes, Book A, 8 April 1853, 6 April 1855, Reorganized Church of Jesus Christ of Latter Day Saints Library–Archives, Independence, Mo.

8. "Conference Minutes," *True Latter Day Saints' Herald* 1 (October 1860): 236.

9. Smith and Smith, *History of Reorganized Church,* 3:276.

10. This has been changed in the handwritten Early Reorganization Minutes, Book A, 6 October 1860. The amendment is recorded in "Conference Minutes," *True Latter Day Saints' Herald* 2 (May 1861): 67.

11. Joseph Smith, Jr., had appointed each of his counselors in the First Presidency in this manner. See Doctrine and Covenants, Sections 80, 99, 107.

12. Ibid., Section 115:1b. W. W. Blair mentioned a prophecy, given in June 1859, that William Marks would be a counselor to the president of the church. See Smith and Smith, *History of Reorganized Church,* 3:317. Section 115 was not approved by vote in 1863—only a resolution was adopted approving Marks's ordination.

13. "Conference Minutes," *True Latter Day Saints' Herald* 7 (15 April 1865): 126; Smith and Smith, *History of Reorganized Church,*

3:432; Jason W. Briggs, "A Condensed Account of the Rise and Progress of the Reorganization of the Church of Latter Day Saints," p. 172, M. H. Forscutt–H. A. Stebbins Letterbook, Reorganized Church Library–Archives.

14. Apostle James Blakeslee had died in 1866; Apostle John Shippy had resigned in 1868; Counselor Philo Howard of the Presiding Bishopric died in 1869; Apostle Charles Derry had resigned in 1870 because he did not truly believe he had been called of God; Apostle Zenos H. Gurley, Sr., had died in August 1871; Smith's counselor in the First Presidency, William Marks, had died in 1872; and Apostle Samuel Powers had died in February 1873. In addition, apostles Reuben Newkirk and David Rasey and one of the bishop's counselors, William Aldrich, had been largely inactive.

15. Smith had told the conference as early as 1870 that he felt "assured the time is not far distant when those who are to fill the positions will be made known by God." *True Latter Day Saints' Herald* 17 (15 April 1870): 243–44. See also similar statements by Smith in 1872 in *True Latter Day Saints' Herald* 19 (1 June 1872): 346. Richard P. Howard has described this development in "On the Background of Section 117," *Saints' Herald* 124 (February 1977): 47.

16. Minutes of the General Annual Conference of the Reorganized Church, 9 April 1873, p. 12; Joseph Smith to G. A. Means, 22 April 1878; Joseph Smith to Zenos H. Gurley, Jr., 10 August 1878, both in Joseph Smith III Letterbook #1, Reorganized Church Library–Archives.

17. Doctrine and Covenants, Section 117; Smith and Smith, *History of Reorganized Church*, 4:5; *Rules and Resolutions of the Reorganized Church of Jesus Christ of Latter Day Saints* (Independence, Mo.: Herald Publishing House, 1964), p. 38; *Kendall County Record* (Yorkville, Ill.), 10 April 1873.

18. Howard, "On the Background of Section 117," p. 47.

19. For an insightful article pointing out this important Reorganization distinction, see Douglas D. Alder and Paul M. Edwards, "Common Beginnings, Divergent Beliefs," *Dialogue: A Journal of Mormon Thought* 11 (Spring 1978): 19.

20. "Common consent" originally stood as a policy of the church established by revelation (see Doctrine and Covenants, Section 25:1b). This emerged in the early Reorganization as a concept important beyond anything witnessed in an earlier day. See the discussion of how important Reorganized Church members considered this topic in *Church Member's Manual* (Independence, Mo.: Herald Publishing House, 1957), pp. 85–86. For excesses see "Annual Conference," *True Latter Day Saints' Herald* 9 (15 April 1865): 122.

21. Joseph Smith and Thomas W. Smith, comps., *A Manual of Practice and Rules of Order and Debate for Deliberative Assemblies of the Church of Jesus Christ of Latter Day Saints* (Plano, Ill.: Herald Publishing House, 1876), preface.

22. Joseph Smith to Charles Derry, 23 October 1866, Joseph Smith III Papers, Reorganized Church Library–Archives.

23. David H. Smith to Joseph Smith, 4 March 1871, Miscellaneous Letters and Papers, Reorganized Church Library–Archives.

24. *True Latter Day Saints' Herald* 18 (15 April 1871): 273.

25. Smith and Smith, *History of Reorganized Church* 3:298.

26. *True Latter Day Saints' Herald* 3 (February 1862): 192, contains the statement that the president will review all matter submitted to the newspaper before it is accepted for publication.

27. Joseph Smith, "An Appeal to the Saints," ibid. 3 (November 1862): 108–9.

28. Joseph Smith, "Salutatory," ibid. 7 (1 May 1865): 129.

29. Leonard Lea, "Editorial," ibid. 81 (6 November 1934): 1407.

30. In the 1860s Plano was a boom town because of the completion of the Chicago, Burlington, and Quincy Railroad line through the community. With the railroad came a large number of businesses and a rapid influx of people. A number of prominent church members lived in the town —Israel Rogers, David Dancer, and Elijah Banta were the most important —and these men were the prime movers in establishing the community as a central congregating point for many church members. See Rev. E. W. Hicks, *History of Kendall County, Illinois, From the Earliest Discoveries to the Present Time* (Aurora, Ill.: n.p., 1877), pp. 298–99; Joseph Smith, "The Memoirs of President Joseph Smith (1832–1914)," *Saints' Herald* 82 (25 June 1935): 817, 82 (30 July 1935): 975–78; 82 (6 August 1935): 1007.

31. Smith, "Memoirs," *Saints' Herald* 82 (13 August 1935): 1040, 82 (20 August 1935): 1071; Joseph Smith, "Autobiography," in Edward W. Tullidge, *The Life of Joseph the Prophet* (Plano, Ill.: Herald Publishing House, 1880), p. 784.

32. The best means of determining the quantity and type of publications issued by the printing house under Smith in the 1860s and 1870s is to survey the entries in Chad J. Flake, ed., *A Mormon Bibliography, 1830–1930* (Salt Lake City: University of Utah Press, 1978), pp. 547–68.

33. "Books, Tracts, &c, For Sale at Herald Office, Plano, Ill," *True Latter Day Saints' Herald* 18 (18 July 1871): 416.

34. "Advertisement," ibid. 16 (1 November 1869): 288.

35. Smith and Smith, *History of Reorganized Church,* 3:433–34, 4:430; *True Latter Day Saints' Herald* 9 (15 April 1866): 125.

36. *Complainants' Abstract of Pleading and Evidence, in the Circuit*

Court of the United States, Western District of Missouri, Western Division, at Kansas City: Temple Lot Case (Lamoni, Iowa: Herald Publishing House, 1893), pp. 156–57.

37. Robert D. Matthews, *"A Plainer Translation": Joseph Smith's Translation of the Bible, A History and Commentary* (Provo, Utah: Brigham Young University Press, 1975), pp. 142–44.

38. Emma Bidamon to Joseph Smith, 20 January 1867, 10 February 1867, Emma Smith Bidamon Papers, Reorganized Church Library–Archives.

39. Joseph Smith to Spencer Smith, 24 June 1868, Joseph Smith III Papers; Joseph Smith, "The Publication Committee," *True Latter Day Saints' Herald* 11 (1 February 1867): 42.

40. Joseph Smith to Charles Derry, 12 January 1867, 18 September 1867, both in Joseph Smith III Papers; Frederick W. Blair, comp., *The Memoirs of President W. W. Blair* (Lamoni, Iowa: Herald Publishing House, 1908), pp. 130, 135–36; *Kendall County Record*, 9 January 1868; Smith and Smith, *History of Reorganized Church*, 3:485; Smith, "Memoirs," *Saints' Herald* 82 (25 June 1935): 818.

41. Early Reorganization Minutes, Book A, 6 October 1862, Reorganized Church Library–Archives; Joseph Smith to A. W. Thompson, 15 June 1881, Joseph Smith III Letterbook #3; *True Latter Day Saints' Herald* 6 (1 October 1864): 108, 7 (1 June 1865): 172, 8 (15 October 1865): 113–15, 9 (15 February 1866): 50, 10 (1 August 1866): 47, 17 (15 November 1870): 688–90; Joseph Smith to Sr. M. J. Stiles, 3 May 1876, Joseph Smith III Letterbook #1; Joseph Smith to William H. Kelley, 24 April 1884, William H. Kelley Papers, Reorganized Church Library–Archives; Joseph Smith to Abner Vernon, 14 November 1879, Joseph Smith III Letterbook #2, Reorganized Church Library–Archives; Joseph Smith to Mrs. A. E. King, 8 June 1881, Joseph Smith III Letterbook #3; Joseph Smith to Samuel M. Reeve, 19 February 1867, Miscellaneous Letters and Papers; Joseph Smith to Joseph Luff, 12 February 1878, Joseph Smith III Letterbook #1; Doctrine and Covenants, Sections 114, 115, 116, 117.

42. Blair, "Moderate Mormons," p. 210.

43. On Smith's legalism see Vlahos, "Moderation as a Theological Principle in the Thought of Joseph Smith III," pp. 4–7.

44. The development of the *Book of Abraham* is an interesting study in itself. A Reorganized Church perspective on this can be found in Richard P. Howard, "Joseph Smith, the Book of Abraham, and the Reorganized Church in the 1970s," in *A Decade of the Best: The Elbert A. Smith Award Winning Articles* (Independence, Mo.: Herald Publishing House, 1972): 186–211.

45. *"The Book of Abraham," Times and Seasons* 3 (15 March 1842):

720–22. The *Book of Abraham* is now in the Utah Latter-day Saint canon on scripture, *The Pearl of Great Price* (Salt Lake City, Utah: Deseret Book Co., 1968), pp. 29–42.

46. Council of Twelve, Minutes, 1865–1928, 2–5 May 1865, p. 12, Reorganized Church Library–Archives.

47. Two instances in which Smith allowed the opposition to air its interpretations were "A Plurality of Gods," *True Latter Day Saints' Herald* 1 (October 1860): 280–83; W. W. Blair, "The Harmony of the Bible, Book of Mormon, and Doctrine and Covenants," *True Latter Day Saints' Herald* 10 (1 September 1866): 69.

48. "The Godhead," *Saints' Herald* 29 (15 April 1881): 234; Zenos H. Gurley, Jr., "The Godhead," *Saints' Herald* 29 (1 May 1881): 246; Joseph Smith to J. Jeremiah, 8 September 1877, Joseph Smith III Letterbook #1; Joseph Smith to Sr. Othilla Grabske, 10 February 1904, Miscellaneous Letters and Papers; Joseph Smith to J. W. Peterson, 10 June 1902, Miscellaneous Letters and Papers; Smith, "Memoirs," *Saints' Herald* 82 (23 April 1935): 527.

49. To mention even a small fraction of the historical literature on Reconstruction, usually considered as the period between 1865 and 1877, is impossible in such a study as this; however, these basic texts provide excellent introductions to the issues and arguments considered during the period. See John Hope Franklin, *Reconstruction: After the Civil War* (Chicago: University of Chicago Press, 1961); Kenneth M. Stampp, *The Era of Reconstruction* (New York: Vintage Books, 1967); John Hope Franklin, *From Slavery to Freedom: A History of Negro Americans* (New York: Alfred A. Knopf, 1967); James M. McPherson, *Ordeal by Fire: The Civil War and Reconstruction* (New York: Alfred A. Knopf, 1982); C. Vann Woodward, *The Strange Career of Jim Crow* (New York: Oxford University Press, 1955).

50. For an account that emphasizes the radical Republican commitment to black equality, see Hans L. Trefousse, *The Radical Republicans: Lincoln's Vanguard for Racial Justice* (New York: Alfred A. Knopf, 1968).

51. Blair, *Memoirs of President W. W. Blair*, p. 113; Diane Shelton, "The 1865 Revelation," unpublished paper presented at the 1978 annual meeting of the John Whitmer Historical Association, Plano, Ill., copy at Restoration History Manuscript Collection, Frederick M. Smith Library, Graceland College, Lamoni, Iowa.

52. Blair, *Memoirs of President W. W. Blair*, p. 113.

53. Ibid.; "Council," *True Latter Day Saints' Herald* 7 (1 June 1865): 163–64.

54. Council of Twelve, Minutes, Book A, 3-4 May 1865, Reorganized Church Library–Archives.

55. Doctrine and Covenants, Section 116. This section was officially canonized by the church at the general conference of 1878.

56. William D. Russell, "A Priestly Role for a Prophetic Church: The RLDS Church and Black Americans," *Dialogue: A Journal of Mormon Thought* 12 (Summer 1979): 39.

57. See the letter of L. F. West, from Escandia County, Alabama, 21 April 1872, published in the *True Latter Day Saints' Herald* 19 (1 August 1872): 469–71, as an example of this issue and the problems it raised. He wrote, "I am not opposed to, nor pregudiced [sic] against the negroes; on the other hand I contended for their liberation from bondage, and I here expressed my determination to make no distinction in word of doctrine; but to break down the middle wall of partition from between the two races is beyond the power of mortal man, this can only be done by time." He asked that the church send a black missionary into the area to work with black converts, concluding, "To cultivate too much familiarity with the blacks, offends the whites, to neglect the blacks, will offend the Lord."

58. *Journal of History* 1 (July 1909): 287–88; Early Reorganization Minutes, Book A, 1 May 1865; Joseph Smith to John M. Kennedy, 6 November 1896, Joseph Smith III Letterbook #6, Reorganized Church Library–Archives.

59. Joseph Smith to L. L. Barth, 26 May 1893, Joseph Smith III Letterbook #4, Reorganized Church Library–Archives.

60. Smith, "Memoirs," *Saints' Herald* 82 (5 February 1935): 177–78, 82 (12 February 1935): 207–8; Smith, "Autobiography," in Tullidge, *Life of Joseph*, pp. 798–800.

61. This ritual had been established by Joseph Smith, Jr., in Nauvoo, Illinois. See Doctrine and Covenants, Sections 107, 109, 110.

62. Council of Twelve, Minutes, 1865–1928, p. 12.

63. Council of Twelve, Resolutions, 1865–1914, p. 3, Reorganized Church Library–Archives.

64. Joseph Smith to Alfred Ward, 9 May 1880, Joseph Smith III Letterbook #3; Joseph Smith to Job Brown, 5 January 1886; Joseph Smith to L. L. Barth, 26 May 1893, both in Joseph Smith III Letterbook #4, Reorganized Church Library–Archives; Joseph Smith to Mrs. N. S. Peterson, 3 May 1894, Joseph Smith III Letterbook #5, Reorganized Church Library–Archives; Joseph Smith to John R. Haldeman, 5 May 1896, Joseph Smith III Letterbook #6.

65. Blair, "Moderate Mormons," p. 222.

66. Doctrine and Covenants, Section 86. For a discussion of health concerns during the 1830s see Lester E. Bush, Jr., "The Word of Wisdom in Early Nineteenth Century Perspective," *Dialogue: A Journal of Mormon Thought* 14 (Autumn 1981): 46–65.

67. Joseph Smith to Joseph Lampert, 22 February 1878; Joseph Smith to Mrs. Maria Falk, 16 July 1878, both in Joseph Smith Letterbook #1; Joseph Smith to M. B. Williams, 10 May 1879, Joseph Smith III Letterbook #2; Joseph Smith to William Hart, 16 May 1877, Joseph Smith III Letterbook #1A, Reorganized Church Library–Archives. Smith was a temperance lecturer on several occasions; see *Kendall County Record,* 4 April 1878, 27 May 1880, 14 July 1881. For discussions of the development of the Word of Wisdom's obedience in the Utah Latter-day Saint movement, see Robert J. McCue, "Did the Word of Wisdom Become a Commandment in 1851?" *Dialogue: A Journal of Mormon Thought* 14 (Autumn 1981): 66–77; Thomas G. Alexander, "The Word of Wisdom: From Principle to Requirement," *Dialogue: A Journal of Mormon Thought* 14 (Autumn 1981): 78–88.

68. Charles Derry, "Autobiography of Charles Derry," *Journal of History* 2 (January 1909): 22.

69. Joseph Smith to Charles Derry, 19 September 1865, Joseph Smith III Papers.

70. Joseph Smith to James Caffall, 12 June 1880, Joseph Smith III Letterbook #3.

71. Early Reorganization Minutes, Book A, 6 October 1860; "Minutes of the Annual Conference," *True Latter Day Saints' Herald* 2 (May 1861): 68.

72. A survey of the conference minutes from the 1860s demonstrates the importance of the appointee reports. For instance, in the semiannual conference of 1863 John Shippy reported his activities to the body, and Joseph Smith stood in his behalf, acknowledging the acceptability of Shippy's work. See "Semi-Annual Conference," *True Latter Day Saints' Herald* 3 (November 1863): 116–19. If one failed to report properly, it could serve as grounds for disciplinary action from the church. See "Conference Minutes," *True Latter Day Saints' Herald* 5 (April 1864): 125.

73. Smith and Smith, *History of Reorganized Church,* 3:333, 430–34, 479–81, 527, 532–35, 540, 548–53, 702–3; David H. Smith to Joseph Smith, 11 September 1868, Miscellaneous Letters and Papers.

74. Charles Derry, "Why I Did as I Did: Reasons for Uniting with the Reorganization of the Church of Jesus Christ of Latter Day Saints," *Saints' Herald* 24 (15 February 1877): 68–69; Joseph Smith to Charles Derry, 27 May 1911, Miscellaneous Letters and Papers; Smith, "Memoirs," *Saints' Herald* 82 (18 June 1935): 784–86, 82 (25 June 1935): 815–17, 82 (30 July 1935): 975; Joseph Smith to Charles Derry, 6 June 1865, 19 September 1865, 1 November 1865, 20 August 1866, all in Joseph Smith III Papers; Joseph Smith, Diary, 11 February 1865–4 April

1865, Reorganized Church Library–Archives; "Biography of Mark Hill Forscutt: Arranged from His Diaries by His Daughter, Mrs. Ruby C. Fowler," *Saints' Herald* 81 (16 January 1934): 75, 81 (30 January 1934): 143–44; Smith and Smith, *History of Reorganized Church,* 3:484, 494, 546, 702–3; Joseph Smith to Mark H. Forscutt, 21 February 1868, Miscellaneous Letters and Papers; "Annual Conference," *True Latter Day Saints' Herald* 11 (1 May 1867): 142.

75. *The Holy Scriptures: Containing the Old and New Testaments, an Inspired Revision of the Authorized Version* (Independence, Mo.: Herald Publishing House, 1944), Jeremiah 31:9.

8

And the Lord Called His People, Zion

While Joseph Smith had been remarkably successful in building a viable religious organization out of the loose confederacy of the early Reorganization during his first years as president—defining doctrine and policy and creating a bureaucracy in response to the needs of the moment—another very important theological question arose that the young prophet had to deal with: the issue of a utopian society. The establishment of what the Saints called Zion had been the most persistent goal of the early Mormon movement. The early Latter Day Saints had believed they were commissioned from among the world to help usher in the triumphal second coming of Christ and the advent of the millennial reign by building a society from which Christ could rule the world. Accordingly, during the 1830s and 1840s they had established Mormon communities to serve as utopian centers, places that would foster a new, righteous social order preparing the earth for Christ's return: Kirtland, Ohio; Independence and Far West, Missouri; and Nauvoo, Illinois. However, in each case the vision dissolved in failure and disillusionment. The reasons for failure were complex but essentially rested on the unwillingness of the Saints to live under the strict laws of the community established by the prophet and on persecution by non-Mormons.[1]

By the time the Reorganized Church had coalesced under Jason Briggs and Zenos H. Gurley, Sr., during the 1850s, many Saints had been forced to reevaluate the church's visions of Zion and the gathering of the righteous in relationship to these past failures, but few rejected the belief outright. Undoubtedly, the majority of the Saints looked with great longing toward the day when the prophet would call them to gather at a selected place and establish Zion on earth. But Briggs and Gurley were conservative leaders who believed they had no authority to dictate policy regarding this question. Consequently, they persuaded the Reorganized Church general conference of 1852 to adopt a very mild policy, directing "that in the opinion of this conference there is no [place] to which the Saints on this continent are commanded to gather at the present time." The conference did not reject the "sacred goal of bringing forth Zion in America," but it adopted a cautious policy that asked the Saints to wait until a more opportune time before beginning a settlement. The policy proposed that the Saints be satisfied for the present "to turn their hearts and their gazes towards Zion, and supplicate the Lord God for such deliverance." This statement underscored the uncertainty of the new Mormon organization during the 1850s, but it also accented the longing of the church to implement the quest for a physical utopian community.[2]

When young Smith assumed leadership over the Reorganized Church, his followers believed that he would begin the long-anticipated gathering of the Saints for the building of a zionic community. But given the young leader's impressions about the nature of the movement's zionic mission, as well as his pragmatic nature, his ideas were different from those of most of his followers. While convinced that his father's approach toward organizing utopian communities was basically correct, Smith realized that the early Mormons had tried to accomplish too much too quickly. He believed that neither the early church members nor the non-Mormons had been sufficiently prepared to overcome their fundamentally selfish human nature and accept an all-sharing utopian life-style: the Saints had lacked the mutual respect necessary for a communitarian society and the personal piety and desire for perfection crucial to the successful establishment of such a Christian utopia; non-Mormons did not understand the significance of such a society to the Mormon movement's millennialism, invariably castigated it, and in some cases sought to destroy it.[3]

Smith believed that the Reorganization's Zion-building effort should be more liberal and all-encompassing than it had been during his father's lifetime. He maintained that the millennial kingdom of God could be initiated only through personal righteousness and moral perfection, and would reach full fruition only if the righteous attacked evil in society. Young Joseph's hope that the Saints would purify themselves and become moral crusaders in the world stood in direct contradiction to his father's zionic program, under which early Mormons had retreated from secular society to create their utopia away from outside influences. The logical conclusion of Joseph Smith's philosophy was an emphasis on Zion's spiritual nature rather than its physical, community-building aspects.[4]

As a result of his personal emphasis upon the inner purity of the Saints and the necessity of working to change the world for the better, the young leader immersed himself in humanitarian reform movements and urged his followers to do the same. In the mid-1860s, he published an editorial in the church's official newspaper, the *True Latter Day Saints' Herald*, that succinctly stated his beliefs: "The church should begin to take a high moral ground in regard to the very many abuses in society, which can only be reached, to correction, by a strong setting upon them of the current of public opinion."[5] He called for a church-wide crusade to eliminate sin, the primary barrier to the establishment of Zion, and for the Saints to move out as reformers. The effort might take decades, even centuries, but Smith believed the church would ultimately triumph if it moved in a cautious, steady, and unified manner. Therefore, Smith agitated in both political and social spheres for the reform of American society.[6]

Joseph Smith III's concern with the spiritual aspect of an earthly kingdom of God did not mean that he totally neglected the church's desire to build communities as it had done in the past. He insisted, however, that this particular quest take a less important role than it had during the early years of the church's existence. Prodded both by church members who longed for the beginning of a utopian experiment and expected the new prophet to act and by non-Mormons in search of gain from a Reorganized Church gathering effort, in the summer of 1860 Smith explored the propriety of establishing a church community. The immediate impetus for this endeavor came from a Quincy, Illinois, lawyer named Godfrey, who saw the prospect of a lucrative legal fee for his services if he could persuade Smith to undertake court action against Missourians who had expelled the Mormon movement from the western part of the state in 1833. Considering the prospect of founding a church-sponsored community in Missouri with reparations from the legal settlement, Smith sent Godfrey to Independence, Missouri, to research the land records at the courthouse and bring back information about the feasibility of a civil suit in Jackson County.

Anticipating victory in such a lawsuit, Smith sent his stepfather, Lewis Crum Bidamon, to Independence to scout the area for property that the church might purchase for a Mormon settlement. Bidamon needed only a few days to realize that the Saints had virtually no chance of obtaining a favorable settlement in the courts. First, the Reorganization possessed no deeds to the church's 1833 property, for which it sought payment, and, consequently, had only the most tentative of claims based on the continuation of the movement and young Joseph Smith's personal status as the son of the early Mormon prophet. Second, many of the Missourians who had expelled the Mormons in 1833 were still living in the vicinity and were still strongly opposed to the church. The Missouri courts which would decide the case certainly would reflect their hostility. Third, even if the Reorganization were to win the case, the Saints moving into the area might well face another forceful expulsion.[7]

Rather than returning to Joseph in Nauvoo with this discouraging news, Bidamon decided to scout for an alternate location for the anticipated Reorganized Church community. He worked his way northward into Iowa looking for land. Everywhere he found landowners and speculators anxious to sell him large tracts for the proposed community. Although Bidamon could make no final arrangements, he informed potential sellers that his stepson would be able to close any business deals. Land promoters from Missouri and Iowa inundated Joseph Smith with offers of land for sale, proposing attractive packages with little money down and liberal terms.

Young Smith was flabbergasted that his stepfather had overstepped his authority so extravagantly, and by the time Bidamon returned to Nauvoo, Joseph had built up weeks of rage, which he vented on him. He told his stepfather that he had been wrong in looking at land outside Jackson County, that the Reorganization had no concrete plans for forming a community of any type, and that Bidamon should inform all promoters that the church had no interest in buying land at that time. Bidamon apologized for his poor judgment and made amends as best he could. In spite of Bidamon's actions, however, his report about the impossibility of a successful lawsuit proved valuable; Smith, always practical, based his decision to halt plans for it on his stepfather's realistic assessment.[8]

Apparently Bidamon's excursion into Iowa reached many more people than just the land promoters to whom he talked during the trip. As a result of the tour Smith began receiving letters from ambitious promoters all over the United States offering to sell their land at very reasonable prices. Most of the offers, such as the one made by the former territorial chief justice of Utah, John R. Kinney, were quickly disposed of by Smith, who replied that the Reorganization had no plans for the establishment of a church settlement anywhere in the immediate future.[9]

Other offers were not easily dismissed. Some were made by old members of the church or friends of Smith's father. Not long after his ordination as president of the church, for example, Smith received an offer from James Arlington Bennet, the debonnaire proprietor of the Arlington House educational institution on Long Island, New York. Bennet had been a friend of Joseph's father during the 1840s and may have joined the church just prior to the prophet's death. In his letter Bennet reminisced about his friendship with the prophet and applauded young Joseph's acceptance of leadership in the Reorganization. Bennet noted that as a small token of the esteem in which he held the church and the Smith family he was willing to help Joseph establish a utopian community for the Saints that would be as important as anything his father had achieved. Smith read this proposal with particular interest. "I am not aware of what property you have in Nauvoo," wrote Bennet, "but if it were necessary & meet to form a nucleus around which the Saints might congregate I have 160 acres of land in Livingston County, Illinois most admirably located between the Grait R. Roads that I would give for the purpose. Here immence numbers of the Saints could repair from all parts of the U.S. including Utah. Where under your plan their respectability and power would soon be felt."[10] Smith considered this offer for a time, but ultimately turned it down. His mother may have influenced him to disregard Bennet's proposal, for she disliked and distrusted him and on one occasion even called him an "old arch hypocrite."[11]

Smith also received a letter from another Bennett, John Cook

Bennett, a man whom the Saints had expelled from the church in 1842 on charges ranging from attempted murder of the prophet to fornication. In June 1860 Bennett wrote the young Reorganization leader from Polk City, Iowa, a small town north of Des Moines, where he was raising chickens for the commercial market. He told Smith that he owned many acres of prime land that he would gladly make available for the church's use as a communal gathering center. As they discussed the possibilities in correspondence, however, Bennett asked that Smith keep their plans secret and that he send him a fictitious name and address so they could communicate in strictest confidence. Smith recalled his reply to Bennett in his memoirs: "I immediately wrote him that any communication addressed to Joseph Smith, Box 60, Hancock County, Illinois, would reach me and be given proper and due consideration," and that he "had but one name and address for the communications of either friend or foe." After this harsh reply Smith never heard from Bennett again.[12] Smith's principles had ensured that he would never associate with someone who would not deal openly. He still adhered to the "Rules of Behaviour" that he had prepared in 1845, in which he vowed to have nothing to do with any activity that could not be conducted in the open.[13]

The aborted lawsuit, the questionable offers from friends of the Saints, and Smith's natural inclination to pursue spiritual purity rather than physical community building prompted the Reorganization leader to drop any thought of beginning a communal experience with the Saints. On 1 July 1860 Smith wrote to his longtime friend in the county, George Edmunds, a young lawyer practicing in Carthage, that he had decided to remain in Nauvoo for at least five years, managing his religious affairs from his home.[14] This letter somehow became public and was misinterpreted to mean that Smith wanted to start a Mormon communal experiment at Nauvoo. During the late summer and early fall various citizens' groups mobilized to ensure that a community like his father had created at Nauvoo in the 1840s did not arise again. This action prodded Smith even further away from any utopian city-building. By the fall of 1860 Joseph Smith had decided to steer clear of conflict with the non-Mormon community by stating an exceptionally cautious policy regarding zionic experiments. In an epistle to the Reorganization he wrote, "There is no command to gather . . . at any given locality." Before any such gathering could take place, he continued, "there are many obstacles to be met by us, which are to be overcome, not the least of which is . . . prejudice."[15] He counseled the Saints to remain in their present homes and to demonstrate their Christian faith there. But while most Latter Day Saints accepted this policy as the most logical for the present, most also apparently considered it only temporary and looked forward to the time when their prophet would announce the gathering of the Saints to a zionic center.[16]

While Smith managed to ignore the members' calls for the beginning of a communal experiment during the early 1860s, pressure from his followers mounted during the decade. A 1863 article in the church newspaper summarized the general belief of the Saints; the author concluded that church members live "daily as strangers and pilgrims on the earth, who look for 'a city which hath foundations, whose builder and maker is God.' "[17] The prophet's move to Plano, Illinois, in early 1866 and the location of most of the church's officials and offices there curtailed much of the membership's demands for the establishment of a separate utopian settlement. For a time, at least, Plano satisfied the Saints communal expectations: its large church population, larger percentage of important church officials, and supporting institutions—printing office, administrative offices, and religious educational activities—served as an official gathering location for the movement.[18]

Plano did not satisfy the membership's desires for long, however, and increasing pressure forced Joseph Smith to respond to the demands that the church begin its "Zion-building mission." He wrote in the *True Latter Day Saints' Herald* in 1868 that he heard from every quarter the constant cry for community building but that the church had not yet accomplished the self-purification necessary to succeed in establishing such a society. "Strife and contention, with disobedience," he chided, "are sure fruit that the gospel, with great witness, had not wrought in us the work of peace, and without peace in our heart we predict that *no perfectness will come in Zion*." He claimed that only when the Saints cease "evil of any and every kind, [and] become champions of truth, [then] there will be no want of definite action of policy" in forming a utopian community.[19] A little over a year later Smith suggested that those who wished to gather together to establish a zionic community should informally settle with others of like mind without waiting for an official pronouncement about location.[20]

Although officially silent about the gathering of the Saints during this period, Smith wrestled with the question. He believed in the zionic mission perhaps as strongly as anyone in the church, but his pragmatism and emphasis on the spiritual made him hesitant to act. In late 1869 Smith began to perceive a way to undertake a form of the old community-building issue accepted by most of the church members without violating the spirit of his more idealistic approach. Smith and other church officials of similar beliefs called for the Reorganization to establish, not a full-fledged communal experiment, but a less ambitious joint stock company that would make land available to Latter Day Saints on terms equitable to both the company and the settlers. In so doing the church would indirectly sponsor a settlement of church members and satisfy the repeated pleadings of many Saints to undertake such an experiment, but it would have neither official church management nor the millenarian overtones of similar settlements established by the Mormons in Missouri and Nauvoo during the 1830s and 1840s. In essence, Smith could publicly emphasize the spiritual aspects of Zion while the community would satisfy the membership's demands for a physical settlement.

The movement toward the founding of the joint stock company and a settlement for the Saints began at the Reorganized Church's general conference in October 1869. During this meeting Smith informed representatives from throughout the movement about the prospects of beginning a company to establish a religious community. He made it clear that he did not intend a full-fledged utopian enterprise; his basic pragmatism dictated an experiment that was marginally legitimate to the membership and enough within the mainstream of American religious experience to be acceptable to those outside the church. Rather, as he told the conference, "it is given as a means to an end, not as the end itself." Nonetheless, Smith called the organization of the corporation, whose express purpose was to establish a Latter Day Saint community, a step toward the full realization of the church's zionic mission. The proposal received enthusiastic support from the conference body, and with this approval Smith moved quickly toward organization of the company.[21]

Immediately after the conference Smith appointed Bishop Israel L. Rogers, the church's chief financial officer, to take charge of the company. During the winter of 1869–70 Rogers and a carefully selected group of associates prepared a proposed constitution for the company. The Order of Enoch—the name was the same used by Joseph Smith, Jr., for the organization that managed the Mormon communal experiment in Independence, Missouri, between 1831 and 1833—was a legally constituted organization empowered to buy and sell land and securities, construct buildings, manufacture machinery, lease assets, and make contracts. The proposed constitution stated that company's purpose: "The general business and object of this corporation shall be the associating together of men and capital and those skilled in labor and mechanics, belonging to the church . . . for the purpose of settling, developing and improving new tracts of land, . . . to take cognizance of the wants of worthy and industrious poor men, who shall apply therefore, and provide them with labor and the means for securing homes and a livelihood; and to develop the energies and resources of the people who may seek those respective localities for settlement." Rogers and his committee recommended that the Order of Enoch's charter specify a twenty-year existence, at which time the shareholders could renew the charter for another twenty years or dissolve the company.[22]

With the details of the Order of Enoch's government drafted, Rogers was ready to begin soliciting support and financial commitments from the church membership. In February 1870 he sent a printed circular to each congregation of the movement explaining in detail the purpose and organizational structure of the new corporation and asking for investments from the Saints. The members responded rapidly, and by May 1870 the Order of Enoch had received pledges of $28,000 with the prospect of even more. Rogers wrote in the church newspaper that this financial response came because the Saints believed "that the *First Order of Enoch* is but the beginning of the prosperity of Zion." [23]

On 15 May 1870 Rogers addressed an open communication to the church, commending them on their generous pledges to the Order of Enoch, and announced formal organization of the company in the fall of 1870. He asked that as many subscribers as possible attend the first meeting of the corporation, to be held in conjunction with the church's general conference in September at Council Bluffs, Iowa. At this meeting, he added, the subscribers were to approve formally the company's constitution and by-laws and elect a board of directors. Joseph Smith was present but took no part when the subscribers met on 19 September 1870 as Rogers had planned. At the meeting they ratified the order's constitution as presented and chose a board of directors consisting of seven faithful Saints, electing Elijah Banta, a giant, amiable man from Sandwich, Illinois, president, and Rogers treasurer of the company.[24]

They then moved on to what many thought the most important and historic event of the meeting, appointment of a committee to seek "a suitable location for the purchase of land & the operation of said company." Elijah Banta; David Dancer, a wealthy businessman from Wilton Center, Illinois; Israel Rogers; and Phineas Cadwell of Magnolia, Harrison County, Iowa, assumed this responsibility.[25] Smith and Rogers believed, as Rogers had written in May 1870, that "the committee will be directed in the search for a location by that Spirit which had charged the affairs of God's people . . . [and] that a step toward the redemption of Zion may be taken, and taken now."[26] As the first annual meeting of the Order of Enoch came to an end, the Saints believed that their dreams of a physical community would soon be realized.

The committee on location went to work immediately after the fall conference looking for the ideal land for settlement. Banta, their prime field operative, began traveling throughout Illinois, Iowa, and Missouri in search of inexpensive but productive land. He stumbled across a large tract of land in Decatur County, Iowa, quite by accident but immediately found that it was exactly what he had been looking for. The Reorganized Church had a strong, active congregation at Pleasanton, Iowa, a few miles east of this land, and Banta had gone there to visit some of the members. Ebenezer Robinson, one of the congregation leaders, told Banta that he experienced a vision in which he had been told that the Latter Day Saints were to gather in large numbers on either side of the state line west of Pleasanton. In this supposed vision, Robinson had heard the voices of angels singing this verse:[27]

> Give us room that we may dwell!
>   Zion's children cry aloud:
> See their numbers—how they swell!
>   How they gather, like a cloud![28]

As a result of Robinson's testimony Banta decided to investigate the prospects of purchasing land immediately west of Pleasanton.[29]

Between 3 October and 24 November 1870 Banta made several visits to Decatur County to look over the land and make arrangements for its purchase. One of its most attractive features, he found, was that a large part of Fayette Township, in which the land was located, could be purchased for as little as eight dollars an acre on liberal credit terms. In addition, the prospects of a railroad being build through a town site there were excellent. After reviewing all its attractions the committee on location decided to purchase the property as soon as the board of directors approved. By 5 April 1871 the board had met, with Joseph Smith present as a matter of courtesy, and sanctioned the purchase. Shortly thereafter Banta contracted on behalf of the Order of Enoch for the purchase of 2,680 acres in one large tract and several smaller parcels in southern Decatur County for the sum of $21,768.84.[30]

Soon after this purchase the Order of Enoch's directors began planning for the land's development. During the summer of 1871 Banta dispatched surveyors to the newly acquired property; the team divided it into eighty- and 160-acre parcels. Meantime, other company officials established priorities for choosing the first colonists and formulated policies for the community. With these activities still underway, the first settlers arrived in covered wagons from Wisconsin during early July 1871. These settlers, the families of Samuel Ackerly and Robert K. Ross, had waited years to "gather" with the Saints and were heartened by the beginning of the Order of Enoch experiment. Soon other similarly enamored settlers followed, and the handful of families on the property began building houses, breaking land, and making other improvements.

Most of these first settlers' farms were purchased outright from the Order of Enoch, but Elijah Banta and the other members of the board offered rental or rental-purchase arrangements to settlers with less money. The Order of Enoch often built one-and-a-half story houses and assorted outbuildings on eighty-acre tracts and rented them to settlers, collecting one-third of the crops for the use of the property. For a larger proportion of the crop yield, however, the Order of Enoch would allow a settler to acquire title to his farm. In this way the order's directors made it possible for families to raise their standard of living and eventually purchase their farms.[31]

When Israel Rogers made his first secretary's report to the Order of Enoch shareholders on 1 September 1871, he enumerated the successes of the company's first year. Most important, Rogers reported that the company was financially secure. After the purchase of the Decatur County property the order had operating capital amounting to $22,731.16, money sufficient to continue developing this property. Rogers also reported that the company's settlers were industriously improving the property: many had already completed "spacious accommodations" and the order had erected twelve houses at the cost of $7,678.40 for property renters. Additionally, Order of Enoch employees and settlers had worked together to break the sod of 1,600 acres, plant hundreds of nursery plants, and make other improvements.[32]

From the community's very inception, the Latter Day Saints settling there considered religious fellowship its most important advantage. Virtually all of the colonists took part in the Reorganized Church congregations nearest their farms. In November 1871, however, fifteen settlers who had been attending the Little River congregation of the church, located in the western part of the county, organized a new group that met on the order's property. This group became known as the Lamoni branch, after a benevolent king in the Book of Mormon.[33] In time this group built a twenty-four-by-thirty-six-foot-long building to meet in; they called it the "sheep shed," partly because they considered themselves sheep of the fold of Jesus Christ but also because, upon seeing the structure, one unimpressed church member remarked, "Humph! It looks like a sheep shed."[34]

After the initial flurry of activity the directors of the Order of Enoch allowed the settlement in Decatur to develop independently, and by 1874 it had grown into a modest farming community with a population of about 200, most of whom were Reorganized Church members. It boasted a general store, a blacksmith shop, a few homes near these shops, and ranging farms. During this time the settlers asked the directors of the order to begin the incorporation of the community as the town of Lamoni to further city development, but little progress was made. The directors did not forcefully manage the experiment during the mid-1870s, and the colony operated virtually autonomously under what might be called a policy of "benign neglect."[35]

Joseph Smith, who had no official role in the Order of Enoch, watched the development of the Lamoni experiment from his

church administrative offices in Plano. The community's establishment had been a boon to the church, giving the members hope for
an expression of the best intentions of the movement. But he had
wanted the Order of Enoch to serve as a crucible out of which
would arise a people with the spiritual unity and moral integrity
needed to begin the establishment of a physical Zion. He was disappointed, therefore, that the order's leadership seemed to allow
affairs at its colony to drift aimlessly. As a result, in his own quiet,
practical way, he prodded its leaders to act more responsibly by
encouraging them at every opportunity and by intimating that in
time the church headquarters would be located in Lamoni.[36]

Smith's efforts to promote more forceful leadership from the
directors of the Order of Enoch were only moderately successful.
These men acted lethargically in all too many cases; for example,
in 1875 they failed to take advantage of an opportunity to allow
a railroad to pass through the company's land, which would have
ensured the settlement's easy access to the outside world and provided a focus for the establishment of an important town. Instead, it
came to nothing. Seeking to goad the order's directors still further,
Joseph Smith persuaded the general conference of April 1875 to
designate a special committee of removal separate from the Order
of Enoch "to arrange for and effect the purchase of land, locate a
town site, and perform such acts as are consistent with the making of such locations" of gathering. This maneuver showed Smith's
skills as a politician: if all else failed, the threat of removing church
support from the Order of Enoch and of placing it elsewhere would
be a powerful lever in influencing its leaders. Smith could either
use the church-authorized committee to support the order's work
or pursue an independent experiment in community-building under
direct church control.[37]

Evidently Joseph Smith had no real intention of withdrawing
church support from the Order of Enoch, but the conference action
served the purpose he intended. The Order of Enoch leaders perceived the new committee as a threat to the welfare of the Lamoni
settlement. This perception was compounded by Smith's apparent
willingness to consider other gathering locations: in the mid-1870s
he met with the town fathers of Nauvoo to discuss the city's proposal that the Reorganization make its headquarters there. As a
result, the order's leaders met with Smith and other church officials

on 11 May 1875, soon after the conference, to discuss the situation. After obtaining these directors' promise to act more responsibly, Smith pledged the church's support for the Lamoni community. Later, on 6 June 1875, Smith privately told the order's leaders that he and several close associates had investigated the possibility of moving the church's headquarters from Plano to Lamoni. As a result, Smith asked David Dancer; W. W. Blair, the prophet's closest advisor; and John Scott, a well-respected church member, to oversee the removal of the church's assets—administrative offices, publishing house, and religious education facilities—to Lamoni as soon as practicable. He cautioned that this committee should not act hastily and that the move should take several years at least. Nonetheless, this decision meant that Smith and the church looked forward to a bright future in Lamoni.[38]

Following this meeting, the directors of the order began to manage the Lamoni settlement more forcefully. When Joseph Smith visited the settlement in August 1877, he was favorably impressed. He said, "The country where the Order of Enoch had located the scene of their operations has been frequently described, but we found a changed land to what we visited and rode over some six years ago. . . . Then, a wilderness of arable land, untouched by the plower; and dotted only here and there by a farm or a grove, greeted the eye; now, a cheerful scene of busy farm life, a wide spread of growing corn and wheat and rye and oats and waving grass was seen everywhere, brown now and then by an interval of untilled land, showing the place yet open to the settler; where the cattle roamed freely, the occupants, literally, of a 'thousand hills.' It was rightly called a rolling country; very fair to look upon, and giving to the careful and industrious husbandman a just reward for his labor."[39]

Following Smith's visit, the order's leaders continued to improve conditions in the Decatur County settlement, but little out of the ordinary happened until 1879, when plans for a railroad through the Order of Enoch property hastened the selection of a formal townsite. The Chicago and Burlington Railroad planned to construct a branch on a nearly straight line between Leon and Mt. Ayr, several miles north of the Latter Day Saint property. Elijah Banta, representing the Order of Enoch, and several influential residents of the settlement met with the railroad officials and agreed that if the company would lay its tracks through the order's property, the order would plat a town on the railroad line, obtain a charter from the state legislature, and provide 200 acres of land for the town. During the spring of 1879, Order of Enoch officials carried out these stipulations, and by the end of the year the railroad had been completed through the property, the first passenger train passing through the townsite on 25 December 1879.[40]

In spite of the favorable activity there, Joseph Smith held off until 1880 on an official announcement of Lamoni as the church's official gathering place, but he let it be known that the church would soon be leaving Plano. Smith often received letters from church members seeking advice about where to move to be with other Saints, and usually replied by asking them to remain where they were but suggesting that if they had to move Plano was a good location. By mid-1879, however, he was telling them not to go to Plano under any circumstances because of the poor economic situation. He wrote one prospective settler in the latter part of 1879, "I would not like to encourage you to come, and then have you no chance to maintain yourself." Instead Smith began advising the Saints to move to Lamoni.[41]

Conditions in Plano worsened during 1880, even as they brightened in Lamoni, and the hard times led Smith to make the final step toward publicly declaring Lamoni as the new church headquarters. He wrote to his closest advisor, W. W. Blair, explaining that Plano was becoming a ghost town and they had to move the church's business center soon: "The bottom is out of the Plano real estate market. Deering is removing, car by car, all he has. The lumber yard is about empty, and the men are being discharged, one by one. Many are making removal to Chicago, and some are going elsewhere; and Plano will soon be a dismally dull business place. I agree with you, *move at once*."[42]

After the official word came that all church administrative offices would be moving to Lamoni, the Saints living in Plano did not take long to leave. By the first of May 1881 most of the church's membership had moved away, the bulk of them settling in the Lamoni area. Even most of those left in Plano were packing. A last general conference met in Plano in April 1881, and most of the Saints approached it with both sorrow at leaving and hope for a better future in Iowa. In a letter to a close friend written in early 1881, Joseph Smith struck the general mood of the Reorganization during these months: "There is now an opportunity to make a striking step forward in our work. . . . I believe that we should take that step. I have made the matter one of constant study and prayer; and have that assurance that makes me bold to go forward."[43]

The Smith family's move in the fall of 1881 signaled the official demise of Plano as a Reorganized Church religious center and ushered in the reign of Lamoni as the church's stronghold. Before leaving Plano, however, the Smith family received a warm send-off from the townspeople. The local newspaper reported the farewell celebration: "The citizens of Plano presented Joseph Smith with a magnificent gold-headed cane on Wednesday evening. J. H. Jenks presented it in a fine speech. The ladies of Plano presented Mrs. Joseph Smith with an elegant silver cake basket. As these were presented by those outside the [Reorganized] church, the speaker being a Methodist, it speaks well for the standing of Elder Smith in particular, and the Mormon people in general." By November 1881 nearly all of the church institutions had been relocated to Lamoni and the little church settlement grew in activity.[44]

The most important Reorganized Church institution to be moved from Plano to Lamoni, after the office of the president itself, was the publishing house. The Herald Publishing House office had been located in Plano since 1863 and had risen to almost legendary status in the church. On 15 October 1881 Joseph Smith, the director of the establishment, announced in the *Saints' Herald* that the printing office was moving and that the next issue of the *Herald* would appear on 1 November as scheduled from Lamoni, Iowa. Once moved, the *Herald* set up temporary quarters in a frame building in Lamoni and later moved to a fine brick office in the heart of the town.[45]

As the church headquarters relocated to Lamoni, the community appeared to take on even more vitality and charisma. Physically it changed because of the buildings required by the large influx of people. In 1881 the population of Lamoni stood at approximately 300; by 1885 it had expanded to 490, to 1,133 by 1895, and by 1900 was a community of 1,540 residents. With this increase came a broadening of business and manufacturing concerns. In 1896 the retail businesses on Lamoni's main streets included three general stores, numerous specialty shops, two drug stores, two banks, four restaurants, two hotels, and a grain elevator. There were also lumber mills, machine shops, and several other manufacturing concerns.[46]

Joseph Smith considered Lamoni one of the busiest little towns he had ever lived in and was proud of his role in creating it. He considered it a wonderful place to live. It was a homogeneous society of politically conservative, morally upright, and economically compatible people. Smith enjoyed living within the church-centered community enormously. He thrived on the activities of the relatively large church congregation established there and looked forward to meeting his followers in everyday affairs. They were his flock, and he took great delight in being pastor in the town. More important, however, Smith came to believe in the 1880s that Lamoni was serving its purpose well. It had become a Reorganized Mormon mecca; a center for gathering for the Saints and a stable, deferential society in which all knew their places and rarely stepped out of them.

But Smith's contentment with life in Lamoni did not mean that he became complacent or parochial in his view of Zion. His commitments were still to the spiritual perfection of the people and the eventual undertaking of other zionic experiments elsewhere. He set his sights on Independence, Missouri, the traditional centerplace of Zion in Mormon thought, as the ultimate location of the church headquarters and encouraged the Saints to live there and to serve as Christian examples to their neighbors. With this interpretation of the Lamoni experience as a way station on the journey towards a spiritual Zion, Joseph Smith had, once again, demonstrated his pragmatic bent. The exciting aspect of this stance, however, was that Smith was incredibly pleased with the results he had seen in Lamoni. Certainly, it was not perfect, Smith recognized that, but Lamoni had been at least a small step in the right direction, if not a giant stride.[47]

Lamoni's position as a stepping stone in the zionic quest, coupled with its genuine success as a community, fostered definite action when the time came for the Order of Enoch's charter to expire in 1890. Joseph Smith III asserted that no further purpose would be served in continuing the commercial corporation for another twenty years. The company's shareholders largely agreed with Smith's conclusion that the order had served its purpose in providing a place where the Saints could live together in relative peace and harmony and asked its board of directors to cease operations and divide the assets among the owners. They did so without remorse, for they were pleased with the success of the experiment and fully convinced that the Lamoni settlement had helped give the Saints strength to move toward the eventual building of a spiritual kingdom of God on earth.[48]

After the dissolution of the United Order of Enoch, Joseph Smith III took no further part in zionic activities until the creation of a second United Order in Independence, Missouri, in 1909. Even so, by that time Smith was in semiretirement and had almost no role in its affairs. The Reorganization prophet remained in his haven in Lamoni until 1906, then he moved to Independence, Missouri, to enjoy the last years of his life. From Lamoni some of the most important activities of the nineteenth-century Reorganized Church were directed—the church's efforts to deal with Utah Mormonism.

NOTES

1. The best analyses of early Mormonism's zionic commitment can be found in Leonard J. Arrington, Feramorz Y. Fox, and Dean L. May, *Building the City of God: Community and Cooperation Among the Mormons* (Salt Lake City, Utah: Deseret Book Co., 1976), pp. 15–40; Klaus J. Hansen, *Quest for Empire: The Political Kingdom of God and the Council of Fifty in Mormon History* (Lincoln: University of Nebraska Press, 1973), pp. 3–71.

2. "Early Reorganization Minutes," Book A, 13 June 1853, Reorganized Church of Jesus Christ of Latter Day Saints Library–Archives, Independence, Mo.

3. Joseph Smith to J. J. Pressley, 31 March 1880, Joseph Smith III Letterbook #3, Reorganized Church Library–Archives; Book of Doctrine and Covenants (Independence, Mo.: Herald Publishing House, 1970), Sections 42, 57, 77, 81; "The Location of Zion," *True Latter Day Saints' Herald* 3 (October 1862): 74; "Questions and Answers," *Saints' Herald* 38 (26 September 1891): 616; John Zahnd, "Room in Zion," *Saints' Herald* 56 (7 July 1909): 638.

4. Joseph Smith to Alfred Hart, 9 May 1880, Joseph Smith III Letterbook #3; Joseph Smith to William H. Kelley, 22 March 1871, William H. Kelley Papers, Reorganized Church Library–Archives.

5. *True Latter Day Saints' Herald* 8 (1 September 1865): 67.

6. Ibid. 27 (18 February 1880): 49, 27 (18 September 1880): 284; Joseph Smith to Rev. F. Wilson, 23 September 1878, Joseph Smith III

Letterbook #2, Reorganized Church Library–Archives; Joseph Smith to David R. Ramsey, 6 August 1879, Joseph Smith III Letterbook #2; *Weekly Argus* (Sandwich, Ill.), 16 July 1881; *Kendall County Record* (Yorkville, Ill.), 8 December 1875, 4 April 1878.

7. Joseph Smith, "Autobiography," in Edward W. Tullidge, *The Life of Joseph the Prophet* (Plano, Ill.: Herald Publishing House, 1880), pp. 775–76; Amboy (Ill.) *Times*, 17 March 1864; *Complainant's Abstract of Pleading and Evidence in the Circuit Court of the United States, Western District of Missouri, Western Division, at Kansas City, Missouri* (Lamoni, Iowa: Herald Publishing House, 1893), pp. 275–78; Joseph Smith, "Editorial," *Saints' Herald* 24 (15 January 1877): 25.

8. Smith, "Autobiography," in Tullidge, *Life of Joseph*, pp. 775–76.

9. Joseph Smith, "The Memoirs of President Joseph Smith (1832–1914)," *Saints' Herald* 82 (16 April 1935): 495.

10. James Arlington Bennet to Joseph Smith, 6 May 1860, Joseph Smith III Papers, Reorganized Church Library–Archives.

11. Emma Bidamon to Joseph Smith, 21 January 1870, Mormon Collection, Chicago Historical Society.

12. Smith, "Memoirs," *Saints' Herald* 82 (8 January 1935): 49–50. On the activities of John C. Bennett, see Robert B. Flanders, *Nauvoo: Kingdom on the Mississippi* (Urbana: University of Illinois Press, 1965), pp. 93–96, 242–77.

13. Joseph Smith, "Rules of Behavior for Youth," February 1845, Special Collection, Harold B. Lee Library, Brigham Young University, Provo, Utah. The importance of this document has been explained in chapter 2.

14. Joseph Smith to George Edmunds, 1 July 1860, Joseph Smith III Papers. See also Thomas Gregg, *History of Hancock County, Illinois* (Chicago: Charles C. Chapman and Co., 1880), pp. 376–77.

15. Joseph Smith, "An Address to the Saints," *True Latter Day Saints' Herald* 1 (November 1860): 254–56.

16. Richard P. Howard, "Images of Zion in the Reorganization," in *Zion: The Growing Symbol*, ed. David Premoe (Independence, Mo.: Herald Publishing House, 1980), pp. 45–49.

17. "The Location of Zion, No. 4," *True Latter Day Saints' Herald* 3 (April 1860): 138.

18. Smith, "Memoirs," *Saints' Herald* 82 (25 June 1935): 817–18, 82 (2 July 1935): 848–50.

19. Joseph Smith, "Pleasant Chat," *True Latter Day Saints' Herald* 13 (1 June 1868): 168–69.

20. Joseph Smith, "Pleasant Chat," Ibid. 16 (1 August 1869): 81, 16 (1 September 1869): 146.

21. Joseph Smith, "What Shall It be Called?" Ibid. 17 (1 March 1870): 144–48.

22. "Proposed Constitution of the First United Order of Enoch," Ibid. 17 (15 February 1870): 126.

23. Israel L. Rogers to Samuel Powers, 10 February 1870, Miscellaneous Letters and Papers, Reorganized Church Library–Archives.

24. Israel L. Rogers, "To the Saints," *True Latter Day Saints' Herald* 17 (15 May 1870): 280–90; "The Order," *True Latter Day Saints' Herald* 17 (1 October 1870): 595; Jason W. Briggs, "A Condensed Account of the Rise and Progress of the Reorganization of the Church of Latter Day Saints," passim, M. H. Forscutt–H. A. Stebbins Letterbook, Reorganized Church Library–Archives.

25. Order of Enoch, Minutes 1870–1882, p. 7, Reorganized Church Library–Archives.

26. Rogers, "To the Saints," p. 290. See also Joseph Smith, "The Movement," *True Latter Day Saints' Herald* 17 (15 July 1870): 435.

27. Frederick W. Blair, comp., *The Memoirs of W. W. Blair* (Lamoni, Iowa: Herald Publishing House, 1908), pp. 174–75. See also "Report of the Board of Directors to the Stockholders of the First United Order of Enoch," *True Latter Day Saints' Herald Supplement* 18 (17 June 1871): 1–4.

28. Hymn 939, *The Saints' Harp* (Plano, Ill.: Herald Publishing House, 1870).

29. Blair, *Memoirs of W. W. Blair*, pp. 174–75; "Report of the Board of Directors to the Stockholders of the First United Order of Enoch," pp. 1–4.

30. Elijah Banta, Journal, Book B, pp. 157–58, Restoration History Manuscript Collection, Frederick Madison Smith Library, Graceland College, Lamoni, Iowa; Order of Enoch, Minutes 1870–1882, pp. 7–12.

31. Pearl Wilcox, "The First United Order of Enoch and the Founding of Lamoni," *Restoration Trail Forum* 6 (February 1980): 4.

32. Israel L. Rogers, "Report of the Secretary of the Order of Enoch," 1 September 1871, Reorganized Church Library–Archives.

33. Asa S. Cochran, "The Founding of Lamoni and the Work of the Order of Enoch," *Saints' Herald* 54 (22 January 1908): 80–83; Order of Enoch, Minutes 1870–1882, pp. 7–12; Larry E. Hunt, *F. M. Smith: Saint as Reformer* (Independence, Mo.: Herald Publishing House, 1982), pp. 150–55.

34. Cochran, "Founding of Lamoni and the Work of the Order of Enoch," pp. 80–83.

35. Order of Enoch, Minutes 1870–1882, pp. 38–48; *History of Ringold and Decatur Counties, Iowa* (Chicago: Lewis Publishing Co., 1887), pp. 782–88; Joseph Smith and Heman C. Smith, *The History of the Reorganized Church of Jesus Christ of Latter Day Saints* (Independence, Mo.: Herald Publishing House, 1969), 4:120.

36. Smith, "The Movement," p. 435; Joseph Smith to David Dancer, 26 November 1877, Joseph Smith III Letterbook #1, Reorganized Church Library–Archives; W. W. Blair, "The Gathering," *True Latter Day Saints' Herald* 23 (1 September 1876): 513; Blair, *Memoirs of W. W. Blair*, pp. 187–88.

37. *True Latter Day Saints Herald* 22 (15 May 1875): 299–300; Joseph Smith to Bro. Hendrick, 4 January 1877, Joseph Smith to J. W. Brackenbury, 6 March 1877, Joseph Smith to William H. Kelley, 22 March 1877, Joseph Smith to Charles Derry, 9 June 1876, all in Joseph Smith III Letterbook #1; Smith, "Memoirs," *Saints' Herald* 82 (5 November 1935): 1424; Joseph Smith, Diary, 18 December 1877, Reorganized Church Library–Archives; *Carthage* (Ill.) *Gazette*, 26 December 1877; *Plano* (Ill.) *Mirror*, 22 June 1876.

38. Joseph Smith to Phineas Cadwell, 8 December 1877, Joseph Smith to Lars Peterson, 9 January 1878, Joseph Smith to David Dancer, 15 July 1878, all in Joseph Smith III Letterbook #1; Joseph Smith to David Dancer, 18 February 1879, 10 March 1879, Joseph Smith III Letterbook #2; Order of Enoch, Minutes 1870–1882, pp. 49–60; Blair, *Memoirs of W. W. Blair*, pp. 191–92.

39. *Saints' Herald* 25 (15 January 1878): 24. See also Smith and Smith, *History of Reorganized Church*, 4:186.

40. Joseph Smith, "Editorial," *Saints' Herald* 26 (15 October 1879): 312; T. J. Andrews, "Impression on Visiting Decatur County," *Saints' Herald* 26 (1 August 1879): 28–31; Joseph Smith, "An Order of Enoch," *Saints' Herald* 26 (15 July 1879): 218–19; "Editorial Items," *Saints' Herald* 26 (1 September 1879): 263; Order of Enoch, Minutes 1870–1882, pp. 61–62.

41. Joseph Smith to Henry Bach, 26 November 1879, Joseph Smith III Letterbook #2.

42. Joseph Smith to W. W. Blair, 30 October 1880, Joseph Smith III Letterbook #3.

43. Joseph Smith to David Dancer, 26 March 1881, Joseph Smith III Letterbook #3. For a general description of the move, see Joseph Smith, "Editorial," *Saints' Herald* 27 (15 October 1880): 322; *Weekly Argus*, 15 May 1880; *Plano Mirror*, 14 April 1881.

44. Smith, "Memoirs," *Saints' Herald* 82 (17 December 1935): 1615–16; Joseph Smith, "Editorial," *Saints' Herald* 28 (1 November 1881): 322. The lengthy quotation is from *Weekly Argus* (Plano, Ill.), 17 September 1881.

45. Joseph Smith, "Editorial," *Saints' Herald* 28 (15 October 1881): 322.

46. James C. Reneau, "A History of Lamoni, Iowa, 1879–1920" (M.A. thesis, University of Iowa, 1953), p. 72.

47. Joseph Smith to F. C. Warrity and the Saints at Independence, Missouri, 22 April 1880, Joseph Smith to Joseph Luff, 22 February 1881, both in Joseph Smith III Letterbook #3; Joseph Smith, "Editorial," *Saints' Herald* 24 (15 January 1877): 25; Joseph Smith to D. S. Mills, 17 July 1883, Joseph Smith to Samuel Brannan, 17 July 1883, both in Joseph Smith III Letterbook #4, Reorganized Church Library–Archives. For a discussion that emphasizes Lamoni's centrality to the Reorganization see Norma Derry Hiles, "Lamoni: Crucible for Pluralism in the Reorganization Church," in *Restoration Studies III*, ed. Maurice L. Draper and Debra Combs (Independence, Mo.: Herald Publishing House, 1986), pp. 139–44.

48. Smith and Smith, *History of Reorganized Church*, 3:583–84, 598, 616, 4:274.

9

The Legacy of Plural Marriage

No issue weighed more heavily upon Joseph Smith III during the nineteenth century than the doctrine of plural marriage, embraced by the followers of Brigham Young as well as by certain other Mormon factions. The Reorganized Latter Day Saints, very early in their history, categorically rejected and condemned the practice of plural marriage. Indeed, many of those who affiliated with the "new organization" during the 1850s, such as Jason W. Briggs and Zenos Gurley, Sr., did so in part because they believed polygamy contrary to the laws of God and deserving of condemnation. Zenos Gurley expressed this conception ably when recounting a spiritual experience during the early 1850s that he believed demonstrated God's displeasure with the practice. In this experience Gurley was told: "Polygamy is an abomination in the sight of the Lord God: it is not of me; I abhor it, . . . and the men or set of men who practice it. I judge them not, I judge not those who practice it. Their works shall judge them at the last day. Be ye strong; ye shall contend against this doctrine; many will be led into it honestly for the devil will seek to establish it and roll it forth to deceive."[1] As a body, therefore, the Reorganized Church denounced the practice and demanded that it be stopped. In all likelihood, it was one of the few questions upon which most church members agreed during the earliest years of the Reorganized Church.

The movement's opposition to this concept solidified after 5 August 1852, when Orson Pratt announced that Brigham Young's faction of Mormondom had been teaching and practicing polygamy as a tenet of the faith since the 1840s.[2] For instance, before publication in January 1853 of the first missionary tract of the infant Reorganization, *A Word of Consolation to the Scattered Saints,* the authors reworked its conclusion to discuss plural marriage. Adding three pages to the original tract, they bitterly condemned Brigham Young for leading his followers into an evil practice and pleaded that all repent of the doctrine. They noted that none of the scriptures of the church countenanced such a practice, concluding that "we have shown in a few words what the law of God is on this subject, and we call upon you both far and near to obey it lest ye be found fighting against God, and receive of his wrath in the day of his indignation."[3] Throughout the 1850s the Reorganized Church continued to denounce plural marriage as evil and to call for the repentance of those involved in it, basing its work on scriptural and moral precedents.

While the Reorganized Church violently opposed the practice of plural marriage as a gross evil, there can be little doubt that it emerged in Nauvoo during the early 1840s.[4] William Clayton, a confidant of Joseph Smith, Jr., recorded in his journal the circumstances surrounding the coming forth of the practice. He noted that on 12 July 1843 Joseph Smith, Jr., in the presence of two witnesses, dictated a revelation commanding the church hierarchy to enter into marriage covenants with more than one wife as a part of God's eternal plan of salvation and a necessary prerequisite for entrance into the Celestial Kingdom. Most students of Nauvoo polygamy assert that the writing down of this document was simply a formality, for Joseph Smith had married several women and had taught the concept to many of his chief associates already. Apparently, the seed of the plural marriage doctrine had germinated as early as 1831 as Smith pondered the meaning of several Old Testament statements about the subject, not recording the revelation until the late date only because he believed the Saints previously had not been capable of accepting the practice. He reportedly commented that it was time finally to give the Saints meat whereas they had only received milk before.[5]

Following this, Joseph reluctantly allowed Hyrum Smith to take a copy of the document to Emma Smith, who he knew was totally opposed to the practice of plural marriage, in order to convince her that it was the will of God. Although Emma never left an account of this meeting and denied her husband's participation in such a principle on her deathbed, others recorded that she severely chastized Hyrum and sent him back to her husband completed chagrined.[6] When he returned, Joseph skeptically commented, "I told you you did not know Emma as well as I did," and put the document in his pocket.[7] Later, after copies had been made, Joseph allowed Emma to burn the original revelation, hoping that it would soothe her anger. Brigham Young told the story of this incident to a congregation assembled in Utah. "Emma took that revelation," he declared, "supposing she had all there was . . . went to the fireplace and put it in, and put a candle under it and burnt it, and she thought that was the end of it, and she will be damned as sure as she is a living woman.[8]

Apparently, Emma Smith's objections to the revelation made little difference. Joseph Smith continued to teach and practice the doctrine, and authorized Hyrum Smith to present the plural marriage document to the Nauvoo High Council on 12 August 1843. According to one of the members present, after Hyrum had read the revelation he said, "Now, you that believe this revelation and go forth and obey the same shall be saved, and you that reject it shall be damned." Some of the members of the High Council—William Marks, Austin Cowles, and Leonard Soby—did reject it and soon divided the council into pro- and antipolygamy factions.[9]

Although some rumors had circulated previously, soon after Hyrum's presentation of the plural marriage revelation to the Stake High Council a myriad of tales, rumors, misrepresentations, charges, countercharges, and denials created dissension within the movement and drew hyperbolic or satirical comments from the outside. While very few of the Latter Day Saints in Nauvoo had any real first-hand knowledge of plural marriage prior to the death of the prophet, without question the prophet was teaching some form of marital experimentation in Nauvoo. There were too many charges of marital irregularity in the city to claim otherwise.[10] One concrete example of these charges appeared in the 7 February 1884 issue of Thomas Gregg's *Warsaw Message*, published a few miles south of Nauvoo. A satirical poem entitled "Buckeye's Lamentation for Want of More Wives" poked fun at the rumor circulating about plural marriage in Nauvoo. A portion of it read:

I once thought I had knowledge great,
  But now I find 'tis small.
I once thought I'd religion too,
  But now I find I've none at all—
For I have but ONE LONE WIFE,
  and can obtain no more;
And the doctrine is I can't be saved,
  Unless I've HALF A SCORE.

A TENFOLD glory—that's the prize!
  Without it you're undone!
But with it you will shine as bright
  As the bright shining sun.
There you may shine like mighty Gods,
  Creating worlds so fair—
At least a world for every WIFE
  That you take with you there.[11]

It would be impossible to conclude how extensively plural marriage was practiced in Nauvoo before the death of Joseph Smith, Jr., but certainly several church officials were intimately involved. Evidence abounded that Joseph Smith, Hyrum Smith, Brigham Young, Heber C. Kimball, Orson Hyde, Parley P. Pratt, William Clayton, and John Taylor married extra wives during the early 1840s. And others probably entered the principle as well.[12] Some of them left concrete documents from the period pertaining to plural marriage. For instance, on 27 July 1842 Bishop Newel K. Whitney performed the marriage of his daughter, Sarah Ann Whitney, to Joseph Smith, Jr. Less than one month later, while in hiding from Missouri extradition officers at the home of Carlos Granger in Nauvoo, Joseph requested that Sarah and her parents clandestinely visit him. He told them that he had a special affection for them as a result of "what has pased lately between us" and needed their company. Then he told them where he could be found, how to approach the house so no one would know, and asked them to avoid his wife, Emma, because of her vocal opposition to plural marriage. He told them:

Let Brother Whitney come a little a head, and nock at the south East corner of the house at the window; it is next to the cornfield, I have a room intirely by myself, the whole matter can be attended to with the most perfect safty, I know it is the will of God that you should comfort me now in this time of afflication, or not atl, now is the time or never, but I hav no kneed of saying any such thing, to you, for I know the goodness of your hearts, and that you will do the will of the Lord, when it is made known to you; the only thing to be careful of; is to find out when Emma comes then you cannot be safe, but when she is not here, there is the most perfect *safty*: only be careful to escape observation, as much as possible, I know it is a heroick undertakeing; but so much the greater friendship, and the more Joy, when I see you I will tell you all my plans, I cannot write them on paper, burn this letter as soon as you read it; keep all locked up in your breasts, my life depends upon it. one thing I want to see you for is to git the fulness of my blessing Sealed upon our heads, &c. you will pardon me for my ernestness on this subject when you consider how lonesome I must be, your good feelings know how to make every allowance for me.

Joseph then told the Whitneys, "I think Emma wont come tonight if she dont dont fail to come tonight." Clearly Joseph was willing to meet his plural wives secretly to avoid Emma because of her well-documented opposition to the practice.[13]

As the plural marriage issue became better known by the Saints, a small group of dissidents, who believed the prophet had departed from the pure religion once taught by the church, organized a rival church that they believed more fully expressed the purity of the restoration. Led by William Law, a former member of the First Presidency, this group included his brother, Wilson Law, Austin Cowles, Robert and Charles Foster, Chauncey and Francis Higbee, and several others. On 7 June 1844 they issued a newspaper, the *Nauvoo Expositor,* to present their views about the church's apostacy. This publication contained three affidavits concerning plural marriage. The first, by William Law, stated: "I hereby certify that Hyrum Smith did, (in his office), read to me a certain written document, which he said was a revelation from God, he said that he was with Joseph when it was received. He afterwards gave me the document to read, and I took it to my house, and read it, and showed it to my wife, and returned it the next day. The revelation (so called) authorized certain men to have more wives than one at a time, in this world and in the world to come. It said this was the *law,* and commanded Joseph to enter into the *law.*—And also that he should administer to others. Several other items were in the revelation, supporting the above doctrines." Law's wife, Jane, also certified by affidavit that "I read the revelation referred to in the above affidavit of my husband, it sustained in strong terms the doctrine of more wives than one at a time, in this world, and in the next." Finally, Austin Cowles published in this newspaper an affidavit describing the presentation of the plural marriage document to the Nauvoo Stake High Council on 12 August 1843. He noted that the revelation described, "1st, the sealing up of persons to eternal life, against all sins, save that of shedding innocent blood or consenting thereto; 2nd, the doctrine of a plurality of wives, or marrying virgins; that 'David and Soloman had many wives, yet in this they sinned not save in the matter of Uriah.' " [14]

Sidney Rigdon, another counselor to Joseph Smith in the First Presidency, also commented on the plural marriage doctrine. After the death of the prophet and his unsuccessful bid for "guardianship" over the church, Rigdon took a small following to Pennsylvania and organized his own Latter Day Saint faction. In October 1844 Rigdon published his observations on the church's demise in the official newspaper of his sect: "It would seem almost impossible that there could be found a set of men and women, in this age of the world, with the revelations of God in their hands who could invent and propagate doctrines so ruinous to society, so debasing and demoralizing as the doctrine of a man having a plurality of wives; for it is the existence of this strange doctrine—worse than the strange fire offered on the alter, by corrupted Israel—that was the root of all the evils which have followed, and are following in the church." [15] In June 1846 Rigdon issued another rebuke of Joseph Smith, Jr., for introducing plural marriage and all of those who continued it: "This [plural marriage] system was introduced by the Smiths some time before their death, and was the thing which put them into the power of their enemies, and was the immediate cause of their death. . . . We warned Joseph Smith and his family, of the ruin that was coming on them, and of the certain destruction which awaited them, for their iniquity, for making their house, instead of a house of God a sink of corruption. . . . The Smiths have fallen into everlasting shame, and disgrace, until their very name is a reproach; and must remain so forever." [16]

Several explanations have been advanced in an effort to understand why the Mormons under Joseph Smith, Jr., adopted plural marriage as a doctrine of the faith. The official explanation of the church that continued the practice was simple: God had given Smith a revelation commanding the practice.[17] Others have argued that Smith's lascivious nature accounted for the practice. It was simply, for these people, a means whereby Joseph Smith could satisfy his lust and promiscuity under a veil of religion.[18] A few have suggested that plural marriage arose in response to the practical problem of providing husbands for female converts to the church and that as the ratio of men to women in the church equalized the doctrine lost impetus and was well on its way to extinction in the latter part of the nineteenth century.[19]

Most other observers have developed arguments based on a variety of factors. They have generally acknowledged the innovative genius of Joseph Smith, Jr., while asserting that plural marriage arose out of a complex series of social relations peculiar to the early nineteenth century. For instance, many of these individuals have noted that the nation was in cultural ferment. Virtually every institution was being seriously questioned during the 1830s and 1840s, and the marriage relationship was no exception. A number of alternatives arose in which groups sought better forms of marriage: the Shakers practiced celibacy, the Oneida Perfectionists under John Humphrey Noyes instituted a group marriage system, and some even preached free love. The Mormons, therefore, offered simply one more solution to a hotly debated question.[20]

While all of these concepts may have some validity (some more than others), in part speculation about the nature of the hereafter may have prompted the development of plural marriage. When the church was organized in 1830, the Saints took as their central mission the establishment of a zionic community upon earth and the aiding of the Lord in bringing about the millennial reign. Certainly, millennial expectations permeated the movement as did nothing else. By the founding of Nauvoo, however, the Saints had been dealt with harshly throughout the nation and had been expelled forcibly from Missouri. The millennial dream in 1839 and 1840 seemed to compare less favorably with the stark realities of life on the frontier than it had in 1830 and 1831. While still recognizing the central importance of the movement's millennial aspirations, many of the Saints were increasingly concerned about the nature of eternity. One should not overdraw the comparison, but perhaps the church began a transformation of ideals similar to that undergone by the Christian church during the centuries following the ascension of Jesus Christ into Heaven. At first the apostles advocated waiting for the Savior to return, with the expectation that His return would take place soon. As time progressed and Christ did not return, they gradually shifted emphasis toward the redemption and triumph of the soul at death.[21]

Apparently the Nauvoo Saints, including Joseph Smith, Jr., were deeply concerned about the nature of the hereafter and speculated about things eternal. The Mormon temple ceremonies that arose during the same period, with the sealing up of blessings for eternity, baptism for the dead, eternal marriage, and other kindred doctrines, certainly suggest this concern on the part of the church. Contrary to the accepted Christian traditions of heaven, during the Nauvoo experience a complex system of eternal relationships emerged that allowed the placing of Mormon marriages and families on a celestial plane with the father ultimately achieving a status of godhood. The elevation of these institutions to an eternal sphere altered greatly the marriage patterns of the members.[22]

The institution of celestial or eternal marriage—marriage not "till death do you part" but forever—about 1842 suggests the Saints' concern for the afterlife. And with the beginning of eternal marriage, polygamy seemed a logical step in the progression. A letter written on 5 January 1844 by Jacob Scott, an elder in Nauvoo, to his daughter in Canada substantiates the Saints' enthusiasm for eternal marriage:

> Several revelations of great utility and uncommon interest have been lately communicated to Joseph and the church. One is that all marriage contracts or covenants are to be *everlasting,* that is, the parties if they belong to the church and will obey the will of God in this relationship to each other, are to be married for both *Time* and *Eternity:* and as respects those whose partners were dead before this *Revelation* was given to the Church; they may have their deceased husbands, or wives (as the case may be) for eternity, and if it is a man who desires to be married to his deceased wife, a Sister in the Church stands as Proxy or as representative of the deceased in attending to the marriage ceremony and so in the case of a widow who desires to be joined in an everlasting covenant, to her dead husband. . . . I intend to be married to the wife of my youth before I go to Ireland,

I would be unspeakably glad to have you all here to witness the second nuptials. . . . many members of the Church have already availed themselves of this privilege and have been married to their deceased partners, and in some cases where a man has been married to two or three wives, and they are dead, he had been married to them all; in the order, in which he was married to them while living and also widows have been married to their dead husbands but only to one husband.[23]

Three months later Hyrum Smith addressed the general conference of the church in Nauvoo upon the development of eternal marriage. Smith said that he was compelled to make these statements because of the 10,000 reports "daily coming in about the spiritual wife doctrine." He explained the concept to the congregation:

I married me a wife, and I am the only one who had any right to her. We had five children, the covenant was made four our lives. She fell into the grave before God shewed us *his* order. God has shewn me that the covenant is dead, and had no force, neither could I have her in the resurrection, but we should be as the angels—it troubled me. Prd. Joseph said you can have her sealed to you upon the same principles as you can be baptized for the dead. I enquired what can I do for any second wife? You can also make a covenant with her for eternity and have her sealed to you by the authority of the priesthood. I named the subject to my present wife, and she said I will act as proxy for your wife that is dead, and I will be sealed to you for eternity myself for I never had any other husband.[24]

In both instances nothing was said about multiple *living* wives, but both Jacob Scott and Hyrum Smith would have more than one with him after death. With the legality of having two or more wives in the hereafter established, it would have been a very short step indeed for the Saints to allow two or more in the present as well.

No matter how the doctrine began, after Joseph Smith III assumed the presidency a dichotomy arose within the Reorganized Church about the church's response to plural marriage in Nauvoo. Although everyone in the movement believed the practice wrong, they differed over how to assess blame for its adoption. Numerous early Reorganization leaders wanted to fix blame for plural marriage upon Joseph Smith, Jr., arguing that the church should admit that he had made a grievous mistake by introducing the principle and demanding that all factions of the church end the practice. Isaac

Sheen, editor of the *True Latter Day Saints' Herald,* published an account of Joseph Smith, Jr.'s involvement in polygamy in the January 1860 issue of that newspaper. Originally issued in the *Saturday Evening Post* of 9 October 1852 this recollection stated: "The Salt Lake apostles also excuse themselves by saying that Joseph Smith taught the spiritual-wife doctrine, but this excuse is as weak as their excuse concerning the ancient kings and patriarchs. Joseph Smith repented of his connection with this doctrine, and said that it was of the devil. He caused the revelation on that subject to be burned, and when he voluntarily came to Nauvoo and resigned himself into the arms of his enemies, he said he was going to Carthage to die. At that time he also said, that if it had not been for that accursed spiritual wife doctrine, he would not have come to that."[25]

This opinion was echoed by William Marks, who was Nauvoo Stake president in the 1840s and in 1863 became young Joseph Smith's counselor in the First Presidency of the Reorganization. In several published statements and one remarkable letter Marks testified:

> Brother Joseph came to me abut two weeks before he was kiled and said Brother Marks I want to talk to you we went by our selves and he sais that this poligamy business in the Church must be stopt or that Church is ruened and we cant stay in the United States I have been deceive[d] in this thing and it must be put down I thought it would be an advantage to Mankind but I find it proves a curse I asked him how it coul be dun he said I must go into the high Council and he would prefur charges agaist those in adultry and i must cut them off and he would go onto the stand and preach against it and thought buy so doing we might put it down but the mob son commenced gathering and there was nothing dun.[26]

Several other early leaders of the Reorganization, among them Zenos Gurley, Sr., and Jason Briggs, also expressed the opinion that Joseph Smith, Jr., had introduced the practice and that the current church should admit it and then continue on with its business.[27]

The younger Joseph Smith, however, could never progress beyond his childhood perceptions of his father as a good man and refused to accept this assessment of the introduction of plural marriage. When Joseph Smith accepted the leadership of the Reorganized Church at Amboy, Illinois, on 6 April 1860, he also announced his unqualified aversion to plural marriage. He told the

Saints at that time: "There is but one principle by the leaders of any faction of this people that I hold in utter abhorrence; that is a principle taught by Brigham Young and those believing in him." The principle was, of course, plural marriage. But he went much further by categorically declaring that his father had not been involved in the practice. "I have been told that my father taught such doctrines," he said. "I have never believed it and never can believe it. If such things were done, then I believe they never were done by divine authority. I believe my father was a good man, and a good man never could have promulgated such doctrines."[28] This could arguably be referred to as the first public statement of what would become Smith's postulate: (1) Joseph Smith, Jr., had been a good man; (2) good men do not practice polygamy; (3) therefore, Joseph Smith, Jr., could not have been involved in Mormon plural marriage.

Throughout the remainder of his life Smith's statements did not waver in this basic proposition. In 1866 Smith wrote in the *True Latter Day Saints' Herald,* "Joseph Smith was *not* a POLYGAMIST in 1843 and 1844, as I have every reason to believe, from every proof I have been able to gather."[29] In 1895 he wrote to Caleb Parker in Lanark, Idaho, along a similar line: "Father had *no wife* but my mother, Emma Hale, to the knowledge of either my mother or myself, and I was twelve years old nearly when he was killed. *Not a child* was born to father, except by my mother, *not one.*"[30] Finally, in more reasoned tones, Smith wrote in his memoirs: "To admit that my father was the author of such false theories as were being taught, or that he practiced them in any form, was not only repulsive in itself to my feelings and strongly condemned by my judgment, but was contrary to my knowledge of, and belief in him."[31] Smith's staunch defense of his father's innocence in the face of considerable opposition represented one of the several instances during his career in which his principles (his belief in his father's innocence of what he was convinced by his moral and legal background was wrong, that is, plural marriage) directed his pragmatic methods of ensuring that his viewpoints were adopted within the Reorganized Church and, at least in a legal sense, outside as well. In this instance, Joseph Smith III was an ideologue who tempered his means of achieving his end so that, once again, he could gain it without undue conflict. That he was not totally successful in this attempt should be acknowledged, but that his efforts were in keeping with his general approach to religious concerns is significant.

At the same time, when Smith was pressed on the matter, his tempering ways did rise somewhat. He sometimes moderated his view by suggesting that the church's position was to oppose polygamy without reference to his father's involvement. For instance, he wrote to J. L. Traughber in 1877, "So far as polygamy or spiritual wifery is concerned, the Reorganization denies its correctness without reference to whether he [Joseph Smith, Jr.] did or did not practice it."[32] On another occasion Smith wrote, "You know that while I believe father was not the author of Utah polygamy I have not and am not now making the battle against the Utah church on that ground but upon the ground that plural marriage is not of God no matter who the revelation, so called, came through or who taught or practiced it."[33] To carry the explanation further, Smith suggested that his father had not been perfect and that if it turned out he had been responsible for polygamy's establishment among the Mormon people he would be punished. He told a J. J. Barbour of Dart Town, Georgia, "While I fully believe that Joseph did not receive the revelation referred to, yet, if he did, it is so directly opposed to the laws already received, that I must [admit] it to have been either of *man* or of the Devil."[34]

As might be expected in such a volatile case as this, without Smith's moderating pragmatism the prophet's policy concerning the origins of plural marriage created considerable turmoil within the Reorganized Church during the 1860s and 1870s. As an example, the divergence of opinions clashed on 2 May 1865 when a joint council of the First Presidency and the Twelve met and considered the question of plural marriage in Nauvoo. The minutes of the meeting noted: "The question arose as to whether Joseph the Martyr taught the doctrine of polygamy. President [William] Marks said Brother Hyrum [Smith] came to his place once and told him he did not believe in it and he was going to see Joseph about it and if he had a revelation on the subject he would believe. And after that Hyrum read a revelation on it in the High Council and he Marks felt that it was not true but he saw the High Council received it."[35] Joseph Smith III could not accept this as a truthful rendition of the facts, but he could not very easily repudiate the testimony of an eyewitness. Consequently, in his typically pragmatic manner he did not confront the matter directly. He was satisfied that the joint council was unable to reach a consensus upon this subject and adjourned without issuing a binding policy upon the origins of polygamy.

The chasm between Joseph and several of the church leaders over the origins of polygamy continued to widen during the remainder of the 1860s. In 1867 another joint council met and reconsidered the subject. One of the members who stood in agreement with Smith advanced a resolution about plural marriage's origination. It said: "Resolved, that we do not believe that the revelation, alleged to have come through Joseph Smith, the Martyr, authorizing polygamy, or spiritual wifery, came from God, neither do we believe that J. Smith was in any wise the author or excusor of these doctrines." Several of the participants in the meeting opposed this resolution "on the grounds that its passage would be more injurious than good because of the almost universal opinion among the Saints that Joseph was in some way connected with it." Recognizing that the opinion that his father had been innocent of teaching plural marriage had little support, Joseph Smith III stepped into the debate and pragmatically suggested that the council should not legislate on this matter. In light of this he expressed the opinion "that the passage of the resolution would do more injury than good." The prophet was probably concerned with internal unity on this matter—the question of unity had been uppermost in his mind almost since taking office in 1860—and realized that the difference of opinion would only be exacerbated by the passage of such a resolution. Certainly some of the leaders would refuse to subscribe to it, and in all practicality it would create considerable turmoil among the Saints.[36]

The issue of Joseph Smith, Jr.'s role in the introduction of plural marriage in Nauvoo remained officially unresolved throughout the rest of the 1860s. There were too many advocates of the prophet's involvement for the younger Smith to enforce his opinion that his father was innocent upon the church, therefore Smith became somewhat less forceful in presenting his ideas, at first taking a position similar to his handling of the complex question of plurality of gods—downplaying the importance of the conception and issuing a mandate against teaching it as official policy. Accordingly, Joseph did not make the innocence of his father concerning polygamy a test of fellowship in the church, and he cautiously used his authority as president to ensure that church-appointed ministers made no official pronouncements about his father's guilt. During this period, therefore, the Reorganized Church took a stand denouncing plural marriage without commenting much on the origins of the practice.[37]

During the 1870s, however, the rivalry between the Reorganized Church and the Utah Mormons intensified, and Joseph Smith and his missionaries began to advance more forcefully than ever before the claims of the movement as the true successor of original Mormonism. Substantiation of these claims necessitated proof that plural marriage had never been a part of the church during the lifetime of Joseph the Prophet and had been a corruption started by others after his death. During the same period the staunchest supporters of Joseph, Jr.'s guilt in beginning plural marriage grew old and began to die: William Marks died on 22 May 1872 and Isaac Sheen passed away on 3 April 1874. This eliminated considerable opposition to Joseph's position, so he could advance claims of his father's innocence more forthrightly without the powerful opposition from the older Saints.[38]

After this time, Joseph Smith worked even more diligently to clear his father's name of all connection with plural marriage. Smith believed the teaching a moral sin, destroying the souls of those who practiced it, and thought, at least from 1860 on, that his father had been wrongfully accused. Moreover, he had enough evidence—based on personal experience and observations by others he trusted—that his position had some foundation. He believed it imperative that he purge his father's memory of this blot; it was his duty as a son. "Is it manly or unmanly for a son to defend his father's good name according to his convictions of honor and truth?" Smith asked only somewhat rhetorically in 1896.[39] In time, it seems that Joseph Smith III came to believe that the only thing humanity ultimately possesses is a legacy, and it should be a positive one.[40] He honestly admitted, therefore, "I have been ambitious of but one thing, so far as human ambition is concerned, and that was to prove by the logic of conduct that my father was not a bad man," and as a result much of his work within the church had largely been directed toward absolving his father of teaching polygamy.[41]

A second reason for Joseph Smith's intense interest in proving his father's innocence was his great concern about the welfare and viability of the Reorganized Church. No one can question seriously Joseph Smith III's fundamental commitment to the Reorganized Church. Its welfare motivated his every decision. He believed that the church's uniqueness and reason for existence was more acceptable with a stance favoring his father's innocence of polygamy. "To me the gospel plan as taught by Joseph Smith," he wrote to Zenos Gurley, Jr., "is not so defensible from the ground that he did preach, teach, and practice polygamy, as upon the basis that he was not its author."[42]

With all due credit to Joseph Smith III's essential honesty, because of his concerns about proving his father's innocence in the plural marriage issue, he was prompted to abandon his temperate, practical approach toward dealing with most issues. As a result, he may not have been an entirely objective investigator into his father's possible involvement in the practice. He did seek out individuals who might have knowledge about Nauvoo during the mid-1840s and asked them for information about plural marriage, and he did receive sufficient affirmative responses to reinforce his belief in his father's innocence of the practice. But he also learned quite well, while studying law in the 1850s, how to ask questions that would supply him with the answers he sought.[43] He framed his questions to reflect his preconceived notions in all too many cases. Usually his questions progressed along these lines: "Was my father married to more than one woman and did they live together as husband and wife?" To the first part of the question, perhaps, a witness could answer with an affirmative but the second part was in complete opposition to the clandestine plural marriage practices of the Mormons in Nauvoo. To be truthful a witness would be forced to answer no to the question.

Apparently Smith was also willing to stretch or misconstrue his evidence, using it to support his position when in fact it was not particularly impressive to those without his particular mindset. Indicative of many of Smith's interviews, all of which he considered as strong evidence acquitting his father of all charges, was a conversation with Melissa Lott Willis, who had lived in Nauvoo during the 1840s. He visited her while on a missionary trip to Utah in 1885 and recorded this exchange in his memoirs:

"Now, Melissa, I have been told that there were women, other than my mother, who were married to my father and lived with him as his wife, and that my mother knew it. How about it?"

She answered rather tremulously, "If there was anything of that kind going on you may be sure that your mother knew about it."[44]

This could not be construed as a particularly firm denial of Joseph Smith, Jr.'s involvement in plural marriage. If one recognizes that Smith recounted this almost thirty years later, after his subject was dead, and that his recitation of the episode had an unconscious bias that might have given Willis's answers a somewhat stronger acquittal than she had intended, the statement should be considered entirely unconvincing.

Moreover, Smith's legal training and his experiences as a child prompted him to accept only rather narrow types of testimony. Early in his career Smith rejected all but eyewitness commentary and urged his associates to do the same.[45] Perhaps one could argue that this was wise—after all, hearsay evidence is not really reliable —but it seems likely that a significant amount of the information he rejected was not second- or third-hand but rather evidence provided by people who were taught the plural marriage doctrine by some of the highest Mormon leadership in Nauvoo. They had learned from such church officials as the Twelve, the Bishopric, and the High Council that Joseph Smith, Jr., had instituted the practice. In many cases they learned of this while still living in Nauvoo. I would think that many were not far removed from the source of the teaching either in time or in space. Nonetheless, Smith ridiculed individuals if they had no eyewitness information directly incriminating his father. This can be seen in an interview with Solon Foster in Utah in 1885. Foster had lived in Nauvoo in 1844 and 1845, for a part of that time in the Nauvoo Mansion, where he and young Joseph III had developed a friendship. He had gained knowledge of plural marriage while still in Nauvoo, and if he had not been taught the practice by Joseph Smith, Jr., he was still intimately acquainted with those that expanded the practice near the time of the prophet's death. Joseph Smith interviewed Foster about his father's involvement. Although Foster remembered the interview differently, Smith's recollection of the incident was recorded in his memoirs:

"Brother Solon, were you ever present at a marriage ceremony of any kind which occurred between my father and any other woman other than my mother, Emma Hale?"

"No; I was not even present at their marriage."

"When you were an inmate of my father's house at occasional stated periods, as you have said, did you ever see any woman there whom you knew to be a wife to my father, other than my mother?"

"No, sir."

"Did you ever meet, in social gatherings anywhere in the city of Nauvoo at any time a woman in company with my father, introduced by him or others as his wife, other than my mother Emma?"

"No, sir."

The interview continued for some time after this exchange, Smith pressing harder with each question. When Foster could not answer as he had promised—that is, by telling Smith "*what he knew*"—the prophet exploded: "I discover that, like others, you know nothing at all, personally, that would convict and condemn him, for you say he never taught you the doctrine; you say you never saw him married to any woman other than my mother."[46]

Of course, there were those, both within and without the Reorganized Church, who regularly told Joseph Smith III that his father had been guilty of teaching plural marriage. For instance, George A. Smith and his other relatives regularly tried to explain to him Joseph Smith, Jr.'s role in the development of plural marriage. One of them, Joseph F. Smith, began to collect affidavits from women claiming to have been the plural wives of the prophet and other types of documentation to prove that Joseph Smith, Jr., had originated the practice. Some of the older Reorganized Church members who had been in a position to learn about the practice in Nauvoo in the 1840s also described for Joseph III plural marriage developments.

Smith seemed to react to these efforts in several different ways, or combinations thereof, depending upon the circumstances. First, in some cases, as in that concerning Solon Foster, he discounted these statements on the grounds that they were not eyewitness accounts. Much, perhaps most, of this evidence he threw out for this reason.

Second, Smith would sometimes try to impeach the testimonies of his witnesses. Leaders of the Utah Latter-day Saints were invariably dealt with in this way;[47] their testimonies were biased by their immoral character in perpetuating polygamy, Smith believed. A more difficult problem arose in dealing with members of the Reorganized Church. For example, Zenos H. Gurley, Jr., the liberal apostle who challenged Smith's authority as well as the Reorganized Church's structural and belief system during the 1870s and 1880s, constantly told Smith that his father had been a polygamist.[48] At first, Smith may have responded by claiming that Gurley had no firsthand knowledge of the situation in Nauvoo, which was true; but in 1888, when Gurley wrote a chapter in a history of Decatur County, Iowa, he inserted an affidavit by his father-in-law, Ebenezer Robinson, who had joined the Mormon church in 1835 and could describe the development of plural marriage in Nauvoo, which said that Joseph Smith had taught him and his wife the doctrine.[49] Smith castigated Gurley and Robinson in his memoirs, quoting approvingly a Methodist minister's statement concerning this affidavit: "Yes, I have seen it, Brother Smith, that article can do you no harm. The writers are too well known, and the effect will be quite contrary to what they anticipate."[50] This conclusion does not seem to be warranted, however; Zenos Gurley was a political leader in Decatur County through the 1890s and well thought of by the majority of voters who repeatedly elected him to office.[51]

Third, if one of the other approaches did not seem to be appropriate, Smith was likely to ignore the issue entirely. He reacted to the testimonies of some of his Utah relatives and fellow Reorganized Church members in this way all too often. He kept silent in the face of challenges from Isaac Sheen, William Marks, James Whitehead, George A. Smith, and others both within and without the church.[52] W. W. Blair, an apostle and later counselor in the First Presidency of the Reorganized Church, met with James Whitehead in April 1874 to ask him about plural marriage in Nauvoo. Blair's diary is revealing: "J[oseph] did te[ach] p[olygamy] and pr[actice] too. That E[mma] knos it too that she put [the] hand—of wives [in] Jos. hand. W[hitehead] says Alex. H. Smith asked him . . . if J[oseph] did P[ractice] and tea[ch] P[olygamy] and he, W[hitehead] told him he did." Blair apparently confronted both Joseph and Alexander Smith with this information, but their responses are not recorded. They seem to have totally ignored it.[53]

Finally, if no other approach worked, Smith sometimes pleaded that he was not sure. Numerous individuals charged Smith with stubbornness concerning his unwillingness to admit that his father had initiated plural marriage. His usual response when pressed to give an answer was similar to what he wrote to Zenos H. Gurley, Jr., in 1878: "I am not positive nor sure that he was innocent."[54] Upon occasion, when pressed further, Smith was known to have reacted more forcefully. Gurley continued to challenge Smith's reasons for believing his father innocent and when he could get no admission of involvement became quite upset. Smith responded to Gurley, "I tell you, brother, I have been cut to the quick, when brethren have affirmed that I did know that my father was guilty of practicing polygamy; and denied it because I was obstinate, and sinned against light and knowledge in so denying."[55] This placed Gurley on the defensive and prompted him to seek a reconciliation.[56] However, Gurley's reconciliation was only temporary; eventually he was removed from his position as an apostle, and in 1886 he withdrew from the movement, in part over the issue of plural marriage.[57]

If all else failed, Smith was pragmatically willing to sanction untruths about the origins of plural marriage if necessary for his purposes. For instance, in an 1882 letter to his uncle, William B. Smith, the prophet suggested that the cause of the church necessitated that certain carefully planted conceptions about the origins of the doctrine not be disturbed. At that time William Smith was writing a book about his career in Mormonism, and Joseph sought to ensure that nothing was said that reflected poorly upon his stand concerning his father's innocence in polygamy: "I have long been engaged in removing from Father's memory and from the early church, the stigma and blame thrown upon them because of Polygamy; and have at last lived to see the cloud rapidly lifting. And I would not consent to see further blame attached, by a blunder now. Therefore, Uncle, bear in mind our standing to-day before the world, as defenders of Mormonism free from Polygamy, and go ahead with your personal recollections. . . . if you are the wise man I think you to be, you will fail [to] remember anything contrary to the lofty standard of character at which we esteem these good men. You can do the cause great good; you can injure it by injudicious sayings."[58] William Smith acceded to his nephew's wishes both in his public statements and private letters, clearing Joseph, Jr., of any involvement with plural marriage even though William had been involved himself.[59]

Such rigid, principled commitment to the position that his father was innocent of plural marriage, coupled with his pragmatic application of its teaching within the Reorganization, gradually ensured that it took effect as the predominant position within the church. By the late 1880s it had certainly been adopted as the official position of the Reorganization. Essentially, the necessity of maintaining a consensus of opinion, at least before those outside the movement, was just as important to Joseph as honesty and integrity. During his presidency, even without consensus on the origins of plural marriage, Joseph Smith III's movement took part in a forceful antipolygamy crusade, designed not only to destroy all vestiges of plural marriage but also to reform Mormonism along more orthodox lines and to gain converts from among the ranks of the Utah Latter-day Saints.[60]

NOTES

1. Zenos H. Gurley, Sr., "History of the New Organization of the Church," *True Latter Day Saints' Herald* 1 (March 1860): 53.

2. "Address on the Opening of the New Year," *Latter-day Saints Millennial Star* (Liverpool, England) 15 (1 January 1860): 1–5; *Deseret News Extra* (Salt Lake City, Utah), 14 September 1852; Jason W. Briggs, "A Condensed Account of the Rise and Progress of the Reorganization of the Church of Latter Day Saints," pp. 157–58, M. H. Forscutt–H. A. Stebbins Letterbook, Reorganized Church of Jesus Christ of Latter Day Saints Library–Archives, Independence, Mo.

3. Jason W. Briggs, Zenos H. Gurley, Sr., and John Harrington, *A Word of Consolation to the Scattered Saints* (Janesville, Wisc.: n.p., 1853), pp. 21–23.

4. The controversy over plural marriage has prompted voluminous studies in recent years. A valuable survey of the literature on this subject is Davis Bitton, "Mormon Polygamy: A Review Article," *Journal of Mormon History* 4 (1977): 101–18. The most extensive studies of the origins of plural marriage are Lawrence Foster, *Religion and Sexuality: Three American Communal Experiments of the Nineteenth Century* (New York: Oxford University Press, 1981); Danel W. Bachman, "A Study of the Mormon Practice of Plural Marriage before the Death of Joseph Smith" (M.A. thesis, Purdue University, 1975); Donna Hill, *Joseph Smith:*

The First Mormon (Garden City, N.Y.: Doubleday and Co., 1977), pp. 335–61; Richard S. Van Wagoner, *Mormon Polygamy: A History* (Salt Lake City, Utah: Signature Books, 1985); Linda King Newell and Valeen Tippetts Avery, *Mormon Enigma: Emma Hale Smith, Prophet's Wife, "Elect Lady," Polygamy's Foe* (Garden City, N.Y.: Doubleday and Co., 1984); James B. Allen, *Trials of Discipleship: The Story of William Clayton, A Mormon* (Urbana: University of Illinois Press, 1987). On the Ohio origins of the doctrine, see Danel W. Bachman, "New Light on an Old Hypothesis: The Ohio Origins of the Revelation on Eternal Marriage," *Journal of Mormon History* 5 (1978): 19–31. The unsettled nature of the practice is demonstrated by Richard S. Van Wagoner, "Mormon Polyandry in Nauvoo," *Dialogue: A Journal of Mormon Thought* 18 (Fall 1985): 67–83. For a Reorganized Church approach to the subject see Richard P. Howard, "The Changing RLDS Response to Mormon Polygamy: A Preliminary Analysis," *Journal of the John Whitmer Historical Association* 3 (1983): 14–29; and Alma R. Blair, "RLDS Views of Polygamy: Some Historiographical Notes," *John Whitmer Historical Association Journal* 5 (1985): 16–28.

5. *Journal of Discourses* (Salt Lake City, Utah), 3:266; Bachman, "New Light on an Old Hypothesis," pp. 19–34; Robert B. Flanders, *Nauvoo: Kingdom on the Mississippi* (Urbana: University of Illinois Press, 1965), pp. 276–77; William Clayton, Journal, 27 April 1843, 1 May 1843, 13 May 1843, 23 May 1843, 23 June 1843, 30 June 1843, 12–13 July 1843, as cited in James B. Allen, "One Man's Nauvoo: William Clayton's Experiences in Mormon Illinois," *Journal of Mormon History* 6 (1979): 44.

6. Joseph Smith, "Last Testimony of Sister Emma," *Saints' Herald* 26 (1 October 1879): 289–90. Emma Smith's rejection of plural marriage was recorded in William Clayton, Journal, 23 May 1843, 12 July 1843, 13 July 1843, 11 August 1843, 16 August 1843, 21 August 1843, 23 August 1843, as cited in Allen, "One Man's Nauvoo," pp. 44–45. On 13 July 1843 Clayton wrote about Emma, "O may the Lord soften her heart that she may be willing to keep and abide by his Holy Law."

7. Andrew Jenson, "Plural Marriage," *Latter-day Saints' Historical Record* 6 (July 1887): 226.

8. Brigham Young in *Journal of Discourses,* 17:159.

9. Jenson, "Plural Marriage," pp. 226–27.

10. In addition to those mentioned in the text, see the following contemporary documents to demonstrate the far-reaching charges leveled against the Mormons about their marriage practices. John C. Bennett, *The History of the Saints; or, An Exposé of Joe Smith and the Mormons* (Boston: Leland and Whiting, 1842), pp. 217–57; *Nauvoo* (Ill.) *Expositor,* 7

June 1844. The denials of marital irregularity are almost as revealing as the charges. See Doctrine and Covenants of the Church of the Latter Day Saints (Kirtland, Ohio: F. G. Williams and Co., 1835), Section 101:4; *Times and Seasons* (Nauvoo, Ill.), 4 (1 December 1842): 32, 3 (1 October 1843): 869, 5 (1 February 1844): 523, 5 (15 March 1844): 474; *Latter Day Saints' Elder's Journal* (Far West, Mo.), July 1838.

11. *Warsaw* (Ill.) *Signal*, 7 February 1844.

12. The most complete study of plural marriage in Nauvoo, including information on those involved in the practice, remains Bachman, "Study of the Mormon Practice of Plural Marriage before the Death of Joseph Smith." One should also review carefully Foster, *Religion and Sexuality*.

13. Joseph Smith, Jr., to Newel K. Whitney, Elizabeth Ann Whitney, etc., 18 August 1842, George Albert Smith Family Papers, Special Collections, Marriott Library, University of Utah, Salt Lake City. The text and the signature of this document are in the handwriting of Joseph Smith, Jr. This document has been reproduced in Dean C. Jessee's masterful *The Personal Writings of Joseph Smith* (Salt Lake City, Utah: Deseret Book Co., 1984), pp. 539–40.

14. *Nauvoo Expositor*, 7 June 1844.

15. Sidney Rigdon to Bro. J. Greig, *Latter Day Saints' Messenger and Advocate* 1 (15 October 1844): 13. Rigdon apparently became most upset over the plural marriage issue when it directly affected his family. In the spring of 1842 the prophet propositioned Rigdon's daughter, Nancy, to become his plural wife. She refused, the family publicly chided Joseph Smith, and a scandal erupted in Nauvoo. The Nancy Rigdon affair has been discussed in F. Mark McKiernan, *The Voice of One Crying in the Wilderness: Sidney Rigdon, 1793–1876, Religious Reformer* (Lawrence, Kan.: Coronado Press, 1971), pp. 113–19.

16. Sidney Rigdon to Ebenezer Robinson, editor, *Latter Day Saints' Messenger and Advocate* 2 (June 1846): 475.

17. The Doctrine and Covenants of the Church of Jesus Christ of Latter-day Saints (Salt Lake City, Utah: Deseret Book Co., 1968), Section 132; William E. Barrett, *The Restored Church* (Salt Lake City, Utah: Deseret Book Co., 1964), pp. 181–83.

18. Literally hundreds of publications of the nineteenth century attributed the plural marriage system to lust. See, as examples, Bennett, *History of the Saints;* Oliver H. Olney, *The Absurdities of Mormonism Portrayed* (Hancock County, Ill.: n.p., 1843); John Hyde, Jr., *Mormonism: Its Leaders and Designs* (New York: W. P. Fetridge, 1857); J. H. Beadle, *Life in Utah; or, The Mysteries and Crimes of Mormonism* (Philadelphia: National Publishing Co., 1870); Wilhelm Wyl, *Joseph Smith, The Prophet: His Family and Friends; a Study Based on Facts and Documents*

(Salt Lake City, Utah: Tribune Printing and Publishing Co., 1886). An analysis of this type of literature is Leonard J. Arrington and Jon Haupt, "Intolerable Zion: The Image of Mormonism in Nineteenth Century American Literature," *Western Humanities Review* 22 (Summer 1968): 243–60.

19. "George Bernard Shaw Speaks," *Improvement Era* (Salt Lake City, Utah) 40 (July 1937): 413; William J. Whalen, *The Latter-day Saints in the Modern World* (Notre Dame, Ind.: University of Notre Dame Press, 1964), p. 129. In view of the more recent demographic information on conversions to Mormonism, this explanation can be dismissed without much consideration. Studies of this type include James E. Smith and Phillip R. Kunz, "Polygyny and Fertility in Nineteenth-Century America," *Population Studies* 30 (November 1976): 465–80; Wayne L. Wahlquist, "Population Growth in the Mormon Core Area, 1847–1890," in *The Mormon Role in the Settlement of the West*, ed. Richard H. Jackson (Provo, Utah: Brigham Young University Press, 1978), pp. 107–34; Stanley S. Ivins, "Notes on Mormon Polygamy," *Western Humanities Review* 10 (Summer 1953): 229–39.

20. Fawn M. Brodie, *No Man Knows My History: The Life of Joseph Smith, the Mormon Prophet* (New York: Alfred A. Knopf, 1972), pp. 418–21; Foster, *Religion and Sexuality*, pp. 128–80. An early study, although outdated and suspect in certain areas that bear upon the same theme, is Isaac Woodbridge Riley, *The Founder of Mormonism: A Psychological Study of Joseph Smith, Jr.* (New York: Dodd, Mead, and Co., 1902).

21. Klaus J. Hansen, *Quest for Empire: The Political Kingdom of God and the Council of Fifty in Mormon History* (Lincoln: University of Nebraska Press, 1974), pp. 3–23; Klaus J. Hansen, *Mormonism and the American Experience* (Chicago: University of Chicago Press, 1981), pp. 98–103; David Premoe, ed., *Zion: The Growing Symbol* (Independence, Mo.: Herald Publishing House, 1980), pp. 22–27, 33–38; H. Roger Grant, "Missouri's Utopian Communities," *Missouri Historical Review* 66 (October 1971): 20–48; Richard Lloyd Anderson, "Joseph Smith and the Millenarian Timetable," *Brigham Young University Studies* 3 (Spring and Summer 1961): 55–66. Howard, "Changing RLDS Response to Mormon Polygamy," pp. 25–29, emphasizes this aspect of the origins of plural marriage, calling it an "accident of history." A direct critique of this position can be found in Imogene Goodyear, "Joseph Smith and Polygamy: An Alternative View," *John Whitmer Historical Association Journal* 4 (1984): 16–21.

22. Book of Doctrine and Covenants (Independence, Mo.: Herald Publishing House, 1970), Sections 107, 109, 110; Lisle G. Brown, "The Sacred Departments for Temple Work in Nauvoo: The Assembly Room and the

Council Chamber," *Brigham Young University Studies* 19 (Spring 1979): 361–74; T. Edgar Lyon, "Doctrinal Development of the Church during the Nauvoo Sojourn, 1839–1846," *Brigham Young University Studies* 15 (Summer 1975): 435–46; Roger D. Launius and F. Mark McKiernan, *Joseph Smith, Jr.'s, Red Brick Store* (Macomb: Western Illinois University Monograph Series, 1985), pp. 23–32.

23. Jacob Scott to Mary Warnock, 5 January 1844, Miscellaneous Letters and Papers, Reorganized Church Library–Archives.

24. Hyrum Smith, Sermon, 8 April 1844, Minutes Collection, Church of Jesus Christ of Latter-day Saints Historical Department, Salt Lake City, Utah.

25. *True Latter Day Saints' Herald* 1 (January 1860): 24.

26. William Marks to Hiram Falk and Josiah Butterfield, 1 October 1865, Paul M. Hansen Papers, Reorganized Church Library–Archives. See also statements by Marks in *Zion's Harbinger and Baneemy's Organ* (St. Louis, Mo.), July 1853, p. 53; *True Latter Day Saints' Herald* 1 (January 1860): 22–23.

27. Even the prophet's brother, David H. Smith, expressed his misgivings about the innocence of their father. He wrote to a Brother Sherman on 27 July 1872: "I know my mother believes just as we do in faith repentance, baptism, and all the saving doctrines, in the books of the church and all, but I do not wish to ask her in regard to polygamy, for fear brother   God forgive me if I am wrong. . . . I believe there was something wrong. I don't know it, but I believe it, the testimony is too great for me to deny." See David H. Smith to Bro. Sherman, 27 July 1872, Miscellaneous Letters and Papers. See also Ebenezer Robinson, "Items of Personal History," *The Return* (Davis City, Iowa), April 1890, June 1890, September 1890, October 1890, April 1891; William E. McLellin to Joseph Smith, July 1872, Miscellaneous Letters and Papers; Joseph Smith to J. J. Cornish, 9 February 1878, Joseph Smith III Letterbook #1, Reorganized Church Library–Archives; Joseph Smith to Zenos H. Gurley, 2 April 1879, 24 July 1879, Joseph Smith III Letterbook #2, Reorganized Church Library–Archives.

28. *True Latter Day Saints' Herald* 1 (May 1860): 103.

29. *True Latter Day Saints' Herald* 10 (15 August 1866): 63.

30. Joseph Smith to Caleb Parker, 14 August 1895, Joseph Smith III Letterbook #6, Reorganized Church Library–Archives.

31. Joseph Smith, "The Memoirs of President Joseph Smith 1832–1914), *Saints' Herald* 82 (2 April 1935): 432. See also Joseph Smith, "Mormons Who Are Not Polygamists," *Everybody's* 25 (September 1911): 427–28; Joseph Smith to Cousin John, 28 December 1876, Joseph Smith III Letterbook #4; Samuel H. B. Smith to George A. Smith, 10

214 Joseph Smith III

July 1860, Special Collections, Harold B. Lee Library, Brigham Young University, Provo, Utah; Joseph Smith to E. C. Brand, 26 January 1884, Joseph Smith III Letterbook #4, Reorganized Church Library–Archives; Joseph Smith to L. O. Littlefield, 14 August 1883, Joseph Smith III Letterbook #4; Joseph Smith to John Henry Smith, 6 January 1886, Joseph Smith III Letterbook #4; Joseph Smith to Deseret News Co., 21 March 1896, Joseph Smith III Letterbook #6; Joseph Smith to Hon. J. C. Barrows, 3 January 1880, Joseph Smith III Letterbook #2, Reorganized Church Library–Archive; Joseph Smith to Hon. G. F. Edmunds, 4 March 1886, Joseph Smith III Letterbook #4; Joseph Smith to Hon. W. F. Hepburn, 9 February 1886, Joseph Smith III Letterbook #4; Joseph Smith, "Ways That Are Doubtful," *Saints Herald* 36 (5 October 1881): 654–57; "Memorial to Congress from a Committee of the Reorganized Church of Jesus Christ of Latter Day Saints, on the Claims and Faith of the Church," *True Latter Day Saints' Herald* 17 (1 June 1870): 321–27; *Chicago Tribune*, 22 February 1880; "Anti-Polygamy: Another Outpouring from Chicago Declares that the Evil Must Go," *Saints' Advocate* 4 (April 1882): 185–87; Joseph Smith to L. O. Littlefield, n.d. [30 July 1883], Joseph Smith III Letterbook #4.

32. Joseph Smith to J. L. Traughber, 13 February 1877, Joseph Smith III Letterbook #1A, Reorganized Church Library–Archives.

33. Joseph Smith to Zenos H. Gurley, 5 March 1886, Joseph Smith III Letterbook #4.

34. Joseph Smith to J. J. Barbour, 15 May 1878, Joseph Smith III Letterbook #1. See also Joseph Smith to Z. H. Gurley, 2 April 1879, Joseph Smith III Letterbook #2; Joseph Smith to James T. Cobb, 19 November 1878, Joseph Smith III Letterbook #2; Joseph Smith to Mrs. D. C. Chase, 7 January 1893, Miscellaneous Letters and Papers, Reorganized Church Library–Archives.

35. Council of Twelve Minutes, 1865–1928, 2 May 1865, p. 11, Reorganized Church Library–Archives.

36. Ibid., 9 April 1867, p. 34.

37. Management of the plurality of gods doctrine has been described in chapter 8, "Forging an Organization." See also Alma R. Blair, "The Reorganized Church of Jesus Christ of Latter Day Saints: Moderate Mormons," in *The Restoration Movement: Essays in Mormon History*, ed. F. Mark McKiernan, Alma R. Blair, and Paul M. Edwards (Lawrence, Kan.: Coronado Press, 1973), pp. 206–30; Roger D. Launius, "Joseph Smith III and the Quest for a Centralized Organization, 1860–1873," in *Restoration Studies II*, ed. Maurice L. Draper and A. Bruce Lindgren (Independence, Mo.: Herald Publishing House, 1983), pp. 104–20.

38. *Saints' Herald* 26 (1 January 1879): 1; "Out of Their Own

Mouths," *Saints' Herald* 26 (15 March 1879): 84–85; Smith, "Last Testimony of Sister Emma," pp. 289–90. Smith's moderate approach to issues has been described in Clare D. Vlahos, "Moderation as a Theological Principle in the Thought of Joseph Smith III," *John Whitmer Historical Association Journal* 1 (1981): 3–11; and Launius, "Joseph Smith III and the Quest for a Centralized Organization, 1860–1873," pp. 104–20.

39. Joseph Smith to Publisher, *Deseret News*, 6 May 1896, Joseph Smith Letterbook #6.

40. Examples of how the prophet applied this approach can be found in Joseph Smith, "A Card from Bro. Joseph Smith," *True Latter Day Saints' Herald* 1 (July 1860): 169–70, particularly the next to last paragraph; Joseph Smith to Charles Strang, 22 July 1882, Joseph Smith III Letterbook #3A. Additionally, Smith may have been motivated by a concern for his fate in the hereafter. Apparently, Smith believed he would have to answer to his father at some future time. As he told E. D. Smith: "Your father is like mine, ever on the other shore; both of us are rapidly going thitherward; the work of our fathers was clear to them; both earnestly engaged in it as the way of life; we shall meet them, and I am going to try to so live that when I may meet them, it will be safe for them to say, 'Joseph, you fought bravely, and though at times the battle seemed to go against you, you rallied well, and we are glad to meet you' " (Joseph Smith to E. D. Smith, 22 July 1896, Joseph Smith III Letterbook #7, Reorganized Church Library–Archives).

41. Joseph Smith to E. L. Kelley, 10 July 1883, E. L. Kelley Papers, Reorganized Church Library–Archives. Joseph Smith was motivated to take his position in favor of his father's innocence concerning plural marriage, also, at least in part, because of what he considered his duty to his father. During this period it was something of a social necessity that a son clear his father's reputation if besmirched without cause. This social background has been described in Stephen Kern, "Explosive Intimacy: Psychodynamics of the Victorian Family," in *The New Psychohistory*, ed. Lloyd deMause (New York: The Psychohistory Press, 1975), pp. 29–53; Peter J. Comins, "Late-Victorian Sexual Respectability and the Social System," *International Review of Social History* 8 (1963): 18–48, 216–50; Phyllis Greenacre, *The Quest for a Father: A Study of the Darwin-Butler Controversy, as a Contribution to the Understanding of the Creative Individual* (New York: Harper and Row, 1963), passim. See also the excellent fictional example of this present in William Faulkner, "An Odor of Verbena," in *The Unvanquished* (New York: Random House, 1965).

42. Joseph Smith to Zenos H. Gurley, 24 July 1879, Joseph Smith III Letterbook #2.

43. Joseph Smith to James Whitehead, 8 September 1884, Joseph Smith III Letterbook #1A; Smith "Memoirs," *Saints' Herald* 83 (18 February 1936): 208–12, 83 (2 June 1936): 689. Smith's brief period of legal training has been described in chapter 3. Smith also served as a justice of the peace while living in Nauvoo between 1858 and 1866, and in Plano, Illinois, prior to 1881.

44. Smith, "Memoirs," *Saints' Herald* 83 (28 April 1936): 530. Alma Blair has analyzed this misconstruing of testimony further in "RLDS Views of Polygamy," p. 20.

45. In writing to J. F. Minton in 1891 Smith commented on this demand for hard evidence: "Don't make statements of which you have not the proof at hand, or know first what it is" (Joseph Smith to J. F. Minton, 13 March 1891, Joseph Smith III Papers, Reorganized Church Library–Archives). See also Joseph Smith to Zenos H. Gurley, 20 August 1879, Joseph Smith III Letterbook #1; Joseph Smith to Zenos H. Gurley, 24 July 1879, Joseph Smith III Letterbook #2. Smith's mother had earlier taken this approach, and he may have adopted it in part because of her attitude. She wrote to Thomas Gregg in 1846, "Everything that has not come within my immediate observation remains doubtful in my mind until some circumstances occur to prove reports either true of false" (Emma Smith to Thomas Gregg, 21 April 1846, Mormon Collection, Chicago Historical Society; Newell and Avery, *Mormon Enigma*, pp. 301–2, 366).

46. Smith, "Memoirs," *Saints' Herald* 83 (24 March 1936): 368.

47. George A. Smith to Joseph Smith, 9 October 1869, Joseph Smith III Papers; Smith, "Memoirs," *Saints' Herald* 81 (8 January 1935): 47–49, 82 (1 October 1935): 1264–66.

48. Gurley's career has been described in Clare D. Vlahos, "The Challenge to Centralized Power: Zenos H. Gurley, Jr., and the Prophetic Office," *Courage: A Journal of History, Thought, and Action* 1 (March 1971): 141–58. His polygamy stand is amply expressed in Zenos H. Gurley to Joseph Smith, 5 December 1873, 23 November 1874, 7 August 1879, Joseph Smith III Papers.

49. *Biographical and Historical Record of Ringold and Decatur Counties, Iowa* (Chicago: Lewis Publishing Co., 1887), pp. 543–44; Charles W. Turner, "Joseph Smith III and the Mormons of Utah" (Ph.D. diss., Graduate Theological Union, 1985), pp. 378–84.

50. Smith, "Memoirs," *Saints' Herald* 83 (11 February 1936): 176.

51. The politics of the county and Gurley's role in it has been described in Alma R. Blair, "A Loss of Nerve," *Courage: A Journal of History, Thought, and Action* 1 (September 1970): 29–36; Roger D. Launius, "The Mormon Quest for a Perfect Society at Lamoni, Iowa, 1870–1890," *The Annals of Iowa* 47 (Spring 1984): 339–41; Roger D. Launius, "Quest for

Zion: Joseph Smith III and Community-Building in the Reorganization, 1860–1900," in *Restoration Studies III*, eds. Maurice L. Draper and Debra Combs (Independence, Mo.: Herald Publishing House, 1986), pp. 327–28.

52. Marks to Butterfield, 1 October 1865; William McLellin to Joseph Smith, July–8 September 1872, Miscellaneous Letters and Papers.

53. W. W. Blair, Journal, 13, 17 June 1874, Reorganized Church Library–Archives; Newell and Avery, *Mormon Enigma*, p. 300.

54. Joseph Smith to Zenos H. Gurley, 15 May 1878, Joseph Smith III Letterbook #1.

55. Joseph Smith to Zenos H. Gurley, 24 July 1879, Joseph Smith III Letterbook #2.

56. Zenos H. Gurley to Joseph Smith, 7 August 1879, Joseph Smith III Papers.

57. He was accompanied by Jason Briggs and several associates. See Vlahos, "Challenge to Centralized Power," pp. 141–58; Alma R. Blair, "The Tradition of Dissent—Jason W. Briggs," in *Restoration Studies I*, ed. Maurice L. Draper and Clare D. Vlahos (Independence, Mo.: Herald Publishing House, 1980), pp. 146–61.

58. Joseph Smith III to William Smith, 11 March 1882, Joseph Smith III Letterbook #3. A similar warning can be found in Joseph Smith to William Smith, 12 July 1879, Letterbook #2.

59. William Smith to Joseph Smith, n.d.; Joseph Smith to William Smith, 26 October 1893, both in Joseph Smith III Papers; William Smith, *William Smith on Mormonism* (Lamoni, Iowa: Herald Publishing House, 1883); Newell and Avery, *Mormon Enigma*, pp. 308–9; Robert D. Hutchins, "Joseph Smith III: Moderate Mormon" (M.A. thesis, Brigham Young University, 1977), pp. 76–77. William Smith's career has been described in Irene M. Bates, "William Smith, 1811–1893: Problematic Patriarch," *Dialogue: A Journal of Mormon Thought* 16 (Summer 1983): 11–23; Paul M. Edwards, "William B. Smith: The Persistent Pretender," *Dialogue: A Journal of Mormon Thought* 18 (Summer 1985): 128–39; E. Gary Smith, "The Patriarchal Crisis of 1845," *Dialogue: A Journal of Mormon Thought* 16 (Summer 1983): 24–39; T. Edgar Lyon, "Nauvoo and the Council of the Twelve," in *The Restoration Movement: Essays in Mormon History*, ed. F. Mark McKiernan, Alma R. Blair, and Paul M. Edwards (Lawrence, Kan.: Coronado Press, 1973), pp. 167–205.

60. These issues have been best addressed in Blair, "RLDS Views of Polygamy," pp. 16–28 and Howard, "Changing RLDS Response to Mormon Polygamy," pp. 14–29.

10

The Utah Mission

At the same time that church authorities disagreed over the origin of plural marriage, the Saints seemed to agree that the Reorganized Church should prosecute a vigorous missionary program and "rescue" those Latter Day Saints enmeshed in what Reorganized Church members believed were "evil practices." Accordingly, Joseph Smith presided over an organization bent on the destruction of all vestiges of plural marriage within the Mormon movement and the cleansing of its stigma from the memory of the church. He wanted to bring the church back from what he considered a gross apostasy, to eliminate all evil in society, and to gain the friendship of other Christian leaders while maintaining the church's individual character.[1] When Joseph Smith joined the Reorganization in 1860, he told the general conference that he held the highest regard for the people who had accepted the leadership of Brigham Young in 1844 and followed him to Utah. He thought they had been misled and were controlled by tyranny. All the Reorganized Church had to do to redeem these people was to offer an alternative, pointing out the errors of plural marriage and other "Utah doctrines."[2]

As a result of these rather simplistic beliefs, the Reorganization prophet undertook a program designed to return the whole of Mormonism to what he thought had been the "pure principles" taught during the 1830s and 1840s. This decision thrust Smith and his sect into the forefront of a national quest to bring Mormonism into line with accepted Christian teachings, principally through the destruction of the institution of plural marriage and the lessening of the Mormon church's political and economic power in Utah. This reformation movement of the latter half of the nineteenth century consisted of diverse elements and strategies. As in the antislavery movement of the first half of the century, the individuals working to solve the "Utah Question" ranged from pious cranks to skilled politicians. Since their motives were oftentimes different and they rarely agreed about methods, they formed an uneasy alliance, to be sure, but one that the Reorganized Church accepted and in time joined fully.[3]

Under Joseph Smith the Reorganized Church participated in this crusade by initiating a two-sided policy toward the Utah Mormon movement that remained in effect with little change, other than emphasis, for over thirty years. The first part of this policy aimed at reconciliation with and conversion of Utah Latter-day Saints, emphasizing the necessity of reforming Mormonism to reflect the purity of the gospel as taught in the early church. The second part of the policy strove for the subjugation of the Utah Mormon church through legal means by working with legislators to pass and enforce antipolygamy legislation and to destroy the political and economic power of Brigham Young's movement. In essence, the first part of Smith's policy was one of the open, velvet-gloved hand, the second part was one of a steel-gloved fist.[4]

These two phases of Smith's Mormon policy operated simultaneously, two sides of the same coin. The attempts at reconciliation and conversion were successful in some measure—several hundred Utah Latter-day Saints were converted to the Reorganization during the Gilded Age—but these successes were at best inconclusive. Therefore, as missionary activities in Utah proved less than fully satisfactory, Smith began to expend more effort in working with other antipolygamists to destroy the practice and Mormon power through federal legislation. The remainder of this chapter will deal with the first part of this antipolygamy policy, the missionary efforts of the Reorganization.[5]

Soon after his ordination Smith forcefully took control of the conciliatory aspects of his Utah policy. Under his direction the church published numerous tracts, pamphlets, magazine articles, and books designed to point out the error of plural marriage to the Saints of the Rocky Mountains. In addition, Smith and others in the

Reorganization made every effort to publicize the church's opinion concerning polygamy to the non-Mormon world in secular periodicals. They also sought to explain the other differences between the two Mormon churches and to cast the Reorganized Church in the best possible light, educating those outside the movement about the religion and demonstrating that the Reorganized Church stood squarely within orthodox American Christianity.[6]

In carrying out this program Smith rarely acted vindictively. He always claimed that his goal was only to educate both the non-Mormons and the Saints of the Great Basin about the errors that had been introduced into the Mormon religion. Early in his presidency Smith worked steadily toward the time when missionaries from the Reorganization would be able to go to Utah personally to work with the people there and bring them back to "orthodox Mormonism."[7] Smith's public attitude toward the Utah Saints was very tolerant—in fact, so tolerant that some Reorganized Church members got the impression that he planned to unite the two churches immediately after his ordination by settling in Utah and taking over. This was, of course, completely without justification, but it became such a widespread rumor that Smith felt compelled to respond to it in the columns of the *True Latter Day Saints' Herald*. He told the Saints that he did not accept the doctrines of the Utah Mormons and that he wished only to aid in bringing them back into the "true gospel." He completely discounted the rumor that he was going to Salt Lake City to unite with Brigham Young, adding, "to those who know me, it is needless for me to state that I am not going to do any such thing while the doctrine of polygamy and disobedience to the laws of the United States are countenanced there."[8]

During the April 1863 general conference Joseph Smith implemented his conciliatory approach in a more tangible manner when he persuaded the body to open a mission to Utah. The mission to the most populous of the factions that had emerged following the death of Joseph Smith, Jr., had been a long time coming. For years there had been importunings from certain residents of the Utah Territory asking for the Reorganization to send ministers into the region. It was reported in 1863, for example, that church officials had received over 500 letters from the Salt Lake Valley alone, "urging young Joseph to send missionaries there."[9] Thus the hands rising in silent affirmation of the resolution providing for two missionaries to be sent to Utah signified for many the coming of age of the Reorganization: the reformed church was finally beginning to call back the scattered elements of the Mormon movement.

The missionaries to be sent into Utah were to preach a three-pronged message of salvation. Their first theme was that the true successor to Joseph Smith, Jr., that is, his eldest son, had taken his rightful place in the presidency of the Reorganized Church. Their second assertion was that Brigham Young was an usurper of authority who ruled as a dictator without legal or spiritual authority. Indeed, a missionary tract published for the Utah Saints summarized this point: "Brethren, you are now without a prophet in the flesh to guide you." Finally, the ministers' last major theme categorically denounced plural marriage as a false doctrine and a means whereby Young held his followers in a bondage every bit as evil and horrible as southern slavery.[10]

The men chosen by Joseph Smith III to open the Utah mission were extremely capable. Edmund C. Briggs, a recently ordained member of the Twelve Apostles, headed the missionary team. He had achieved dazzling success in Iowa in the early years of the Reorganization, baptizing over 100 new members and organizing six new branches.[11] He brought a peculiar brand of religious conviction, missionary skill, and administrative ability to the mission. Originally C. C. McIntosh was to have accompanied Briggs but for some reason was unable to undertake the mission and was replaced by Alexander McCord. McCord had been a member of the early church, had served as a sergeant in the Mormon Battalion in 1846–47, and after being mustered out of the service had settled in Utah, only to become completely disillusioned and bitter over what he considered the excesses of church government under Brigham Young and the apostles. As a result, McCord returned to the Midwest in 1847 and later joined the Reorganized Church when its missionaries visited his home near Galland's Grove, Iowa.[12] These two men were to be only the opening wave of Reorganization missionaries sent by Joseph Smith to Utah. Briggs, for instance, left with the expectation that three or four more men would follow within a few months.[13]

Briggs and McCord left the Midwest in July 1863 and, after traversing some 1,000 miles by wagon, arrived in the "City of the Saints" on 7 August 1863.[14] They promptly began to preach in the streets of Salt Lake City. "Arise, shake off your sins; turn once again to the Lord and serve him with all your might and strength," they proclaimed to its inhabitants. But this call to repentance made by two dusty and trail-worn street preachers did little to endear them to the church leaders in the city, and soon it provoked action to stop the missionary endeavors.[15]

On 11 August Brigham Young and about thirty other members of the hierarchy held a meeting with Briggs and McCord. The Reorganization missionaries declared their purpose for being in the territory and asked for permission to speak in the Latter-day Saint Tabernacle and meeting houses. They were forbidden to preach in any building in the territory; in fact, Young and his advisors warned the two that they might not even be safe on the streets of Salt Lake City and that the Utahans "would not be responsible for [their lives] on the streets for a single hour."[16] With enmity clearly showing between the two factions, the meeting broke and the missionaries declared that they would continue their work no matter what the price.

In addition to preaching, both in the streets and in a few homes of non-Mormons, Briggs began writing for the non-Mormon periodicals in the area. In the *Daily Union Vendette*, published at Fort Douglas, Utah, an army post, Briggs outlined the main tenets of the Reorganization and asked for a greater opportunity to speak to the inhabitants of the region. At this same time, Briggs sent McCord to begin missionary work in Ogden, a Mormon community about forty miles north of Salt Lake City, while he continued working in the core area.[17]

A few weeks after arriving, Briggs attended a religious meeting in which Brigham Young addressed his people on the subject of the Reorganization. In the course of the sermon, Briggs arose and defended his movement—an act of either great courage or unmitigated foolhardiness. Neither Young nor the others in the meeting could silence him, and only after the police had arrived was order restored. As the police escorted Briggs from the building, he is said to have turned to the officer next to him and commented that "he recognized his authority but not that of Brigham Young."[18] Notwithstanding the limited opportunities with which Briggs had to contend in Salt Lake City, he was moderately successful and held the first baptismal service for the Reorganized Church in Utah in the city on 6 September 1863. At that time sixteen people joined his movement, and during the following month Briggs was able to add another four to that total.[19]

In November 1863 Edmund Briggs baptized possibly the most important convert to come out of the initial missionary visit to Utah —George P. Dykes. Dykes was immediately ordained an elder and began preparing for missionary service. As a longtime resident of Utah and a highly capable and devout convert, Dykes was able to talk to many people in the region who would have refused to listen to outsiders like Briggs and McCord. Largely through his assistance the membership of the Utah mission grew from zero in August 1863 to over 300 by the spring of 1864. In late 1863 Dykes also opened the California mission for the Reorganized Church and was highly successful there as well.[20]

On 26 January 1864 McCord and Briggs proudly officiated in Joseph Smith's stead at the organization of a branch of the church in Salt Lake City, a congregation that grew from thirty-five members to over 100 by 6 April 1864.[21] That same April these missionaries presided over the organization of the Utah district and the ordination of several men to priesthood offices, thus creating an able local leadership base. This activity marked the beginning of the first continuous religious activities held in the territory by any group other than Utah Latter-day Saints.[22]

The Reorganized Church continued to grow effectively during the remainder of Briggs's stay in Utah. Before he left, on 12 August 1864—when he went to California to review the activities underway there—Briggs reported back to Joseph Smith, commenting that he was "happy to inform [him] that the work of the Lord in this territory is onward with rapid strides to the spiritual observer, and I feel every day more and more encouraged with the prospects before me of the triumph of the gospel of Jesus."[23] The first Reorganized Church mission to Utah had been moderately successful, and Joseph Smith was quite pleased. Indeed, upon reflection it appeared that Briggs and McCord had succeeded beyond all expectation. Edmund's brother, Jason Briggs, writing about the first mission some ten years later, remarked somewhat caustically, "The footprints of the first missionaries of the Reorganized are still visible, and all the soft soap of the Tabernacle works can not wash them out."[24]

During the next several years Smith kept missionaries operating throughout the Great Basin. They converted hundreds of Utah Mormons to the Reorganization by preaching the same threefold message: the true successor to Joseph Smith, Jr.—that is, his eldest son—had taken his rightful place in the presidency of the church; Brigham Young was an usurper of authority who ruled as a dictator; plural marriage was a false doctrine and a means whereby Young held his followers in bondage. The converts gained for the Reorganization became some of the most effective leaders of the movement—including Edmund C. Brand, Glaud Rodger, and Charles W. Wandell, all of whom made significant contributions in the church's mission fields.[25] Although these later Reorganization missionaries, like Briggs and McCord, were moderately successful, Smith was disappointed that the Reorganization did not seem to be building a viable organization in the Great Basin.

Smith realized that there were several reasons for the only moderate success in the Utah mission. Without a doubt the Utah Mormon authorities tolerated a certain amount of unofficial persecution of Reorganized Church converts by their former brethren. In all cases converts were likely to be subjected to several forms of economic pressure: if one worked for another Latter-day Saint, he might be fired from his job; or if one owned a business, Mormons might boycott it. Additionally, a convert's children could be teased by their peers and the entire family ostracized. Occasionally converts reported that they had been physically threatened although instances of actual violence were rare. But each of these actions served to discourage Utah Mormons from joining the Reorganization, even if they were initially attracted to the movement.[26] Consequently, those who decided to affiliate with the Reorganization quickly found Utah a very inhospitable place to live, and nearly every spring during the 1860s, after the mountain passes cleared sufficiently for safe travel, wagon trains of converts left for the more attractive Midwest. During one winter in the 1860s virtually the entire village of Coalville, Utah, consisted of Reorganized Church converts who wintered there in anticipation of returning eastward in the spring. This exodus hindered the Reorganization's efforts toward building standing congregations in the territory during the first decade of missionary work there.[27]

As a direct result of this apparent lack of success, Joseph Smith asked the 1866 general conference to appoint his younger brother,

Alexander Hale Smith, as the head of the Pacific Slope mission, which included the Great Basin. Smith believed that the stature of the martyr's son functioning for the Reorganization in Utah would intensify the missionary effort and help build a solid base of Latter Day Saints in the intermountain West. Accepting this call, Alexander Smith and two companions left Nauvoo, Illinois, on 20 May 1866 for the West, arriving in Salt Lake City during the late summer. As Smith had hoped, the Mormons did want to see the martyr's son, and they flocked to hear his first sermons in Salt Lake City. Brigham Young grew increasingly concerned about this development and told his followers on several occasions to avoid these "heretics." Almost immediately, attendance at Alexander's meetings dropped, causing the missionaries to journey to California for the winter because of the more cheery prospects there. Just before the snows closed the passes, Alexander Smith slipped over the Hastings Cutoff to carry on missionary work in the Golden State, not to return to Utah for another three years.[28]

In 1869 Joseph Smith began another phase of the Reorganized Church's missionary program in Utah. He sent both his brothers, Alexander and David Smith, to the territory on an extensive missionary venture. The prophet designated Alexander mission president; twenty four-year-old David would presumably act as evangelist, igniting interest in the Reorganization with his sermons. Whereas Alexander looked like a younger edition of his older brother—medium height, portly, brown hair, deep penetrating eyes, full beard, and a less-than-entrancing speaking ability—David eerily reminded most people of his dead father. Tall, slim, and light-complected, David even possessed, it was said, many of his father's mannerisms. He displayed acute sensitivities which he expressed beautifully in poetry, art, and music, but most important for this trip was his charming charisma.[29] It was said that, even though unprepared, he could stand before a crowd and move them to tears or laughter with his eloquent speech. Neither of the older Smith boys had such personal appeal as David, and Joseph had apparently called him to this mission to capture the interest and good will of the people of Salt Lake City.

Born on 17 November 1844, eleven days after his brother Joseph's twelfth birthday, David Hyrum Smith had never known his father. He had been considered at birth a child of promise by the Nauvoo Saints, "a means of performing a Mighty work for the glory of God and Prince Forever," as Zina Huntington had recorded at the time. These mystical expectations did not die easily, and Joseph presumably sought to capitalize on them in the Great Basin by sending his brother there in 1869.[30] Joseph had already experienced David's magnetism in 1863 when some of the Saints asserted that Joseph should abdicate his position as church president in favor of his younger brother. Although David never entertained notions that he could demand the presidency from Joseph, the matter was an issue of some importance until David published an eloquent poem in the April 1863 issue of the *True Latter Day Saints' Herald* called "A Word of Advice to Those Who Look for Me to Be the Prophet."

Little Herald, stop a moment
    Ere you journey on your way;
I have something of importance
    That I wish that you would say
Unto those who, not contented
    With the leader God hath sent,
Still declare that I shall lead them,
    Though I gave them no consent.

Go and tell them I am loyal
    To the Counsels of the Lord;
Tell them I have no desire
    To dispute His mighty word.
Joseph is the Chosen Prophet
    Well ordained in God's clear sight;
Should he lose it by transgression,
    Alexander has the right.

Joseph, Alexander, David,
    Three remaining pillars still;
Like the three remaining columns
    Of the Temple on the hill!
Joseph's star is full and shining,
    Alexander's more than mine;
Mine is just below the mountain,
    Bide its time and it will shine.[31]

Without doubt, this unequivocal statement ended any speculation by members of the Reorganized Church about David's succession of his brother. While David was in Utah in 1869, however, this question arose among the Mormons there, and he just as unequivocably laid it to rest, telling an interviewer of the *Utah Daily Reporter*, "My free will, independence, unfaltering service, faith, and influence, I give to my brother Joseph." [32]

The Smith brothers arrived in Utah aboard the newly completed transcontinental railway, reaching Salt Lake City on 15 July 1869. They soon learned that there was a municipal law against preaching in the streets. Only somewhat disappointed with this development, they began searching for a building where they would be welcome. They knew that upon a few occasions the Tabernacle had been made available for preaching, and arranged an interview with Brigham Young to ask permission for its use. They called upon Young at the appointed time but were kept waiting for more than two hours. When finally ushered into Young's office, the two young men found Young and some twenty others waiting for them. A debate followed for some time thereafter, with Young calling Emma Smith "the damndest liar that ever lived" and condemning the Reorganized Church. When he finally responded to the original request for the use of the Tabernacle, Young reportedly said, "No, David, we do not think it best to let you have the tabernacle." [33]

Instead, the Smith brothers accepted offers to speak in buildings owned by the anti-Mormon Walker brothers, substantial businessmen in Salt Lake City, and in the hall of William S. Godbe and his followers, the Liberal Institute.[34] They remained in Salt Lake City from 15 July until 23 August 1969, preaching in these buildings. Then they took a short trip to Malad, Idaho, where there was a thriving Reorganized Church congregation. There followed some three months of solid missionary work in Salt Lake City. David did most of the speaking and attendance was usually excellent. His eloquent preaching services became one of the great social and intellectual events of the city; the Mormons who saw him generally concluded he was the most impressive of the martyr's sons. He tried to be tactful in his sermons and communicated with less hostility than had most other Reorganization ministers, including his brother Alexander.[35] These efforts were moderately successful, and the Salt Lake City congregation grew larger.

After several months of preaching, on 5 December 1869 the Smith brothers boarded a train for San Francisco. While there, a sudden illness incapacitated young David and brought his mission to a close. They moved from place to place to help David's recovery. Finally, although David did show some improvement, Alexander cut the mission short after receiving word that his wife was dangerously ill. It was just as well, for when Alexander returned to Illinois in March 1870, David was still too incapacitated by illness for the field.[36]

When Joseph met his brothers at the local train station, he was naturally worried about what might become of David. Alexander had wired ahead about the condition, and rumors about the young man's illness were circulating throughout the area. Joseph apparently blamed himself for sending his talented younger brother to Utah and subjecting him to such disease, for he took David to his home and patiently nursed him back to health. Within a few months David had recovered sufficiently to return to missionary work for the church, but Joseph tried to lighten his religious duties to allow eventual full recovery.[37]

Although David seemed to be fine for several years after this undefined and debilitating illness, and even undertook additional missions to Utah, without warning in 1876 he suffered a relapse. Joseph once again kept David at his home, trying to nurse the young man back to health. His efforts this time failed, however; David's illness grew worse and he became unmanageable. At times he seemed perfectly rational, but at other times he seemed to imagine all manner of wild things. Once, for instance, David left the Smith home and went to the Plano telegraph office, where he cabled the home office of the Atlantic and Pacific Railroad to send him the Board of Directors' official train. In 1876, after David had begun to grow violent and had threatened several members of the Smith family, Joseph took steps to commit his brother to a hospital where he could be cared for professionally. Consequently, in January 1877 Joseph reluctantly allowed David to be committed to the State Asylum for the Insane at Elgin, Illinois. He remained there the rest of his life, passing away in this hospital in 1904. Upon learning of David's confinement, several Utah Mormon officials accused Joseph Smith of locking his brother away so that he could never be a challenge to the prophetic office, but this charge was groundless, for no one who had seen David Smith during his last months outside the hospital doubted that he was mentally disturbed.[38]

Throughout his younger brother's illness, Joseph Smith continued to carry on his plans for the conversion of the Latter-day Saints in Utah. Alexander had been singularly ineffective as a mission president, and from about 1873 on David was too incapacitated to continue work there. Accordingly, during the early 1870s Smith had sent other ministers to Utah to continue this work. The most effective of these was Jason W. Briggs, president of the Quorum of Twelve, who journeyed to the Great Basin in 1874 to take over direction of the Utah mission. In November 1874 he founded the Reorganization's first newspaper in Salt Lake City, *The Messenger*, which for a time was a forceful voice for Smith's movement in the Great Basin. But Briggs became increasingly unorthodox during his missionary stint in Utah and had to be recalled. He returned to his home in Fremont County, Iowa, on 2 July 1877.[39]

Joseph Smith decided that, to continue effective ministry in Utah, he would have to go there himself. During his nineteenth-century career, Joseph Smith made four trips to Utah. The first only a few weeks long, took place in the late fall of 1876. The second, as well as the most extensive, took place during the summer and fall of 1885. In both of these Smith spent considerable time attending to church affairs and preaching to the Mormons. The latter two trips were not nearly as involved. The third trip took place during the winter of 1887–88, but Joseph Smith remained in Utah only a few days and had very little contact with people outside the church and his family. Last, Smith went to Utah in 1889, met with political leaders and his cousins, but held virtually no speaking engagements. These trips educated Joseph Smith about the conditions in Utah and helped him understand the reasons behind the Reorganized Church's only moderate successes there. The first two trips seemed to be missions to convert the Mormons. When his own efforts, like those of earlier missionaries, failed to win many converts, Smith recognized that the Reorganization's message did not entice the Mormons the way he had hoped. After 1885, he apparently shifted drastically his approach toward the "Utah Question," and his latter two trips to Utah were aimed more at political ends.[40]

Even while still looking after David in his home, in 1876 Joseph made plans to attend a church reunion—a family-centered religious retreat lasting about one week—scheduled for the late summer at Santa Ana, California. Although he planned to spend most of his time in California, Smith decided to return to Plano by way of Salt Lake City and attend to missionary work there. When Smith arrived in California in August 1876, he made the rounds of the Saints, preaching in homes, schools, public buildings, and the Reorganization's chapels at every opportunity. To build good will for his movement, he visited many of the most important secular and religious leaders of the state. In addition, Smith went into several of the Mormon settlements, particularly San Bernadino, a city that had been founded by the Mormons a quarter century earlier, to preach to the followers of Brigham Young. As always when ministering to those inside the Utah movement, Smith taught the three-fold message developed by the Reorganization nearly fifteen years earlier. He pointed out the errors of Young's authoritarian regime, the evil of polygamy, and lauded the legitimacy of the Reorganization. By 1 November 1876 Smith had completed his work in California and embarked on a train for the East. Although he stopped in Carson City, Nevada Territory, for several days to visit and preach to the miners in the region, Smith soon pushed on toward his important and dramatic appointment in Salt Lake City. At last the leader of the principal Mormon dissenting movement was invading the stronghold of the largest faction of the church.[41]

The train from Nevada bearing Joseph Smith arrived in Ogden on 22 November. Peter Reinsimar, a recent convert to the Reorganization, met him at the train station and drove him in his wagon to his Salt Lake City home. As he traveled through the city to the Reinsimar home, he surveyed the "City of the Saints" and concluded that it was a tidy, attractive place in which to live. But he immediately saw that the people living there avoided him either because he represented the Reorganized Church or because they were naturally clannish. Smith wrote to his teenage daughter about the "cold-shoulder" he received from many of the people of Salt Lake City, commenting that "almost everybody one sees on the street is shy, and does not appear so frank and fearless as in Plano."[42]

It was just as well that most people in Salt Lake City ignored Smith during his first days there, for the arid, cold mountain climate had caused him to have the first of many attacks of neuralgia. Smith had never experienced such excruciating pain before, and although he recovered sufficiently to go about his duties quickly, the ailment flared up periodically ever after. Known as the "suicide sickness" during the nineteenth century because the terrible pain presumably drove the sufferer to suicide, the largely hereditary disease was caused by a nerve growing directly into the skull without the usual tissue shielding it from contact with the bone. It was particularly painful whenever the weather changed dramatically, and sometimes even when it did not, making it difficult for the sufferer to talk, eat, or even move his head. In 1876 virtually nothing could be done to treat the malady; those unfortunate enough to inherit it just had to suffer. Because of his illness Smith could do very little during his first week in Salt Lake City except catch up on his correspondence, study, rest, and see a few visitors.[43]

Some individuals, however, were excited that Smith had come to Salt Lake City. For instance, the day after his arrival the *Salt Lake Tribune,* a non-Mormon controlled publication that had proven a source of turbulence for Brigham Young and his lieutenants since its initiation, published a notice of Smith's arrival:

> Joseph Smith, Jr., the true head of the Mormon Church, arrived in this city yesterday from the West, and is now stopping with Mr. Peter Reinsimar of the Eighth Ward. We welcome him to Utah, and feel sure for him and his co-laborers. Thousands of Mormons who had been swindled and deceived by the arch impostor, Brigham Young, are now awakening to the fact that he intends to perpetuate his own dynasty by the elevation of his two unworthy sons to the highest place in the Church. But his followers are not prepared for quite so much slavery and they will revolt. The time for Joseph Smith, Jr., to put in the sickle is come, and we trust he will do it vigorously, that the power of Brigham may be broken.[44]

The next day the *Tribune* sent a reporter to interview Smith at Reinsimar's home, and a lengthy and favorable article was published in the 24 November edition of the newspaper. The reporter asked the prophet a variety of questions about his church, his career as religious leader, and about his visit to the Great Basin. Smith told him that he sought to reclaim the lost Saints of the Mormon religion, to show them the heinous nature of their practices, and to bring them back into the pure Latter Day Saint religion that had been taught by his father and that was still a part of the Reorganization. The reporter commented: "That part of the Mormon people in Utah who have not yet compromised themselves by becoming polygamists, he thinks will be ready to listen to him and weigh the reasons he presents. It is his intention also to visit his cousins, who are quite numerous in Zion, and many of whom occupy positions in the priesthood under Brigham Young."[45]

Within two weeks of this interview Smith had recovered sufficiently to begin his espoused purpose, scheduling a series of four preaching services at the Liberal Institute. This organization had been founded by the Godbeite splinter group from Young's church. William S. Godbe had rejected Young's "tyrannic" rule, and with the support of several influential writers, newspapermen, intellectuals, and businessmen had founded the institute as an alternative to Young's theocracy. The institute fostered intellectual freedom in both thought and expression and offered a safe haven for dissenters of every stripe from Mormonism. At one time or another during its existence, virtually every Mormon or pseudo-Mormon with a real or imagined grievance against Utah Mormonism preached in the Liberal Institute. Joseph Smith, of course, was only one such person among many. That orthodox Mormons disliked the Liberal Institute and all it stood for seems obvious. Charles Walker, a fearless supporter of Brigham Young and Mormon orthodoxy, expressed the feelings of most Latter-day Saints toward the Liberal Institute. "Now those who pretend to worship at the Liberal Institute," he wrote in his diary, "are chiefly apostate. . . . They think they are especial favorites of God, and the entire Church of God and its leaders are all wrong and have gone astray and are continually finding fault with the chosen of God, and are trying all in their power to shed the blood of the Lords anointed and despoil the saints of their peaceful homes and bring trouble and destruction upon the Saints of God."[46] Joseph Smith, contrary to the remarks of Walker, found the Liberal Institute an oasis of religious investigation in a desert of narrow ideas. He delighted in the services held there, preaching to a few eager Reorganized Church members who had come from miles around to hear their prophet, a wide variety of interested non-Mormons, some disgruntled Latter-day Saints, and an assortment of curious listeners who apparently came to see the son of the great Mormon prophet.[47]

While Joseph Smith stayed in the city, several of his relatives met with him informally. For the most part none of his Utah cousins had seen Joseph since the summer of 1860, and the reunion was heartwarming for all. The first relative that Joseph met was John

Smith, oldest son of Hyrum and presiding patriarch of the Mormon church. They spent an afternoon together discussing their boyhoods in Nauvoo, their growing families, and other noncontroversial subjects. In their conversation they avoided topics touching on the Mormon religion, plural marriage, and Brigham Young's leadership. Other relatives also invited Joseph into their homes for brief visits; again in most cases Joseph refrained from discussing religious differences.

One relative in the Great Basin, however, seemed to avoid Joseph during his first weeks in Salt Lake City. Joseph F. Smith, an apostle in the movement and the member of the family with the most authority in the Mormon hierarchy, was antagonistic toward the Reorganization and had taken a lead in defending plural marriage from its attack. He had begun in 1869 collecting evidence of Joseph Smith, Jr.'s involvement in the institution, and eventually compiled several hundred affidavits of witnesses and other documents demonstrating his complicity. Considerable animosity apparently existed between Joseph Smith and this Utah cousin. Joseph F. Smith may also have shunned Joseph Smith III because of comments attributed to the Reorganized Church president in the *Tribune*. In discussing the succession question of the Utah Mormon church, Smith had told a *Tribune* reporter that he thought that when Brigham Young died several men could assert claims to the prophetic office. Smith believed that Brigham Young, Jr., known derogatorily as "the fat boy"; John Taylor, the able president of the Twelve Apostles; and Joseph F. Smith would each try to attain the office. But Smith accused his cousin of hungering for power, for he "will claim the leadership, as the most faithful one nearest of kin to the original prophet." Joseph F. may well have been upset by this obvious defamation.[48]

Smith did finally meet and talk with his cousin, but he did so under rather unexpected circumstances. Smith had scheduled a meeting in a rented auditorium in the northern part of the city in December, expecting the same type of modest turnout he had previously attracted at the Liberal Institute and at other sites. When he arrived, however, he found a house packed with orthodox Mormons, government officials, and other dignitaries. Smith recognized in the audience an ex-territorial governor of Utah, the territorial secretary, several judges, a few attorneys, and local officials. Suddenly, as Smith was surveying this assembly, the back door opened and Joseph F. Smith stepped inside. Smith watched as the Mormon leader glanced around the room and casually strolled up the center aisle to the front pew, where seven middle-aged women appeared to be saving him a seat. Joseph Smith felt a sinking feeling as he concluded from this scene that his cousin had come to this meeting to debate him about plural marriage and that the women in the front row were probably ladies who claimed to have been married to his father in Nauvoo.

The service began promptly at half past seven, and the room was silent as Smith arose to speak. He recited his familiar speech setting "forth plainly the views of the Reorganized Church upon marriage and the marriage relation." He argued that his father, to his knowledge, had not taught plural marriage, but even had he done so, it was still counter to everything that Christianity held most dear and therefore a false doctrine. At every point in his sermon Smith expected to be interrupted by his cousin, but neither he nor anyone else heckled him or made any attempt to rebut his argument. When he had finished, he asked if the audience had any questions, fully expecting his cousin to rise in response, but again nothing happened. When the meeting adjourned the seven women in the front row left quietly and Joseph F. Smith came up to pay his respects, neither condoning nor condemning the Reorganized Church's president's remarks.[49]

During this first meeting with Joseph F. Smith, the Reorganized Church prophet was invited to have dinner with his cousin. This was perhaps Joseph Smith's first close-up look at polygamy. When Smith arrived at his cousin's pleasant Salt Lake City home, the two chatted for a little while before supper was announced. When they went into the dining room Smith was introduced to his three hostesses, all plural wives of Joseph F. Smith. Smith recorded his impression in his memoirs:

> To me the situation in which I found myself seemed very strange. For the first time in my life I was permitted to see thus at close range the domestic relations of a polygamous family and the actual operation of a doctrine which had so long been unspeakably repulsive to me. The very fibers of my being seemed to cry out in protest, and so strong was my prejudice and antipathy that I seemed to feel almost physically ill as I contemplated the scene. There, at one board, sat

a complacent man, surrounded by three wives and a large number
of children—just how many I do not now recall, though I seem to
remember that he had some there who belonged to his deceased sister
Sarah.

Smith admitted that although he had gone to Utah with a heavy bias
against plural marriage this incident galvanized it even further.[50]

A few days after this incident, on 11 December 1876, Smith departed Salt Lake City to return to Illinois, reaching home a few days
before Christmas. His first western mission had lasted just over five
months, and while it had been a difficult trip, Smith believed it
had been rewarding. He had traveled thousands of miles by every
conceivable means of transportation of the period, had preached
over seventy times, and had baptized ten new members. More important, perhaps, Smith had visited Utah for the first time, giving
clear proof that the sons of the prophet stood as one in condemnation of Brigham Young's movement and in offering the Utah Saints
a viable alternative religion. While Smith's brief visit in Salt Lake
City did not yield impressive numbers of converts immediately, he
counted it a successful venture for it gave him an opportunity to
learn more about the people and to open doors that would one day,
he believed, serve to convert thousands to the Reorganization.[51]

Joseph Smith's 1876 visit to Salt Lake City came at a crucial
time in the history of the Latter-day Saint movement. Smith was
the acknowledged successor of his father, and even Brigham Young
had stated publicly that he would welcome him to the movement if
he repented of the evil designs the Utah Saints thought him propa-
gating through the Reorganization. By this time Young had grown
old and feeble, and everyone in the Great Basin knew that he would
die soon and that a successor would have to be chosen. Several candidates were readily available, and there was no reason to believe
that Smith could not be one of them. While in Salt Lake City, perhaps in an effort to hint at his availability, he had told a reporter
from the *Tribune* that while John Taylor, Brigham Young, Jr., and
Joseph F. Smith could all make strong cases for their succession to
the presidency, "the successful claimant will be a man chosen by
the people themselves." Again, there was no reason to believe that
Smith could not be that person, reforming the Mormon church and
uniting the factions under the theology of the Reorganization.[52]

An opportunity to make a significant step in this direction presented itself in the late summer of 1877. The question of succession in the presidency, already an important issue for the Latter-day Saints, emerged as the critical concern of the church when Brigham Young died on 29 August 1877.[53] Immediately after his burial several claimants came forward vying for control of the church, and the central administration that had functioned so effectively under Young was unable to settle the question promptly. Young had very much wanted to appoint Brigham, Jr., to succeed him, but many in the church's hierarchy opposed the establishment of a dynasty, so the matter was not formally resolved for several years.[54]

During the succession struggle following Young's death, Joseph Smith's name arose as a candidate for the prophetic office, although it was not seriously considered in official circles. L. R. Freeman of Ogden, Utah, wrote Smith in September 1877, explaining that the Mormon hierarchy was in chaos and that, with his prestige as the son of the prophet and the designated successor to the presidency, he might come to Utah, proclaim his authority, and take over. While always interested in such schemes, Smith saw little chance of success and never seriously considered the matter after returning from the territory in 1876. "There are three sides of this question," he replied to Freeman, "the church in Utah, the element called there the outsiders or Gentiles, and the one we occupy as a church." He went on to explain that "what may seem feasible and proper from your standing ground, may not be so from ours, all things considered." Smith did not categorically dismiss Freeman's idea, however, concluding only that "the times are ominous and changes are imminent."[55]

Smith apparently considered returning to Utah during the next several weeks but could not reach a firm decision. For instance, he wrote to Judge J. B. Van Cleave in Chicago on 13 September explaining that he had not yet decided what course to pursue but that there was a possibility that he might go to the Great Basin to carry out a reunification and reformation of Mormonism. By December Joseph's caution had all but paralyzed him, but he tried to discount his indecision. He wrote to Magnus Fyrando, a Reorganized Church missionary in Utah, that he would make no trips to the area until the next spring. When spring came, however, Smith put off making a decision once more. All the while the Utah church presidency was far from settled. Finally, the opportunity—if it had actually existed, which was unlikely—slipped away, for John Taylor was ordained president in late 1880 after more than three years of indecision and interim church government. In later years Joseph regretted having been so hesitant, whimsically wishing that he had acted more forcefully but thankful that the Reorganization was still intact and growing.[56]

Having chosen, probably wisely, not to become involved in the Mormon succession controversy, Smith waited several years before returning to the Great Basin for missionary activity. In the interim his missionaries had continued their efforts there and in California, enjoying moderate success among the Latter-day Saints. Perhaps it was appropriate that Smith did not return to Utah for almost a decade. During his first visit he had discovered that the Mormon authorities were not the autocrats he had expected, that the people there followed them willingly, and that the people as a whole had embraced and defended the practice of plural marriage. He realized that Utah was not the fruitful field he had anticipated.[57]

Finally, however, on 12 June 1885 Joseph Smith did leave Lamoni, Iowa, on a Union Pacific train for Utah. After arriving there he met often with the Reorganization members, held several public meetings in a rented opera house in the heart of Salt Lake City, and met with his relatives. In many respects Smith found a city very different from what he had experienced in 1876. He noted that everyone seemed more open and friendly and there did not appear to be the siege mentality that had previously cast a gloomy tint over the entire territory in spite of federal efforts to end polygamy. John Taylor was much more tolerant of conflicting viewpoints than had been his predecessor, allowing his followers to believe and say very much as they wished. The result was a blossoming of society that impressed Smith greatly. He engaged in a constant round of missionary activities, took every opportunity to meet residents of the city, and relaxed by visiting some of the tourist attractions. In late July, for example, he went to an exclusive resort on the Great Salt Lake. He wrote to his daughter about his afternoon's dip in the lake, saying "it is hard to swim in it, though one can stand up, lie down in it and float. Large as I am, I could hardly sink in it. It is considered the fashionable thing here to go to the lake."[58]

Early in August 1885 Smith and some companions left Salt Lake

City to visit other parts of Utah Territory and meet the Saints there. He took a two-month trip through Ogden and went as far north as Butte, Montana, returning to Salt Lake City on 1 October. Upon his return he continued his extensive round of interviews, speaking engagements, and social activities. After a stay in Mormon country of several months, Smith determined that he should return to Lamoni and resume his administrative duties. He arrived home just before New Year's Day 1886, somewhat discouraged that his mission did not prove any more successful than the trip in 1876.[59]

Joseph Smith returned to Utah again in late 1887, but this time he stayed in Salt Lake City less than a month, to meet with a few old friends, associates, and gadflies, before journeying on to California. The trip should probably be considered more a personal and social visit than a missionary sojourn, for Smith held only a few religious services. He later recalled that "I made no effort to reach many outside our own circles on this winter visit to Salt Lake City, but enjoyed my stay there very much, indeed." Toward the end of January 1888 Smith boarded the train for California to tour the mission field there, returning to Lamoni in time for the April 1888 general conference. He made one final trip to Utah in the nineteenth century, in early 1889, again without holding many public meetings.[60] Thereafter, Reorganized Church missionaries operated there under his direction.

Instead of reaping a rich harvest of Latter-day Saints, as Smith had expected when he began ministry in 1860, the Utah mission was never fully successful. After an ambitious start, by the end of 1863 the Reorganized Church had grown to some 300 members. By 1880 the census registered 820 Reorganized Church members in the territory, and by 1890 the members were no more than 1,000 in the Mormon coreland.[61] In spite of the work of Smith's hand-picked representatives, that of his brothers and himself, and the publications prepared for the Mormon audience, nothing seemed to demonstrate a satisfactory progress, and Smith became increasingly dissatisfied with the missionary efforts in the territory during the 1870s and 1880s. Smith gradually came to realize that the arguments of the Reorganization were insufficient to move many Mormons toward rejection of polygamy and acceptance of a more moderate form of Mormonism. He perceived that the wide breaches between the two churchs' theologies could not be broached with mere words. Where once Smith had believed that most of the Utah Saints had been duped into following what he considered the authoritarian leadership of Brigham Young, he came to understand that Young's followers for the most part accepted his leadership without misgivings. He had been a stern father-figure, to be sure, but the Utah Saints had given their obedience to him willingly. Smith found that it was difficult to break the chains of bondage from a slave to a master when those chains did not truly exist. These realizations, coming over a period of years, brought a subtle and gradual shift of Smith's policy toward the Utah Mormons from one of compassion and pity to one oriented toward legal action to bring about the end of plural marriage.[62]

NOTES

1. Several analyses of this theme in early Reorganization history are available. Among the best are Alma R. Blair, "The Reorganized Church of Jesus Christ of Latter Day Saints: Moderate Mormons," in *The Restoration Movement: Essays in Mormon History,* ed. F. Mark McKiernan, Alma R. Blair, and Paul M. Edwards (Lawrence, Kan.: Coronado Press, 1973), pp. 206–30; W. Grant McMurray, "The Reorganization in Nineteenth Century America: Identity Crisis or Historiographical Problem?" *John Whitmer Historical Association Journal* 2 (1982): 3–11; Clare D. Vlahos's intriguing article, "Images of Orthodoxy: Self-Identity in Early Reorganization Apologetics," in *Restoration Studies I: Sesquicentennial Edition,* ed. Maurice L. Draper and Clare D. Vlahos (Independence, Mo.: Herald Publishing House, 1980), pp. 176–86; Richard P. Howard, "The Reorganized Church in Illinois, 1852–1882: Search for Identity," *Dialogue: A Journal of Mormon Thought* 5 (Spring 1970): 63–75; Clare D. Vlahos, "Moderation as a Theological Principle in the Thought of Joseph Smith III," *John Whitmer Historical Association Journal* 1 (1981): 3–11.

2. *True Latter Day Saints' Herald* 1 (May 1860): 103. See also Joseph Smith to Caleb Parker, 14 August 1895, Joseph Smith III Letterbook #6, Reorganized Church of Jesus Christ of Latter Day Saints Library–Archives, Independence, Mo.; Samuel H. B. Smith to George A. Smith, 10 July 1860, George A. Smith Papers, Special Collections, Harold B. Lee Library, Brigham Young University, Provo, Utah. The most thorough, if at times trite and pedantic, study of the Mormon–Reorganized Church relations during the lifetime of Joseph Smith III is Charles W. Turner,

"Joseph Smith III and the Mormons of Utah" (Ph.D. diss., Graduate Theological Union, 1985).

3. The general antipolygamy crusade began in 1856 when the Republican party declared in its platform that polygamy along with slavery were the "twin relics of barbarism" and that the party would work to abolish them. This crusade has been described in Gustive O. Larson, *The "Americanization" of Utah for Statehood* (San Marino, Calif.: Huntington Library, 1971); Richard D. Poll, "The Mormon Question Enters National Politics, 1850–1856," *Utah Historical Quarterly* 25 (April 1957): 117–31; Charles A. Cannon, "The Awesome Power of Sex: The Polemical Campaign Against Mormon Polygamy," *Pacific Historical Review* 43 (February 1974): 61–84.

4. Richard Lyle Shipley, "Voices of Dissent: The History of the Reorganized Church of Jesus Christ of Latter Day Saints in Utah, 1863–1900" (M.A. thesis, Utah State University, 1969), passim; A. Karl Larson and Katherine Miles Larson, eds., *The Diary of Charles Lowell Walker* (Logan: Utah State University Press, 1980), 1:122.

5. On these phases see E. C. Briggs, Journal, 7 October 1863, Reorganized Church Library–Archives; *Weekly Argus* (Sandwich, Ill.), 26 March 1881; *New York Times*, 30 May 1865; Larson and Larson, *Diary of Charles Lowell Walker*, 2:771; *Saints' Herald* 24 (1 January 1877): 1; Joseph Smith to E. L. Kelley, 10 July 1883, Joseph Smith III Papers, Reorganized Church Library–Archives; Joseph Smith to E. C. Brand, 26 January 1884, Joseph Smith III Letterbook #4, Reorganized Church Library–Archives; Joseph Smith to Mrs. D. C. Chase, 7 January 1893, Miscellaneous Letters and Papers, Reorganized Church Library–Archives; Edward W. Tullidge, *The Life of Joseph the Prophet* (Plano, Ill.: Herald Publishing House, 1880), p. 657.

6. These ideas have been expressed in *Brighamite Doctrines* (Plano, Ill.: Herald Publishing House, n.d.); *Rejection and Succession* (Plano, Ill.: Herald Publishing House, 1878); Joseph Smith, *Reply to Orson Pratt* (Plano, Ill.: Herald Publishing House, 1870); *Chicago Tribune*, 22 February 1882; "Anti-Polygamy: Another Outpouring in Chicago Declares that the Evil Must Go," *Saints' Advocate* 4 (April 1882): 185–87; "Anti-Polygamy: A Meeting at Plano Addressed by Joseph Smith," *Saints' Advocate* 4 (April 1882): 198–99; Edmund L. Kelley et al., "Polygamy a Crime—Not a Religion," *Saints' Advocate* 5 (July 1882): 217–33; *New York Times*, 9 April 1886; Joseph Smith, "Ways That Are Doubtful," *Saints' Herald* 36 (5 October 1889): 654–57.

7. "News from Utah," *True Latter Day Saints' Herald* 2 (June 1861): 92–93; Joseph Smith, "The First General Epistle of the President of the Reorganized Church of Jesus Christ of Latter Day Saints, to All the

Scattered Saints," *True Latter Day Saints' Herald* 2 (August 1861): 121–24.

8. Joseph Smith, "A Card from Bro. Joseph Smith," *True Latter Day Saints' Herald* 1 (July 1860): 169–70.

9. See the letters in Ibid. 1 (July 1860): 195–96; 1 (August 1860): 208–10; 3 (May 1863): 196–98; 4 (15 November 1863): 146.

10. Edmund C. Briggs and R. N. Attwood, *Address to the Saints in Utah and California* (Plano, Ill.: Herald Publishing House, 1869 rev. ed.), pp. 31, 39.

11. Robert Bruce Flanders, "Mormons Who Did Not Go West: A Study of the Emergence of the Reorganized Church of Jesus Christ of Latter Day Saints" (M.S. thesis, University of Wisconsin, 1954), p. 27.

12. Joseph Smith and Heman C. Smith, *The History of the Reorganized Church of Jesus Christ of Latter Day Saints* (Independence, Mo.: Herald Publishing House, 1967), 3:772. See also C. V. Waite, *The Mormon Prophet and His Harem* (Cambridge, Mass.: Riverside Press, 1866), pp. 6–7, which, although an exposé of Brigham Young, contains an affidavit by McCord describing his difficulties in Utah in 1847.

13. Charles Derry, "The Autobiography of Charles Derry," *Journal of History* 4 (January 1911): 38; Smith and Smith, *History of Reorganized Church*, 3:320.

14. *True Latter Day Saints' Herald* 4 (15 September 1863): 89–90; Inez Smith Davis, *The Story of the Church* (Independence, Mo.: Herald Publishing House, 1976), p. 481.

15. Briggs and Attwood, *Address to the Saints*, p. 69.

16. Quoted in Shipley, "Voices of Dissent," pp. 24–25. Apparently, General Patrick Edward Connor, commander of the army unit stationed at Fort Douglas, guaranteed Briggs's and McCord's safety. See Joseph Smith, "The Memoirs of President Joseph Smith (1832–1914)," *Saints Herald* 83 (24 March 1936): 369.

17. *Daily Union Vedette* (Fort Douglas, Utah), 18 December 1863; Smith and Smith, *History of Reorganized Church*, 3:339; Davis, *Story of the Church*, p. 483.

18. Vida E. Smith, *Young Peoples' History of the Church*, 2 vols. (Lamoni, Iowa: Herald Publishing House, 1918), 2:267–68.

19. Smith and Smith, *History of Reorganized Church*, 3:334.

20. Ibid., 3:339; *Daily Union Vedette*, 18 December 1863; Davis, *Story of the Church*, p. 483.

21. Smith and Smith, *History of Reorganized Church*, 3:373–784.

22. *True Latter Day Saints Herald* 5 (15 May 1864): 155; Orson F. Whitney, *History of Utah* (Salt Lake City, Utah: George Q. Cannon and Sons, 1898), 3:311.

242 Joseph Smith III

23. *True Latter Day Saints' Herald* 6 (15 October 1864): 124.

24. *The Messenger* (Salt Lake City, Utah) 1 (December 1875): 10.

25. Smith, "Memoirs," *Saints' Herald* 82 (10 September 1935): 1170; Davis, *Story of the Church*, p. 484; Roy A. Cheville, *They Made a Difference* (Independence, Mo.: Herald Publishing House, 1970), pp. 228–36.

26. The best analyses of the Reorganized Church's difficulties in the Utah mission include Turner, "Joseph Smith III and the Mormons of Utah," and Shipley, "Voices of Dissent."

27. Joseph Smith to John Codman, 15 December 1884, Joseph Smith III Letterbook #4; Joseph Smith to Zenos H. Gurley, Jr., 20 August 1878, Joseph Smith III Letterbook #1, Reorganized Church Library–Archives; Shipley, "Voices of Dissent," pp. 15, 41–43, 49–52.

28. Larson and Larson, *Diary of Charles Lowell Walker*, 2:771; Davis, *Story of the Church*, p. 517.

29. Considerable recent efforts have been made to understand the life of David H. Smith. Paul M. Edwards's sensitive essay, "The Sweet Singer of Israel: David Hyrum Smith," *Brigham Young University Studies* 12 (Winter 1972): 171–84, outlined David's life and work and suggested that his creative genius made him susceptible to mental illness. Later in the year F. Mark McKiernan, in "The Tragedy of David H. Smith," *Saints' Herald* 119 (December 1972): 20–22, asserted that David was not mentally ill at all but suffered from acute hypoglycemia, which could not be treated by physicians of the nineteenth century. This interpretation sparked a historical debate that has yet to be settled. As an indication of the responses to this argument, see "Letters to the Editor," *Saints' Herald* 120 (February 1973): 8. McKiernan published two other articles on David Smith, discussing his poetry and art: "David H. Smith: A Son of the Prophet," *BYU Studies* 18 (Winter 1978): 233–45, and "David H. Smith—Artist, Poet, Musician," *Saints' Herald* 127 (1 January 1980): 18–20. Finally, Valeen Tippetts Avery has written "Insanity and the Sweet Singer: A Biography of David Hyrum Smith, 1844–1904" (Ph.D. diss., Northern Arizona University, 1984), from which was drawn her "Sketches of the Sweet Singer: David Hyrum Smith, 1844–1904," *John Whitmer Historical Association Journal* 5 (1985): 3–15.

30. Maureen Ursenbach Beecher, ed., "'All Things Move in Order in the City:' The Nauvoo Diary of Zina Diantha Huntington Jacobs," *Brigham Young University Studies* 19 (Spring 1979): 298. See also Briggs, Journal, 7 October 1863; Larson and Larson, *Diary of Charles Lowell Walker*, 1:343–49.

31. David H. Smith, "A Word of Advice to Those that Look to Me to Be the Prophet," *True Latter Saints' Herald* 3 (April 1863): 199. See also

"The Son of the Prophet," *Autumn Leaves* 25 (November 1912): 507–12; John Hawley, "The Life of John Hawley Written from Memory, January 1, 1885," p. 44, Miscellaneous Letters and Papers; Fred Ursenbach to Joseph Smith, 31 July 1866, Joseph Smith III Papers.

32. *Utah Daily Reporter* (Salt Lake City, Utah), 15 August 1869.

33. Vida E. Smith, "Biography of Alexander H. Smith," *Journal of History* 5 (1912): 259–65; "The Son of the Prophet," pp. 502–5; Avery, "Sketches of the Sweet Singer," p. 8.

34. A valuable analysis of this dissenting movement can be found in Ronald W. Walker, "The Commencement of the Godbeite Protest: Another View," *Utah Historical Quarterly* 42 (Summer 1974): 216–44.

35. "The Son of the Prophet," pp. 505–6; Avery, "Sketches of the Sweet Singer," pp. 8–9.

36. See note 35; Smith and Smith, *History of Reorganized Church*, 3:527–30, 547; *True Latter Day Saints' Herald* 17 (1 March 1870): 180.

37. David H. Smith to Joseph Smith, 19 November 1871, 14 March 1872, Miscellaneous Letters and Papers; Larson and Larson, *Diary of Charles Lowell Walker*, 2:702–3. Insights in the close feelings Joseph Smith III had for David can be gathered from Roger D. Launius, "The Relationship of Joseph and David Hyrum Smith," *Restoration Trail Forum* 6 (November 1980): 1, 5–6.

38. Joseph Smith to Charles Derry, 24 January 1877, Joseph Smith III Papers; Joseph Smith to Dr. E. A. Kilbourne, 4 January 1877, Joseph Smith III Letterbook #1; Joseph Smith to Zenos H. Gurley, Jr., 20 January 1877, Joseph Smith III Letterbook #1A, Reorganized Church Library–Archives; Joseph Smith to L. D. Hickey, 7 September 1877, Joseph Smith III Letterbook #1; Joseph Smith to G. C. Tomlinson, 3 September 1910, Joseph Smith III Papers; "In the Matter of David H. Smith, an Insane Person: Warrant to Commit David H. Smith to the Northern Illinois Hospital for the Insane," 17 January 1877, Probate Records, Kendall County Courthouse, Yorkville, Ill.; Joseph Smith to George L. Matthews, 4 March 1881, Joseph Smith III Letterbook #3; Avery, "Sketches of the Sweet Singer," pp. 8–14.

39. Alma R. Blair, "The Tradition of Dissent—Jason W. Briggs," *Restoration Studies I*, pp. 146–61, is the only work of substance on this individual. On his Utah mission see Smith and Smith, *History of Reorganized Church*, 3:74, 79–80, 82, 87, 91, 119, 166, 180.

40. These trips are described in Smith, "Memoirs," *Saints' Herald*, published serially between 1934 and 1937; Turner, "Joseph Smith III and the Mormons of Utah," pp. 289–300, 360–78, 388–90, 394–401.

41. Joseph Smith to Audentia Smith, 4 November 1876, Joseph Smith

III Papers; Smith, "Memoirs," *Saints' Herald* 82 (3 September 1935): 1135–38, 82 (10 September 1935): 1167–70; 82 (17 September 1935): 1199–1200, 82 (24 September 1935): 1231–33.

42. Joseph Smith to Carrie Smith, 1 December 1876, Rebecca Weld Nolan Collection, Reorganized Church Library–Archives. See also the general account in Smith, "Memoirs," *Saints' Herald* 82 (24 September 1935): 1233.

43. Smith, "Memoirs," *Saints' Herald* 82 (24 September 1935): 1233, 83 (16 June 1936): 754; interview with F. Mark McKiernan, 4 November 1979, Independence, Mo. The likelihood of Joseph Smith, Jr., having the same affliction is considerable. Since he died a relatively young man, it never appeared sufficiently for diagnosis, but Lucy Mack Smith quoted a statement made by Hyrum Smith concerning the incarceration in Liberty Jail in the winter of 1838–39 which demonstrates that Joseph Smith, Jr., experienced symptoms of neuralgia. "Several others made similar expressions, in the agony of their souls," Hyrum wrote, "but my brother did not say anything, he being sick at the time with the toothache, and ague, in his face, in consequence of a severe cold brought on by being exposed to the severity of the weather." Lucy Mack Smith, *Biographical Sketches of Joseph Smith the Prophet and His Progenitors for Many Generations* (Lamoni, Iowa: Herald Publishing House, 1912), p. 304.

44. *Salt Lake* (Utah) *Tribune*, 23 November 1876.

45. Ibid., 24 November 1876.

46. Larson and Larson, *Diary of Charles Lowell Walker*, 1:348–49. See also Walker, "Commencement of the Godbeite Protest," pp. 216–44.

47. Smith, "Memoirs," *Saints' Herald* 82 (1 October 1935): 1263–64; Joseph Smith, "Autobiography of Joseph Smith," in Tullidge, *Life of Joseph*, pp. 785–86.

48. *Salt Lake Tribune*, 24 November 1876. The evidence Joseph F. Smith had collected is contained in Joseph F. Smith, Affidavit Books, A through D, Church of Jesus Christ of Latter-day Saints Historical Department, Salt Lake City, Utah. See also Eliza R. Snow to Joseph F. Smith, n.d., Joseph F. Smith Collection, Latter-day Saints Historical Department.

49. Smith, "Memoirs," *Saints' Herald* 82 (1 October 1935): 1264–65, 82 (8 October 1935): 1299–1300.

50. Ibid., 82 (8 October 1935): 1299–1300.

51. *Saints' Herald* 24 (1 January 1877): 1; Joseph Smith to Zenos H. Gurley, Jr., 27 August 1877, Joseph Smith III Papers; Joseph Smith to Bros. Hanson and Overstreet, 6 January 1877; Joseph Smith to D. F. Miller, 15 March 1877, both in Joseph Smith III Letterbook #1.

52. Joseph Smith to Heman C. Smith, 19 September 1878, Joseph Smith III Letterbook #1; *Salt Lake Tribune*, 24 November 1876.

53. The ambiguities of orderly succession to the presidency for John Taylor, who followed Brigham Young in the office, have been caustically described in Samuel W. Taylor, *The Kingdom or Nothing: The Life of John Taylor, Militant Mormon* (New York: The Macmillan Co., 1976), pp. 133–38, and more sympathetically in B. H. Roberts, *The Comprehensive History of the Church of Jesus Christ of Latter-day Saints* (Salt Lake City, Utah: Deseret Book Co., 1930), 3:160–315, and Stanley B. Kimball, *Heber C. Kimball: Mormon Patriarch and Pioneer* (Urbana: University of Illinois Press, 1981), pp. 292–95.

54. Roberts, *Comprehensive History*, 5:524; *Salt Lake Tribune*, 6–10 April 1877; John D. Lee, *Mormonism Unveiled; or, The Life and Confessions of the Late Mormon Bishop* (St. Louis: Bryan, Brand, and Co., 1877), pp. 404–5; Leonard J. Arrington, "The Settlement of the Brigham Young Estate," *Pacific Historical Review* 21 (February 1952): 1–20.

55. Joseph Smith to L. R. Freeman, 8 September 1877, Joseph Smith III Letterbook #1.

56. Joseph Smith to Judge K. B. Cleave, 13 September 1877; Joseph Smith to Magnus Fyrando, 6 December 1877, both in Joseph Smith III Letterbook #1; Zenos H. Gurley, Jr., to Joseph Smith, 21 July 1878, Joseph Smith III Papers; Joseph Smith and W. W. Blair to Heman C. Smith, n.d., Joseph Smith III Letterbook #7, Reorganized Church Library–Archives.

57. Joseph Smith to James Whitehead, 8 September 1884, Joseph Smith III Letterbook #1A; Joseph Smith, "The Editor Abroad," *Saints' Herald* 32 (4 July 1885): 427.

58. Smith, "Memoirs," *Saints' Herald* 83 (18 February 1936): 209–10, 83 (25 February 1936): 242–44, 83 (10 March 1936): 305–6, 83 (24 March 1936): 267–70, 83 (31 March 1936): 399–400; Joseph Smith to Audentia Smith, 19 June 1885, 3 August 1885, 5 August 1885, Joseph Smith III Papers; *Deseret News* (Salt Lake City, Utah), 19 June 1885; Joseph Smith to Bro. George, 20 June 1885, Miscellaneous Letters and Papers.

59. Smith, "Memoirs," *Saints' Herald* 83 (28 April 1936): 527–30, 83 (5 May 1936): 559–62, 83 (2 June 1936): 687–89.

60. Joseph Smith, Diary, 3 January 1888, Reorganized Church Library–Archives; Joseph Smith to E. L. Kelley, 24 February 1888, Joseph Smith III Papers; Smith, "Memoirs," *Saints' Herald* 83 (16 June 1936): 752, 83 (23 June 1936): 784; Turner, "Joseph Smith III and the Mormons of Utah," pp. 388–90, 394–401.

61. Howard, "Reorganized Church in Illinois," p. 73; F. Henry Edwards, *The History of the Reorganized Church of Jesus Christ of Latter*

Day Saints (Independence, Mo.: Herald Publishing House, 1973), 5:92; Edward W. Tullidge, *The Life of Joseph the Prophet* (Plano, Ill.: Herald Publishing House, 1880), p. 657; "The World Mistaken," *Deseret News* (Salt Lake City, Utah), 7 October 1863, 6 September 1882; Briggs, Journal, 7 October 1863.

62. Joseph Smith to E. L. Kelley, 10 July 1883, Joseph Smith III Papers; Joseph Smith to J. F. Minton, 13 March 1891; Joseph Smith to Zenos H. Gurley, Jr., 5 March 1886, Joseph Smith III Letterbook #4; Joseph Smith to J. J. Barbour, 15 May 1878; Joseph Smith to Mrs. D. C. Chase, 7 January 1893; Blair, "The Reorganized Church," pp. 218–21. This frustration was recognized by all the leadership of the Reorganization, and at least one suggested that they had only to blame themselves for the lack of success in Utah. W. W. Blair wrote to Heman C. Smith sometime between 1893 and 1896: "I *know,* and so does elder Anthony, that the continued failure of the Church from the fall of 1880 to suitably sustain the Utah mission caused the falling off in interest and progress in every direction. One of the most sinful and humiliating periods of my ministerial life was that of from the Spring of 1881 to the fall of 1884. With the advantages had by us from Nov. 1879 to May 1881, it miserably used, the Church could have planted its work in every part of Utah and contiguous regions" (W. W. Blair to Heman C. Smith, n.d. [but sandwiched between letters dated 1893 and 1896], Joseph Smith III Letterbook #7, Reorganized Church Library–Archives).

CHAPTER
11

Politicking against Polygamy

"I may never see you, and you may never hear from me again," Joseph Smith wrote to James A. Garfield in June 1880, "but I could not forbear writing you just once." He added, "I am not a politician, but I am engaged with others in what is called the 'Josephite or Anti-polygamic wing of the Mormon Church'; and am doing what I can to exorcise the Utah cancer from the fair feature of American civilization." This excerpt from Smith's letter to the Republican presidential candidate of 1880 succinctly stated Smith's and the Reorganized Church's great crusade: from the 1850s onward the destruction of all vestiges of plural marriage within the Mormon movement was perhaps the greatest passion of the Reorganization. Its ultimate realization in 1890 was probably the motivating factor in many of the policies of the movement.[1]

Gradually, as he realized that the Reorganization's missionary program was less than fully successful in Utah, Joseph Smith began to emphasize a political solution to the problem of Mormon polygamy. As a result, throughout the latter quarter of the nineteenth century the Reorganized Church took an ever increasing interest in the politics of the antipolygamy crusade. In so doing, Smith involved the church with a wide diversity of individuals, many of whom had differing goals but most of whom appear to have feared that the Mormons were trying to build a theocratic nation in the Great Basin. The creation of a peculiar society and culture, of which plural marriage was a prominent part, seemed to these people the means whereby the Latter-day Saints would succeed in their quest. Consequently, the issue of Mormon disloyalty to the United States was also a serious question of the settlement of the polygamy question. Joseph Smith, therefore, dealt with the related questions of theocracy and polygamy among political circles during this period to create a unique Reorganized Church response to Utah Mormonism.[2]

The first instance of the Reorganization's political involvement in actions against the Utah Mormon theocracy and all that it implied came in 1863 when Joseph Smith and his chief assistants wrote a "Declaration of Loyalty" for the United States Congress, pledging their church's unqualified support of the federal government's position in prosecuting the Civil War. This document subtly stated that, while Utah Mormonism's allegiance could be questioned, the moderate Mormons of the Reorganized Church stood behind Lincoln and his efforts to save the Union. With this one memorial to Congress Smith forever rejected the idea of a theocracy as embodied in the State of Deseret and adopted the more acceptable American ideal of separation of church and state.[3] Also, it signified that the Reorganization was willing to accept conventional religious conceptions rather than such practices as Mormon polygamy.

Because of his special position as son of the dead Mormon prophet and as a result of his church's missionary activities in Utah, Joseph Smith quickly won the interest and, in many cases, the respect of several prominent Washington officials concerned about the Mormon theocracy and polygamy. In early May 1866 Republican Congressman James M. Ashley of Ohio asked Smith to come to the Capital to confer about the Utah question with members of the House Committee on Territories. Most concerned about the Mormon church's apparent disregard of federal authority, the committee was in the process of framing legislation to bring the territory in line with other western jurisdictions. Ashley hoped, in addition, to persuade Congress to pass legislation that would put teeth in the almost unenforceable Morrill Antibigamy Act of 1862.[4] Smith had long wanted to talk about the Morrill Act; consequently, he and Elijah Banta—a huge, amiable church official—left for Washington on 30 May 1866.[5]

On 6 June 1866 Smith met with Ashley to consider the Utah question in detail before the committee's formal hearings. After discussing the issue for some time Ashley pointedly asked the young Reorganization leader what legislation he would recommend to deal with the situation in Utah. Smith immediately offered several suggestions, impressing Ashley with his grasp of the problems in the territory. Consequently, the congressman asked Smith to put his suggestions in a written report to aid the committee in its planning. After several more informal meetings with Ashley and other members of the committee, Smith gave Ashley his report.

In this report to the Committee on Territories Smith summarized the history of the Mormon church from 1830 to 1846 and affirmed that until his father's death the church had obeyed the laws of the land.[6] However, Smith asserted that since the split in the church the Utah-based faction had constantly sidestepped the law and had not been forced back into line and that "such failure and neglect of duty on the part of the executive officers of the various States and the Nation have given rise to a conviction upon the part of some of the [Utah] church members that there was no disposition to so enforce the laws of the land." Smith argued that the Mormons had been allowed to rule themselves as they saw fit for so long that they honestly believed they should hold this power forever, even if their practices ran counter to the laws of the United States. He added that therefore it was time that the government officials assert their legitimate authority over Utah Territory. Smith shocked Ashley, though, when he concluded that no further laws establishing federal jurisdiction need be enacted. As Smith put it, "The Constitution was very plain about where final secular power rested, and no legislation need extend their basic right."[7]

Knowing the religious leader's strong opposition to the practice, Ashley had specifically asked Smith to comment on the polygamy issue. He asked if Smith thought Congress should pass further anti-polygamy legislation, and if so what forms these bills should take. Ashley cautioned Smith, however, to remember that the Constitution expressly forbade the proscription of religious freedom. Wanting to determine the legality of the practice in Mormon theology and tradition, Ashley asked whether polygamy was a religious tenet and thereby inviolate under the law? Smith's written response was cautious and tactful. Although acknowledging the right of every citizen to worship as conscience dictated, Smith asserted that plural marriage was not a Christian principle. It was not substantiated in either scriptures or the history of Christianity and positively contradicted all for which Jesus Christ had stood. Moreover, Smith insisted that the original Mormon faith, as a part of Christianity, could never have adopted such a tenet, producing some of the evidence he had gathered which suggested that it had been virtually unknown during his father's lifetime.[8]

Smith went on to restate his personal opinion that polygamy had been the invention of lascivious and lustful men after the death of his father. The doctrine, he insisted, had to be destroyed quickly before it contaminated others who might enter the practice. Even the defenders of slavery were on more solid ground in rebutting the abolitionists with the Bible than were the polygamists, he added. Furthermore, the best means of destroying polygamy, Smith noted, was not by the passage of additional legislation. The current laws on the subject were sufficient; they were not, however, being properly enforced. As a final note Smith chastized Congress: "No additional legislation upon the part of congress was really needed to eliminate [polygamy] . . . if they would only insist upon a strict, just, and persistent enforcement of the laws already included in their statutes."[9]

When Smith left Washington on 11 June 1866, he was satisfied that he had presented his viewpoint on the Utah question rationally and that he had convinced Ashley and his committee that his approach to political control of the Mormons was the most logical and could be the most successful approach. However, because of the inherently slow and circuitous nature of government activity, Smith was skeptical of the outcome of this trip. When asked to comment on the accomplishments of the visit to Washington, Smith described the many meetings with committee members and restated his views but added that probably little would result from the episode.[10] This appraisal proved correct; in spite of Smith's analysis of the Utah question, Washington politicians did not accept his argument, and for months after his visit to the Capital, Congress continued to debate the necessity of new antipolygamy legislation. However, it eventually reached a stalemate and decided, almost by default, to enforce the laws already on the books and to forget for the present about additional antipolygamy laws.[11]

With this decision, however unintended it might have been, one of the most pressing concerns of governmental policy makers became the appointment of territorial officers who could carry out the laws that already existed. On 7 September 1850 the United States Congress had passed legislation providing for the creation of the Utah Territory; a few days later President Millard Fillmore signed it into law. The law creating the Utah Territory followed the established territorial precedents of the time, providing for the appointment of a governor, a secretary, a chief justice and two associate justices, an attorney, and a marshal by the president of the United States. These officers, who served at the pleasure of the president, were the representatives of the federal government in the territory. The governor, for instance, acted as the president's alter ego in the territory, carrying an absolute veto over bills passed by the popularly elected territorial legislature and providing for the enforcement of all laws within his jurisdiction.[12] The Mormons in Utah had experienced a virtually endless round of trouble with federal authorities almost since the creation of the Utah Territory in 1850. The most important such episode took place between 1857 and 1863, when United States troops were sent to the territory to maintain order and enforce the governor's edicts.[13]

Knowing well the generally unsympathetic way in which most Americans viewed the Latter-day Saints of the Great Basin, the Reorganization made it very clear that it was completely and undeniably loyal to the federal government. The 1863 "Declaration of Loyalty" was one such attempt to demonstrate the differences between the two Mormon factions. In 1870 Joseph Smith persuaded the Reorganized Church's general conference to issue a similar statement of loyalty, this time adding a comment on the claims and faith of the church so that Americans could more easily delineate differences between Utah Latter-day Saints and Reorganization members.[14]

Partly because of the admirable personal reputation of Joseph Smith III among non-Mormons, partly because of the Reorganization's solid support of the civil government in all matters affecting the question of church and state, and partly because of the church's opposition to the major doctrinal bone of contention between the Mormons and the rest of the United States—plural marriage—a movement arose in the 1870s to appoint Joseph Smith the territorial governor of Utah. Such a movement was perhaps unsurprising to many within the Reorganization. After all, when Smith had joined the Reorganized Church in 1860, he had been hailed by many as the individual who would reform Mormonism. "Joseph is said to be a strong man of good strong sense," one newspaper reported from the 1860 general conference, adding that he was "opposed to polygamy, and all manner of depredations upon the Gentiles." This writer then added somewhat prophetically, "Under his head undoubtedly the church would be purged of the outrageously bad practices which have brought it such disrepute with all law abiding citizens." The young prophet's leadership would, claimed the reporter, "materially affect us not only as individuals but as a nation." [15]

When the territorial governor of Utah, J. Wilson Shaffer, fell ill and died suddenly in October 1870, many people in the territory as well as elsewhere petitioned President Ulysses S. Grant to appoint their political friends to the office.[16] David Hyrum Smith, brother of Joseph and a keen observer of the Mormon scene, wrote to his brother in November, telling him that many members of the non-Mormon community in Utah, various antipolygamy crusaders elsewhere, and even a few liberal Latter-day Saints thought the head of the Reorganization would make a good replacement for Governor Shaffer. There was no question about Joseph Smith's position concerning polygamy and Mormon theocratic government, and he had long been a proponent of strictly enforcing the existing laws in the territory. To many people, apparently, Smith seemed the perfect candidate. David wrote to Joseph, "If a movement should arise recommending you to Pres. Grant appointing you to the governorship of Utah, do not fight the idea." [17]

This draft did not materialize; those who were politically astute knew it was a stillborn movement. In January 1871 President Grant appointed Oregon Governor George L. Woods, who took office from Vernon H. Vaughn, an interim governor. Woods's appointment did not discourage Smith's supporters, however, and whenever the governorship opened in Deseret thereafter, they vocally supported his appointment to the office. They made a strong case for Smith, arguing that his personal morality, the respect he enjoyed in Utah because of his status as the son of the Mormon prophet, and his determination to stamp out polygamy made him an exceptional candidate. From a purely political standpoint, they added, Smith was a staunch Republican and his appointment would help the party's efforts in the territory. An Illinois newspaper summed up the matter succinctly: "If the government would make Joseph Smith governor of that territory, it would wipe out at once polygamy and fair Utah would take her place among the states, with no blot upon her face."[18]

The advocates of the appointment of Joseph Smith to the Utah territorial governorship continued their efforts for several years thereafter. On 19 October 1879, for instance, Edward W. Tullidge, the iconoclastic Mormon historian who had affiliated with the Reorganized Church a few months earlier, wrote a letter to President Rutherford B. Hayes, urging Joseph Smith's appointment to the Utah governorship.[19] He said that Smith would be able to destroy the "Polygamic Theocracy" in the Great Basin. With Smith as governor and with some 200 projected Reorganized Church missionaries working in the territory, Tullidge predicted that it would be a short time before 20,000 to 50,000 Utah Mormons would join the crusade to abolish plural marriage.[20] Additionally, in late 1881 the editor of the *Weekly Argus,* published in Sandwich, Illinois, not far from the church headquarters at Plano, issued a lengthy statement supporting Joseph Smith III's governorship of Utah. Under the title "Mormonism" the editor wrote:

> *The Argus* had frequently pointed out a remedy [to the Mormon question], which is on the frontiersman's principle of a backfire. Opposed to these [objectionable] religious practices, while holding the general principles of the Mormon faith, is the "Reorganized Church" with Elder Joseph Smith at its head; a body of eminent, able men, already making inroads on the Brighamites, and to aid them in promulgating the new faith in Utah should be the aim of the general government.
>
> In the end it would be wise to appoint Elder Joseph Smith—who had the character and the ability for the position—as governor of that territory, an appointment which would receive the approval of his own branch fully, and largely of the other, and would divide the power of the Brighamites as to enable this branch successfully to combat the crime at its central point. Mr. Smith is a true, loyal citizen, a practical Christian, a temperance man, an able leader, and bitterly opposed to the "peculiar institution."[21]

A week later the *Argus* ran a letter signed simply "A" from Mendota, Illinois, which also addressed the question of Smith's appointment to the Utah governorship. The statement read: "A recent number of *The Argus* had an article in reference to [the Mormon question], or more definitely polygamy, as that is the bone of contention in the case. In this appointment of Pres. Smith the chief and leader of the antipolygamous branch of the Mormon church was advocated." The author claimed that Smith's appointment might be reasonable but also desired the passage of more stringent antibigamy laws. The editor replied to this letter with the following:

> All the laws suggested by our correspondent are now on the statute books, but cannot be enforced in Utah until backed by a strong public sentiment.
>
> The appointment of Joseph, the president of the Anti-Polygamous element of the church, as Governor of Utah, would give a power, about which the opposition could crystalize to enforce the law. Mr. Smith is as much opposed to the "peculiar institution" as our correspondent.[22]

There is no evidence, however, to indicate that these proposals were seriously considered in Washington.

Although Smith reflected the mores of most Americans of the Victorian era and might have been acceptable to the president otherwise, the governorship of the Utah Territory was a political plum of significant importance and was given to a party stalwart in recognition of services rendered. Smith's Republicanism was strict in that he voted the ticket, but in most other ways he was apolitical. Therefore, he did not have the necessary political friends and had not performed the necessary services to the party to gain such an appointment. Consequently, he never really had much of a chance at appointment and there is no evidence to suggest that the president seriously considered his candidacy.[23]

Indeed, Joseph Smith's reaction to the various bids to make him Utah governor ranged from apathy to revulsion. He recognized that, as a religious leader, he had little business in secular affairs; he probably understood that the position would have been impossible for him to fill successfully with his other duties, and certainly he could not have resigned from the church's presidency. He recalled his feelings about this issue in his memoirs: "The governorship of Utah was the position neither desirable nor practicable for me, in that my work lay entirely outside the field of politics, and that I had no ambition whatever for secular honors. I pointed out that such a position for me would avail nothing of good to the people of Utah, for as a people they would regard it as but one more attempt to fasten upon them an unwelcome rule."[24] However, Smith did support for the governorship another Reorganization member, Phineas Cadwell, an Iowa legislator who had hopes of gaining the executive office of Utah. As in Smith's case, there is no evidence to suggest that the administration seriously considered Cadwell for the governorship either.[25] Eventually, the idea died.

Because of their antipolygamy stand Joseph Smith and the Reorganized Church always enjoyed relatively respectable relations with the secular world. This acceptability increased in 1880 when Smith's organization won an impressive court case which affirmed the movement's status as the "lawful" successor to the original Mormon church. The case involved the property rights to the Kirtland Temple, a large house of worship that had been constructed under his father's direction between 1833 and 1836. After the majority of the Latter Day Saints had left Kirtland, Ohio, in 1838, the building had fallen into disrepair and was eventually sold to settle some of Joseph Smith, Jr.'s local debts. In 1862 Russell Huntley, who became a Reorganized Church member, bought this property and in 1873 deeded it to Joseph Smith and Mark H. Forscutt. Following this transaction Smith began paying taxes on the building, financed some renovations, and allowed his followers in the local area to hold services there.[26]

The Kirtland Temple Suit arose out of complex land transactions associated with the first "House of the Lord" built by the early Mormon church.[27] Since the church during the 1830s was not a legal entity—that is, it was not incorporated—it could not hold property. To facilitate ownership the church used a form of the common legal vehicle of "trustee in trust," which appointed an officer to oversee organizational property. In this instance, Joseph Smith, Jr., received authority to act as trustee in trust for the church during his life, his successor in the church presidency to continue these duties. He was vested "with plenary power . . . to receive, acquire, manage or convey property, real, personal, or mixed, for the sole use and benefit of said Church." When a trustee in trust died, his heirs were required by law to convey the property held in trust to the legal successor. The difficulty with the Kirtland Temple property revolved around which organization was the legal successor.[28]

The heirs of Joseph Smith, Jr., failed to transfer legally any property to any of the many factions that arose during the 1840s and 1850s. Indeed, Emma Smith, the prophet's widow, refused to have any association with any of these groups. At the same time she apparently took no interest in the Kirtland Temple, for had she asserted herself, she possibly could have advanced claims to ownership. As it stood, however, no organization claiming the legacy of early Mormonism held either legal or equitable title to the property for more than a few years. The tenuous claims they put forth during this period derived solely from possession of the building.[29]

The ownership of the Kirtland Temple remained in this unsettled condition until 29 October 1860, when the probate court of Lake County, Ohio, the site of the property following the splitting of Geauga into two units in 1840, began liquidating the real property of the Mormon prophet.[30] On 18 April 1862 William L. Perkins, a businessman from Painesville, Ohio, purchased the entire Smith acreage in Kirtland, including that upon which the temple stood, acquiring an administrator's deed from the probate court of Lake County.[31] On the same day of his purchase, Perkins sold by quit claim deed to Russell Huntley for $150 a small portion of the former Latter Day Saints holdings "being the same premises on which the 'Mormon Temple,' so called, stands, and which was this day deeded to said Wm L. Perkins by H. Holcomb, as Administrator of Joseph Smith Jr. deceased."[32]

Huntley was delighted with his purchase. The Kirtland Temple held special significance for him because of the religious activities that had taken place there and the opportunities it held for continued worship. He spent over $2,000 to stabilize the exterior of the building, appointed a caretaker, and allowed the Reorganized Church branch and civic organizations to hold activities. Even so, it was still in disrepair years later.[33] In the early 1870s Russell Huntley decided that the time had come for him to give up ownership of the temple, that there were other individuals who could oversee it more efficiently and provide funds for restoration. As a result, he opened negotiations with his friend Mark H. Forscutt and Joseph Smith III toward selling the property. On 17 February 1873 Huntley and Forscutt and Smith completed their transaction. Smith and Forscutt purchased for $150 the quit claim deed held by Huntley to the building.[34]

The details of this transaction are unknown. Huntley probably believed that his transfer of the temple to Smith and Forscutt meant that the property was in the hands of the church. It seems apparent, however, that neither Smith nor Forscutt thought of the building as anything more than personal property to be done with as they believed most prudent. Without question, these men purchased the temple from Huntley with the intention of immediately selling it to offset overburdening financial obligations.[35] Joseph Smith III wrote to his mother about the possibilities of this sale 8 March 1872: "I was made glad by the receipt of your letter, and so much was your mind like my own upon the matter that I at once wrote to Kirtland, offering the Temple for sale. Should I be able to sell for the price offered I will be able to get out of debt, for which I shall feel profoundly grateful to the Lord. However, I dare not build any air castles, they are such cob house affairs."[36]

To carry out his plan, Joseph Smith visited Kirtland during July 1875 to meet with a Mr. Carpenter, a local government leader. They formulated plans to transfer the building to the city of Kirtland as a town hall or school for a sale price of $2,500. When Smith met with local leaders and reviewed the transaction, Carpenter discovered that Smith held only a quit claim deed and that other individuals and organizations had claims to the property. Smith commented in a letter to Alexander Fyfe in 1881: "I went to Kirtland in the latter part of July to complete sale and make out papers, when Mr. Carpenter informed me that the Town would not buy, as the *title* was not *in* Eld. F[orscutt] & I. But if we would perfect the title and get a deed from the *church*, they might talk with us."[37]

Joseph Smith III returned to his home in Plano, Illinois, soon thereafter. Apparently, he met with Presiding Bishop Israel L. Rogers, the chief financial officer of the church, and asked Rogers to give him a quit claim deed for the property. Rogers refused, according to Smith, because "the Bishop and some others always held that Bro. Huntley had no title, and that the Temple belonged to the *church*, not to Elds. F[orscutt] and I."[38] Then Bishop Rogers asked Smith and Forscutt to deed the temple to the incorporated church, but they refused. Smith remembered many years later that "from Bishop Rogers and others came strong importunities to make the title to the Temple property over to the church, outright." He added that at the next Reorganized Church conference, held in

April 1876, "we were again presented with the idea it was our duty to make the title over to the church, and were strongly urged to that step. I held my ground, absolutely refusing to be moved in that direction, and stating emphatically that the church could secure such title only at the end of lawsuit. I could see that to *assume* ownership, such as would be implied were we to execute a deed of transfer, would be to lay ourselves open to a contest involving the channel through which we had come into possession, viz., through Mr. Huntley."[39] With the issue stalemated, the Reorganization's general conference voted to allow church authorities to investigate the claims of all parties to the Kirtland Temple and report back with a recommended course of action.[40]

They secured an abstract of title and at the next general conference, on the basis of study of this document, Israel Rogers recommended that the church take legal action as an institution to acquire title to the temple. The representatives referred the abstract to a committee consisting of E. L. Kelley, Elijah Banta, and J. W. Chatburn for further review. Later in the conference these men reported "that there was a cloud upon the title and recommended that the Bishop be authorized and instructed to take proper steps to remove the cloud." The representatives approved this action and the church began legal action. The bishop secured the services of George Paine, the individual who had prepared the title abstract, and he, along with attorneys from the church, prepared a case.[41] According to Henry A. Stebbins, church secretary, they wished to establish two points: "One the right of the Church of Jesus Christ of L.D.S. to the property against the deeds made to persons, the present holders of which are Joseph Smith and M. H. Forscutt. The second is that of who is the church, a matter of principle and precedent." To prove these points Reorganized Church officials wanted to establish that the temple should, by law, belong to a Mormon religious faction and that their particular faction was the successor to the one that built the temple.[42]

Whatever the desires of Smith and Forscutt to sell the Kirtland Temple in 1875, there is no doubt that they supported the efforts of the church to clear its title. In January 1879 Smith wrote to George Paine, a Painesville, Ohio, attorney who had been placed on retainer for the case, explaining that he and Forscutt "are perfectly willing to be made parties in defense to an amicable suit to determine the title. It is with us, not a question of $s and cts, but the equitable and moral claim to proper and legal succession, as a church, to the body which Joseph Smith was trustee, at the time the property was deeded, or attempted to be deeded to the church." He added that neither he nor Forscutt had any intention of contesting the case, and the only expected opposition might come from the leadership of the Church of Jesus Christ of Latter-day Saints, the most successful of the factions arising out of the early Mormon movement. "But should they," Smith continued, "we shall make a stubborn fight of it; and we think we can make a successful showing to the claim we make to the rightful succession."[43] For Smith, a decision in favor of the Reorganized Church in this case would serve as an important rationale for arguing that his faction was the lawful continuation of his father's religious institution, and that it adhered to the beliefs and practices of the early church.[44] The Reorganization argued, of course, that, since plural marriage had not been practiced in the 1830s and 1840s, the Utah faction could not legitimately claim to be the successor to Joseph Smith's movement.

The Reorganized Church's case was heard during the February term of the court of common pleas. None of the defendants appeared to contest the case on the appointed day, however, and Judge L. S. Sherman retired to his chambers to prepare a decision. On 23 February 1880 Judge Sherman announced his decision in this lawsuit, ruling that the Reorganized Church had clearly established its position as the legal successor to the early Mormon organization founded by Joseph Smith, Jr., that plural marriage was not an original tenet of the faith and therefore invalidated Utah Mormon claims to succession, and that the Reorganized Church was heir to all the rights of the earlier possessions of the earlier organization. The Judge's opinion further stated: "And the Court do further find that the Plaintiff, the Reorganized Church of Jesus Christ of Latter Day Saints, is the True and Lawful successor of, and successor to the said original Church of Jesus Christ of Latter Day Saints, organized in 1830, and is entitled in law to all its rights and property."[45] The determination of this issue was critical for the leadership of the Reorganized Church: it legitimized the movement and increased its prestige with those outside of Mormondom.

But the court went further. It ruled that the supposed sale of the temple by the probate court of Joseph Smith's estate in 1862 was void and that all titles to the temple obtained from this action were invalid. Judge Sherman added that legal title to the temple was vested in the heirs of the prophet through legal trustee-in-trust practices. He wrote: "And the Court further finds that the legal title to said property is vested in the heirs of said Joseph Smith in trust for the legal successor of said organized church." Since the Reorganized Church had been recognized as the legal successor in the same case, the heirs were obligated by law to assign their rights to the property to the church corporation. This decision was also acceptable to the Reorganized Church counsel.[46] However, in a surprise ending that church leaders did not anticipate, Judge Sherman concluded that "the Court finds as matter of law that the Plaintiff is not entitled to the Judgment or relief prayed for in its petition. And thereupon it is ordered and adjudged that this action be dismissed at the costs of the Plaintiff." Although on the surface it might appear that the case settled nothing, since the Reorganization was not granted the relief sought, on further analysis Judge Sherman's final action was the only option available to him, given the circumstances of the case and the nature of the action brought by the church.[47]

As a matter of law it was indeed true that, after the court found that the Reorganized Church was the "True and Lawful successor" to the original Mormon church and that the title of the Kirtland Temple was vested in the heirs of Joseph Smith, Jr., as a trusteeship, the legal duty rested upon the Smith family to transfer the trusteeship to the church corporation. As a result, the Reorganized Church as a corporation had no right in law to win a judgment for possession of the temple against one of the trustees, in this case Joseph Smith III. Therefore, Judge Sherman had no choice but to dismiss the case. This ending could have been avoided if the Reorganized Church attorneys had brought the action against all other parties in the name of the trustee instead of the church corporation and had sought only to "quiet title" rather than ask for possession of the property.[48] Nonetheless, the outcome of the Kirtland Temple Suit gave the Reorganized Church legal ownership of the property, because soon after the case Joseph Smith III exercised his legal requirements as trustee of the property in lieu of his father, signing it over to the church corporation.

Even with the unforeseen decision, the outcome of the court case was favorable to the Reorganization. Smith had been very lucky indeed. The case had been uncontested; had the Utah Latter-day Saints offered a defense, there is no way of determining in what direction the court's opinion might have gone. The timing had also been excellent. The Reorganization capitalized on a national tide of opposition to plural marriage, one that would very quickly bring it into the national political arena with a new vigor. Along with that came an opposition to Mormonism, and this case represented an opportunity to at least add some impetus to the attack. Just how much the judge was reacting to the arguments of the Reorganized Church's case and how much he was striking a blow against Utah Mormonism is unclear.

Whatever the case, the Reorganized Church benefited. Unquestionably, the outcome of the Kirtland Temple Suit boosted the morale of the Reorganization and raised the status of the church among non-Mormons. Even as the case was underway, during January 1880 Joseph Smith accepted a speaking engagement in the Carthage Jail, the very site of his father's murder. He took tremendous satisfaction in this episode, taking it as a sign that he and the Reorganized Church were becoming ever more respectable in the eyes of Americans. In part, he believed, the Kirtland Temple Suit was responsible for this change.[49] Additionally, once the case was concluded, Joseph Smith III exploited the court's decision as much as he dared, sending copies of the opinion to numerous newspapers and making speeches about the ruling, emphasizing that the Reorganization had been declared by a court the legal successor of his father's movement.[50] It was a jubilant period and a major milestone in the development of the Reorganized Church, for it brought greater prestige to the movement and helped win favor among the antipolygamy elements of the nation.

Smith took great pride in this opinion, for the court had vindicated his work and gone on record as saying that his father had not initiated the practice of plural marriage. He could thereafter use the court's opinion in seeking to stamp out polygamy, for now it could be proven, at least if one revered the verdict of the American judicial system as Smith did, that the doctrine had not been a part of the Mormon faith during his father's lifetime and could not be protected under the freedom-of-religion clause of the Constitution. His publicity campaign had the desired effect of making the American public more aware of the work being done by the Reorganized Church to eliminate polygamy. Smith commented a few years later that the decision had "certainly drawn the attention of the world upon us as nothing else [had] ever done."[51]

Almost immediately after the court case had been decided, Smith began to receive offers, as head of the church, to take a more prominent role in the secular antipolygamy campaign from people who had previously been uninterested in his movement's activities. Some longtime anti-Mormon crusaders wrote to express their sympathy for the blow Smith and the Reorganization had struck against the Utah Mormon church and to pledge their support of the prophet's activities. The large transcontinental railroads granted Reorganized Church missionaries free passes to ride their trains as they became more aware of the movement's activities within Mormonism. On one occasion Smith was even solicited by officials in Mexico for advice in dealing with members of the Utah faction who were settling in some of the country's northern provinces and causing quite a stir in the region.[52]

At the same time that Smith's publicizing efforts were at their height, the national tenor began turning more unfavorable toward the theocratic system that fostered polygamy. People who had not previously shown much interest in the antipolygamy reform movement became active agitators during the 1880s. Consequently, politicians began to listen with more interest to the antipolygamists lobbying for harsher legislation in Washington. Smith's role in this agitation was vocal and constant. Throughout the 1880s, as the crusade heated up nationwide, Smith became increasingly influential in the nation's capital. He kept up a running correspondence with many of those concerned about the "Mormon Question," including Congressman James M. Ashley of Ohio, Congressman William F. Hepburn of Michigan, President Rutherford B. Hayes, President James A. Garfield, Senator George F. Edmunds of Vermont, Governor Eli H. Murray of Utah Territory, and several politicians of lesser note. His advice was monolithic—destroy plural marriage and Mormon theocratic power—but he urged caution to avoid unlawfully depriving individuals of religious freedom.[53]

The snowballing power of the antipolygamy crusade was evident when James A. Garfield delivered his inaugural address in 1881. Influenced at least partially by his contact with Smith and other agitators, Garfield demanded that Congress act to eliminate the Mormon problem with stricter and better enforced laws. Near the same time Smith also made recommendations to Senator George F. Edmunds of Vermont on the framing of legislation that eventually passed in 1882 as the Edmunds Act, providing for the arrest and prosecution of those engaging in plural marriage, or as the law called it, "unlawful cohabitation."[54] Still later Smith met and discussed the enforcement of this legislation with Governor Eli H. Murray of Utah Territory, who agreed with Smith that the more than ninety percent of Mormons who did not practice plural marriage should not suffer along with offenders. Murray promised a tough but fair enforcement policy and with some notable exceptions he delivered.[55]

Despite Joseph Smith's constant agitation for antipolygamy enforcement, he and his lieutenants tried to act justly toward the Mormon people in general. Therefore, he was especially troubled by an incident he witnessed while visiting Salt Lake City on 4 July 1885—an incident that colored his perspectives even more negatively toward the Latter-day Saint leadership. The apparently insignificant incident became a touchstone for his belief that the Mormon institution was disloyal to the United States. On the morning of the Fourth of July non-Mormons in Salt Lake City discovered that the watchman at the city hall had hoisted the nation's flag only to half-staff, as if in mourning. Smith noted that within an hour the city was in turmoil. When he arrived at the city hall, a crowd was already there, milling about and watching a squad of Regular Army troops attempting to raise the flag while another group of city officials and police tried to prevent the raising. One of the city officials declared that the Mormon people had nothing to celebrate on that national holiday and would not permit the flag to be raised.

The forces stalemated for a time, and finally Governor Eli Murray arrived at the scene. Smith remembered that "by the calm and dispassionate exercise of his good judgment and authority, trouble was averted, the flag was taken down and was not hoisted again during the day." This did not end the affair, however, for territorial officials, fearing that some altercation might arise during the Fourth of July festivities, called out the Army from Fort Douglas to keep order. Smith remembered that he was stirred by the presence of these troops and their ability to ensure order. "[W]hen I viewed the little company of soldiers in their blue uniforms, rifles on shoulders, filing past me down the street to their place of encampment," he commented, "I could not repress a strong feeling of exultation . . . As a citizen of the United States and of one of the sovereign States of that Union, and as a free man, at liberty to come and go in that city and Territory where priestly domination prevailed, I could not help a thrill of joy passing through me, as I realized that that company of uniformed and steadily marching men represented the power and authority of a still higher government—the Republic." He became convinced from then on that the goals of the Reorganized Church—to destroy plural marriage and bring Mormondom within the purview of government authority—could not fail.[56]

At the same time, Smith recognized that not all Mormons were polygamists or disloyal to the United States and should not be persecuted. For this reason, when in 1886 Senator Edmunds proposed a bill stiffening antipolygamy laws and destroying the political identity of the Mormon church, Smith took a leading part in trying to temper its wording and enforcement to ensure against violation of any individual's freedom of worship.[57] "Unwise legislation in the present crisis can not fail to be productive of evil," he warned Representative William F. Hepburn of Michigan concerning this proposed bill. "No scheming for mere political effect ought to be for the moment tolerated," he added in an obvious reference to using the polygamy issue both to build political support among the people involved in the crusade and to disfranchise Utahns. "Solid work for the benefit of the people governed and the maintaining of the supremacy of the institutions and laws of the Country ought to be sought after," rather than political favor, Smith warned.

Smith asked Hepburn to remember that an ironclad oath proposed by the Edmunds bill, by which all Mormons would have to disavow any connection with their temple beliefs and forsake other religious commitments as a prerequisite for suffrage, stood very close to a violation of freedom of religion. He pleaded with Hepburn to make Congress understand that it must "wisely discriminate between acts of disloyalty and that which is belief preparatory to the life beyond." Smith's closing comments summed up his impression of the Edmunds bill and his belief concerning the delicate matter of religion's relationship to the state. The polygamy question aside for the moment, Smith discussed the legality of the bill's forcing Mormons to denounce their religion: "I acknowledge the right of the government to define largely what the rights may be to control my civil actions [as it does regarding plural marriage]; but certainly deny the right to impose oaths upon me that ask me to renounce my allegiance to god in any sense; as this oath by Senator Edmunds may be construed to do."[58] A month later Smith wrote to Edmunds personally to explain his position on the Utah problem with greater clarity. He told the senator that he favored moderation in dealing with nonpolygamist Mormons, allowing them all the rights and privileges of full United States citizenship.

This did not mean, however, that he was turning soft on plural marriage itself. He remained as steadfastly opposed to this doctrine as he had ever been but did not want to persecute innocent people for their fellow church members' crimes. His natural practicality prompted him in this direction. He may have also been concerned about the legislation being used against his followers, but there is insufficient evidence to be sure on this point. Whatever the case he had no sympathy for polygamists. Smith told Senator Edmunds: "The hand of Government has too long been clothed in silk; those who had attempted legislation have feared to hurt; this made the leaders of the polygamists bold and aggressive, and they presume upon the old time plea of 'persecution, oppression, religious intolerance, the rights of conscience,' &c." If Edmunds restricted his activity to antipolygamy legislation, leaving other aspects of the religion alone, Smith counseled, there would be little trouble with nonpolygamist opposition to the bill. If he persisted in attacking the Mormon church as a whole, however, Congress would find itself with a huge Mormon war on its hands. He explained that it would cost millions of dollars to subdue the Rocky Mountain Saints if the government carried through this program in Utah. In addition, there would be great loss in property and quite probably in human life. Certainly, ill-feelings would persist for generations after the "Cohab Hunts" had ended.[59]

When the Edmunds-Tucker Act passed Congress in February 1887 and became law with presidential signature, Joseph Smith received it with mixed emotions. At least part of his argument about fairness to Mormon church members had been heard, but in many respects the act was disappointing. The law, as Smith had hoped would be the case, was directed at polygamists. It provided for more strict enforcement and stiffer prison sentences, loosened the confines of legality under which federal marshals worked, and permitted certain types of circumstantial evidence to be admitted in court cases dealing with plural marriage. All of these results of the Edmunds-Tucker Act were acceptable to Joseph Smith. But he seriously questioned some of its other sections. The act disincorporated the Mormon church and provided for the seizure of all church property in excess of $25,000. It called for a test oath of allegiance to the United States government before any Utahns could serve in public office or exercise their franchises. Smith had already protested the oath's inclusion to Senator Edmunds and he accepted the rest of the provisions of the act only with reservation. Once it was enacted, however, Smith supported its enforcement, concluding that while it was not the best tool to resolve the Utah question it was the only one available and therefore had the potential of ending the half-century-long practice of polygamy.[60]

Smith was correct in this assessment. Under the new, tougher law United States marshals rounded up most of the polygamists who did not flee outside the nation and placed them in prison. Finally, after four years of harsh and in some cases ruthless enforcement, and only after thousands of lives had been ruined and much property destroyed, a new Mormon church president, Wilford Woodruff, realized that his people could not survive much longer in the underground society they had erected to forestall the federal assault on polygamy. Woodruff decided to make a compromise. On 6 October 1890, after guarantees of peace had been made by federal authorities, Woodruff issued a manifesto declaring that the church would henceforth abide by the laws of the land. In effect, the church swore it would no longer sanction polygamist marriages, meaning that within a generation the practice would officially die out, with the understanding that no further prosecution would be undertaken.[61]

Although Joseph Smith had mixed feelings about the suffering of the Utah Saints at the hands of federal officials, he took great pride in the elimination of plural marriage as a tenet of the religion. After a thirty-year struggle it was one step toward the complete elimination of evil and a great stride toward realizing the goal of his father's quest for an earthly utopia. He believed it was worth doing; however, he wished it had not been necessary. It signified for Smith that his efforts were indeed reforming the Mormon movement; although the Reorganization actually had little to do with the Utah Mormon decision to end plural marriage, Smith believed that he could take a fair measure of credit for the action. He summarized his belief about the ending of polygamy in a letter to Congressman Moses Thatcher of Utah upon the state's entrance into the Union: "I have watched the course of the events as it had appeared to the public and have been anxious to see the right vindicated." With the passing of plural marriage, Smith was convinced, the right *had* been vindicated, justice had triumphed, truth had prevailed, and, moreover, the church had been cleansed of its most prevalent blemish.[62]

NOTES

1. Joseph Smith to James A. Garfield, 18 June 1880, Joseph Smith III Letterbook #3, Reorganized Church of Jesus Christ of Latter Day Saints Library–Archives, Independence, Mo.

2. For further information on the antipolygamy crusade see Charles A. Cannon, "The Awesome Power of Sex: The Polemical Campaign Against Mormon Polygamy," *Pacific Historical Review* 43 (February 1974): 61–84; Gustive O. Larson, *The "Americanization" of Utah for Statehood* (San Marino, Calif.: Huntington Library, 1971), passim.

3. Joseph Smith, Jason W. Briggs, and W. W. Blair, "The Declaration of Loyalty to the Government of the United States, by the Church of Jesus Christ of Latter Day Saints," *True Latter Day Saints' Herald* 3 (May 1863): 201–2. For a discussion of questions of loyalty among the Mormons of Utah during the Civil War see E. B. Long, *The Saints and the Union: Utah Territory During the Civil War* (Urbana: University of Illinois Press, 1981).

4. James M. Ashley to Joseph Smith, 10 May 1866, Joseph Smith III Papers, Reorganized Church Library–Archives.

5. Joseph Smith and Heman C. Smith, *The History of the Reorganized Church of Jesus Christ of Latter Day Saints* (Independence, Mo.: Herald Publishing House, 1967), 3:349; Joseph Smith, "The Memoirs of President Joseph Smith (1832–1914)," *Saints' Herald* 82 (16 July 1935): 912.

6. Smith, "Memoirs," *Saints' Herald* 82 (16 July 1935): 912–13; Nels Anderson, *Deseret Saints: The Mormon Frontier in Utah* (Chicago: University of Chicago Press, 1966), pp. 263–65.

7. See note 6. Smith had long been involved in seeking to prove that his father was not a polygamist. For excellent discussions of how this affected the Reorganized Church's development and relations with outside

organizations, see Richard P. Howard, "The Changing RLDS Response to Mormon Polygamy: A Preliminary Analysis," *Journal of the John Whitmer Historical Association* 3 (1983): 14–29, and Alma R. Blair, "RLDS Views of Polygamy: Some Historiographical Notes," *John Whitmer Historical Association Journal* 5 (1985): 16–28.

8. Smith, "Memoirs," *Saints' Herald* 82 (16 July 1935): 912–13. Some of Smith's sources, cited for Representative Ashley in support of his father's innocence concerning plural marriage, were *Nauvoo* (Ill.) *Neighbor*, 19 June 1844; *Times and Seasons* (Nauvoo, Ill.), 5 (15 March 1844): 474.

9. Smith, "Memoirs," *Saints' Herald* 82 (16 July 1935): 912–13.

10. Joseph Smith, "Pleasant Chat," *True Latter Day Saints' Herald* 9 (15 July 1866): 177–78; Joseph Smith to Charles Derry, 29 June 1866, Joseph Smith III Papers.

11. *Deseret News* (Salt Lake City, Utah), 8 January 1868; Edward W. Tullidge, *The History of Salt Lake City* (Salt Lake City, Utah: Star Printing Co., 1886), chapter 42; B. H. Roberts, *A Comprehensive History of the Church of Jesus Christ of Latter-day Saints* (Salt Lake City, Utah: Deseret News Press, 1930), 5:220; Anderson, *Desert Saints,* pp. 264–68.

12. *Congressional Globe* (Washington, D.C.), 21:1772–76; J. Kenneth Melville, *Conflict and Compromise: The Mormons in Mid-Nineteenth Century Politics* (Provo, Utah: Brigham Young University Press, 1974), pp. 93–94.

13. The story of this conflict is analyzed in James B. Allen and Glen M. Leonard, *The Story of the Latter-day Saints* (Salt Lake City, Utah: Deseret Book Co., 1976), pp. 295–320; Richard D. Poll, "The Mormon Question Enters National Politics, 1850–1856," *Utah Historical Quarterly* 25 (April 1957): 117–31; Norman F. Furniss, *The Mormon Conflict, 1850–1859* (New Haven, Conn.: Yale University Press, 1960); Long, *The Saints and the Union*; LeRoy R. Hafen and Ann W. Hafen, eds., *The Utah Expedition, 1857–1858: A Documentary Account of the United States Military Movement under Colonel Albert Sidney Johnston, and the Resistance by Brigham Young and the Mormon Nauvoo Legion* (Glendale, Calif.: Arthur H. Clark Co., 1982).

14. Smith, Briggs, and Blair, "Declaration of Loyalty," pp. 201–2; Joseph Smith, Alexander H. Smith, Mark H. Forscutt, W. W. Blair, and Josiah Ells, "Memorial to Congress from a Committee of the Reorganized Church of Jesus Christ of Latter Day Saints, on the Claims and Faith of the Church," *True Latter Day Saints' Herald* 17 (April 1870): 321–27.

15. *Amboy* (Ill.) *Weekly Times,* 11 April 1860.

16. Roberts, *Comprehensive History,* 5:353; H. H. Bancroft, *History of Utah* (San Francisco: The History Co., 1889), pp. 661–62; *Latter-day*

Saints Millennial Star (Liverpool, England), 33:112; Anderson, *Desert Saints*, pp. 264–68.

17. David H. Smith to Joseph Smith, 12 November 1870, Miscellaneous Letters and Papers, Reorganized Church Library–Archives.

18. *Weekly Argus* (Sandwich, Ill.), 21 June 1879.

19. A remarkable individual, Edward W. Tullidge was a professional writer who specialized in church history. First involved with Utah Mormonism in the latter 1870s, he converted to the Reorganization. His stormy career has been described in William Frank Lye, "Edward Wheelock Tullidge, The Mormons' Rebel Historian," *Utah Historical Quarterly* 28 (January 1960): 57–75. Tullidge's role in the Utah dissenting movement, the Godbeites, during the 1870s has been accented in Ronald W. Walker, "Edward Tullidge: Historian of the Mormon Commonwealth," *Journal of Mormon History* 3 (1976): 55–72. His work within the Reorganized Church has been described in Richard P. Howard, "Edward W. Tullidge: RLDS Enigma," *Saints' Herald* 125 (October 1978): 50, 125 (November 1978): 52, 125 (December 1978): 52, and Roger D. Launius's brief essay, "Edward W. Tullidge and the Reorganization," *Restoration Trail Forum* 10 (February 1984): 1, 4–6.

20. Edward W. Tullidge to Rutherford B. Hayes, 19 October 1879, Letters Received Regarding Polygamy, United States Department of the Interior, microfilm in Utah State Historical Society, Salt Lake City, Utah; Walker, "Edward Tullidge," p. 67.

21. *Weekly Argus*, 10 September 1881.

22. Ibid., 17 September 1881.

23. *New York Tribune*, 19 January 1880; *Salt Lake* (Utah) *Daily Herald*, 12 December 1879; *Deseret News*, 20 January 1880; *Weekly Argus*, 10 September 1881; Anderson, *Desert Saints*, pp. 309–10; Richard D. Poll, ed., *Utah History* (Provo, Utah: Brigham Young University Press, 1978), pp. 694–96.

24. Smith, "Memoirs," *Saints' Herald* 83 (11 February 1936): 177.

25. See Joseph Smith's correspondence on Cadwell's behalf. Joseph Smith to President R. B. Hayes of U.S., n.d., Joseph Smith III Papers; Joseph Smith to Hon. R. J. Oglesby, 23 August 1878; to Hon. P. C. Hayes, 23 August 1778; to Hon. B. F. Marsh, 23 August 1878; to Hon. Alvin Saunders, 23 August 1878; to Henry M. Pollard, 23 August 1878, all in Joseph Smith III Letterbook #1, Reorganized Church Library–Archives.

26. Joseph Smith to George E. Payne, 27 April 1876; Joseph Smith to Joseph F. McDowell, 16 June 1876, both in Joseph Smith III Letterbook #3; Joseph Smith to George E. Payne, 31 January 1879; Joseph Smith to Frederick Y. Mather, 23 December 1879, both in Joseph Smith III Letterbook #2, Reorganized Church Library–Archives; William H. Bohnard,

"Kirtland Temple Report," April 1934, Project 25, District 22, Northern Ohio, Historic American Buildings Survey, Kirtland File, Lake County Historical Society, Mentor, Ohio; Vida E. Smith, *Young People's History of the Church*, 2 vols. (Lamoni, Iowa: Herald Publishing House, 1918), 2:129.

27. George E. Paine, "Abstract of Title," 5 January 1878, copy in Historical Files, Kirtland Temple Historic Center, Kirtland, Ohio.

28. Joseph Smith, Jr., *History of the Church of Jesus Christ of Latter-day Saints*, ed. B. H. Roberts (Salt Lake City, Utah: Deseret Book Co., 1976), 4:286–87.

29. On Emma Smith see Linda King Newell and Valeen Tippetts Avery, *Mormon Enigma: Emma Hale Smith, Prophet's Wife, "Elect Lady," Polygamy's Foe* (Garden City, N.Y.: Doubleday and Co., 1984). The insufficient nature of legal claims advanced by some Mormon factions have been challenged in Israel A. Smith, "The Kirtland Temple Litigation," *Saints' Herald* 90 (9 January 1943): 8–11, 22, and Elbert A. Smith, comp., *The Church in Court* (Lamoni, n.d.), pp. 3–6.

30. "Abstract of Title and Encumbrances: To Land in the Township of Kirtland, County of Lake, and State of Ohio," The Clark and Pike Company, Abstractors and Engineers, Willoughby, Ohio, copy in Historical Files, Kirtland Temple Historic Center.

31. Ibid.; Paine, "Abstract of Title," 5 January 1878; "Estate of Joseph Smith, Jr., Deceased," Administrative Docket A, p. 240, Lake County Courthouse, Painesville, Ohio; Real Estate Record S, p. 526, Lake County Courthouse.

32. Real Estate Record S, p. 371, Lake County Courthouse; Paine, "Abstract of Title," 5 January 1878.

33. Smith, *Young People's History*, 2:129.

34. Real Estate Records, 4:67, Lake County Courthouse; Paine, "Abstract of Title," 5 January 1878; Joseph Smith III, Diary, 17 February 1873, Reorganized Church Library–Archives.

35. Joseph Smith III to Israel A. Smith, 17 February 1898, 26 December 1898, Miscellaneous Letters and Papers; Joseph Smith III to Cousin Mary B., 4 December 1877, Joseph Smith III Letterbook #1A, Reorganized Church Library–Archives.

36. Joseph Smith III to Emma Bidamon, 8 March 1872, Miscellaneous Letters and Papers.

37. Joseph Smith III to Alexander Fyfe, 9 July 1881, Joseph Smith III Letterbook #3, Reorganized Church Library–Archives; "Electra Stratton to Editor," *True Latter Day Saints' Herald* 22 (1 February 1875): 86.

38. Smith to Fyfe, 9 July 1881.

39. Smith, "Memoirs," *Saints' Herald* 82 (3 December 1935): 1553; Smith to Fyfe, 9 July 1881; Smith and Smith, *History of Reorganized Church*, 4:148, 172.

40. Joseph Smith to George E. Paine, 27 April 1876; Joseph Smith to Joseph F. McDowell, 16 June 1876; Joseph Smith to Mark H. Forscutt, 22 February 1878; Joseph Smith to Collector of Taxes for Kirtland, 23 February 1878, all in Joseph Smith III Letterbook #1A.

41. Smith and Smith, *History of Reorganized Church*, 4:172.

42. Henry A. Stebbins to George E. Paine, 14 January 1879, Forscutt–Stebbins Letterbook, Reorganized Church Library–Archives.

43. Joseph Smith to George E. Paine, 31 January 1879, Joseph Smith III Letterbook #2, Reorganized Church Library–Archives. See also Joseph Smith to Frederic Y. Mather, 23 December 1879, Joseph Smith III Letterbook #2.

44. Common Pleas Record, Book T, 18 August 1879, pp. 482–83; Lake County Courthouse.

45. Reorganized Church of Jesus Christ of Latter Day Saints vs. Lucius Williams, et al., Common Pleas Record, Book T, 23 February 1880, p. 488; "The Reorganization in Court," *Saints' Herald* 27 (15 March 1880): 89.

46. See note 45.

47. See note 45.

48. Affidavit of Carroll L. Olson, Attorney at Law, 24 June 1969, copy in Historical Files, Kirtland Temple Historic Center; Israel A. Smith to Francis E. Lawler, 22 September 1947, copy in Historical Files, Kirtland Temple Historic Center.

49. Smith, "Memoirs," *Saints' Herald* 82 (3 December 1935): 1551–52.

50. "Kirtland Temple Suit," *Saints' Herald* 27 (15 March 1880): 236; Smith, "Memoirs," *Saints' Herald* 82 (3 December 1935): 1553–54; Joseph Smith to Publisher, *Tribune*, 2 March 1880; Joseph Smith to Publishers, *New York Times*, 2 March 1880, both in Joseph Smith III Letterbook #3; *Chicago Tribune*, 22 February 1880.

51. Joseph Smith to E. L. Kelley, 10 July 1883, Joseph Smith III Papers.

52. *Saints' Advocate* 4 (April 1882): 185–87, 198–99; Joseph Smith to E. F. Cragin, 18 February 1882; Joseph Smith to Charles Strang, 22 July 1882, both in Joseph Smith III Letterbook #3A, Reorganized Church Library–Archives; Joseph Smith to T. L. Kimball, 20 October 1879, Joseph Smith III Letterbook #2; Joseph Smith to John Codman, 15 December 1884; Joseph Smith to General E. A. Maxia, 5 August 1884, both in Joseph Smith III Letterbook #4, Reorganized Church Library–Archives.

53. Joseph Smith to Hon. J. C. Barrows, 29 December 1879, 3 January 1880, Joseph Smith III Letterbook #2; Smith, "Memoirs," *Saints' Herald* 83 (7 January 1936): 15–16.

54. Joseph Smith to Robert Warnock, 20 March 1882, Joseph Smith III Letterbook #2; *Congressional Globe* (Washington, D.C.), 15 February–14 March 1882; James D. Richardson, ed., *The Messages and Papers of the Presidents* (Washington, D.C.: Bureau of National Literature and Art, 1897), 7:11.

55. Joseph Smith to Bro. George, 20 June 1883, Miscellaneous Letters and Papers; Thomas F. O'Dea, *The Mormons* (Chicago: University of Chicago Press, 1957), p. 246; Smith, "Memoirs," *Saints' Herald* 83 (3 March 1936): 274.

56. Ibid. 83 (3 March 1936): 274, 83 (10 March 1936): 305–6.

57. Joseph Smith to William H. Kelley, 14 January 1886, William H. Kelley Collection, Reorganized Church Library–Archives.

58. Joseph Smith to Hon. W. F. Hepburn, 9 February 1886, Joseph Smith III Letterbook #4.

59. Joseph Smith to Hon. G. F. Edmunds, 4 March 1886, ibid.

60. Kenneth W. Godfrey, "The Coming of the Manifesto," *Dialogue: A Journal of Mormon Thought* 5 (Autumn 1970): 11–25; *United States Statutes at Large*, 22:635–41 (1887); *Salt Lake* (Utah) *Herald*, 20 February 1887, 11 March 1887.

61. Roberts, *Comprehensive History*, 6:146–301; Henry J. Wolfinger, "A Reexamination of the Woodruff Manifesto in the Light of Utah Constitutional History," *Utah Historical Quarterly* 39 (Fall 1971): 32–49.

62. Joseph Smith to Hon. Moses Thatcher, 18 December 1896, Joseph Smith III Letterbook #7, Reorganized Church Library–Archives.

12

Crisis in the Ranks

Even as Joseph Smith worked to concentrate more authority in his presidential office, to make a meaningful response to the church's zionic ideal, and to deal with the polygamy question, the Reorganization began to experience certain internal difficulties that erupted during the latter 1870s. The delicate balance of unity in policy and doctrine that Smith so laboriously worked to achieve during the middle part of the decade was jeopardized by the activities of a small group of Latter Day Saints who were concerned with questions of authoritarianism, political power, and theological dogmatism. Led by two influential apostles—Jason W. Briggs, one of the prime movers of the movement since the 1850s, and Zenos H. Gurley, Jr., the son of another early Reorganized Church leader—this faction struggled with Joseph Smith for the better part of a decade.[1]

Both Briggs and Gurley were theologically liberal for their time and recognized the necessity of subjecting religious teaching to the most rigorous of tests. They asked themselves whether a doctrine was reasonable, what the writer of the scripture upon which it was based might have intended, and what factors of evolutionary thought might have changed it from its original meaning. Briggs's and Gurley's approach to religious questions was, no doubt, quite modern. It was also anathema to Joseph Smith III and most of the other Latter Day Saints, individuals who had, for the most part, little religious training and who adopted a very literal and legalistic interpretation of the scriptures.[2]

During the latter 1870s both Briggs and Gurley took the opportunity to express their liberal theological ideals. In October 1874 Jason Briggs founded *The Messenger*, a Reorganization newspaper based in Salt Lake City and intended as a missionary tool to be used in converting the Saints of the Great Basin. While *The Messenger* may have been aimed initially at the Mormons, Briggs quickly turned it on the conservative, dogmatic Reorganized Church members, using it as a personal vehicle for the presentation of his ideas about church history, doctrine, and policy.[3]

In the paper's pages Briggs challenged the most cherished tenets of the Reorganization's doctrine, including many teachings peculiarly Mormon in conception. He attacked the Mormon concept of the preexistence—a spiritual existence with God before the physical creation—which had been expounded by Joseph Smith, Jr., and accepted as a keystone of the faith since the 1830s.[4] Briggs claimed that a belief in man's existence before the physical creation implied that God did not create mankind and, therefore, was less than all powerful.[5] Briggs concluded that Joseph the Prophet had been wrong about this question and that if he had been deceived about "preexistence how do we know that he was not" also deceived about "half the truths he claimed to reveal?"[6]

Briggs also challenged Joseph Smith, Jr.'s conception of the gathering of the Saints into a close-knit community for the building of Zion. In a series of *Messenger* essays he claimed that belief in a literal gathering of God's elect was completely without scriptural foundation and in practice had proved foolhardy.[7] He contended that throughout the movement's history every "attempt in gathering and locating Zion had been a failure. Shall we give rise to a tradition that in coming generations shall reproduce these attempts?" He, of course, told the church that it should discard its zionic ideal because the past "failure [had] resulted from the theory." Again Briggs noted that past prophetic leadership had been wrong, calling into serious question the work of Joseph Smith, Jr.[8]

Finally, Briggs laid siege to the most important doctrine governing the Mormon movement—the addition of revelation through a living prophet to all the world's previous scripture. On the basis of the newly emerging discipline of higher criticism, Briggs insisted revelation, whether spoken or written, was intended for a specific time and place and was not necessarily universally applicable. Briggs declared that written scripture was not the literal word of God but rather the work of individuals who had written what they believed God had told them, which was not always what He may have actually intended.[9] This same caution applied to the modern revelation of the Mormon prophets as well. To support his assertions Briggs described inconsistencies in the Old Testament, maintaining that these writings must be analyzed against the history of the Hebrew people and the cultural factors that shaped Israel's peculiar *Weltanschauung* or world view.[10]

Nor was Briggs content only with criticisms of the Bible; he cast aspersions on the unique Mormon scriptures—the Book of Mormon and the Doctrine and Covenants—as well. He did not object to these works themselves, accepting the possibility and even probability of divine revelation to a modern prophet, but he questioned the church's uncritical belief that if the prophet claimed a statement as divine revelation it was necessarily God's eternal truth. In essence, Briggs said, "revelation corresponds with the experience and does not transcend it, though it may seem to." The revelatory experience, therefore, was an incredibly ill-defined and difficult means of explaining the divine encounter. Briggs urged the Saints to consider, not just prayerfully but also critically, every statement made in the scriptures for reasonableness and applicability to current situations. This was the only manner in which the church would be able to avoid apostasy, he insisted, because all revelation to any prophet evolved gradually from the germ of an idea to full explanation.[11] Briggs summarized his sophisticated position in an 1876 essay entitled "Inspiration." He wrote: "Any other view which makes inspiration absolute, a divine deposit, whether in the ark, or the tables, or in the canon of scriptures, subjects us to the crushing force of objections, based upon those errors, contradictions, and improprieties, that 'neither we nor our fathers could (or can) bear,' and our children will not attempt it." [12]

While Jason Briggs was the spokesman for the new liberalism within the Reorganized Church during the 1870s, Zenos Gurley was its politician. Both wanted to change the thrust of the church's theological development along lines more rational, urbane, and intellectual. They had a handful of followers, many of them close friends and relatives. For instance, Ebenezer Robinson, a man who had joined the Mormon movement in Kirtland in 1835 and affiliated with the Reorganized Church in 1863, supported the position of Briggs and Gurley, but he did so not so much because of the liberal theological ideas they espoused as because Zenos Gurley was his son-in-law. Although the two leaders' goals were similar, Briggs and Gurley pursued independent methods of accomplishing them. Briggs was completely apolitical and aimed at demonstrating to the Saints a more rational system of belief. Gurley believed this an acceptable approach as far as it went, but he was much more politically minded and sought to work within the Reorganized Church's administrative system to effect change.[13]

During the latter 1870s, both Briggs and Gurley made every effort to assert their complex ideas; of course they attracted the attention of more orthodox church members who did not understand their theology and distrusted their motives. Accordingly, Joseph Smith received complaints from throughout the church demanding that he stop the presentation of what many considered the heretical teachings of the two apostles. As in all cases of internal dissensions, Smith took a cautious and tolerant approach toward both positions.[14] He told the Saints that Briggs and Gurley had the right of self-expression and suggested that their comments had perhaps been misinterpreted. Convinced that a consensus position had already been adopted, he asked the membership to be patient and the problem would work itself out. Then Smith urged the two apostles to be more circumspect in the presentation of conceptions that ran counter to the accepted position. After hearing Smith's admonitions for more moderation several times, Jason Briggs sent a caustic letter to William Kelley, exclaiming that "there is but little encouragement for an Elder who thinks as well as feels."[15]

While these theological questions were important, Briggs and Gurley were reacting, at least in part, to the greater degree of administrative authority Joseph Smith III had brought to the prophetic office. Beginning in the 1870s first Briggs and then Gurley began questioning the church membership's unbending devotion to the Smith family and obsequious obedience to the president of the church. In 1875 Briggs complained to a fellow member of the Quorum of Twelve Apostles, William H. Kelley, that the movement seemed to be leaving itself open to the establishment of a dynastic royal family that could rule dictatorially through the church presidency if it so chose. He decried what he called the incipient "Family Worship" of members of the Smith family and asked for a reevaluation of the prophetic office with the intention of redistributing ecclesiastical power among the various priesthood quorums. Essentially, Briggs desired a return to the more democratic governmental system of the early Reorganization at the expense of the authority that Joseph Smith had so cautiously gained during the preceding fifteen years. On one occasion in 1877 Briggs's fear of Smith's centralized authority led him to charge the Reorganization president with "Caesarism."[16]

Of course this challenge set off Smith, but he reacted even more strongly when Briggs and Gurley publicly attacked the integrity of his father, charging that Joseph Smith, Jr., had been the originator and chief practitioner of polygamy in the early church. Both Briggs and Gurley insisted that Joseph III and the Reorganized Church were acting hypocritically by trying to purify the name of the elder Smith and that the church should take the honest position that the prophet had been involved, that he had been wrong, and that God would punish him for his transgressions. Joseph Smith III had no sympathy for this position. He had long sought to vindicate his father by clearing him of any involvement in the practice of plural marriage. This vindication would be a hollow victory, however, unless Smith could achieve united support for his position within his own movement.[17]

Unable to accept the conceptions of Briggs and Gurley regarding this issue, Joseph Smith III tried to stop them. On one occasion in the spring of 1879, for instance, Zenos Gurley tried to publish an article in the *Saints' Herald* charging Joseph Smith, Jr., with plural marriage. When Smith refused to publish the piece, Gurley fumed to him:

> I have felt somewhat sore and chagrined at the attempts made through the Herald to establish the innocence of your father touching polygamy, as though the work of God depended in any sense upon his innocence or guilt, and I may say here that *many* others in the church have expressed similar feelings to me, but have and do feel too delicate to speak with you upon the matter because it's your father. I however have more confidence in your good sense and judgment to allow such feelings preventing me, will you open the columns of

the Herald to the other side of the story? And have I not a right as a member of the Body to demand it? The impression is obtaining that the object of those statements and articles are to build up family name—hence selfish interests and is militating against you.

I believe firmly in your father's guilt and think it susceptible of proof, and have for years. . . . all the assertions you have made relative to your father cannot change the facts one iota, nor benefit him nor you, but eternity *will reveal* them. I believe then that your mission is something higher than that, however I will not question your right to follow the bent of your own mind. But I ask equal privilege for myself and others; that of being heard.[18]

Smith had little sympathy for Gurley's position. He appealed to the apostle's sense of mission and interest in maintaining unity within the church but then went on with a rigorous explanation of his unwillingness to allow the *Saints' Herald* to be used for a debate on the origins of plural marriage. "So far as the opening of the columns of the Herald to a discussion of the guilt of Joseph Smith from your pen is concerned," he wrote to Gurley, "were I to choose, I should much prefer to open them for Orson Pratt, John Taylor, or Joseph F. Smith for the obvious reason, that they hold that the dogma of polygamy is true, and that while Joseph Smith was its author he was innocent in so being; and to my mind the influence upon the church and upon the world would be infinitely less harmful by such a course; than would be the presentation of the same discussion by you or others in the Reorganization who believe the doctrine to be evil, but believe him to have been its human author."[19] Essentially, the necessity of maintaining a consensus of opinion, at least to the view of those outside the movement, was just as important for Joseph Smith as any other consideration. This issue remained a sore point between the prophet and the two liberal apostles for the rest of their lives.[20]

Unfortunately, Briggs and Gurley refused to temper the presentation of their ideas along the cautious lines suggested by the president, and as the situation continued unabated, even more protests reached Smith. Early in 1877 Joseph finally realized that he had to take action more forceful than simple counsel. Since the chief vehicle for the dissemination of Briggs's ideas was *The Messenger,* published by the church in Salt Lake City, Smith decided to end its publication. He defended his decision against protests by Jason

Briggs, saying that too many church members had been aroused by its columns; it was causing dissension within the movement, something he could not allow. Smith told Briggs in a letter of 22 January 1877: "I assume no right to dictate, but have supposed from the actions of the conferences since 1852, that if a matter was decided by the plain teaching of the books it was settled for all members of the Church. If this is not correct, nothing is gained by organization, for the word alone means nothing. However, I am a man of free speech and free inquiry, howbeit, he who mistakes *belief* for liberty will have a hard row to hoe."[21] Smith cautioned Briggs to ensure that his public discourses were orthodox. The goal of his presidency, Smith stated, was concensus and unity among the membership and he would not tolerate for long those who sought to destroy it.

Two days after Smith sent this letter, Briggs mailed a defense of his position to William H. Kelley. He acknowledged that he had received complaints about his ideas. "Some thoughts expressed by me others condemn I suppose," Briggs told Kelley, but "then they ought to show my errors, for which I have waited and still wait. . . . I ask no quarter of the intellect, or criticism, of any who choose to take exceptions. The avenues of light are open to us all, and I do not propose to shut my eyes—because everyone else shuts theirs."[22]

The breach between the two apostles and their supporters and Smith and most of the rest of the church widened during the conference of October 1877 when the representative body exercised its right by voting not to sustain Jason Briggs in his apostolic office. It did, however, choose to sustain Zenos Gurley, because he had largely taken a position in the background and his support of Briggs had not yet become public knowledge. The vote of no confidence, which placed Briggs's priesthood in an inactive status, was the first public statement made by the movement as a whole that it would not allow the teaching of such liberal conceptions and served as an important symbol of the church's conservative nature. During the months following this conference a committee appointed by the representatives assembled evidence against Briggs for a court of inquiry, reporting back at the April 1878 convening of the Saints. Joseph Smith, who had viewed the censure of Briggs with mixed feelings, urged the Saints to act tolerantly and mercifully toward the accused, recommending that the matter be dropped. Partially in deference to Smith's plea for compassion and partially because of insufficient evidence, the conference decided to dismiss the case against Briggs and restore him to his priesthood office. Although this confrontation came to nothing, it demonstrated the resolve of the majority of the church membership to disallow the teaching of ideas that ran counter to certain accepted beliefs.[23]

At the fall conference of 1878 a second public confrontation took place between Smith and the more conservative Saints and the two apostles, this time with Zenos Gurley taking a decidedly more public stand. At least partly in response to the perceived threat from liberal reformers, this conference passed a set of resolutions affirming the church's acceptance of the inspired revision of the Bible, the Book of Mormon, and the Doctrine and Covenants "as the standard of authority on all matters of church government and doctrine, and the final standard of reference on appeal in all controversies arising, or which may arise in the church of Christ."[24] Both Briggs and Gurley had already seriously challenged the revelatory experience and the absolute authority assigned to these scriptures by the church; therefore they protested the resolution. They claimed that it would force all church members of good conscience to proclaim their acceptance of the scriptures in their entirety without the opportunity to disregard certain parts that were unhistorical or without current application.[25]

Joseph Smith, to be sure, understood the crisis of conscience of these men, but he believed that there was nothing in the resolution that a loyal Latter Day Saint could not publicly avow. He suggested to these apostles that it had been merely a routine affirmation of the belief that the scriptures contained the word of God and would serve as the means of measuring all doctrinal ideas. Zenos Gurley was not persuaded by Smith's argument and asked to be removed from the Quorum of Twelve because he could not accept such a resolution. Jason Briggs, on the other hand, continued to serve as an apostle, all the while voicing protests against the church government. At the April 1879 conference he was charged with heresy; however, Joseph Smith intervened to see that the trial was postponed indefinitely, asking Briggs to curtail his espousal of doctrines that ran counter to the Reorganization's accepted canon or risk excommunication from an angry conference. He intimated that if Briggs maintained a low profile the whole controversy would soon be forgotten.[26]

Just as Smith believed he had brought the problem to a close, Zenos Gurley became involved again. After the April 1879 conference he had begun speaking throughout southern Iowa, explaining his position and calling for a reformation of the church. This brought a wave of protest from the more conservative membership. Stephen F. Walker, one of the leading citizens of the church's colony at Lamoni, complained to Smith in May 1879 about Gurley's "heretical" teachings. Smith replied that he appreciated Walker's information and promised action. "I am so glad you wrote me about Zenos," he told Walker; "I have been waiting for two years for some strange act from him." [27] At the same time, perhaps encouraged by Gurley's activity, Briggs also resumed his forceful pleas for liberal reforms within the Reorganization.

Clearly Joseph Smith had to deal with this situation, for the two influential leaders were creating too much dissension among the membership and he believed the crisis could bring anarchy. He did not want to let them join forces in any sort of internal political struggle, for they had a significant following within the church, and even if Smith was the victor, it would probably create a damaging rift within the movement. Nor did Smith want to act harshly, for it would not be Christianlike—a very important concern for the president—and, almost equally important, it would make martyrs of Briggs and Gurley and might bring on further conflict. He would have to deal with the conflict promptly but without malice, and Smith succeeded admirably.

Briggs was the dissenter most clearly in violation of church policy and Smith decided to settle the question of his "heresy" first; in doing so, he believed that Gurley would recognize his folly and return to orthodoxy. [28] During the fall conference of 1879 Smith implemented his newly formulated policy of controlling the Briggs-Gurley attack. Jason Briggs's case arose almost immediately after the convening of the first session; at Smith's direction the matter was referred to the Council of Twelve for resolution. He had previously discussed the Briggs affair with several members of the quorum, asking each to consider carefully the facts of the case and to treat him justly. He was sure that the apostles would decide that Briggs was guilty of heresy and deserving of censure. His expectations were fulfilled within two days: the conference voted that Briggs "stand rejected from the Quorum of the Twelve, and that he be forbidden to act in any of the offices of the church. And that he be so suspended until he makes restitution to the church." The chastized apostle was quite chagrined with this action and remained so through most of the next year.[29]

As Smith intended, the action taken by the conference in the Jason Briggs case prompted Zenos Gurley to be more circumspect in his public statements. Moreover, the censure made Gurley more willing to compromise, and Smith and other members of the church's hierarchy used this to bring Gurley back into the Twelve. Since the problem with Gurley rested essentially with the resolution affirming the scriptures, at the October 1879 conference Smith gained passage of an amendment to the document that stated, "It is not the intent and meaning of the said resolution to make a belief in the revelation in the Book of [Doctrine and] Covenants, or the abstract doctrines possibly contained in it, a test of reception and fellowship in the church, but that the things therein contained relating to the doctrine, rules of procedure and practice in the church should govern the ministry and elders as representatives of the church." Gurley, who wanted to return to the active ranks of the church, accepted this position and was readmitted into the Apostolic Quorum on the last day of the conference.[30]

As a result of the prophet's activities at the October 1879 conference, the two dissidents were separated in standing and their arguments diffused. Gurley, once more a member in good standing, was pleased to return to the fold, although he still disagreed with much of the church policy. Briggs, on the other hand, was a disgruntled outsider who tried to regain his position as a member of the Twelve. Joseph Smith sought to prohibit this restoration until Briggs admitted his faults and made amends. He explained his position in a letter of 25 May 1880 to Apostle Thomas W. Smith: "There is no parallel between Jason's offense and Zenos'. One [Jason Briggs] was defiant, scornful of public teaching; the other was a manly statement that he could not *Teach* [what he thought the church demanded concerning the scriptures]. One [Briggs] remained and does silently oppose notwithstanding the findings *of his peers:* the other made a frank statement through the accredited *officer* of the church, he *stood* with the church thus pledging himself, as his subsequent acts show, a consistent co-worker."[31] Finally, after Briggs had promised to curtail his excessive activities concerning the beliefs of the church, Smith and the general conference of

October 1880 restored him to full fellowship in the church and the Quorum of Twelve Apostles, because Briggs "stated to his quorum that in general he was in accord with the faith of the Reorganization and stood with us, on the findings of the Pres. last fall, as did Zenos."[32]

Although the controversy between the two apostles and the majority of the church was largely submerged after the restoration of Briggs's office in late 1880, the differences between the two systems of belief were very real and resulted in further difficulties during the mid-1880s. The rebellion of these two men was different this time, however, for it was led by Zenos Gurley and was manifested in a political maneuver to take authority from the hands of the prophet. Following the settlement of the first conflict in 1880 Joseph Smith had continued his consolidation program in an effort to gain enough authority to carry out the collective goals of the church efficiently. Gurley's attack, which emerged full-blown in 1884, directly challenged this program by urging a return to the more democratic church structure of the early Reorganization and charging the prophet with exercising authoritarianism. He then translated his challenge of the prophetic office into an assault on the conservative doctrines that he and Briggs had so long questioned.[33]

Unlike Briggs, who had no systemic method of changing the church into the movement he desired, Gurley developed a set of tactics that could achieve his goal. First, he enlisted support for change by questioning the programs, goals, and even the legitimacy of Joseph's administration. Next, he demanded the opening of the columns of the *Saints' Herald* to completely free debate on any question of importance to the movement for one year, during which time the church would presumably be informed of all various opinions, including his own. Gurley was convinced that if he had a forum for presenting his beliefs the rationality of his argument would convince even the most hard-nosed skeptic and lead to a better and more democratic church. Gurley also demanded that, following this free discussion, the general conference make a definitive statement concerning the position of the Reorganization on all religious questions of importance and that the membership adhere to this credo ever after.[34]

By early 1884 Gurley's demands for opening the *Saints' Herald* had been made public, and while his unique appeal had won some support from a few members of the Reorganized Church, notably from Jason Briggs and others of similar mind, the prophet and the other leading officials had flatly refused him access to the inter-- nal newspaper. Joseph Smith, aware that he was dealing with a far different protagonist than Briggs, adopted a policy of watchful caution. He had no intention of allowing the apostle to succeed in his quest, but his natural sense of pragmatism prompted him to avoid open confrontation which could divide the church. As a result, Smith created what could be called a safety envelope be- tween Gurley and the rest of the church. He would allow Gurley to push only so far before taking any action, and if he pushed progres- sively harder into forbidden territory, stirring up significant internal dissension, Smith would take increasingly more strident action to counteract him. Only as a last resort, as in the case involving Jason Briggs in 1879 and 1880, would Smith seek a public victory over Gurley.[35]

During the winter of 1884–85 Zenos Gurley challenged the pro- tective envelope that Smith had erected to shield the church from his potentially divisive demands. Smith, as editor of the *Saints' Her- ald,* had shown his tolerance of the situation by allowing Zenos Gurley to publish several theological articles in the church news- paper. Although Smith considered these articles quite harmless, some of the more conservative church members questioned the con- cepts presented and demanded the opportunity to respond. These responses prompted Gurley to write rebuttals, and before Smith could put a stop to the affair, the *Herald* had become a battleground for the liberal and conservative theologians of the movement. Dur- ing the debate Gurley challenged the supremacy of scripture as the absolute word of God, the authority of the prophet as the only means of gaining the will of God, the nature and purpose of the gathering, the meaning of Zion, the law of tithing, and doctrines stemming from the church's Nauvoo experience. The rank-and-file membership countered by defending the traditional conceptions of the movement and by charging Gurley with heresy.[36]

As winter became spring and the situation grew more heated, Smith moved to maintain the stability and harmony of the Reorga- nized Church. He believed that if such strife continued it could de- stroy the movement. Many Latter Day Saints demanded that action be taken against Gurley, but Joseph Smith was unwilling to take

Zenos H. Gurley, Sr., close associate to Jason Briggs in the founding of the Reorganization. He died in 1871. Courtesy Library–Archives of the Reorganized Church

Zenos H. Gurley, Jr., became an apostle of the Reorganized Church during the 1870s. From this office he mounted a liberal reform effort at the church structure. Like Briggs, he was stripped of his priesthood office in 1885 and withdrew from the church in 1886. Courtesy Library–Archives of the Reorganized Church

Jason W. Briggs, one of the founding members of the Reorganized Church during the early 1850s, became one of Joseph Smith III's problems during the 1880s, as he espoused liberal ideas that challenged church practice and doctrine. He was stripped of his apostolic rank in 1885 and resigned from the movement in 1886. Courtesy Library–Archives of the Reorganized Church

Isaac Sheen, first editor of the *True Latter Day Saints' Herald*, the official publication of the Reorganized Church. It was first issued in January 1860 and has enjoyed continuous publication to the present. Courtesy Library–Archives of the Reorganized Church

The chapel of the Reorganized Church built in Plano, Illinois, in 1868, the flagship congregation of the church during Smith's residency in Plano (1866–81). The chapel is still used by the Reorganized Church congregation in Plano. Courtesy Library–Archives of the Reorganized Church

Elijah Banta, primary field operative for the United Order of Enoch, Lamoni, Iowa, during the 1870s and 1880s. Courtesy Reorganized Church Library–Archives

Main Street in Lamoni, Iowa, circa 1905. Courtesy of Alma R. Blair

Home of David Dancer, Lamoni, Iowa. Dancer was a primary figure in the Reorganized Church corporation, the United Order of Enoch, which founded Lamoni. Photograph by author

Earliest photograph of the Kirtland Temple, circa 1875. This building, constructed by the early Saints in the 1830s, was acquired by Joseph Smith III in 1872. Following the Kirtland Temple Suit of 1880, it was transferred to the corporation of the Reorganized Church. The small building to the right of the Temple was a Methodist meeting house. That building was later acquired by Reorganized Church Apostle Gomer T. Griffiths for use by the Reorganization. Courtesy Library–Archives of the Reorganized Church

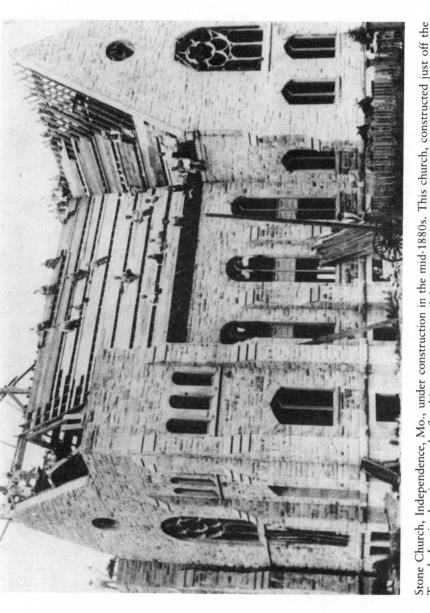

Stone Church, Independence, Mo., under construction in the mid-1880s. This church, constructed just off the Temple Lot in the city, was the flagship congregation of the Reorganized Church in Independence. For Joseph Smith III this building's construction signaled a coming of age of his movement and a return in force to the area from which Mormonism had been expelled in 1833. Courtesy Library–Archives of the Reorganized Church

On tour in England (l–r): British official J. E. Meredith; Joseph Smith III; R. C. Evans, ambitious member of the First Presidency; and Apostle John W. Rushton. Courtesy Library–Archives of the Reorganized Church

direct action until he learned that Gurley was himself planning a political maneuver for the April conference. Soon thereafter, the prophet decided that he would have to settle the matter once and for all. In February 1885 he wrote to William H. Kelley about the controversy. He said, "There are rumors that there will be something out of the ordinary line attempted, or done at the April conference [by Gurley and his supporters]. What is in the *Herald* seems to be only a prelude." Joseph admitted that he had tried "to avoid the hurt that might ensue if it [the conflict] came to the surface. But it seems that prudence had been construed to be *fear*, and, like Banquer's ghost, the thing 'will not down.' " He then confided that he intended to exercise his authority as president of the church to settle the conflict, telling Kelley that, although he did not know entirely what others wanted him to do, "I think, however, that my own course is determined upon." [37]

The conference body that convened in Lamoni, Iowa, on that April morning of 1885 was as surly a lot as ever seen in the church. They wanted to punish Gurley and his followers for what they considered an abuse of the high office and calling tendered. As a result, Joseph Smith was not surprised that, when the time came to sustain the church's presiding officers, the delegates to the conference voted overwhelmingly against both Gurley and Briggs as members of the Twelve Apostles. The body then asked Joseph Smith what the fate of these men should be—a moderate reprimand or harsh punishment. In an effort to mitigate tensions, Joseph declared that "they are still members of their quorum, and hold priesthood; but by reason of the vote not to sustain, are not authorized to act as ministers for the church, until such time as the disability imposed by the vote of conference is removed." [38]

After Joseph's mild reprimand the conference passed a resolution that was obviously directed against the two dissidents, making it impossible for them ever to be restored to full fellowship in the church. It read, "Resolved, That it is the sense of this body, that any man who accepts appointment and ordination as a representative of the church is under the obligation to teach, sustain, and seek to establish the faith of the church; and no one, be he whosoever he may be, has any right to attack the divinity of the faith in part, or as a whole, as said faith is set forth in the Bible, Book of Mormon, and Doctrine and Covenants." [39] While the official chastisement of

Briggs and Gurley had been mild, this resolution prohibited them from ever being in good conscience active members of the church.

As a result of these actions, at the general conference in April 1886 Briggs and Gurley, as well as several supporters, asked to be allowed to withdraw honorably from the Reorganized Church. Joseph Smith remarked in his memoirs that this episode in 1886 was shown to him in a spiritual experience that pointed the direction for his action. In this experience Smith said that he and his counselor in the First Presidency, W. W. Blair, were "engaged in tending three charcoal pits, such as are used in making charcoal. They were very well located, and we had carefully fitted our plates and built our fires, but for some reason difficulty arose in one of the pits; it kept burning out, . . . perhaps because of some flaw in the formation of the pit." He noted that the smoke and steam inside threatened to destroy the wood rather than char it as planned. Smith remembered that he decided to sacrifice some of the wood in the charcoal pit to correct the problem, hammering a large hole into the pit and allowing it to burn until it was under control. He wrote, "Thus the trouble threatened was avoided and the pit saved from destruction." Smith's practical bent of taking an approach that he believed most expeditious and least detrimental to church polity in the long run is pointed up well in this episode.

When Smith arrived at the 1886 general conference and was confronted with the Briggs and Gurley withdrawal request, he exclaimed to W. W. Blair, "Here is our unruly coalpit! I am prepared to act in this emergency; how about you?"[40] They decided that it was in the best interest of all that Gurley and Briggs and their supporters be allowed to withdraw without conflict, and Smith was convinced ever after that this "pruning" was necessary for the further development of the movement. Accordingly, Joseph Smith and his movement weathered their most serious internal crisis of the nineteenth century and emerged intact with an even stronger presidency and great resolve to press forward with the goals of the movement Smith had identified during his first years in office.[41]

NOTES

1. Two fine studies of the liberal-conservative split within the church during the 1870s and 1880s have been published. See Alma R. Blair,

"The Tradition of Dissent: Jason W. Briggs," in *Restoration Studies I: Sesquicentennial Edition*, ed. Maurice L. Draper and Clare D. Vlahos (Independence, Mo.: Herald Publishing House, 1980), pp. 146–61; Clare D. Vlahos, "The Challenge to Centralized Power: Zenos H. Gurley, Jr., and the Prophetic Office," *Courage: A Journal of History, Thought, and Action* 1 (March 1971): 141–58.

2. A useful critique of this basic conservatism can be found in William D. Russell, "Beyond Literalism," *Dialogue: A Journal of Mormon Thought* 19 (Spring 1986): 57–68, which describes the historical approach of Mormonism toward questions of higher criticism, scriptural conservatism, and revelatory literalism, challenging these long-standing traditions.

3. On Jason W. Briggs's Utah mission and *The Messenger* see Joseph Smith and Heman C. Smith, *The History of the Reorganized Church of Jesus Christ of Latter Day Saints* (Independence, Mo.: Herald Publishing House, 1967), 3:74, 79–80, 82, 87, 91, 119, 166, 180.

4. The question of preexistence has been important to Reorganized Church members to the present. See the discussion in Maurice L. Draper, *Credo: I Believe* (Independence, Mo.: Herald Publishing House, 1983), pp. 56–66, for a recent challenge to the preexistence doctrine.

5. Book of Mormon (Independence, Mo.: Herald Publishing House, 1966), Mosiah 1:97–102, Alma 9:65–70; *True Latter Day Saints' Herald* 6 (September 1864): 65–67.

6. *The Messenger* (Salt Lake City, Utah) 1 (October 1875): 45–46. See also *The Messenger* 2 (November 1875): 3–4, 2 (December 1875): 6–7, 2 (January 1876): 10, 2 (July 1876): 30; Blair, "Tradition of Dissent," pp. 153–54.

7. Briggs's belief concerning the principle of the gathering of the Saints and the establishment of zionic communities was not so very different from that of Joseph Smith III. Although he accepted the theory behind the doctrine, Smith was cautious and pragmatic about its implementation. Accordingly, he acted hesitantly in creating communities for the Reorganization. This caution has been discussed in chapter 9 and in Roger D. Launius, "Quest for Zion: Joseph Smith III and Community-Building in the Reorganization, 1860–1900," in *Restoration Studies III*, ed. Maurice L. Draper and Debra Combs (Independence, Mo.: Herald Publishing House, 1986), pp. 314–32; Roger D. Launius, "The Mormon Quest for a Perfect Society at Lamoni, Iowa, 1870–1890," *Annals of Iowa* 47 (Spring 1984): 325–42.

8. *The Messenger* 3 (February 1977): 3; Blair, "Tradition of Dissent," pp. 152–53.

9. At the very heart of the theology of the Reorganization was the belief in divine revelation. Concerning the nature of the revelatory experi-

ence as understood by Joseph Smith, Jr., one should review Richard P. Howard, "Latter Day Saints Scripture and the Doctrine of Propositional Revelation," *Courage: A Journal of History, Thought, and Action* 1 (June 1971): 209–26, and Clare D. Vlahos, "Joseph Smith, Jr.'s, Conception of Revelation," *Restoration Studies II*, ed. Maurice L. Draper and A. Bruce Lindgren (Independence, Mo.: Herald Publishing House, 1983), pp. 63–74. Sharon Welch, "Revelation in the Restoration Movement," *Commission*, September 1979, pp. 27–32, traces the evolution of the revelatory concept, while Geoffrey F. Spencer, "Revelation and the Restoration Principle," in *Restoration Studies II*, pp. 182–92, describes a useful perspective from which to analyze revelation and doctrine arising from it.

10. Briggs's ideas on this subject can be found in *The Messenger* 1 (April 1875): 23–24; Jason W. Briggs, "The Past and the Present," *True Latter Day Saints' Herald* 2 (February 1861): 25–31, 21 (1 October 1874): 584, 22 (15 January 1875): 47; Blair, "The Tradition of Dissent," pp. 155–57.

11. The best work explaining the development of the Reorganized Church's scriptures can be found in Richard P. Howard, *Restoration Scriptures: A Study of Their Textual Development* (Independence, Mo.: Herald Publishing House, 1969). See also William D. Russell, "History and the Mormon Scriptures," *Journal of Mormon History* 10 (1983): 53–63, for a criticism of the scriptural authority granted in Mormonism.

12. Jason W. Briggs, "Inspiration," *The Messenger* 2 (September 1876): 41.

13. Charles W. Turner, "Joseph Smith III and the Mormons of Utah" (Ph.D. diss., Graduate Theological Union), pp. 378–84.

14. On Smith's tolerant nature see Clare D. Vlahos, "Moderation as a Theological Principle in the Thought of Joseph Smith III," *John Whitmer Historical Association Journal* 1 (1981): 3–11.

15. Jason W. Briggs to William H. Kelley, 15 October 1876, William H. Kelley Collection; Joseph Smith to Charles Derry, 21 January 1877, Joseph Smith III Papers, Reorganized Church Library–Archives; Joseph Smith to E. C. Briggs, 7 February 1877, Joseph Smith III Letterbook #1, Reorganized Church Library–Archives; Joseph Smith to Zenos H. Gurley, Jr., 24 March 1877, Joseph Smith III Letterbook #1.

16. Jason W. Briggs to William H. Kelley, 31 October 1875, 2 April 1877, William H. Kelley Collection, Reorganized Church of Jesus Christ of Latter Day Saints Library–Archives, Independence, Mo. This was in part the result of Smith's centralizing efforts. See Roger D. Launius, "Joseph Smith III and the Quest for a Centralized Organization, 1860–1873," *Restoration Studies II*, pp. 104–20.

17. Evidence of this conflict within the church can be found in Joseph

Smith to J. J. Cornish, 9 February 1878, Joseph Smith III Letterbook #1; Zenos H. Gurley, Jr., to Joseph Smith, 23 November 1874, Joseph Smith III Papers; Zenos H. Gurley, Jr., to *Herald*, 5 December 1873, Joseph Smith III Papers; Joseph Smith to Zenos H. Gurley, Jr., 24 July 1879, 2 April 1879, Joseph Smith III Letterbook #2, Reorganized Church Library–Archives; Joseph Smith to Jason W. Briggs, 5 April 1877, Joseph Smith III Letterbook #1. For a Reorganized Church approach to the subject see Richard P. Howard, "The Changing RLDS Response to Mormon Polygamy: A Preliminary Analysis," *Journal of the John Whitmer Historical Association* 3 (1983): 14–29, and Alma R. Blair, "RLDS Views of Polygamy: Some Historiographical Notes," *John Whitmer Historical Association Journal* 5 (1985): 16–28.

18. Zenos H. Gurley, Jr., to Joseph Smith, 25 March 1879, Joseph Smith III Papers, Reorganized Church Library–Archives.

19. Joseph Smith to Zenos H. Gurley, Jr., 2 April 1879, Joseph Smith III Letterbook #2.

20. Howard, "RLDS Views of Polygamy," pp. 17–19. See also chapter 9 for a fuller discussion of Smith's views on this issue.

21. Joseph Smith to Jason W. Briggs, 22 January 1877, Joseph Smith III Letterbook #1.

22. Jason W. Briggs to William H. Kelley, 24 January 1877, 11 March 1877, 20 April 1877, William H. Kelley Collection.

23. "Semi-Annual Conference," *Saints' Herald* 24 (1 November 1877): 312–13; Joseph Smith to J. L. Traughber, 29 November 1877, Joseph Smith III Letterbook #1; Joseph Smith to Zenos H. Gurley, Jr., 15 December 1877, Joseph Smith III Letterbook #1; Joseph Smith and Heman C. Smith, *The History of the Reorganized Church of Jesus Christ of Latter Day Saints* (Independence, Mo.: Herald Publishing House, 1967), 4:194–96, 213–17.

24. *Rules and Resolutions* (Independence, Mo.: Herald Publishing House, 1964), Resolution 215.

25. Joseph Smith to Zenos H. Gurley, Jr., 23 October 1878; Joseph Smith to E. C. Brand, 23 October 1878, both in Joseph Smith III Letterbook #1; Zenos H. Gurley to Fred Johnson, 18 June 1886, Miscellaneous Letters and Papers, Reorganized Church Library–Archives.

26. Smith and Smith, *History of Reorganized Church*, 4:255–61; Joseph Smith to W. W. Blair, 20 January 1879, Joseph Smith III Letterbook #2; Joseph Smith to R. M. Elvin, 30 January 1879, Joseph Smith III Letterbook #1A, Reorganized Church Library–Archives; Joseph Smith to Jason W. Briggs, 17 February 1879, 10 May 1879, Joseph Smith III Letterbook #2; *Weekly Argus* (Sandwich, Ill.), 12 April 1879; "Annual Conference," *Saints' Herald* 26 (15 April 1879): 130.

27. Joseph Smith to Stephen F. Walker, 13 May 1879, Joseph Smith III Letterbook #2.

28. Vlahos, "Challenge to Centralized Power," pp. 147–49.

29. Joseph Smith to Thomas W. Smith, 24 May 1879, Joseph Smith III Letterbook #2; Joseph Smith to Unknown Addressee, 25 May 1880, Joseph Smith III Letterbook #3, Reorganized Church Library–Archives; Jason W. Briggs to William H. Kelley, 22 February 1880, William H. Kelley Collection.

30. Smith and Smith, *History of Reorganized Church*, 4:385–86; *Rules and Resolutions*, Resolution 222.

31. Joseph Smith to Thomas W. Smith, 25 May 1880, Joseph Smith III Letterbook #3.

32. Joseph Smith to W. W. Blair, 20 October 1880, Joseph Smith III Letterbook #3; "Conference Minutes," *Saints' Herald* 27 (1 October 1880): 318.

33. Zenos H. Gurley, Jr., to Council of Twelve, 26 March 1884, Miscellaneous Letters and Papers; Vlahos, "Challenge to Centralized Power," pp. 141–44.

34. Zenos H. Gurley, Jr., to Unknown Addressee, 14 June 1882, Miscellaneous Letters and Papers; Gurley to Twelve, 26 March 1880.

35. Vlahos, "Challenge to Centralized Power," p. 149.

36. W. W. Blair, "Tithing, Gathering, and Revenge," *Saints' Herald* 32 (3 January 1885): 9–10, 32 (10 January 1885): 25–27, 32 (17 January 1885): 42–43; W. W. Blair, "The Issue Reviewed," *Saints' Herald* 32 (28 February 1885): 153–55; Zenos H. Gurley, Jr., "The Issue," *Saints' Herald* 32 (10 January 1885): 57–58; Zenos H. Gurley, Jr., "The Gathering," *Saints' Herald* 32 (21 March 1885): 184–89, 32 (28 March 1885): 200–203, 32 (11 April 1885): 225–29.

37. Joseph Smith to William H. Kelley, 25 February 1885, William H. Kelley Collection.

38. "General Conference," *Saints' Herald* 32 (16 May 1885): 305; Book of Doctrine and Covenants (Independence, Mo.: Herald Publishing House, 1970), Section 121:2b; Smith and Smith, *History of Reorganized Church*, 4:481–83.

39. Smith and Smith, *History of Reorganized Church*, 4:477–78.

40. Smith, "Memoirs," *Saints' Herald* 83 (9 June 1936): 719–20.

41. Ibid.; *New York Times*, 12 April 1886; Zenos H. Gurley, Jr., to Mr. Dillon, 1 April 1893, Miscellaneous Letters and Papers.

CHAPTER
13

The Golden Years

The twenty years that followed the withdrawal of Jason Briggs and Zenos Gurley from the Reorganized Church were in many respects the most rewarding and satisfying in the entire career of President Joseph Smith. During this period Joseph enjoyed great respect from both his own followers and the secular world; he held unchallenged, and most of the time even unquestioned, authority within the movement; and he witnessed the blossoming, and some cases completion, of many of the projects and procedures that he had nurtured from the beginning of his presidency. From the viewpoint of long-term goals, the period between 1886 and Joseph Smith's virtual retirement in 1906 was without question a golden age in the Reorganized Church's history. Physically, in 1886 Joseph looked every bit the patriarch who had ruled the Reorganized Church with a firm but moderate hand for almost thirty years. Much admired by the majority of the membership, and certainly respected by the rest, Joseph guided the church during this period in a much more steady and sure course than in the past. The conclusion of the Briggs and Gurley affair seemed to give him greater confidence—the security as the supreme earthly leader of the church that Joseph needed to press more forcefully toward his goals.[1]

Under Smith's direction the movement had first attained the self-discipline—wrought through the creation of an efficient and authoritative church administration—necessary to move outward with missionary activity, but Joseph had always believed that, since his father's religious dream had gone sour near the time of his death, he had to make reform his central goal. As a result, he had charted an unwavering path toward the restoration of the early Latter Day Saint movement as he believed it had existed under his father during the 1830s and 1840s.[2] Moreover, as Joseph Smith worked toward this "noble goal," he made sure that church-sustained officers were constantly at work among the various Latter Day Saint churches. He had asserted very early in his career that the Saints had the duty of bringing back together the "lost souls of Zion" who had forsaken the truth and abdicated all religious authority.[3] "The Priesthood rightly considered signified a body of men rightfully holding power to administer in the name of Jesus Christ for the conferring of spiritual blessings upon men," Smith contended, but it should never "be conceded to mean a class of men holding power from God to contravene the laws which have been given him for the government of all, or to do that which places in jeopardy or destroys the people and their liberties."[4] This, the Reorganized Church advocates asserted, was exactly what other groups had done.

Under the direction of the prophet, therefore, the Reorganized Church had begun intensive efforts among the various Mormon factions. During the first years of Smith's ministry almost all of this missionary activity had taken place in the Midwest, near the strength of the movement. Many converts were gained in western Iowa from among those who had abandoned Brigham Young's emigration trains en route to the Great Basin or had returned eastward after becoming disgusted with the situation in Deseret. Besides these ex-Mormons, the Reorganization's missionaries attracted many of the followers of other Latter Day Saint factional leaders such as Charles B. Thompson, Alpheus Cutler, James J. Strang, Lyman Wight, and James Colin Brewster.[5] Additionally, but with less enthusiasm, the Saints made contact with people outside of Mormondom who were attracted to their claims of a restoration of New Testament principals, the Book of Mormon, the zionic enterprise, and the continuing revelation of God through the movement's prophets.[6]

Even though the Reorganized Church was seeking largely to reclaim old Mormons, its growth during the nineteenth century was impressive. In late 1860 the total church membership was probably not more than 1,000, but by the next year it was over 1,800, and in mid-1863 the church's bishop estimated the membership at 2,500. Almost all of these members were living in the Midwest and constituted a relatively solid base of support from which to carry on more efficient and far-reaching missionary efforts.[7] In mid-1863 Joseph Smith sent the church's first missionary team to work among the Mormons of the Great Basin, and within six months they had built a mission of over 300 members. By 1880 that number had grown to 820, and in the 1890s membership in Utah had risen to over 1,000.[8] At the same time, the Reorganized Church moved into California and enjoyed remarkable success among the followers of Brigham Young who had settled in the Golden State. Within ten years after the opening of the Pacific Slope mission the Reorganization had developed a following of almost 1,000 members.[9]

Joseph Smith also led the Reorganized into the foreign mission field for very nearly the first time, and over the next score of years the prophet presided over an invigorating overseas operation. In February 1863 Charles Derry, an Englishman converted to the church in 1861, went to Great Britain to tell his countrymen the message of the Reorganized Church. He immediately began working among the followers of Brigham Young in the country, many of whom he had known before emigrating to the United States. Although initially unsuccessful, within a year after embarking on this missionary venture Charles Derry had established a thriving congregation of over 400 members, most of them converted from the ranks of Utah Mormonism. Thereafter, Joseph Smith oversaw a prosperous mission in the British Isles, building a very successful foreign organization throughout the rest of the nineteenth century.[10] As a result of Smith's emphasis on proselytizing at home and abroad, by 1870 his church's membership had reached 6,900. Slightly more than 70 percent of these members lived in the Midwest, but Smith believed that the sect required this strong base of support for his expansion efforts and took pride in the success of the church's efforts.[11]

Still directing its efforts principally toward Mormon splinter groups and especially toward Utah Mormons, during the 1870s Joseph Smith moved the church even more resolutely outward into new missionary fields. In mid-1872 Joseph instructed John Avondet, an ex-Utah Mormon, to open a mission to Switzerland. A native of Pinerolo, Italy, who had converted to Mormonism as a young man and migrated to America, Avondet spoke good German and French and understood Swiss culture. In 1873 Smith asked Avondet to move from Switzerland into Italy and open a mission there. This missionary established the first congregations of the Reorganized Church in both these nations.[12] Meanwhile, Joseph Smith sent two other ex-Utah Mormons from California to the Society Islands and Australia to establish missions there. They were quite successful and both areas became well known for the number and fortitude of the members.[13] In 1874 Smith dispatched John L. Bear, yet another ex-Utah Mormon, to his native Germany to work among his people; Bear organized congregations of Latter Day Saints not only in Germany but also in Denmark and Sweden.[14] In every instance, Joseph Smith was pleased with the harvest of converts moving into the Reorganized Church. During the decade of the 1870s the church's membership nearly doubled, being registered at 11,951 by 1880. The trend continued during the 1880s, as Smith presided over an ever more forceful missionary program, and the membership rose to 23,951 by 1890.[15]

Because of the peculiar nature of the Reorganized Church's missionary program—directed as it was toward the far-flung remnants of the early restoration church—most of the converts were of a common type. They had been basically disgruntled members of small Mormon splinter groups or dissident Utah Mormons looking for an opportunity to associate with a more moderate and democratic Mormon faction. Many of them were poor, although some men of property and standing were a part of the Reorganized Church, invariably rising to status within the organization. Notable among those of wealth and power was David Dancer, a prosperous farmer and businessman who had been a mainstay behind the United Order of Enoch and the building of Lamoni, and David F. Walker, who was also involved heavily in the Lamoni experiment.[16]

Like the majority of Americans of the period, many of the Reorganized Church converts were farmers. Although relatively poor, these people generally owned their own property and worked for themselves. In Great Britain and other more industrialized nations of Europe, the converts were usually working-class people without great economic power. These people were generally not well educated, but they were usually literate and certainly inquiring. Conversions during this period were many times intellectual, as had been the case with many in the early church, coming often through reading the Book of Mormon and studying doctrine rather than through emotional oratory or spiritual experience.[17]

Geographically, the primary base of the Reorganized Church was the American Midwest, which still contained some 43 percent of the church's total membership as late of 1890. It was there that the early Mormon church had grown so large and it was the traditional stronghold of Mormonism. There also was Independence, Missouri, the Mormon centerplace of Zion, where many of the Saints wished to reside. The Midwest was also the cradle of the Reorganization, the location where the church had sprung anew in the 1850s and where Joseph Smith III lived and attracted those Saints who wanted to be closer to the prophet and to the seat of church government. The second most important area of concentration was the Pacific Slope; there missionaries in the Great Basin and California had succeeded in building significant concentrations of members. By 1890, additionally, there were smaller clusters of Saints in England, Australia, the Society Islands, Canada, and continental Europe. Of the members of the Reorganized Church in 1890, for instance, 22,851 were residents of the United States or Canada. These members were located in 30 of the 44 states of the union and in Ontario, Nova Scotia, and Manitoba. The states or provinces with more than a thousand members were Iowa, 5,283; Missouri, 3,080; Illinois, 1,909; Ontario, 1,519; California, 1,387; Michigan, 1,352; Kansas, 1,060; and Nebraska, 1,058. Finally, there were 1,176 more members in the Society Islands, 969 in the British Isles, 329 in Australia, and 43 scattered throughout Europe.[18]

Although the missionary efforts of the Reorganized Church during the first thirty-eight years of its existence had been relatively successful, Joseph Smith began to alter its emphasis gradually after 1890. Perhaps partially because the Utah Mormons had publicly denounced the practice of plural marriage, thereby ridding the movement of that distinctive stigma; perhaps because of the Reorganization's increasing maturity as a religious movement; perhaps for other more intangible reasons, during the 1890s the prophet presided over a gradual shift in relations with other churches, moving toward the common ground of understanding rather than contention.[19]

In large measure, prior to the 1890s Joseph Smith had pursued something of a defensive policy toward other religious groups. Having been subjected to ridicule because of his religion on several occasions and in at least a few instances threatened with physical violence, Joseph had reason to be defensive. For example, while on a missionary trip to Utah in 1885, Smith attended a patriotic meeting at the Methodist church in Salt Lake City on the Fourth of July. The territorial governor, Eli H. Murray, presided at this meeting, and when he saw Joseph Smith enter the church, he asked him to sit on the stand with other dignitaries. Murray introduced Smith to the other people on the rostrum, and most were cordial, but Smith reported that R. G. McNeese, pastor of the Presbyterian church in Salt Lake City, "rudely turned his back upon me." McNeese then complained to Governor Murray about Smith's presence and demanded that Smith be asked to leave. Smith and Murray were both chagrined by the ruckus. Joseph offered to leave but Murray, possibly to assert his authority before the crowd of people watching the affair, refused to back down and allowed him to stay. It was an embarrassing moment for all concerned, and certainly such incidents caused Joseph to be wary of those outside the church who lumped all factions of Mormonism together. It should be added that Murray did not invite Smith to occupy the stand at any other public meetings in Salt Lake City.[20]

In mid-1888 officials of the Reorganized Church were asked to attend an ecumenical meeting in Cincinnati, Ohio. Because of past snubs Joseph hesitated in sending a delegation to the conference. Only after long and agonizing study did he finally allow a representative to meet with the conference.[21] This defensive nature and hesitancy seemed to decline, albeit slowly and cautiously, during the 1890s. One exceptional example of Smith's stretching to overcome sectarianism took place in 1893. In September of that year the World's Parliament of Religions met in conjunction with the Chicago Columbian Exposition, and the prophet and several associates attended the meetings, pleased to be a part of such an important event. In spite of signs of prejudice among certain other participants, Smith sent glowing reports about the parliament to the Saints and reprinted many of the proceedings in the *Saints' Herald*. When it was over, Smith wrote to a friend in Washington, D.C.: "What a wonderful thing it was. Would the time come when all the world were akin in faith."[22]

Joseph Smith's broadening attitude toward other Christian denominations was also apparent in his changing approach toward Utah Mormonism. After the Woodruff Manifesto Smith noted that, to be fair to the Utah Latter-day Saints, such a change was necessary. He commented in 1892: "I am of the opinion that this change requires not only careful thought, but it requires a little difference in presentation. For instance: Until of late when the question was asked, we have stated the chief difference between us and the Utah organization. It is now being forced upon the people of America that they have abandoned polygamy. Our ministry must be prepared for this change. Our ministry must exercise as much charity, forbearance, and courtesy as possible in urging our views upon the people." [23] Where once his missionaries had been directed to attack the "Utah heresy," Smith urged that the Saints deemphasize plural marriage and concentrate on other differences, such as the continuing church-state issue in Utah as well as the dialectics relating to such Mormon doctrines as baptism for the dead, the temple ceremony of "adoption," and esoteric rites designed to prepare a Mormon for celestial glory in the afterlife.[24] Still, he continued to preach that the Reorganized Church had always condemned plural marriage and that it had been no part of the early Mormon movement.[25]

While maintaining the truthfulness of the Reorganized Church and the special message that it had for the world, Joseph Smith admitted that the religions of the Utah Latter-day Saints and other Christian denominations had merit. In an 1894 sermon Smith gave in Lamoni, he suggested that the Reorganization must accept its Christian nature above all else and work with other religious movements for the good of all humanity. As he told his congregation:

> We are not necessarily antagonistic to the truth that they of different faiths may have. We have a right to examine all of them, one by one; we have a right to select that from them that is true. We have a right to accept or use it; and if it be true and antagonistic to that which we personally hold, we are under obligations to drop our opposition to it and conform to that which is true that we may find elsewhere. We have the right to maintain our own faith; but differing faiths should be friendly, but not for a compromising character. We should not strike hands with error, with wickedness, or corruption; but we may easily strike hands with men so far as their truths are concerned, and

walk side by side with them in friendliness. . . . One of the problems of the day that we have to solve, one of the difficulties we have to meet, is extreme faith; I mean by this that peculiar kind of faith that men have in the world that makes them bigots.[26]

Thus during the 1890s Joseph increasingly stressed the commonality of his church's message with the majority of other Christian denominations rather than arguing that the Reorganized Church was "not Mormon" and fully Christian. As a result a conciliatory policy toward Mormonism began to emerge in the early 1890s, and while never predominent in the life of the church it was a liberalizing influence that could not be denied. When traveling in Utah in 1905 Smith personified this more dignified approach, acting without malice and with greater respect toward the Latter-day Saints of the Great Basin.[27]

Smith also exhibited this more conciliatory approach to Utah Mormonism during the controversy over the seating of Reed Smoot, a Mormon apostle who had been elected to the Senate. Between 1903 and 1906 anti-Mormon elements tried to prohibit Smoot from retaining his office on the ground that he could not serve both the Mormon church and the United States government. Joseph Smith and the Reorganized Church hierarchy became involved in the controversy almost immediately after it arose and expressed support of Smoot's position, claiming that service to God and service to country were not necessarily mutually exclusive. In a November 1903 editorial in the *Saints' Herald* Smith asserted that no person should be denied public office simply on the basis of religion and found a dangerous precedent in "the making of any man's religion a cause of war against him when no overt act of outrage against the laws" had taken place.[28]

The Senate investigating committee subpoenaed Joseph Smith, as an expert on Mormon affairs, to testify about the possibility of Mormon allegiances beyond the United States government. He went to the capital in January 1906 and met with Senator James C. Burrows of Michigan, chairman of the investigating committee, and several other congressmen. He told Burrows, whom he had known from his involvement in the antipolygamy crusade, about his opinions and suggested that it would be a travesty to deny Smoot his legally acquired seat in Congress. On 9 February 1906, after the completion of these informal interviews, the investigating committee released Smith and he returned to his home in Lamoni. Thereafter, Smith continued to make his beliefs about the affair known and took it as a personal triumph when the Senate voted in 1907 to allow Reed Smoot to assume his seat in Congress.[29]

In many respects, Smith's increasingly conciliatory attitude toward other religious factions was the result of a personal easiness he began to feel in his position at the same time. More than at any other time previously, Joseph was comfortable in his role as president of the Reorganization and was confident of his and the church's ability to accomplish the goals set in the conferences. Always before Smith had acted cautiously and with great patience and reserve, but during the 1890s he began to move more authoritatively. The success of his missionary program, the triumph over the plural marriage issue, the consolidation of Smith's presidential authority demonstrated in the Briggs-Gurley affair, and the increasing acceptance of the church among other religious leaders all contributed to this heady environment and prompted Smith to move forward boldly with new programs and projects. More important, perhaps, Smith and the Reorganization had essentially grown up together, maturing as the years passed. By the 1890s Smith was the grand old man of the movement who had more than thirty years of leadership and experience to guide him. He knew his followers very well and rarely stepped beyond their good graces.[30]

One striking example of this shift in emphasis and alteration of approach was the realization of a dream toward which Joseph had long worked. Smith valued learning and wanted every young person in the church to have an opportunity to gain an education under conditions that would foster both free intellectual inquiry and Christian ideals. As a result, during the 1890s, Smith and the Reorganized Church established a liberal arts college at Lamoni. Named Graceland College, it was entirely nonsectarian—an embodiment of the shift in Smith's approach to religion. As Smith wrote in the *Saints' Herald,* defending the creation of this new institution, "The Saints need an institution of the kind where their children and the children of others can be educated without contact with sectarian bigotry, [or] denominational dogma." He asked that the Reorganized Church demonstrate to the world with this institution "that a college can be successfully operated purely as an educational institution, free from denominational bias or sectarian taints or intermingling."[31] So pleased was Joseph with the nonsectarian nature of the church-supported college that he boasted of it in his memoirs. He remembered that when the cornerstone of the first building "was laid, speeches delivered, and prayers offered for the success of the enterprise, on that stone stood, plainly chiseled, the word, 'Non-Sectarian,' which stands today to indicate the character the institution had borne from the first."[32]

If the nonsectarian nature of Graceland College was different from Smith's earlier defensive approach toward other religions, it was also a monument to the prestige, authority, and ease Joseph Smith had gained in his presidential office. Joseph had begun suggesting the establishment of a church college as early as 1864, but every time the question arose, the general conference refused to approve the project. His opponents argued that the Reorganization was a small movement and had neither the fiscal resources nor the potential students necessary for the successful chartering and operation of a college. Such financial inadequacies took on added importance during the depression of the 1890s, and when Smith raised the subject again near the beginning of the decade, many within the church opposed the proposal as inexpedient. Smith was not dissuaded, however, and during the first three years of the 1890s he cajoled, begged, and borrowed until he had sixty-four acres of land in Lamoni as a base for the college and $10,000 in working capital with which to build classrooms and begin operations.[33]

After considerable debate in the general conference of 1893 Joseph Smith received approval to begin a college facility. He assumed leadership of the committee charged with the school's creation himself and took an active part in the construction of the school's first building. Smith commissioned Charles Dunham, a local church member, to serve as architect for this building. Dunham's design, a three-story brick building of Gothic Revival and Victorian architecture, impressed Joseph Smith with its stately presence and he quickly approved it. Unfortunately, Dunham's design was structurally unsound, and the building contractor had to rethink and rework the entire plan as it was constructed so that it would be usable. In one case, for instance, the contractor had to reinforce the flooring in the upper levels with metal rods before it was considered safe. All of this alteration more than doubled building costs, and several church members suggested that Joseph Smith was not properly managing the college's money—a dangerous charge because of the tight economic situation of the 1890s. Although dissatisfied with the progress on the building, Smith could only defend himself. He did so repeatedly throughout the rest of his life, even remarking in his memoirs that "I did not err purposely in these matters, nor through egotism or an unwillingness to listen to the opinions of others."[34] In some respects, the church's chastisement of Smith was repayment for his forceful means of gaining acceptance for the creation of the college.

Within a few years after beginning the project, Smith had corrected the errors and paid the extra bills incurred by poor planning and management. As a result within a relatively short period most of the church membership forgot about the difficulties of beginning Graceland College. The prophet, installed as chairman of Graceland College's Board of Trustees in 1893, continued in this capacity through 1898, and each year the institution gained in enrollment, quality of education, and donations. Joseph Smith showed his support of Graceland College not only as an organizer and solicitor but also as a parent of students: he sent his two oldest sons, Frederick M. and Israel A. Smith, to Graceland College in 1895 and took proper pride in Frederick's graduation as the first alum of the new college in 1898.[35]

Smith's subtle shift in emphasis and style of leadership also resulted in a new boldness in his direction of the affairs of the church administration. Although he was by no means a dictator who monopolized the system and ruled as he saw fit, Joseph dropped his hesitancy of former years, acting more forcefully when he deemed it necessary, as in the case of Edmund C. Briggs. In the fall of 1899 Briggs was relieved of his field responsibilities as a member of the Quorum of Twelve Apostles because of a complaint from his quorum that he had failed to resolve a procedural question as directed by superiors. The charges of the quorum were altered somewhat during the winter of 1899–1900 but remained unresolved and created considerable ill-will among some of the leading officials of the church. During this period Briggs, a long-time and dynamic missionary, was essentially inactive within the church. Briggs's case was finally brought before the general conference of 1900, but Joseph Smith sought to prohibit its investigation of the issue. After considerable protest he was able to put off consideration of Briggs's improper conduct, and when the minutes of the 1900 conference were being prepared for printing, Smith instructed the secretary of the church to omit that part of the report which dealt with E. C. Briggs. The church secretary protested, but Smith overruled him and no mention of the case appeared in the records of the 1900 conference, although the intensity of the conference was shown by the fact that 1,000 copies of the record of debate on the Briggs affair were privately published and made available to delegates.[36]

The matter rested until the next year, albeit with considerable concern by church officials who believed Smith had acted outside his bounds of authority. At the next year's conference Smith was directed by the body to explain his actions, which he said rested on several factors: Briggs's right of appeal had not been exhausted; therefore, the conference should not act on the case until all other avenues had been tried. Briggs had been in poor health and was unable to defend himself adequately. The Twelve had acted without proper jurisdiction in passing judgment on what was essentially an *ex parte* case. Moreover, Briggs was a long-time missionary whose length of service to the church should be considered in any case against him. Finally, Smith noted that his own conviction that publishing the debate would serve no useful purpose and might lead to internal strife prompted him to act as he did. These explanations—particularly the last one, which seemed to demonstrate Joseph Smith's willingness to bend rules at whim—created considerable controversy among the church's leadership. They discussed the matter for weeks thereafter. Finally, the conference body voted to accept Smith's decision, an act that showed how firmly in control of the membership he was, and later in the conference, E. C. Briggs made a satisfactory adjustment with the Twelve and was restored to his office.[37] Certainly this incident pointed up the much more forceful nature of Smith's leadership; he would never have acted in such an authoritative fashion thirty years earlier.

In 1901 Smith again exercised this new, bold leadership. He was concerned about an inspired document that he was prepared to deliver to the church at the annual conference. Because it contained sections that would limit the authority of the ruling quorums of the church, the prophet feared that a message he was convinced was divinely inspired would not be accepted by the movement. After agonizing over this possibility for several days, Smith decided to bend the administrative rules to ensure passage. He completely circumvented the priesthood quorums, where he believed much of the contention over the revelation would be, and took the message directly to the general conference rank and file, telling the church he had been "bidden" to do so by God.[38] The conference approved the document, but only after considerable debate.

In line with this action, Smith also took forthright steps to clarify long-standing administrative and procedural questions. Many of his answers were unpopular with certain church officials who lost authority as a result; however, when challenged in some of his reorganizational activities, Smith asserted that he was acting properly but offered no substantive rationale for his actions. He only suggested that as president of the church he was privy to information making clear the necessity of such changes and was acting within the confines of his sacred trust to govern the church properly. Perhaps his most important alteration during this period was a redirection of the emphasis in some of the priesthood quorums away from the details of administration and toward missionary planning and the extension of the church's outreach into the world. At the same time Smith centralized many of the nonfiscal administrative duties within the First Presidency, creating a more clearly focused organizational structure with most of the decision-making authority under his control.[39]

Although many of the members of the Twelve Apostles and other leading priesthood quorums disliked Joseph's centralization efforts, complaining of "creeping authoritarianism," the prophet had no intention of undermining the democratic tendencies of the church and used restraint in implementing his ideas. Moreover, even if these officials had wished to go beyond mere criticism and challenge Smith's alterations—and there is no evidence to indicate that any really wanted to do so—the prophet's position within the movement was so secure that they would have certainly failed. The lesson of the Briggs-Gurley case was still hauntingly vivid in the minds of many, and the prophet's actions prompted only the weakest of protests. In most instances church officials silently tolerated Smith's administrative changes. In later years, after Joseph brought his strong-willed son into the church's administration, these changes provided the vehicle for Frederick M. Smith's forceful leadership— a leadership that was increasingly resented during the early 1920s and led to internal dissension and defection.[40]

Smith's increasingly robust leadership also showed in the prosecution of a civil action known as the Temple Lot Suit, brought by the Reorganized Church against the Church of Christ to gain title to property of special significance to the Latter Day Saints. In 1867 the Church of Christ, led by Granville Hedrick, had established a small congregation in Independence and reclaimed sections of the land that the church had abandoned when it was expelled from the region in 1833. The most important tract was a 1.5 acre plot—a small portion of a total of 63.27 acres in the center of the city—that Joseph Smith, Jr., had designated in 1831 as the site upon which the Saints' holy temple would be built.[41] Joseph Smith and other members of the Reorganization had long wanted to acquire this Temple Lot in Independence because of its tremendous religious significance for the entire Mormon faith. Since the announcement of the doctrine in 1831, the Saints had believed that this temple would be the location to which Jesus Christ would make his triumphal return and that it would serve as the seat of government during the Christian millennium. As the self-styled inheritors of the early Mormon legacy, the Reorganized Church membership naturally believed it should have possession of the Temple Lot and the opportunity to build the sacred structure on the location where Joseph Smith, Jr., had laid the cornerstones of the temple.[42]

With the resolve brought by years of contemplation, Joseph Smith III began moving cautiously to acquire this property. During the 1880s large numbers of Reorganized Church members moved into the Independence area, and their interest in the Temple Lot created the climate needed to begin acquisition. Accordingly, under Joseph's direction the church purchased a number of sections in the 63-acre tract but was unable to buy the small plot belonging to the Hedrickites. Therefore Smith asked the general conference to appoint a committee to confer with the Church of Christ about the possibility of rectifying their doctrinal differences and merging the two sects. This committee's first meeting took place in 1885, without much success, but the two churches met intermittently thereafter.[43]

By 1887 Joseph clearly realized that there were too many differences between the two churches for any satisfactory merger agreement to be reached. While continuing the negotiations to see what good they might bring, Smith decided that if he wished to acquire the Temple Lot immediately he would have to undertake court action. Ever since the 1860s Smith had been convinced, as he noted in his memoirs, that the Reorganized Church "would be called to stand before the great American Jury in the civil Courts of the Republic definitely arrayed against the hierarchy known as the Mormon Church in Utah." The church had been remarkably successful in 1880 with the Kirtland Temple Suit, although the Utah Latter-day Saints had not contested the action, and Smith saw another opportunity to gain a favorable decision. He recalled in his memoirs: "I was impressed that the facts, arguments, and evidences upon which the Reorganization based its position as a religious body must be measured against their opponents of similar or other name, and the truth or error of that position be ascertained before the august tribunals recognized as the Courts of law and justice, established by the American claimants in their rights. The idea that this contest would inevitably come became so firmly fixed in my mind that I am quite willing to admit it assumed almost the proportions of a prophetic obsession, so sure was I that it would come to pass."[44] Clearly, Joseph Smith was convinced of the necessity of gaining a second ruling in legal action declaring the Reorganized Church the legal successor of the early Mormon movement. Indeed, in 1891, when the church was reincorporated in Iowa, he had inserted into the legal document a statement claiming succession from the original Latter Day Saint church organized on 6 April 1830.[45]

At a most opportune time, during the summer of 1887, a deed to the Temple Lot surfaced among the descendents of Oliver Cowdery, one of the early church's most influential members. This document recorded a transaction in which Edward Partridge, bishop and trustee for the church, turned the Temple Lot over to Cowdery and three minor children for the sum of $1,000. On 9 June 1887 the Reorganized Church purchased this deed as well as two quit-claim deeds from Elizabeth Ann Cowdery, widow, and Maria Louise Johnson, daughter of Oliver Cowdery.[46] Smith believed that he had bought the legal title to the property with these documents and would finally be able to acquire possession of the Lot.

Two days after obtaining these deeds the Reorganized Church filed an injunction against the Church of Christ to force them from the Temple Lot, but the Hedrickites refused to withdraw and the dispute entered a long legal process. At the same time Smith began working with George Edmunds, a long-time friend who served as legal counsel for the church, to plot a strategy for legal action. He asked whether, if the Church of Christ fought the case and held a legitimate deed, the Reorganization could still gain possession as the true Mormon church in succession of the primitive organization. Edmunds noted that there were three central issues to be determined before an estimate of success could be made: (1) was the title held by Edward Partridge, which the Reorganized Church had obtained, a personal one or one held in trust for the church; (2) could the Reorganization prove itself the true successor to the original Mormon church if contested by other Mormon factions; (3) was the church too late in pressing its claims? Smith was convinced that all but the last point could be successfully argued. As he put it: "As to the right to the succession of the Church, I have not a particle of doubt; but as to the result of the lapse of years, the mutations of changing claimants, the vicissitudes of destruction of records; and last but more fatal of all, the almost criminal ignorance and careless administration of the agents, or trustees of the original church, I am in grave doubt. And am prepared in mind for adverse judgments, on account of the last named conditions." He planned to use the Extermination Order issued by Governor Lilburn W. Boggs in 1838, which said that Mormons would be driven from the state or "exterminated," as a counter to arguments based on the statute of limitations.[47]

Obtaining no satisfaction from other actions, on 6 August 1891 Joseph Smith's associates filed a "bill of equity" against the Church of Christ in the circuit court of western Missouri "to establish a trust in and recover certain trust property at Independence, Jackson County, Missouri, publicly known as the Temple Lot."[48] As expected, the Reorganization challenged the Hedrickites' claim to the property on essentially two grounds. First, the church contended that it was the "owner in fee simple, by title absolute" through the deeds obtained in 1887 from the Cowdery heirs. This title and the two quit claim deeds, the church claimed, overrode a long set of transactions, legally recorded and accepted by the state since 1848, stating that the property belonged to the Church of Christ. Second, the Reorganization argued that at the death of Joseph Smith, Jr., in 1844 the Mormon hierarchy had splintered and the Reorganized faction was the only legitimate successor to that early movement and should have a right to its predecessor's property.[49]

Smith took a keen interest in the progress of this case through the judicial system of the United States but was disappointed in the final outcome. During the trial, which opened on 6 February 1894 before Judge John F. Phillips of the United States Circuit Court at Kansas City, Missouri, the Reorganized Church's claim that the deeds it had purchased from the Cowdery family were legitimate was dealt a staggering blow by the defense. The Church of Christ's attorneys presented evidence that the deed of Edward Partridge to Oliver Cowdery and three of his children was not an original instrument, that it contained no valid signature or legal date, and that it was not registered in Jackson County until twenty-one years after its supposed execution. Moreover, the defendents showed that on the alleged date of the legal transaction, 25 March 1839, neither principal party was in Missouri. Cowdery, who had left the state in 1838, was in Tiffin, Ohio, and Partridge was in Quincy, Illinois. The defense also demonstrated that the three children named in the deed—John Cowdery, age seven, Jane Cowdery, age three, and Joseph Smith Cowdery, age one—had never existed. In light of this evidence the defense asked the court to rule that the deed was bogus and dismiss the case.[50]

After this setback the Reorganized Church's attorneys, led by George Edmunds, pressed to establish the church's right to the property on the ground that it was the legal continuation of the original Mormon movement and had been illegally driven from the land it held in 1833. Without question, the Reorganized Church brought forth strong evidence supporting the contention that it was the lawful successor to the original Mormon church, arguing that the early church held the same doctrinal, organizational, and procedural beliefs as the present movement and that Joseph Smith, Jr., had set apart his son to lead the church after his death.[51]

On 3 March 1894 Judge John F. Phillips awarded the Reorganization the Temple Lot property. His opinion represented a complete victory for the Reorganized Church. First, he found that the 1839 deed to the Cowdery children was valid and took precedence over those produced by the Church of Christ. Second, he further found that the property in question had been vacant and unoccupied prior to 1882; the suit had not been inaugurated after the accepted ten-year statute of limitations had passed, therefore defense based on the legal concept of laches was not an issue. Third, Judge Phillips affirmed that the Reorganized Church was "similar" to the original Mormon church in doctrines and beliefs, and it was therefore entitled to a decree as "successor" to early Mormonism. All of this established that "equitable title" to the Temple Lot rested with the Reorganized Church: the court ruled in favor of the Reorganized Church, "enjoining respondents from asserting title to the people, and awarding possession to the complainant." [52]

Joseph Smith had anticipated this favorable decision. He recalled in his memoirs that on 3 March, as he walked to his office in Lamoni, Iowa, from his home west of town, he heard a voice say: "The decision of the Court will be in favor of the Reorganized Church on every point." Later in the day he received a telegram confirming his intuition. The membership of the Reorganized Church considered the decision a great victory: they had gained possession of the Temple Lot and had been legally declared the successor to the early church. Smith had Judge Phillips's decision reprinted in a pamphlet and later had the complainant's abstract of evidence issued in book form by the institutional press. He also commented on the favorable decision privately and publicly in both written and spoken form. [53]

The church's victory, however, was short lived. On 4 June 1894 the Church of Christ filed bond for an appeal. As Joseph Smith well knew, Judge Phillips's decision disregarded the very important fact that the Reorganization's deed was a questionable instrument, thus providing an excellent point for the Church of Christ to appeal. Moreover, the Reorganized Church's claim to be the original Mormon church rested largely on a refutation of the Utah Mormon movement's doctrines, especially polygamy, not on the Church of Christ's belief system. As a result the Hedrickites could challenge on the grounds that they were more attuned to the early church than Smith's organization. Finally, Joseph realized that in American judicial tradition a court could not appropriately judge the validity of the religious claims of contending sects. Any of these points could provide sufficient justification for an appeal, and in several instances the prophet tried to prepare his followers for a higher court's reversal. At the April 1894 general conference, for instance, Smith told the body that "the decision awarding the lot to the Reorganized Church may be reversed in that [Appeals] Court, in which case it will be for us to either appeal to the Supreme Court or accept the situation and acquiesce in such reversal." [54]

The Temple Lot Suit appeal was heard by the United States Court of Appeals at St. Louis in January 1895. Joseph Smith III was a spectator in the courtroom during the arguments by counsel and returned to his home in Lamoni after these concluded on 26 January 1895. On 30 September 1895 the three-judge panel reviewing the case handed down its ruling. In the majority opinion Judge Thayer altered the lower court's decision. First, the court found that the Reorganization had no grounds for a suit in chancery because such suits could only be brought to recover property from adverse possession when seeking legal title or seeking to obtain alleged equitable title. In stating its case the Reorganized Church had denied that the Church of Christ held any title to the property, and therefore the emphasis of the case was incorrect. Second, the court ruled that the Reorganized Church had not prosecuted the case soon enough to avoid the statute of limitations, or laches. Judge Thayer wrote, "We think that the plaintiff church and those whom it claims to represent have been guilty of such laches as should bar them from all relief in the form of equity." All counter-arguments were rejected by the court and the Church of Christ would retain its property. The court did not, however, alter the lower court's ruling about the legitimacy of the Reorganized Church, concluding that it "is as this day the legitimate successor of the original beneficiary" of the property. Judge Thayer did not question the propriety of the lower court's opinion about the validity of religious claims made by contending churches.[55]

After this verdict Smith asked the church's attorneys to file for a rehearing of the case, but the court denied this on 9 December 1895 on the ground that all facts were in and there had been no violation of official procedures during the original suit. Then Smith instructed the church's lawyers to petition the United States Supreme Court to hear the case, but in January 1896 it refused, on the grounds that no constitutional questions were challenged. This refusal left standing the appellate court's decision in favor of the Church of Christ.[56]

Joseph Smith was personally disappointed with the failure of the Temple Lot Suit; instead of gaining the key portion of this important property, all he had was bills for court costs and public embarrassment. Nonetheless, he tried to cast the defeat in its most favorable terms for both the church membership and the general public. He claimed that while the church had been vindicated in the courts, because of its ruling that the Reorganization was the "successor" to the "original church," it could not obtain possession because of a legal technicality—the principle of laches, a failure to assert a legal claim on a timely basis. In his memoirs Smith expressed this positive approach well: "We as a church body and members have been obliged to content ourselves with the verdict rendered by the Court of Appeals, even while we had indubitably established the fact that we were the church lawfully in succession to the one organized in 1830. . . . The decision gave our defeat in large measure the color and texture of victory, since its adverse nature was determined upon a technicality which, from the conditions surrounding it, prevented us from carrying the case further in litigation. Hence, we could but feel gratified over certain phrases of the result in spite of our disappointment."[57] Regardless of any appeal's outcome, to undertake such a legal action forced Smith to rethink his position. The potential for internal strife and external criticism because of the case was quite real. Smith's willingness to become involved in such a speculative venture was evidence of his increasing ease in the prophetic office and his security with the leadership of the church.

The twenty years between 1886 and 1906 were some of the most productive and rewarding of Joseph Smith's presidency in the Reorganization. Largely because he had a unified church organization that granted him wide latitude in directing the movement, Smith became increasingly forthright and persuasive in his leadership style. Out of this came several tangible benefits, among them expanded missionary activities, a well-organized and efficient administrative bureaucracy, the building of Graceland College, and the construction of such social institutions as the "Old Saints' Home" in Lamoni and the Sanitarium and Hospital in Independence, Missouri. As he surveyed the events of the preceding forty-five years, Joseph Smith could not help but take pride and satisfaction in the knowledge that he had achieved much as the head of the Reorganized Church.[58] There had been failures, but the successes far outweighed those. This general feeling of accomplishment, coupled with the fact that in 1906 he was seventy-four years old and increasingly less capable of strenuous activity, caused Smith to enter into semiretirement in Independence, Missouri, the church's "centerplace." Except on rare occasions, during the rest of his long life Joseph Smith concerned himself with family affairs, the writing of the history of his life, a few critical church duties, and the succession of his son to the prophetic office.

NOTES

1. Joseph Smith, "The Memoirs of President Joseph Smith (1832–1914)," *Saints' Herald* 83 (9 June 1936): 720, 84 (22 May 1937): 658, passim.

2. Alma R. Blair, "The Reorganized Church of Jesus Christ of Latter Day Saints: Moderate Mormons," in *The Restoration Movement: Essays in Mormon History,* ed. F. Mark McKiernan, Alma R. Blair, and Paul M. Edwards (Lawrence, Kan.: Coronado Press, 1973), pp. 218–26.

3. Ibid., 209–10; Early Reorganization Minutes, 1852–1873, 1 May 1865, Reorganized Church of Jesus Christ of Latter Day Saints Library–Archives, Independence, Mo.; Joseph Smith to O. F. Attwood, 12 October 1883, Joseph Smith III Letterbook #4, Reorganized Church Library–Archives; Joseph Smith to Caleb Parker, 14 August 1895, Joseph Smith III Letterbook #6, Reorganized Church Library–Archives.

4. Joseph Smith, "Priesthood," *Saints' Herald* 24 (1 June 1877): 168; Charles Derry, "Why I Did as I Did: Reasons for Uniting with the Reorganization of the Church of Jesus Christ of Latter Day Saints," *Saints' Herald* 24 (15 February 1877): 68–69.

5. Joseph Smith to L. D. Hickey, 30 April 1894, Joseph Smith III Letterbook #5, Reorganized Church Library–Archives; Blair, "Moderate Mormons," p. 217; Joseph Smith and Heman C. Smith, *The History of the Reorganized Church of Jesus Christ of Latter Day Saints* (Independence, Mo.: Herald Publishing House, 1967), 3:3–256.

6. The approach taken by Reorganized Church missionaries in dealing with non-Mormon prospects was similar to that taken by the early Mormons. They preached a revivalistic message, told about the Book of Mormon, and spoke of the special relationship members of the church had with God that was not enjoyed by individuals associated with other faiths. The result was a feeling of being better than one's fellow man in the case of many converts. Indeed, a favorite hymn of the church during this period bespoke this attitude:

I have found the glorious gospel that was taught in former years,
  With its Gifts and blessings all so full and free;
And my soul is thrilled with gladness, and banished are my fears,
  Since the precious angel message came to me.

Then praise the Lord, O my soul! Abundant mercy, oh, how free!
  In joyful song my spirit doth accord,
Since the precious angel message came to me.

I wandered long in darkness, yet sought the narrow way,
And my life was like the surging of the sea;
But now I am rejoicing in this the latter day,
Since the precious angel message came to me.

See Hymn 284, *The Hymnal* (Independence, Mo.: Herald Publishing House, 1955). The Reorganized Church did insert significant rhetoric into their missionary program aimed at showing the difference between their movement and the larger and better known Utah-base Mormon church. See, as a case study, Roger D. Launius, "W. W. Blair Contributed Much to Reorganization," *Restoration Trail Forum* 4 (May 1978): 1, 6.

7. H. H. Bancroft, *History of Utah* (San Francisco: The History Co., 1889), p. 645; *Saints' Herald* 57 (29 January 1910): 100; Blair, "Moderate Mormons," pp. 228–30.

8. *Daily Union Vendette* (Salt Lake City, Utah), 18 December 1863; F. Henry Edwards, *The History of the Reorganized Church of Jesus Christ of Latter Day Saints* (Independence, Mo.: Herald Publishing House, 1973), 5:92; Edward W. Tullidge, *The Life of Joseph the Prophet* (Plano, Ill.: Herald Publishing House, 1880), p. 657; "The World Mistaken," *Desert News* (Salt Lake City, Utah), 7 October 1863, 6 September 1882; E. C. Briggs, Journal, 7 October 1863, Reorganized Church Library–Archives, Smith and Smith, *History of Reorganized Church*, 3:339.

9. The California mission was quite successful, the Reorganized Church reaping a rich harvest of dissident Latter-day Saints who had refused to live in Utah. By 1894 Mormon missionaries in the Golden State were complaining they could gain no converts because of the strength of the Reorganization there. See A. Karl Larson and Katherine Miles Larson, eds., *The Diary of Charles Lowell Walker* (Logan: Utah State University Press, 1980), 2:771.

10. Inez Smith Davis, *The Story of the Church* (Independence, Mo.: Herald Publishing House, 1976), pp. 469–80; *New York Times*, 5 August 1912. The standard histories of the Reorganized Church in the British Isles include Geoffrey T. K. Holmes, "The Restoration in Britain," *Saints' Herald* 124 (July 1977): 12–14; a condensation of his *History of the Church in the British Isles* (Birmingham, England: British Isles Region of the Reorganized Church, 1977). Focusing on the role of leaders in Great Britain, F. Henry Edwards contributed "British Leaders," *Saints' Herald* 124 (July 1977): 20–24; Geoffrey T. K. Holmes wrote "Thomas Taylor— Pioneer of the Reorganization," *Saints' Herald* 124 (July 1977): 25; and Nephi Dewnup, Jr., produced, "The Dewnups—Historic Church Family [in England]," *Saints' Herald* 124 (July 1977): 34–35. On Charles Derry the only recent historical study is Norma Derry Hiles, "Charles Derry:

A Palimpsestic View," *John Whitmer Historical Association Journal* 4 (1984): 22–29, a disappointing presentistic survey of the life of a most interesting member of the Council of Twelve and High Priests' Quorum.

11. Richard P. Howard, "The Reorganized Church in Illinois, 1852–1882: Search for Identity," *Dialogue: A Journal of Mormon Thought* 5 (Winter 1970): 73.

12. Davis, *Story of the Church*, pp. 507–15; Gregory S. Savage, "Into All the World: Germany," in *Restoration Studies I: Sesquicentennial Edition*, ed. Maurice L. Draper (Independence, Mo.: Herald Publishing House, 1980), pp. 58–68.

13. Davis, *Story of the Church*, pp. 524–45, 562–67; F. Edward Butterworth, *Roots of the Reorganization: French Polynesia* (Independence, Mo.: Herald Publishing House, 1977), pp. 94–149. F. Edward Butterworth, *The Adventures of John Hawkins, Restoration Pioneer* (Independence, Mo.: Herald Publishing House, 1963), traced the life and career of an important missionary in the Pacific between 1844 and the 1870s. On the Australian and New Zealand churches see Maurice L. Draper, "The Australian Mission in Review," *Saints' Herald* 116 (August 1969): 24–26; idem., "The New Zealand Mission in Review," *Saints' Herald* 117 (February 1970): 30–32; Floyd Potter, "Mission in the Making," *Saints' Herald* 121 (January 1974): 20–21, 23, 31; John D. Imrie, "Religion in Australia—Its Origins and Prospects," *Restoration Studies I*, pp. 31–41. Glaud Rodgers and Charles W. Wandell were the first Reorganized Church missionaries to Australia in the 1870s; the story of their mission has been related in Winifred Sarre's "The Wandell-Rodgers Saga," *Saints' Herald* 121 (January 1974): 24–29, 121 (February 1974): 22–25, 31, 51.

14. Joseph Smith to John L. Bear, 8 January 1877, Joseph Smith III Letterbook #1; Savage, "Germany," pp. 58–63; Davis, *Story of the Church*, pp. 506–15.

15. Howard, "Reorganized Church in Illinois," p. 73.

16. As yet there is no demographic study of the membership of the early Reorganized Church. Except for isolated instances the data must be compiled from primary sources, especially the manuscript census returns of the respective jurisdictions. My observations, at best speculative, are based on preliminary analyses of the population schedules of the United States manuscript census returns for 1870, 1880, 1900, and 1910 for Fayette Township, Decatur County, Iowa, and the Iowa manuscript census of population for 1875, 1885, 1895 for the same jurisdiction. Fayette Township was the site of Lamoni, the church's headquarters between 1881 and at least 1906.

17. See note 16.

18. Howard, "Reorganized Church in Illinois," p. 73; F. Henry

Edwards, *The History of the Reorganized Church of Jesus Christ of Latter Day Saints* (Independence, Mo.: Herald Publishing House, 1973), 5:92.

19. For a succinct discussion of the shift in Reorganized Church policy after 1890, as it related to the Utah Mormon church, see Charles W. Turner, "Joseph Smith III and the Mormons of Utah" (Ph.D. diss., Graduate Theological Union, 1985), pp. 426–30.

20. Joseph Smith, "The Memoirs of President Joseph Smith (1832–1914)," *Saints' Herald* 83 (10 March 1936): 305.

21. Joseph Smith to W. W. Blair, 6 May 1888; Joseph Smith to E. L. Kelley, 28 May 1888, both in Joseph Smith III Papers, Reorganized Church Library-Archives.

22. Joseph Smith to Mrs. D. C. Chase, 25 October 1894, Miscellaneous Letters and Papers, Reorganized Church Library–Archives. See also Joseph Smith to E. D. Smith, 22 July 1896, Joseph Smith III Letterbook #7; Joseph Smith to George Updike, 18 June 1894, Joseph Smith III Letterbook #5, both in Reorganized Church Library–Archives; "The Parliament of World's Religions," *Saints' Herald* 40 (21 October 1893): 670–71, 40 (28 October 1893): 688–90, 40 (4 November 1893): 706–708, 40 (11 November 1893): 720–21, 40 (18 November 1893): 736–37, 40 (25 November 1893): 751–53; Smith, "Memoirs," *Saints' Herald* 83 (26 September 1936): 1202, 83 (3 October 1936): 1233–34. For an exceptional study of Mormonism as related to this meeting, see Davis Bitton, "B. H. Roberts at the World Parliament of Religion, 1893, Chicago," *Sunstone* 7 (January–February 1982): 46–51.

23. *Saints' Herald* 39 (30 April 1892): 274.

24. "Baptism for the Dead," *Saints' Herald* 40 (25 February 1893): 115; "Adoption," *Saints' Herald* 41 (2 May 1894): 274; "Building Temples," *Saints' Herald* 41 (4 July 1894): 421; "Joseph Smith's Charge to the Twelve," *Saints' Herald* 42 (14 August 1895): 518; "Are They Untrue?" *Saints' Herald* 43 (22 January 1896): 49; "That Prophecy of the Seer Concerning the Settlement of the Saints in the Rocky Mountains," *Saints' Herald* 43 (29 January 1896): 65–66.

25. The official approach taken by the church toward plural marriage and its origins has been astutely described in Alma R. Blair, "RLDS Views of Polygamy: Some Historiographical Notes," *John Whitmer Historical Association Journal* 5 (1985): 16–28.

26. Joseph Smith, "The Purpose of the Reorganization," *Saints Herald Supplement* 2 (14 March 1894): 87.

27. Joseph Smith, Journal, 4 February 1904, Reorganized Church Library–Archives; Smith, "Memoirs," *Saints' Herald* 84 (8 May 1937): 590–95, 84 (15 May 1937): 625–26, 84 (22 May 1937): 655–56; Joseph Smith to Audentia Anderson, 17 October 1904, Joseph Smith III Papers, Reorganized Church Library–Archives.

28. Joseph Smith, "Men and Things," *Saints' Herald* 50 (4 November 1903): 1026. For a fuller discussion of the Reed Smoot issue see M. Paul Holsinger, "For God and the American Home: The Attempt to Unseat Senator Reed Smoot, 1903–1907," *Pacific Northwest Quarterly* 60 (July 1969): 154–60.

29. Joseph Smith to Israel A. Smith, 30 January 1906, 10 February 1906, Miscellaneous Letters and Papers; Smith, "Memoirs," *Saints' Herald* 82 (23 July 1935): 944–46, 84 (22 May 1937): 657–68.

30. The maturation of Joseph Smith III in the prophetic office can be seen well in his advice to his son, Frederick M. Smith, in 1914. See chapter 15 for a discussion of this.

31. Joseph Smith, "Lamoni College," *Saints' Herald* 36 (12 January 1889): 17.

32. Smith, "Memoirs," *Saints' Herald* 83 (17 October 1936): 1296.

33. Joseph Smith and W. W. Blair to Church n.d., Edmund L. Kelley Papers, Reorganized Church Library–Archives; Joseph Smith to G. J. Waller, 27 March 1896, Joseph Smith III Letterbook #6; Edwards, *History of Reorganized Church* 5:140, 220, 271, 372.

34. Graceland College Board of Trustees Minutes, 1895–1898, pp. 4–34, Reorganized Church Library–Archives; Joseph Smith to W. W. Blair, 20 December 1893, Joseph Smith III Letterbook #5; Smith, "Memoirs," *Saints' Herald* 83 (17 October 1936): 1296.

35. Graceland College Board of Trustees Minutes, 1895–1898, p. 34; Ruth C. Smith, *Concerning the Prophet: Fredrick* [sic] *M. Smith* (Kansas City: Burton Publishing Co., 1924), pp. 27–28, 46–47, 52–54, 61.

36. Edwards, *History of Reorganized Church* 5:472, 485–88, 527–53.

37. Ibid.

38. Book of Doctrine and Covenants (Independence, Mo.: Herald Publishing House, 1970), section 125.

39. Ibid., sections 120, 122, 125; Smith, "Memoirs," *Saints' Herald* 84 (31 July 1937): 975–78. On one occasion Joseph Smith wrote to his son, Israel A. Smith, boasting of how he had handled the reorganization of some of the church's leading quorums. He said, "I have never been so well satisfied with the makeup of the leading quorums, mine and the Twelve. The latter quorum is a strong one, stronger than ever before. . . . I am glad that it [general conference] is over, and that we are not to have another year of another swelling committee round the Bishop's office [to audit books]. It had got to be a nuisance" (Joseph Smith to Israel A. Smith, 25 April 1902, Miscellaneous Letters and Papers).

40. Joseph Smith to E. L. Kelley, 23 January 1891, Joseph Smith III Papers; Joseph Smith to Heman C. Smith, 23 April 1895, Joseph Smith III Letterbook #6. For discussions of the way in which Frederick M. Smith ran the church see Paul M. Edwards, "Theocratic-Democracy:

Philosopher-King in the Reorganization," in *The Restoration Movement,* ed. McKiernan, Blair, and Edwards, pp. 341–57; Larry E. Hunt, *Frederick M. Smith: Saint as Reformer,* 2 vols. (Independence, Mo.: Herald Publishing House, 1981).

41. Edwards, *History of Reorganized Church,* 3:53; Tom Bennett, "The Church in Court (The Temple Lot Case)," *Saints' Herald* 120 (November 1970): 23–24; Turner, "Joseph Smith III and the Mormons of Utah," pp. 406–26.

42. See note 41. On the early development of the temple lot and the temple concept see Ronald E. Romig and John H. Seibert, "Jackson County, 1831–1833: A Look at the Development of Zion," in *Restoration Studies III,* ed. Maurice L. Draper and Debra Combs (Independence, Mo.: Herald Publishing House, 1986), pp. 286–304; Ronald E. Romig and John H. Seibert, "A Close Look at the City of Zion and the Concept of Temples," study in possession of author.

43. Smith and Smith, *History of Reorganized Church,* 4:480–81. A synopsis of these meetings can be found in Joseph Smith to Stephen Maloney, 12 July 1893, Joseph Smith III Letterbook #3A, Reorganized Church Library–Archives.

44. Smith, "Memoirs," *Saints' Herald* 83 (12 September 1936): 1137.

45. The 1891 Articles of Incorporation contained a statement, Article 6, which said: "All property now held or owned by said church, in the name of any person or persons, as trustees or otherwise, including the publication establishment of said church, shall vest in said corporation. And all persons holding such property in trust for said church are hereby directed and required to transfer and convey the same to said corporation, as the property of said church. And said corporation shall by operation of law succeed to all property now owned by said church or held for its use, and may sue for and recover the same in the name of corporation." This article, along with Article 1, which declared the Reorganized Church as successor of the early Mormon movement, laid a foundation for a lawsuit to recover property held in trust for the original church. See Turner, "Joseph Smith III and the Mormons of Utah," p. 609.

46. W. W. Blair to E. L. Kelley, 12 May 1887, Edmund L. Kelley Papers, Reorganized Church Library–Archives; Reorganized Church of Jesus Christ of Latter Day Saints vs. Church of Christ et al., 60 *Federal Reporter* 937 (1894), 935–41.

47. Joseph Smith to George Edmunds, 29 June 1887, Joseph Smith III Papers, Reorganized Church Library–Archives. See also Joseph Smith to George Edmunds, 18 June 1887; George Edmunds to Joseph Smith, 22 June 1887, both in Joseph Smith III Papers; Joseph Smith to E. L. Kelley, 14 June 1887, 6 July 1887, Miscellaneous Letters and Papers.

48. Reorganized Church vs. Church of Christ, 60 *Federal Reporter* 937 (1894), 935.

49. *Complainant's Abstract of Pleading and Evidence in the Circuit Court of the United States, Western District of Missouri, Western Division, at Kansas City, Missouri* (Lamoni, Iowa: Herald Publishing House, 1893), pp. 6–10.

50. Joseph Smith to E. L. Kelley, 17 January 1890, Joseph Smith III Papers; Smith, "Memoirs," *Saints' Herald* 83 (16 September 1936): 1169; Joseph Smith, Jr., *The History of the Church of Jesus Christ of Latter-day Saints*, ed. B. H. Roberts (Salt Lake City: Deseret Book Co., 1976), 3:260–89; Turner, "Joseph Smith III and the Mormons of Utah," pp. 410–17.

51. See note 50; *Saints' Herald* 39 (3 September 1892): 566–67; "President Smith in Detroit," *Saints' Herald* 47 (25 July 1900): 478; Edwards, *History of Reorganized Church*, 5:236–37. Fully three-fourths of all the testimony in the Temple Lot's abstract of evidence deals in one way or another with proving the church's line of authority from the time of Joseph Smith, Jr., to 1890. See *Complainant's Abstract*, passim.

52. Reorganized Church of Jesus Christ of Latter Day Saints vs. Church of Christ et al., 60 *Federal Reporter* 937 (1894); *Kansas City Times*, 4 March 1894; "Opinion of Judge Phillips, in Temple Lot Case," *Saints' Herald* 41 (14 March 1894): 161–62; Turner, "Joseph Smith III and the Mormons of Utah," pp. 418–22.

53. Smith, "Memoirs," *Saints' Herald* 83 (12 September 1936): 1137; "Temple Lot Decision," *Saints' Herald* 41 (14 March 1894): 164; *In the Circuit Court of the United States for the Western Division of the Western District of Missouri: Decision of John F. Philips [sic], Judge in Temple Lot Case: The Reorganized Church of Jesus Christ of Latter Day Saints versus the Church of Christ, et al.* (Lamoni, Iowa: Herald Publishing House, n.d.); "Abstract of Evidence in Temple Lot Suit," *Saints' Herald* 41 (4 July 1894): advertisement on back cover; *Saints' Herald* 41 (21 March 1894): 177; "Deseret News on the Temple Lot Suit," *Saints' Herald* 41 (19 September 1894): 597; "Disclaimer of Interest in Temple Lot Suit," *Saints' Herald* 42 (20 February 1895): 114; Turner, "Joseph Smith III and the Mormons of Utah," pp. 422–23.

54. Edwards, *History of Reorganized Church*, 5:240.

55. Joseph Smith, Journal, 22–25 January 1895, Reorganized Church Library–Archives; "Temple Lot Suit before United States Court of Appeals, in St. Louis," *Saints' Herald* 42 (6 February 1895): 83–84; Church of Christ vs. Reorganized Church of Jesus Christ of Latter Day Saints et al., 70 *Federal Reporter* 179–88 (1895); "Temple Lot Suit Reversed," *Saints' Herald* 42 (6 November 1895): 711.

56. Church of Christ at Independence, Missouri, et al. vs. Reorganized Church of Jesus Christ of Latter Day Saints, 71 *Federal Reporter* 250 (1895); Church of Christ at Independence, Missouri, et al., vs. Reorganized Church of Jesus Christ of Latter Day Saints, 163 *US* 314 (1896); "Editorial Items," *Saints' Herald* 42 (18 December 1895): 808; "Temple Lot Suit," *Saints' Herald* 43 (29 January 1896): 69; *Saints' Herald* 43 (5 February 1896): 85.

57. Smith, "Memoirs," *Saints' Herald* 83 (19 September 1936): 1168–69. See also Joseph Smith to J. W. Peterson, 10 June 1902, Miscellaneous Letters and Papers.

58. See the statement of satisfaction expressed in Joseph Smith to Israel A. Smith, 9 May 1901, Miscellaneous Letters and Papers.

CHAPTER 1

14

Joseph at Home

Over the years Joseph Smith III's duties as president of the Re-organized Church took a tremendous amount of time away from his family, and he regretted not being able to have a more normal home life and relationship with his wife. His long missionary trips to Utah and the Pacific Coast, numerous missions to the East, and innumerable jaunts throughout the Midwest took him away from home more than he would have liked. Even while he was home, either in Plano or Lamoni, church affairs consumed most of his time. On one occasion during his most active years he confided in his diary that he was very tired of this "ceaseless activity which only a strong man can endure."[1] Understanding that his time was not his own because of his religious commitments, Joseph Smith's mother wrote in 1869 to console him by pointing out that his father's experience had been the same. "I do not expect you can do much more in the garden than father could," Emma told her oldest son, "and I never wanted him to go into the garden to work for if he did it would not be fifteen minutes before there would be three or four, or sometimes half a dozen men around him and they would tramp the ground faster than he could hoe it up."[2]

Notwithstanding his broad religious responsibilities, Joseph made every effort to build a stable, caring family relationship. To a considerable extent he succeeded. Over the years he became something of a patriarch to his family as well as to the church, ruling as a benevolent dictator who demanded good order, obedience, proper manners, high morals, and a proper religious reverence from the rest of the family. Emmeline, his first wife, converted to the Reorganized Church in 1866, and this aided greatly in family relations, for thereafter she supported his ministry rather than merely tolerating it.[3]

By 1866 Joseph and Emmeline Smith were the parents of three daughters—Emma, named for her grandmother, nine years old and tomboyish; Carrie, five, plump, happy, and energetic; and Zaide, aged three, the baby spoiled by her father. One daughter, Eva, had died as an infant in 1859, and a son, Joseph Arthur, died on 12 March 1866. Smith recalled in his memoirs the tragedy of his son's death. Joseph Arthur, born on 12 October 1865, was only three months old when the family moved from Nauvoo to Plano. Joseph recalled that about March 1866 his wife became homesick and he sent her back for a visit. As the Smiths waited for the train that would take Emmeline and the baby boy toward Nauvoo, Smith wrote that "the knowledge came to me, with all the force and certainty could possibly attend an event before it happens, that I should never see the two alive again." Smith was upset by this premonition, but said nothing of it to Emmeline. A short time later Joseph received a telegram explaining that his son was ill and asking that he go to Nauvoo immediately. When he arrived he learned that Joseph Arthur had died the day before. This tragedy provided the impetus for his wife's baptism into the Reorganized Church.[4]

The move to Plano, Illinois, was an important step in the family life of the Smiths. During the early part of 1866 Smith and his family packed their few belongings into a wagon and moved from Nauvoo to the new church headquarters at Plano. Once there the Smith family moved into a comfortable, two-story, frame house that Bishop Israel L. Rogers had donated to the church for the prophet's use. In Plano the Smith home became something it had never been before—a way station for almost every traveler who wanted to meet the prophet. By the 1860s Nauvoo was far off the beaten track: it had no railroad near it, few came there to do business, and as a result prior to his move Joseph had largely been isolated from the rest of the church and much of the world. Plano, on the other hand, had a large church population, a growing Reorganized Church bureaucracy, and access to the rest of the nation through the Illinois Central Railroad that passed through the town.

Visitors, both Saint and nonmember, constantly came calling on the Saints. These visits were so frequent that the prophet's wife began to set at least one extra place at the table for anyone that might be visiting at the moment, "for seldom," Joseph remembered, "were we without some guests at mealtime."[5] Additionally, as often as not missionaries in the town on business stayed at the Smith home and there were usually a few long-term guests living in the house.[6]

In 1869 tragedy struck Smith as it never had before: he lost his wife of thirteen years. Emmeline, never a sturdy woman, had been ill with increasingly debilitating maladies during much of their marriage. Early in 1869 she had suffered a miscarriage that forced her into bed, and after a prolonged confinement, on 25 May 1869 Emmeline finally died. She was thirty-four at the time of her death. For the first time in many years Joseph cried as he took his wife's body back to Nauvoo for burial. The loss was devastating for Joseph; in writing to a Latter Day Saint more than thirty years later, he admitted that Emmeline's death made him ponder seriously God's plan for the world, asking himself, "My Lord, Why, Oh Why?" did He allow Emmeline to die.[7]

The church members at Plano tried to comfort Joseph Smith and his young family, but the prophet rejected their overtures of sympathy and wallowed in deep depression for several months. The family of Mark H. Forscutt, an old friend, moved into the Smith home to keep Joseph company, but they were unable to cheer up the prophet. Although the Forscutts served as Joseph's companions, his greatest comfort came from a twenty-six-year-old woman, Bertha Madison, who had joined the household during Emmeline's illness to help with the housekeeping. After Emmeline's death Bertha stayed on to take care of the prophet's children and maintain the house. As could be expected, the presence of an unmarried woman in a widower's home excited gossip in Plano, and the prophet's relationship to Miss Madison quickly became an item of intense interest. The rumors of an affair between Joseph and Bertha flew throughout the community, and although the prophet became aware of the situation, he chose to ignore it. He was finally forced to deal with the gossip one day after coming home from the Herald office unexpectedly and finding Bertha quietly crying as she sewed for one of the children. When he asked Bertha what was wrong, she hesitated to talk about it but eventually told of the hurt brought on by the gossip. She offered to give up her housekeeping job in an effort to end the harsh talk, but Joseph absolutely refused because nothing illicit had taken place, and such a move would have given the mistaken impression that they were ending a relationship as a result of outside pressure.[8]

Nonetheless, Joseph was concerned about the gossip, for it greatly affected his ability to carry on his ministry and hindered the couple's standing in the community. Smith considered simply ignoring the rumors, but the pressure wrought by the idle gossip increased until some action was necessary. In the depths of despair over this situation Joseph asked God for guidance. Eventually, Joseph became convinced that he should remarry so that he would not have to employ a housekeeper and would have companionship for himself and a mother for his children, but the question of who would be his bride remained. Two young ladies, members of the Plano Reorganized Church congregation, were suitable and the prophet considered both carefully; one of them was Bertha Madison. Finally, after confirmation by divine revelation Joseph began to court and eventually married Bertha. The couple's wedding took place in Smith's home on 12 November 1869, Joseph regaining the companionship he had lost several months earlier. The gossip continued for a while thereafter, some arguing that the marriage was a belated attempt to cover a scandal with a thin cloak of respectability. The rumors about Joseph's and Bertha's relationship appear to be without foundation, however, for there was not a shred of evidence implicating the two in any promiscuity and they quietly rode out the problem. Within a few weeks after the wedding most of the talk had ceased.[9]

In many ways Bertha Smith was the exact opposite of Joseph's first wife. Emmeline had not been raised in Mormonism and had refused to be associated with it most of her life, joining the church only three years before her death. Bertha, on the other hand, had been a member of the church since childhood and was devoted to the movement. Additionally, Emmeline had always been a frail, oftentimes ill young woman while Bertha was generally strong and robust. Moreover, Emmeline had been delicately beautiful, with a dainty body and striking dark features. Bertha, however, was a large, somewhat heavy-set woman who had more of a handsomeness than a feminine beauty. Finally, whereas Emmeline had been reserved and quiet in most instances, Bertha was extroverted and loved to meet people. She was always willing to open her home to the Latter Day Saints, to take charge of social activities, and to live in the limelight that her husband attracted in his position as president of the Reorganized Church. More important, perhaps, unlike Joseph's first wife, Bertha seemed never to resent Joseph's long absences from home or his frequent nights away preaching the gospel. She accepted her husband for what he was, a minister, and supported him in his role as president of the church.[10]

Within a short time after their marriage Joseph and Bertha Smith had developed a mutually acceptable relationship that served them throughout the rest of their lives. Although Joseph and Bertha felt both love and respect for each other, the powerful romance between Joseph and his first wife was not repeated with nearly as much intensity in his second marriage. Smith had found Emmeline exciting; he considered Bertha comfortable. Emmeline had been Joseph's love of youth; Bertha, his love as a mature adult. The two relationships were necessarily different because of the women involved and the events that had altered Joseph over the years.[11]

Joseph soon grew to appreciate his new wife and the kind of life she gave him. "I found my second wife to be a most capable woman," he recalled matter of factly—"one in whom I could place the most implicit confidence, and in whose care I always felt it safe to leave my home affairs without question, when I entered into the ministry of my work which required me to go upon near or distant trips. I felt an assurance that she would not only do the best she could but that she possessed the natural ability to discharge the duties of her position honorably and acceptably." [12] His letters to Bertha were not filled with the syrupy confessions of endless love that had been present in some of his correspondence with Emmeline. Bertha did not need constant reassurance, nor did he desire to write to her in such a vein. Instead, Joseph's letters home were filled with news of the trip, reporting on his safe arrival, estimating when he would return, detailing the success of his work, and perhaps reciting a humorous incident. Still, not so much with words as in the tone, Joseph's letters betrayed the love he and Bertha shared.[13]

The full expression of the couple's close relationship was expressed in two poems which Joseph wrote to celebrate their wedding anniversaries. On their sixth anniversary he wrote:

Six years along life's rugged road
   We've passed in quiet pace together;
And held for each the same regard
   through frosty, rough, and pleasant weather.

Six times the sun his annual course
   Has gone, for earth, in joy or sadness;
And days successive, good or worse,
   Have filled the years with grief or gladness.

Three times in joy, our married tie
   For us has budded, bloomed and fruited;
Nor have the years, in passing by,
   Proved yet for each unsuited.

Then may the years that are before,
   as have the past, in peace be tarried,
That looking back to "days of yore."
   We'll ne'er regret that we were married.

Ten years later he redeclared his fondness for Bertha with this poem:

'Tis sixteen years today, Good Wife,
   This bright, though chill, November
Since we in bonds began our life,
   And I as husband, you as wife,
Pledged each the other in time's strife;
   Oh! that I still remember.

And hand in hand we've held our way
   Through fair and stormy weather;
'Mid skies of blue, or skies of gray,
   In stint of toil, or need of play,
We've been in each a staff and stay
   In joy and grief—together.
. . . .

And as the years have waxed and waned,
   Our lives being blended,
Our life's treasures earned and gained,
   By joys been pleased, by sorrows pained,
And thankful been for grace obtained
   When each sad grief-time ended.

Thus, Bertha dear, I call to mind
   That day in chill November,

We made the vows whose ties still bind,
    The bonds made sweet by lives entwined,
    As at the first, by God designed,–
    And trust you still remember.[14]

Soon after their marriage the Smiths began to develop a routine that served well for many years. Joseph allowed Bertha complete charge of the house and the family, while she permitted Joseph wide latitude in carrying out his affairs outside the home. Nonetheless, both catered to the other as much as possible, Bertha molding the household routine as much as practicable to Joseph's wishes and Joseph trying to conform to requests by Bertha.

The household routine that emerged during this period remained relatively static until Bertha's death in 1896. Joseph, who liked to be the first person to rise in the mornings, was usually active in the house before five a.m. In the winter he always stoked the furnace about that time to warm the house, put on a tea kettle, and drew fresh drinking water from the well in an old brass-bound cedar bucket. Upon occasion Joseph cooked breakfast for the family, usually preparing pancakes with a healthy side order of steak. When breakfast was ready, Joseph would ring a bell that rested on a table in a central hallway, and the other members of the family were expected to be in the dining room within five minutes or be lectured on the "sin" of tardiness. After a blessing on the food everyone settled down to a huge breakfast.

Joseph Smith routinely left the house to walk to the Herald office before nine o'clock, and except for some instances when he came home for lunch, Joseph seldom returned before six in the evening unless there was some emergency. The supper routine was much like that for breakfast but with a few more guests and conversation sparked by the day's events. After this meal the men and small children would carry out the chores necessary to maintain the quasi-farm that Joseph liked to operate, while Bertha and the older girls cleaned up in the kitchen. When those things were done, all the household gathered in the parlor. Sometimes they met around the heavy piano and the girls took turns playing and singing. At other times the children put on little plays or shows. More often, however, the family played games, read magazines or books, or worked on handicraft projects. Lucy Smith, one of Joseph's daughters, remembered that as a girl she often sat by the fire on autumn evenings, polishing apples while someone read a story to the family. Audentia Smith, another daughter, mentioned that her father often sat in the corner of the parlor "patiently shaping and sandpapering new bows and arrows for the boys" during the evenings.[15] At nine o'clock every night Smith called the household together to read a chapter from the big family Bible that rested on a table in the parlor; then they all knelt in prayer before retiring for the night.[16]

The positive home environment enabled Joseph Smith to build a close rapport with his children in spite of his frequent trips away from home. At every opportunity Joseph taught his children, both by example and precept, the difference between right and wrong and urged them to make the most of their unique talents. Although he did not have the resources to provide them with many physical things, he ensured that their basic needs were met and tried always to see that they had the opportunity to develop their full potentials. For instance, Joseph encouraged all his children, especially his daughters, to develop musical talents, spending large sums over the years for music lessons, study with well-known musicians, and even music camps. Additionally, he urged his children to develop technical skills. Frederick Madison Smith, Joseph's eldest son, showed considerable interest in the field of electronics, as well as physics, photography, and mechanical engineering. Joseph fostered these investigations by providing a machine shop and photographic darkroom in their home.[17]

Equally important, Joseph early made preparations for each of his sons' educations—he would also have done so for his daughters but did not possess the resources—borrowing heavily to obtain tuition. When he sent Frederick to school at Iowa State University in 1894, he jokingly gave him one last bit of fatherly advice: "I am proud, and I know, my son, that you will not let them make of you a learned incapable."[18] While Frederick was at the university, Joseph sent him a bank draft each month to pay legitimate expenses, occasionally managing to forward a few extra dollars for "splurge money." Frederick's education, however, used up so much of the family's funds that it nearly prohibited Israel, the second son, from attending. As a result, when Israel asked to go to college in 1897, Joseph decided to arrange his appointment to the United States Military Academy at West Point. A man well-known in Iowa, Joseph Smith used his influence with the congressman from his district to assist in the appointment.[19] Although the representative wanted to help, Israel was twenty-three years old by this time and therefore ineligible for the academy. Joseph managed, however, to send Israel to the church's Graceland College in Lamoni.[20]

When he was away from home, Joseph wrote to his children, always urging them to act uprightly and to work hard to accomplish admirable goals. While on a western tour in 1876, for instance, Joseph wrote to Audentia, then four years old, a simple block-printed note that said much about the values he tried to instill in his children. It read: "Your letter was a good one. Pa was glad to get it. Be a good girl and learn fast, so that you can always write long letters to pa when he is away."[21] On another occasion in 1879 when Joseph was away from home on an extended trip, he wrote each of his children short letters reminding them to act rightly. In each instance he ended with the admonition: "Be good children, help mama all you can: be good natured with each other and keep happy."[22]

In many of his letters to his children Joseph Smith described elaborately the locations he visited, especially when he traveled throughout the arid west, where the terrain was so different from anything with which his children were familiar. His letters often contained lessons on botany, natural history, and geography in addition to moral lessons. For instance, in one letter written in 1885 he gave a brief geography lesson. He told Audentia, "I am now fifteen, yes 25 miles north, almost 40 miles south of the head of the Missouri river. Get your map find Bozeman [Montana], and 15 miles north of that I am now."[23] In another letter to Audentia during his 1885 Utah trip he also gave a short lesson on the earth's rotation:

> Audie Daughter: There are many things in this country I wish you could see. If you could only go out on the lawn in front of the house and jump high enough and stay up long enough to let the earth turn around under you till you was [sic] over Salt Lake City and then jump down. Stay till you wanted to go back and then jump back; would not that be nice; would not cost you a cent see![24]

On other occasions Smith pointed out proper or improper actions or made other observations designed to teach his children everything from morality to grammar.[25]

Joseph Smith betrayed a certain restrained wit and humor that told much about the basically positive relationship he enjoyed with his children. In correspondence with his offspring, he tended to poke fun at what he called the "absurdities of life" and encouraged them to enjoy and even relish comic scenes as relief from mankind's common existence. When writing to Audentia from Utah in 1885, for example, Smith tried to explain the complicated family ties between his immediate family and some of their Utah relatives. With much intermarrying and the practice of polygamy in the West, his explanation was hopelessly confused. Finally, almost with a sigh of relief at getting through the convoluted explanation, Joseph wrote, "let that pass," and went on to another subject.[26]

On another occasion, a missionary trip to the East in 1897, Smith told his family about the prospect of attending an organ concert in Washington, D.C. "I expect to be bored," he complained, "as usual in one of these high toned concerts."[27] A few days later he wrote about a recent visit with one of the local church women to the Library of Congress. They toured the building and entered the rotunda, where Hiram Powers's famous sculpture *The Greek Slave*, an elegant nude that had raised complaints of immorality when first displayed, was on exhibition. Joseph described the embarrassing episode as his companion tried to maintain proper Victorian decorum while viewing this art: "Just fancy your Papa looking at a statue of the Greek slave; the statue of a beautiful woman in cold marble, as naked as woman can be, with not a thing on her but a chain to hold her to a ring in the floor, by the side of a good looking, well dressed, warm flesh and blood woman palpitating with life will you. But I give Sr. Bloom credit for not once looking at the nude statue, and pictures, that I could see."[28] Smith certainly saw the humor in such needlessly embarrassing moments.

He also enjoyed what were apparently "in-family" jokes. He often commented on his own rather overweight size, as well as the rotundity of some members of his family. He wrote to the somewhat plump teenage Audentia in 1885 by prefacing his remarks with, "Dear, though fat, Daughter." He closed the letter with "Your father—fat, J. Smith."[29] In another 1885 letter, this time to Carrie, another daughter, he commented on the rigors of missionary work. "We were there [in Beaver, Utah] eleven days and held eleven meetings and eat [sic] eleven dinners at eleven different tables. And I am not yet dyspeptic, though I do breathe hard."[30]

Whenever Joseph traveled he tried to send or take home some little gift for each child in the household. Usually these were inexpensive, but his family came to cherish these, not so much because of the value of the gift but because of Joseph's thoughtfulness. Lucy Smith, a daughter born in 1884, remembered that "he often sent a tiny trinket we might keep, rocks, soil or shells, a sheet of music or a flower pressed to enjoy." On special occasions the gifts might be a bit more valuable, she recalled, perhaps consisting of "a bolt of fabric for the new dresses that pleased us so much," or perhaps clothing or toys unique to the area in which he was traveling.[31] In September 1885 Smith wrote to Audentia, "I have a nice lot of specimens to send you and will send them by express as I fear to carry them with me all the time. They may wear my satchel out. The smaller pair of moccasins are for Miss Audentia Smith. Do you know such a girl? I am, dear girl, your loving Papa."[32]

In 1881 Joseph and Bertha Smith moved from Plano to the Reorganized Church settlement at Lamoni, Iowa, as part of the removal of the organization's headquarters. They planned together the house they built in the community and were very proud of Liberty Hall. It was a large, Victorian farmhouse with some twenty rooms built on a patch of rolling prairie about a mile west of the town. Constructed of the finest Michigan lumber by a master builder, Thomas Jacobs, a church member who lived with the Smiths for years thereafter, work on Liberty Hall began during the summer of 1881 and by late fall was ready for occupancy.[33]

The family quickly learned to love Liberty Hall, and the house began to take on the character and power of its inhabitants. Bertha furnished the rooms for maximum utility as well as proper Victorian elegance. The house had a well-used formal parlor for special occasions, a less formal living room filled with plants and the furniture most used by the family—especially a large piano. It also had a study and office to aid Joseph in his work, complete with bookshelves from floor to ceiling on three walls to shelve his extensive library. Additionally, the family enjoyed a well-planned, modern kitchen, a lavish dining room, and upstairs wings with suites for rooms for the boys, girls, parents, and guests. Outside, the Smiths planted an extensive orchard and vineyard that rivaled anything else in the community. Finally, Joseph fenced the remainder of the forty acres upon which Liberty Hall sat, farmed some of it and had cattle on a small pasture.[34]

As Smith's children matured at Liberty Hall, the family had to deal with many of the normal problems of adolescence. Joseph and Bertha tried to assist them through this difficult period of adjustment but, like most other parents, were only partially successful in dealing with the complicated situations that arose. In all too many cases Joseph offered fatherly counsel when none had been asked and was not wanted. One of his pet sermons included a powerful admonition to work hard, to pay debts promptly, and to assume full responsibility for personal obligations. This belief arose out of Joseph's personal experience, for he had been heavily in debt since 1862, when he was left with an insolvent farm partnership at the death of his brother, Frederick, and he did not want his children to become enmeshed in such difficulties.[35]

For the most part Joseph's children followed his advice concerning personal responsibility, but in one notable instance involving his son Israel A. Smith, born in 1876, such was not the case. During the mid-1890s Israel became rebellious and with a small group of friends engaged in a bit of drinking and carousing. Over the course of several months of living in a manner of which his father disapproved, Israel ran up a substantial bill at the local grog shop and at other stores in Lamoni. Joseph tried repeatedly to persuade his son to curb his activities, but he was unable to convince Israel to change his ways and became quite depressed. To make matters worse, Israel decided to leave town without paying his bills. The young man's action infuriated Joseph, and it was at least two years before the two were on intimate terms again. By that time, it should be noted, Israel had abandoned his wild lifestyle, accepted adult responsibilities, and made amends to his father.[36]

Additionally, Joseph gave his children considerable advice about the conducting of their lives once they left home. He continued to dwell upon the necessity of acting responsibly and justly at all times. He also harped upon planning and executing an upright course of action in spite of opposition from outside forces or from other individuals. When Israel took a new job as a salesman in the eastern states in 1899, for instance, Joseph repeatedly wrote to him explaining the necessity of working hard and acting forthrightly. This viewpoint was expressed in March 1899 when Joseph told his son not to "hesitate to do what they ask of you, if it is not dishonest. But don't consent to anything dishonorable, come home first. Just tell them you will not do it, and they will never ask a second time." [37]

As time passed, Joseph became increasingly satisfied with and proud of his children. He believed that all were working to achieve their fullest potentials, and he remarked often about his pleasure at their accomplishments. In March 1899, for instance, he wrote to Israel, who was then living in West Virginia and by this time was closer to his father than he had ever been when living at home, that "I am getting to be rather proud of my Sons, Frederick and Israel, and hope that you will stick to business." [38] A few months later Smith wrote to Audentia with a similar tone: "Life has had none too many bright episodes for me, but I am thankful that the sweets of friendship and filial [love] are mine. My children have stood by me under conditions that have driven other men's from them—God bless them everyone." [39]

As their children grew up and left home and the Smiths began to ease into a graceful old age, tragedy struck Joseph and his children as never before. In September 1896 Bertha had driven her team and buggy on an errand; during the trip the horses had been frightened, had run off at a gallop, and had thrown her from the buggy. She was stunned and bruised but did not seem seriously injured and within a few minutes had gone on with her daily routine. A few weeks later, however, Bertha went on another errand, and although Joseph protested that the team was skittish and should not be trusted, she insisted that she would have no trouble using the same horses. After a short discussion, in which Bertha let it be known that she would not be cowed by one instance of a runaway team, she departed. Joseph's worst fears were realized, however, for just as she returned home, the horses became frightened again, reared, and took off at a gallop. The buggy tipped over and Bertha tumbled out onto a pile of firewood stacked by the kitchen door. Joseph helped her to her feet. She did not appear hurt, but when she sat down to supper a few minutes later, she fainted and had to be carried to bed. [40]

Bertha was quite ill for several days thereafter, the doctor reporting that she had sustained some internal injuries but that they should heal eventually. Everyone was pleased that by the first part of October Bertha appeared to have all but recovered. Consequently, Joseph felt safe in leaving her to attend to church business away from Lamoni and had been gone ten days when he received word that Bertha was bedridden again and appeared to be on the verge of death. Nothing could be done for her, neither medicine nor prayer seemed to have any effect, and Bertha died quietly on 19 October 1896.[41]

Bertha's death was a tremendous shock to Joseph and their children. He had always believed that she would outlive him, but now he and the rest of the family had to adjust to life without the woman whom they had all loved and on whom they had all depended so heavily for so many years. Joseph expressed his grief in a letter to a friend two weeks after Bertha's funeral. "I have been passing under the rod," he confided, "by losing my companion in wedlock, October 19th, which, with a multiplicity of cares; had kept me from writing. And even now, I hardly know what to write; so varied are the emotions pressing on the mind in consideration of the field of gospel requirements."[42] In December he wrote to another old friend about his relationship with Bertha. "My wife & I lived together over 27 years with not a quarrel, or mischievous misunderstanding in all the long time," adding that "our life was a scene of mutual trust, each of the other. I realized this when my wife and I were wed, and I believe she did; so under this sense of its sacredness our lives passed, until she left me."[43]

In his memoirs written fifteen years later Smith reflected that the months after the death of Bertha "passed on leaden feet" for the entire household. His daughter Audentia, by this time married and with a family of her own, moved back into Liberty Hall to take charge of the domestic routine, reestablishing much the same pattern that her mother had followed. Smith immersed himself in his work, hoping to forget some of his grief and loneliness. He did not plan to marry again: he was sixty-four years old, his children were almost all grown, he had a well-established household functioning under his daughter's direction, and he had ample companionship from his children and friends in Lamoni. Apparently none of the reasons for which he had presumably remarried in 1869 seemed to apply in this instance; besides, Joseph recalled, no one could replace Bertha and the warmth her love had brought to his life.[44]

In spite of these rationalizations the prophet began to change his mind, quite by accident, in the fall of 1897. For some unknown reason he had accepted an invitation to preside at a Reorganization conference in Toronto, Canada—the type of church meeting he

Emmeline Griswold Smith, wife of Joseph Smith III from 1856 until her death in 1869. Courtesy of the Library–Archives of the Reorganized Church

Joseph Smith III as he appeared about the time of his ordination as president of the Reorganized Church, 6 April 1860. Courtesy Library–Archives of the Reorganized Church

Joseph Smith III home in Plano, Illinois, Reorganization Church headquarters between 1866 and 1881. Courtesy Library–Archives of the Reorganized Church

Bertha Madison Smith, wife of Joseph Smith III from 1856 until her death in 1896. Courtesy of the Library–Archives of the Reorganized Church

Joseph Smith III about 1885. Courtesy of the Library–Archives of the Reorganized Church

Home of Joseph Smith III in Lamoni, Iowa, 1881–1905. Named Liberty Hall, the residence was a center of social and religious activity in the community. This photograph was taken about 1900. Joseph Smith III is standing with members of his family in front of the house. Courtesy Library–Archives of the Reorganized Church

Ada Rachel Clark Smith, wife of
Joseph Smith III from 1898 until
his death in 1914. Courtesy of the
Library–Archives of the Reorganized
Church

Painting of Joseph Smith III about
1910. Courtesy of the Library–
Archives of the Reorganized Church

Last home of Joseph Smith III, located on Short Avenue in Independence, Mo.,
less than one block from the Temple Lot which his father had consecrated in 1831
for the building of Zion. Smith lived in this residence from 1906 until his death
in 1914. Photograph by author

The man who would be prophet, the oldest son of Joseph Smith III, Frederick Madison Smith (1872–1946). This painting depicts Smith as he appeared about the time of his ordination as president of the Reorganized Church in 1915. Courtesy of the Library–Archives of the Reorganized Church did not normally attend. Joseph arrived in the city in mid-October 1897, a few days before the start of the conference. The apostle in charge of the area, a young, charismatic Canadian named R. C. Evans, had arranged for him to stay in the home of Alexander Clark, one of the local church officials. There he renewed a brief acquaintance with Clark's twenty-nine-year-old daughter, Ada Rachel.[45] In late October Smith wrote back to Audentia at Liberty Hall about how he began to make friends with Ada.

> While at supper, yesterday evening, Ada Clark, a still older maid, sister to Mable came in. She is employed as a helper in Bellvue Avenue Hospital for women; and having the evening out, came to the house to go to prayer meeting to be held in Sr. Anderson's Hall, a good fifteen minutes walk away. A Sr. Minnie Faulds, married woman was also there. When we started for the meeting Sister Faulds Mable Clark   and Mary Jackson, closed up in rank and left Ada, to my care. So, accepting the challenge, I walked with her to Sr. Anderson's. She is tall; I have to look straight out of my eyes, level headed to look her in the eyes. She is not very broad, but weighs 190 lbs. Her eyes are grey, if I have seen them right. She had a plentiful head of hair something the color of your own, is not very handsome as beauty goes, but is good looking, having a bright intelligent countenance.[46]

Over the course of the next few weeks Joseph and Ada were constant companions, and gradually the two expressed their love for each other and decided to marry. In what must have been a comic episode, the aged Joseph Smith asked Ada's father, a man who was the prophet's contemporary, for his permission to wed his daughter. Nonetheless, Alexander Clark gladly gave his sanction. Worried about his offspring's reaction to his bringing home a new wife—one no older than some of his children—Joseph wrote his sons and daughters to explain that he had fallen in love in Toronto and had decided to remarry. He masked some of his uneasiness with the situation in subtle humor. He told Audentia:

> I write to inform you that I have arranged to bring over from Queen Victoria's dominion a bundle of goods, wares, and Canadian products, properly labeled and directed to pass inspection at the Customs House on the border, provided too many questions are not asked.
> The principal piece will be labeled Mrs. Ada Smith, before being

started over the border; and I hope to arrive with it in my possession
or in my companionship, Jan. 14 or 15th unless blockaded enroute.[47]

He seemed almost to beg his children to accept Ada when he wrote,
"I will be much pleased if my chosen companion pleases my children when you see and know her."[48]

With the decision to marry accepted, at least in principal, by the prophet's children, on 12 January 1898 Apostle R. C. Evans performed a simple wedding ceremony for Joseph and Ada in the home of her father. The couple then went to Toronto for an overnight honeymoon and the next day caught the train for Chicago. From Chicago they traveled via the railroad to Lamoni, arriving there on the afternoon of 15 January. No one was at the station to meet them, invoking a certain forboding in the prophet's mind about the marriage's acceptance in the community and among his family. Joseph then hired a driver to take them to Liberty Hall and was understandably anxious as the wagon pulled up in front of the stately home. Apparently he was prepared for a cold reception. Instead, his brother Alexander and several others warmly greeted the couple at the front door and ushered them into the main room, where they became the guests of honor for a huge welcome-home party. With obvious amazement Smith described the events of that evening in his memoirs: "As the broad door swung open, there they were revealed, old and young, kith and kin, the whole family clan, extending smiling greetings, loving hand-clasps, and affectionate caresses! It was indeed a royal and characteristic welcome, and did much to reassure the young woman who had consented to become so intimate a member of the family hitherto unknown and strange to her."[49]

Not everyone was as thrilled with Joseph Smith's marriage as his family appeared to be, for it aroused, once again, a fair degree of gossip. Non-church members, who generally looked upon it as scandalous behavior, certainly what should be expected from the Mormons, censured Smith severely. Many of the Saints, additionally, thought it terrible that such an old man should marry such a young woman. These people expressed a certain puritan ideology in concluding that two wives in one lifetime were enough and a third at such an old age reprehensible. A few even suggested that Joseph was setting a poor example for the young people of the church, that he was giving the movement a poor public image, and that he was demonstrating a lustful, if not lascivious, nature to the world. Apostle Francis M. Sheehy, unlike many of these more serious Saints, thought the marriage rather humorous. In a letter to his quorum president, William H. Kelley, written just before the wedding, Sheehy expressed his feelings: "Say—Much comment is being made upon that recent act of the Revelator. You know who the bride is dont you   she is that monstrous big girl that played the organ at Kirtland Conf[erence]. . . . I presume now another generation of Smiths will appear. It does seem as if Joseph might have got a wife that would more nearly correspond with his age   she will draw all the sap out of him."[50] Joseph did not let the gossip bother him, and Ada held up very well, also. Again the talk was short-lived, and the couple soon settled down to a regular lifestyle at Liberty Hall much like the routine that Bertha had established nearly thirty years earlier.

By all evidence available Joseph and Ada enjoyed a happy married life. Joseph remarked upon several occasions that his love for Ada was parallel to that he had felt for Emmeline so many years before, and perhaps the marriage was a way of recapturing a portion of his youth. Certainly, Francis Sheehy's prediction about another generation of Smiths proved correct. Ada and Joseph had three sons during their marriage—Richard Clark, 26 December 1898; William Wallace, 18 November 1900; and Reginald Arthur, 8 January 1908. One of these boys, William Wallace, succeeded to the presidency of the Reorganization in 1958 and served until 1978. Finally, as Joseph grew older and more infirm, Ada, who was still relatively young and healthy, served as his nurse, confident, and friend as well as his wife.[51]

NOTES

1. Quoted in Audentia Anderson, "Joseph Smith—A Biographical Sketch," in *Joseph Smith, 1832–1914: A Centennial Tribute*, ed. Audentia Anderson (Independence, Mo.: Herald Publishing House, 1932), p. 24.

2. Emma Bidamon to Joseph Smith, 1 August 1869, Emma Smith Bidamon Papers, Reorganized Church of Jesus Christ of Latter Day Saints Library–Archives, Independence, Mo.

3. Joseph Smith, "The Memoirs of President Joseph Smith (1832–

1914)," *Saints' Herald* 82 (26 February 1935): 273–74. See also these biographical studies of Emmeline Griswold Smith: Carolyn Edwards, "The Women of Liberty Hall," *Restoration Trail Forum* 4 (August 1978): 5–6; Frances Hartman Mullikin, *First Ladies of the Restoration* (Independence, Mo.: Herald Publishing House, 1985), pp. 41–50.

4. Smith, "Memoirs," *Saints' Herald* 82 (26 February 1935): 271–74; Carolyn J. Edwards, "The Family Side of the Smiths at Plano, Illinois," unpublished address delivered at the Annual Meeting of the John Whitmer Historical Association, Plano, Illinois, September 1978.

5. Smith, "Memoirs," *Saints' Herald* 82 (2 July 1935): 850.

6. Ibid.; Eighth United States Census, 1870, Population Schedules, Kendall County, Illinois, 39, Vol. 16, National Archives and Records Administration, Washington, D.C.; Joseph Smith, Journal, 13 December 1866, Reorganized Church Library–Archives.

7. Smith, "Memoirs," *Saints' Herald* 82 (26 February 1935): 273–74; Joseph Smith to G. C. Tomlinson, 3 September 1910, Miscellaneous Letters and Papers, Reorganized Church Library–Archives.

8. Emma M. Phillips, *33 Women of the Restoration* (Independence, Mo.: Herald Publishing House, 1960), pp. 58–59; Smith, "Memoirs," *Saints' Herald* 82 (26 February 1935): 274, 82 (5 March 1935): 303; Mullikin, *First Ladies of the Restoration*, pp. 55–63.

9. Smith, "Memoirs," *Saints' Herald* 82 (26 February 1935): 274, 82 (5 March 1935): 303.

10. Mary Audentia Anderson, *Ancestry and Posterity of Joseph Smith and Emma Hale* (Independence, Mo.: Herald Publishing House, 1929), p. 570.

11. Smith, "Memoirs," *Saints' Herald* 82 (5 March 1935): 303.

12. Ibid.

13. See, as examples, Joseph Smith to Bertha Smith, 4 April 1872, Joseph Smith III Papers, Reorganized Church Library–Archives, and the correspondence between Joseph Smith and Bertha Smith during the prophet's 1885 visit to Utah.

14. Anderson, *Ancestry and Posterity*, pp. 571, 573–75.

15. Lucy Lysinger, "Joseph Smith in the Home," in Anderson, *Joseph Smith, 1832–1914*, pp. 40–42; Audentia Anderson, "Some Memoirs of Our Presidents," *Saints' Herald* 107 (28 March 1960): 315.

16. Notes on Joseph Smith III by Frederick M. Smith, pp. 1–12, Joseph Smith III Papers, Reorganized Church Library–Archives.

17. *Kendall County Record* (Yorkville, Ill.), 14 January 1875; Joseph Smith to Zaide Smith, 11 July 1879, 15 July 1879, 19 July 1879, Miscellaneous Letters and Papers, Reorganized Church Library–Archives. This sense of encouragement and support of his daughters is graphically illus-

trated in Norma Derry Hiles, "Joseph Smith III: Letters Home," *Saints'*
Herald 130 (1 July 1983): 12–13, 21, 30.

18. Quoted in Ruth C. Smith, *Concerning the Prophet: Fredrick* [sic]
Madison Smith (Kansas City: Burton Publishing Co., 1924), p. 157.

19. Joseph Smith to William P. Hepburn, 17 March 1897, 31 March
1897, Joseph Smith III Letterbook #7, Reorganized Church Library–
Archives.

20. Norma Derry Hiles, "Joseph Smith III: Letters Home," 21, 30, correctly points out that Smith was supportive of his children's educational
efforts. She errs, however, in asserting that there was a fundamental difference in the manner in which he dealt with his two oldest sons, Frederick
and Israel, because Frederick was the oldest and the heir apparent to the
prophetic office of the Reorganized Church. She suggests that Smith pam-
pered Frederick in his youth and took a more forceful hand in ensuring his
proper education. This appears unlikely for two reasons. First, Smith did
see that Israel attended college: he graduated from Graceland as did his
brother. He also took steps to help him with an enrollment in West Point.
Second, Smith dealt with Israel somewhat differently than with Frederick
only because of the personality differences of the two. Frederick had been,
according to all available evidence, a model son who had accepted his
responsibilities without complaint. Israel had rebelled against his father
and had acted irresponsibly. See Joseph Smith III to Israel A. Smith, 2 February 1897, 31 March 1899, 16 October 1899, Miscellaneous Letters and
Papers, Reorganized Church Library–Archives, for discussions of these
difficulties. The letters Derry cites to support a difference of approaches
toward the two sons must be viewed from the perspective that Joseph was
trying to teach Israel, perhaps harshly at times, to act responsibly.

21. Joseph Smith to Audentia Smith, 4 November 1876, Joseph Smith
III Papers.

22. Quoted in Norma Derry Hiles, "The Smiths: Letters from Home,"
p. 9, unpublished paper in possession of author.

23. Joseph Smith to Audentia Smith, 26 August 1885, Joseph Smith III
Papers.

24. Ibid., 19 July 1885.

25. Ibid., 4 November 1876, 17 October 1885, 29 October 1885, 17
May 1889, 3–4 July 1889; Joseph Smith to Carrie Smith, 1 December
1876, Carrie Smith Weld Papers, Reorganized Church Library–Archives;
Joseph Smith to Israel A. Smith, 1 November 1889, Miscellaneous Letters
and Papers.

26. Joseph Smith to Audentia Smith, 5 September 1885, Joseph Smith
III Papers. See also Lysinger, "Joseph Smith in the Home," p. 41; Joseph
Smith to Audentia Smith, 3 August 1885, Joseph Smith III Papers.

27. Ibid., 26 November 1897, Miscellaneous Letters and Papers.

28. Ibid., 7 December 1897.

29. Joseph Smith to Audentia Smith, 15 August 1885, Joseph Smith III Papers.

30. Joseph Smith to Carrie Smith, 21 November 1885, Carrie Weld Smith Papers, Reorganized Church Library–Archives.

31. Lysinger, "Joseph Smith in the Home," p. 42.

32. Joseph Smith to Audentia Smith, 16 September 1885, Joseph Smith III Papers.

33. *Kendall County Record,* 13 October 1881; Joseph Smith, "Editorial," *Saints' Herald* 28 (1 November 1881): 332; Clara B. Stebbins, "My Neighbor, Joseph Smith," in Anderson, *Joseph Smith, 1832–1914,* p. 50.

34. Alma R. Blair, "Liberty Hall Lives Again," *Restoration Trail Forum* 4 (August 1978): 7–8; interview with Alma R. Blair, director of the restoration efforts at Liberty Hall, Lamoni, Iowa, 24 January 1976.

35. Joseph Smith to Israel A. Smith, 17 February 1898, 26 December 1898, 6 March 1899, Miscellaneous Letters and Papers.

36. Ibid., 2 February 1897, 17 February 1898, 6 March 1899, 31 March 1899, 8 December 1899, 12 December 1899, 20 December 1899, 3 May 1903, Miscellaneous Letters and Papers; Joseph Smith to Audentia Smith Anderson, 27 January 1897, Miscellaneous Letters and Papers; Joseph Smith to Cousin Mary B., 4 December 1877, Joseph Smith III Letterbook #1A, Reorganized Church Library–Archives.

37. Joseph Smith to Israel A. Smith, 16 January 1899, Miscellaneous Letters and Papers. See also Joseph Smith to Israel A. Smith, 6 March 1899, Miscellaneous Letters and Papers.

38. Ibid., 6 March 1899.

39. Joseph Smith to Audentia Smith Anderson, 26 August 1899, Miscellaneous Letters and Papers.

40. Smith, "Memoirs," *Saints' Herald* 82 (5 March 1935): 304–305.

41. Ibid.

42. Joseph Smith to William H. Kelley, 7 November 1896, Joseph Smith III Papers.

43. Joseph Smith to Sr. E. F. Adamson, 17 December 1896, Joseph Smith III Papers.

44. Smith, "Memoirs," *Saints' Herald* 82 (5 March 1935): 305.

45. Joseph Smith to Lucy Smith, 25 October 1897, Miscellaneous Letters and Papers; Smith, "Memoirs," *Saints' Herald* 82 (5 March 1935): 305, 82 (12 March 1935): 335.

46. Joseph Smith to Audentia Smith Anderson, 28 October 1897, Miscellaneous Letters and Papers.

47. Joseph Smith to Benjamin and Audentia Anderson, 10 December 1897, Miscellaneous Letters and Papers.

48. Joseph Smith to Carrie Smith Weld, 10 December 1897, Carrie Smith Weld Papers.

49. Smith, "Memoirs," *Saints' Herald* 82 (12 March 1935): 335–36.

50. Francis M. Sheehy to William H. Kelley, 7 January 1898, William H. Kelley Papers, Reorganized Church Library–Archives.

51. Mullikin, *First Ladies of the Restoration*, pp. 69–75; Smith, "Memoirs," *Saints' Herald* 82 (12 March 1935): 336.

CHAPTER

15

Twilight

For a few years after Joseph Smith returned home with his new bride in 1898, he continued his far-reaching presidential duties in the church much as before. He made numerous missionary trips, presided at general conferences, and performed a variety of administrative and prophetic chores with his characteristic efficiency. Although Joseph still felt quite well most of the time and worked much as he had for more than thirty-five years, he recognized that he was becoming an old man and would not live a great deal longer.[1] During the 1890s, therefore, Joseph Smith farsightedly began preparing for the transfer of church leadership to a successor.

Joseph remembered vividly the turmoil the Latter Day Saint church had endured at the death of his father in 1844. In large measure unified until that time, Mormonism had fragmented into a myriad of different factions because, as Joseph had gradually come to realize throughout his presidential tenure, his father had not officially stated a succession policy. In addition, the church's body of law as recorded in the Doctrine and Covenants had been ambiguous and open to widely divergent interpretations.[2] Joseph Smith certainly did not want the same problem to arise upon his death and began planning for an orderly succession.

Several convictions underlaid his plans for the succession in the presidency. First, Smith firmly believed that God had to call any president of the church by divine revelation through His prophet. In his case Joseph believed this had been accomplished first in the

Liberty Jail in 1838–39 and had been reaffirmed not only in the Red Brick Store sometime in 1843 or 1844 but also in the parlor of the Nauvoo Mansion just prior to his father's departure for Carthage in June 1844.[3] Furthermore, Joseph believed that God had manifested the divine call to him during the late 1850s, thus precipitating his entrance into the Reorganized Church. As a result Joseph saw that this rule of succession was squarely implanted into the church's procedural law so that there could be no question as to its validity. In 1894 he achieved this purpose by gaining acceptance from the general conference for a resolution which asserted that "the President [of the Church] is primarily appointed by revelation."[4]

Although convinced that his successor would be chosen by revelation, Joseph Smith's second conviction wedded him to the doctrine of lineal succession in the presidency. This concept had been most enthusiastically urged by William Smith, Joseph's uncle, during the 1840s and 1850s and had been endorsed by Zenos H. Gurley, Sr., and other members of the early Reorganization. It held that a direct descendent of Joseph Smith, Jr., should by birthright become the president of the church. Ideally, the two requirements for succession—divine appointment and lineal succession—pointed to the same person, as Joseph believed had been the situation in his case. Smith believed the two would not conflict upon his death either, concluding that his oldest living son, Frederick Madison Smith, should succeed him by virtue of both heredity and revelation. Frederick, of course, already met one requirement—lineage—and during the period between 1895 and 1902 Joseph implored God for a revelation that would call him as successor.[5]

Freddy, as Smith called his son until he became a member of the church's official quorums, was a rambunctious lad. Handsome, intelligent, athletic, college educated and eager to earn a graduate degree, young Frederick was his father's greatest pride.[6] He wanted to pass the presidency on to him but was disturbed by his son's apparent lack of interest in church affairs, believing that his son's unworthiness had prohibited the divine call from being given. Smith told the church's general conference in 1902 that God would provide for presidential succession in His own way and would ensure a proper selection: "I have been importuned to settle the question as to who should be my successor. We have advanced upon the hypothesis of lineal priesthood in this regard, and while I believe in it, I believe it is connected with fitness and propriety, and no son of mine will be entitled to follow me as my successor, unless at the time he is chosen he is found to be worthy in character, . . . for he should be called to serve in the church who has proved himself to be worthy of confidence and trust."[7] All that Smith could do was caution his son about "worldly affairs," explain to him his potential as a servant of God, and encourage his development as a leader.

A major step in Frederick's preparation to take his father's place came when Joseph delivered a divinely inspired document to the general conference of 1897. It stated that the leading officials of the church had functioned in the administration for many years and were rapidly growing old, and it was time for younger men to be brought into the hierarchy in their places. Joseph was pleased with this revelation, because carrying it out would require ordaining and appointing to positions of power the sons of many of these church leaders, including Frederick, and he believed that the thrusting of responsibility on his son would force him to mature faster and more fully. Possibly Joseph had his own son in mind when he wrote in the document: "These sons of my servants are called, and if faithful shall in time be chosen to places whence their fathers shall fall, or fail, or be removed by honorable release before the Lord and the Church."[8]

In keeping with this commandment, a month later the Lamoni congregation called Frederick and the son of W. W. Blair to serve as elders in the church. The position of elder was not to be taken lightly. Men who held that priesthood office were the standing ministry in the individual congregations of the church, and a call to the office signified not only that Frederick had been called by God to serve but also that he was willing to accept responsibility and carry it out to the best of his ability. A few Saints objected that Frederick and the younger Blair should not have been ordained, for the "two young men (whom it will be conceded), have not been active church workers in the past" had given little indication that they would become active in the future.[9]

Apparently Joseph Smith harbored some of these same apprehensions, for in 1900 he approached Frederick concerning his feelings toward church service and his succession to the presidency. "My boy," Joseph told his son, "if you do not think you wish to stand the trials and disappointments that you have had to see me endure [as president of the church], now is the time for you to withdraw." Frederick, although hesitant, finally answered his father by declaring that he knew of no better way to serve humankind than as president of the church and would function diligently in whatever capacity the Lord wished.[10] Thereafter, Frederick began to exhibit a somewhat greater enthusiasm for the church than Joseph had perceived before. The prophet interpreted his son's positive response as a quickening by the Lord, evidence of a future prophetic call.

A great step toward the realization of this prophetic call came in 1902, when Smith prepared an inspired document directing that Frederick and the iconoclastic but capable apostle R. C. Evans serve as counselors in the First Presidency. Smith's previous counselors had long since vacated the office, and the prophet had been functioning almost entirely alone since 1896.[11] At this conference Joseph reported to the assembly that he had experienced a vision in which he "saw in the Presidency two known to the Church, but who have not hitherto been connected with the Presidency." He said further that he welcomed their youth and exuberance but at first questioned why God had placed two inexperienced men in the quorum at the same time. He was told "that it was for the purpose that before the Presidency should be invaded by death these younger men should be prepared by association to be of assistance to whosoever should be chosen as the President upon the emergency which should occur."[12]

Smith's choice of assistants not only brought his son into the First Presidency, the ruling body of the church, it also excited the considerable ambition of R. C. Evans. Short, dark-featured, starkly handsome, and startlingly charismatic, Evans was a forty-one-year-old Canadian who had demonstrated remarkable abilities as an orator. His talents had been put to good use as a member of the Seventy, a missionary organization, and as a member of the Quorum of Twelve Apostles.[13] Joseph had long held deep affection for Evans, partially because of his superior talents and partially because he had introduced him to Ada Clark Smith, the prophet's third wife, in 1897. Everyone in a position of power in the church predicted trouble would come into the Presidency when Evans was ordained to the quorum, for the able leader had an obnoxious manner and a swelled ego that needed constant feeding. Anything but an amiable colleague, Evans had never failed to arouse controversy and animosity among the leaders of the church.[14]

When Joseph called him into the First Presidency and failed to make clear his wishes concerning the succession of his son to the prophetic office, Evans apparently took it as a sign that he might assume the office within a few years. Evans, like Joseph Smith, recognized that lineal succession was a possibility, but he also understood that nothing in the church's body of law excluded others outside the Smith family from becoming president. He reasoned that a hereditary restriction would be nothing more than a feeble attempt by man to limit God's choice of president and, consequently, saw no reason to exclude himself from consideration. Evans further maintained that he had served the Reorganization many years in various leadership offices and in every instance had exceeded expectations. What other relatively young man in the church, Evans asked himself, had served so faithfully and with such effectiveness? By mere process of elimination the self-confident Evans concluded that if the presidency were filled on the basis of merit he had few competitors.[15]

Evans's ambitions were further excited in 1903 by Joseph Smith's request that he accompany him on a missionary journey to Great Britain. He readily agreed, taking great satisfaction in the fact that he, rather than Frederick, whom he considered a rival, had been asked to go. They left New York City on 7 June 1903 bound for Great Britain, the two men extending their already warm relationship during the voyage. Once in England Smith and Evans worked closely together to enjoy the visit and provide the Saints there with ministry. Joseph Smith, who because of his age tired from traveling and preaching easily and suffered increasingly from facial neuralgia, limited much of his activity to informal gatherings with the Saints who longed to meet the prophet and to sight-seeing excursions into the countryside. He passed most of the formal ministerial work on to the younger and more dynamic Evans. In most cases both Smith and Evans occupied the platform, but Joseph usually stood and made only a few brief remarks and then turned the meeting over to Evans, who preached a series of long, evangelistic sermons during the tour.[16]

When Smith and Evans returned from Great Britain in September 1903, Evans apparently had convinced himself that he was the prophet's protegé. He had cemented an already close relationship with the older man during the trip and believed that Joseph loved him as a son. This conclusion heightened his expectations even more; he seemed bent on attaining the prophetic office upon the death of Smith. Evans's expectations were also fostered by the fact that after his ordination Frederick had returned to school to work on a graduate degree, in effect abandoning his responsibilities within the First Presidency and leaving most of the work of the quorum in the hands of his father and Evans. Obviously, concluded Evans, Joseph could not entrust the church's presidency to someone who had not the inclination to perform lesser tasks properly.[18]

At the same time that R. C. Evans was creating his grand dreams of a succession to the presidency that would never come about, Joseph Smith began to grow weaker and more infirm and realized he had to move promptly and forthrightly to ensure an orderly succession. During the previous two years the prophet had become increasingly ill: his obesity, failing eyesight, recurring facial neuralgia, and weakened constitution kept him bedridden on a sustained basis for the first time in his life.[18] The fact of his own mortality came to Joseph as it never had before when he returned from a grueling missionary trip to the American northwest in November 1905, completely exhausted and ailing from a multitude of maladies.[19] He was forced to his bed for weeks, and although he eventually recovered, the time in bed drove home the point that he was growing old rapidly and could not possibly live much longer.

As soon as he was well enough, Smith decided to move from Liberty Hall into Lamoni in order to be closer to other church officials and to his office in the Herald building. He realized that if he tried to come and go between Liberty Hall and Lamoni every day in his weakening condition the winter could kill him. As soon as he told Bishop E. L. Kelley that he wanted to move into town, the bishop found the Smiths a house and saw that they were moved in before Christmas. In mid-January 1906 Joseph arranged for the sale of Liberty Hall to the church for $3,000. The bishop turned it into a home for the aged.[20] It grieved Smith to sell his elegant home. It had been the only house he had ever had built and the memories attached to a twenty-five-year residency were great, but he recognized it was a necessity.

During the winter of 1905–6 Joseph kept his duties to a minimum so as not to exhaust himself any further. He turned much of the editorial work on the *Saints' Herald* over to assistants, and he persuaded Frederick to return from school and assume more of the duties of the First Presidency. Consequently, Joseph supervised the work of his two subordinates within the First Presidency—of Frederick, who was on hand in Lamoni to manage the daily affairs of the church's administration, and of Evans, who operated from his base in London, Ontario—without involving himself in the details as previously. Joseph was convinced of his imminent death during this period, even preparing a last will and testament in February 1906, but he was intent on living until God spoke through him to designate formally a successor to the presidential office. He knew that if he died with the issue yet unclear the struggle for power between Frederick and R. C. Evans could splinter the Reorganization.[21]

When the April 1906 general conference convened in Independence, Missouri, Joseph was present and prepared to name a successor. This would clarify the issue and unify the church, Smith believed. The prophet, claiming inspiration from God, said, "In the case of the removal of my servant now presiding over the church by death or transgression, my servant Frederick M. Smith, if he remain faithful and steadfast, should be chosen, in accordance with revelations which have been hitherto given to the church concerning the priesthood."[22] This statement laid to rest any questions church members might have about who would succeed Joseph.

R. C. Evans was visibly upset over this revelation. While he made no public comments about the younger Smith's designation, he certainly resented it, for he left in a huff immediately after the meetings had come to a close. Evans considered resigning from the First Presidency in 1907, partially in response to this development, but when he talked to Joseph Smith, according to Evans, the prophet "wept over me and begged me not to insist, to wait till the Lord would speak."[23] Evans heeded Smith's request and did not resign, but he also virtually stopped functioning in his office. In many respects his presence in the First Presidency became a hindrance to action rather than an aid.[24]

While at the 1906 general conference in Independence Joseph Smith had stayed with John D. White in his comfortable home not far from the Mormon Temple Lot. He had talked to White a great deal during the conference and expressed a desire to move into the city. White told Joseph that the overwhelming desire of the Saints in the city was to have their prophet live among them in his last years, and the result of these meetings brought Joseph to the decision to discuss with Bishop E. L. Kelley the possibility of moving his family there. Independence was considered by most of the Saints to be the "centerplace" of Zion, the location for the capital of the promised kingdom of God on earth, and as such it had always been presupposed that the church's headquarters would eventually be located in the city. This would necessitate Joseph's moving to Independence as the first step for this relocation, and the prophet was ready to make such a move so that he could, as he said, "die in the goodly land."[25]

White made the move easy for Joseph Smith and his family, offering his house to the prophet at a very reasonable price. In May Joseph wrote to his son Israel about the possibility of moving to Independence. "I might as well be there as here for all the good I am," he stated. "I have been pretty well out of the running for the last 6 or 7 months." Smith added that there was not much left for him in Lamoni anyway. "It will be 25 years next October since I moved here and made a home. Sixteen of those years your mother was with us. The home is gone into other hands, and I may as well move on and at least lay my hooves in *Zion*."[26]

In mid-July Smith, Bishop Kelley, and John White completed plans for the church to purchase White's Independence house for the prophet. Within the month Joseph and Ada had made arrangements for their belongings to be shipped by train to the city, and by 8 August the family had moved into their new home.[27] Smith liked Independence from the first. He already had many close friends there—mostly church members—and he was delighted to live so close to a place he considered a holy land upon which God's temple would one day stand. He also enjoyed the modern conveniences which the city afforded, joking about the "tokens of civilized life about us" with his daughter, Audentia.[28]

With Joseph Smith settling down to virtual retirement in Independence, and R. C. Evans confining his activities to the Canadian mission, the only person functioning in the First Presidency was Frederick M. Smith, who found himself called upon to shoulder increasing responsibility for the organization. For several years after

1906, when Joseph's illness first forced Frederick to accept more responsibility in the First Presidency, the young man developed impressively and honed his leadership skills. By early 1909 Frederick had taken over most of his father's duties, presiding at general conferences and quorum meetings, attending to routine administrative matters, and handling most of the church's publishing decisions. Increasingly after that time Joseph presided more in name than in fact, being called on for his experience and wisdom gained in years of service whenever the situation required. Not that the prophet minded this arrangement in the twilight of his life, for he was rapidly declining physically, and the infirmities of age prohibited the kind of intensive activity that had been his nature in the past.[29]

By the time of the general conference of 1909 Frederick had mastered most of the duties of his office and had the First Presidency running smoothly without the aid of R. C. Evans and oftentimes without his father. Evans's continuation in the quorum, therefore, was not only unnecessary but in all too many cases proved to be a liability, for he and Frederick clashed over virtually every issue. Furthermore, Evans's continuing obnoxious manner and his apparent refusal to recognize the policies and administrative procedures of the church had led many of the other church leaders to demand his dismissal. As a result, in late March 1909 the Quorum of Twelve formally petitioned the president for Evans's removal, claiming that they could no longer support him in the First Presidency.[30]

Joseph initially discussed the problem with his son, and Frederick agreed that the time had come to release R. C. Evans from the First Presidency. Not long before the April church conference, therefore, Smith met with both his counselors and discussed the matter further; at the meeting Evans told the prophet he agreed that the time had come for him to be relieved of his role in the quorum and intimated that he could serve the church better as bishop of Canada.[31] Most of the church leadership was relieved when Joseph Smith brought an inspired document which dealt with the situation to the general conference on 18 April 1909. It said: "The voice of the Spirit to me is: Under conditions which have occurred it is no longer wise that my servant R. C. Evans be continued as counselor in the Presidency; therefore it is expedient that he be released from his responsibility and another be chosen to the office. He has been earnest and faithful in service and his reward is sure." Evans received his wish, however; he was ordained bishop of Canada on the same day he was released from the presidency. As Evans's replacement Smith chose his nephew, Elbert A. Smith, the young and talented son of David H. Smith, who had died in 1904 in the mental hospital in Elgin, Illinois. With another functioning member of the First Presidency ordained at this conference, Frederick felt more free to continue his pursuit of an advanced degree and returned to the university part time.[32]

Although Evans could never challenge Frederick effectively for the presidency after 1909, and most of the church probably accepted Joseph's oldest son as heir apparent, the old prophet still had doubts about the probability of a smooth transition. For one thing, Smith wanted not only to secure his son's place in the presidency upon his death but also to establish the precedent for orderly succession in future years. As a result he offered to abdicate his office in favor of Frederick so that there would be no questions about the propriety of the change, but Frederick refused to take over the presidency officially until the death of his father.[33]

To ensure the plan of succession, in 1912 Joseph Smith prepared one more document that bore upon the issue. In January 1912 he circulated a questionnaire among the leaders of the church, asking their opinion about the nature of the prophetic office, the role of the Quorums of Twelve and the First Presidency in the event of a prophet's death, and other procedural and legal considerations in making a succession decision. Joseph then compiled the responses and, based upon them, prepared a comprehensive plan for succession called the "Letter of Instruction," issued on 4 March 1912.[34] The Letter of Instruction was, without a doubt, the most authoritative document on Mormon presidential succession published up to that time. On his deathbed Joseph Smith commented that it was "one of the most important documents that had ever been presented to the church."[35] But it was not binding on the church, and the Quorum of Twelve responded to it by resolving that "we do not commit ourselves to the terminology nor all the conclusions contained in the 'Letter of Instruction.'"[36] The presidents of Seventy acknowledged the statement only as "opportune counsel," although they willingly endorsed the succession of Frederick. This same position was adopted by the general conference which, when it considered the Letter of Instruction in April 1912, decided not to endorse it as the official policy of the Reorganization.[37] Nonetheless, this document was the position of the First Presidency, and Joseph received enough support from the church hierarchy to see that the central message of it, the succession of his son to the prophetic office, would be carried without difficulty.

Satisfied that the affairs of the church were in his son's capable hands, convinced that the church would set Frederick apart as its next prophet, and aware that as an old man of eighty years he had little time left, Joseph turned his attention to a project he had long wanted to complete—the writing of his memoirs. He believed that an understanding of past events and motivating factors was necessary to the continued development of the church. He also believed that the example of his life would serve as a testimony to the Saints of conviction and faith. Moreover, the church would never be truly free of the stigma of Utah Mormonism until it had its own identity, and perhaps the best means of achieving that identity was the writing of history.[38]

The writing of his memoirs was not his first foray into historical study. He had long had a keen interest in the subject because of its potential to create a collective identity and to build church unity. As early as 1871 he expressed concern for the recording of the movement's history. Furthermore, in 1880 he had overseen the publication of a revised edition of Edward W. Tullidge's *Life of Joseph the Prophet* by the church press as a history of the movement. Tullidge was a convert to the Reorganization from Utah Mormonism, and the work had too much influence from the Great Basin for the Saints, but it contained a 200-page history of the Reorganized Church (about fifty of which was an autobiography of Joseph Smith III) and was the first book-length historical work issued by the movement.[39] During the 1890s Joseph, with Apostle Heman C. Smith, was listed as coauthor of a four-volume history of the church that was largely documentary but reshaped the corporate memory and redefined the movement's character.[40] Finally, during the first decade of the twentieth century Joseph Smith supported efforts to publish records and historical articles in a quarterly magazine, the *Journal of History*, that first appeared in January 1908 and ceased publication only in 1926.[41]

The climax of this reinterpretation of the movement's history, Joseph thought, would be his personal memoirs. Although he had started to collect his thoughts for the project earlier, Smith had made no significant progress in writing his memoirs until 1912 when he asked his son Israel to come to Independence and act as his secretary for the project. By this time Joseph was completely infirm. His vision was all but gone, his hearing was quickly declining, and his overall health forced him to stay at home. Clearly, he could not complete the task of preparing his memoirs alone and needed the help of a trusted and loyal friend. As a result, in early 1913 Israel moved near his father's home so that he could take dictation for the memoirs.[42]

During much of the last two years of Joseph's life, 1913 and 1914, Israel went to his father's home about nine o'clock in the morning, "and remained with him until he tired, usually at noon or middle afternoon," working on the memoirs. Israel was never simply a scribe, however; he was a research assistant and editor as well. Usually Israel surveyed all the documents that his father possessed on a given period or event, read the most pertinent material to the older man and summarized the rest, and waited for Joseph to think about it. After the prophet had considered this information for several days, he would announce that he was ready to dictate his reflections upon it and, sitting in a huge, overstuffed armchair, would tell with remarkable speed stories about people and events bearing upon the theme. Thereafter Israel edited the material and put it into a more readable form.[43]

In spite of Joseph's apparent speed, when the actual writing began, the overall production of the memoirs was ploddingly slow because of Joseph's frequent illnesses. Sometimes the work would be interrupted for weeks at a time because Joseph was bedridden. Moreover, even when Joseph dictated his memoirs, he often digressed from the subject under examination and talked at some length about people and events that had only tangential bearing upon the main subject. Israel tried to edit some of these digressions out as they progressed, but he found that many were worthwhile stories, simply too good to omit. The result was a disjointed narrative that circled back and forth across an eventful eighty-year life.[44] When these memoirs were completed in about the middle of October in 1914, Joseph proudly turned them over to Frederick for publication, but he apparently filed them away and ignored them for several years. It was only through the efforts of his sister,

Audentia, that the memoirs were eventually published some twenty years later; they ran serially in the *Saints' Herald* between 1934 and 1937.[45]

With the completion of his memoirs in late 1914 Joseph had accomplished, as he believed, his final official church duty. Although he had been prepared for death for several years, after this time he was finally ready and fully expected "to leave the earthly existence." Perhaps it was happenstance, or possibly it was Joseph's mind controlling his body, but just as Joseph completed the memoirs, his health began to decline from its already precarious position. During the late fall of 1914, just as the world plunged into a war that would lead it to a new age, Joseph began a final bout with infirmity and old age.

On 26 November 1914, Joseph Smith, the president of the Reorganized Church for more than fifty years and admired by thousands, suffered a heart seizure in his Independence home. He was put to bed and doctors were called, but their examinations revealed that his death was imminent. Ada called Joseph's children and asked them to return home, and a dramatic two-week-long deathbed scene followed. Over the course of this period Joseph's bedroom became the focus of the Saints' attention. When he was awake, the prophet held interviews with important church members and gave advice for conducting affairs. Much of this information was taken down by secretaries charged with preserving the details of this history-making event. Newspapermen waited around Smith's home, providing periodic accounts in the national press.[46]

The day after his seizure Joseph, anticipating death, dictated his last official message to the church. He reaffirmed his faith in the gospel of Jesus Christ and the mission of the Reorganized Church and told the Saints he was prepared finally to meet the Lord, whom he had tried to serve for so many years. He also said that the spirit that surrounded him in 1914 was the very same that had first prompted him to appear before the conference of the church at Amboy in 1860 and ask for acceptance into the movement. He also admitted that he had not been a perfect man and had certainly made stupendous mistakes as the church's president—some of them he had regretted for many years—but declared that he had always tried to do what he believed right. He finally told his followers, "I have not consciously wronged any man or woman. I have no fear to go beyond the vale. . . . I have no fear. If a man can be happy in dying and leaving a home like mine and friends like mine, such a host of them for the Master's cause, I can die happy. O blessed rest! Blessed rest!"[47]

On 29 November Frederick arrived in Independence from the East and was quietly ushered into his father's bedroom. When Joseph was told that his successor was in the room, the prophet grabbed his hand, pulled Frederick to him, and hugged him. Then he began talking. Joseph said he had some very important advice to relay, and while still holding his son's hand, he began. "Fred," Joseph said, "a great opportunity lies before you. Better in some respects than lay before me, for, as I look back over history and the revelations that have been given to the church and are on record since I have been presiding they show me very clearly that a great many things which have been left open to misunderstanding have been cleared up in the revelations and in the letter of instruction." At the same time Smith urged his son to exercise patience in his relationship with the membership of the church. "Be steadfast and if the people are heady, if the church is heady, the eldership are heady and take the reins in their hands as they have done a little especially on the rules and regulations, rules of representations," he told Frederick, "don't worry, let it pass, let the church take the consequences and they will after a while grow out of it. . . . It is better that way than to undertake to force them and coerce. That would be bad trouble."[48]

By the first week of December Joseph's condition had improved little, and although hope for his recovery was kindled by the way he seemed to linger on, the doctors predicted a very slim chance that he would leave his bed alive. In the early afternoon of 10 December 1914 Joseph took a decided turn for the worse and died within a few minutes after experiencing another seizure. Even though his death had been expected for weeks, the Saints were struck with sadness at his passing. Brother Joseph, as the Saints almost universally called him, had been the only president most had ever known. His personality had been unalterably stamped upon the Reorganization, and the sense of loss was everywhere apparent. Immediately following his demise the two remaining members of the First Presidency, Frederick and his cousin Elbert, officially informed the church that the president had died. The leading quorums then met together to draft formal epistles to the Saints about Joseph's death and the church's plans for the future.[49]

Before his death Joseph had left explicit instructions concerning his funeral, and they told a great deal about the faith, commitment, and character of the prophet. He requested that he be buried in a plain wooden casket painted black, similar to the type used to bury Saints who died in poverty at the church's home for the aged in Lamoni. He also asked that no more money than absolutely necessary be spent on the funeral. He considered it a waste of funds, and as stewards of God's possessions while on earth, to waste money was wrong. He did not want the services of a high-priced choir— in fact, he did not want a choir at all—and saw no reason to hire an expensive undertaker or use an impressive hearse. Furthermore, he requested that no one send flowers to the funeral because that too was a waste of resources. Instead, Joseph asked that those who might have wished to send flowers give the money to the poor. Most of all, Joseph said he wanted to keep the affair simple, for he had come into life simply and wished to go out the same way. He even went to the trouble to dictate his funeral dress, asking that he wear one of his old suits, quickly adding, however, "I do not want my black suit used for that purpose, as it had been no favorite of mine." [50]

The funeral was held on the afternoon of 13 December, with sunny but crisp weather. The whole city seemed to turn out for the services, the people passing the casket containing the prophet's remains as it laid outside in state, as he had also requested. Apostle Joseph Luff gave the funeral sermon, striking a positive note for the large number of church members in attendance. He told the congregation: "Let us now, brethren, go on with the great work left for us to accomplish,—undivided, with mutual trust and good fellowship and with greater faith and consecration. There is no occasion for doubt or fear, no cause for division or confusion. There is every reason to have confidence and courage. Good men and well-loved men pass, but God remains. His work must prevail. The living must redouble their efforts in his service. May his favor and blessing abide with us." [51]

Immediately after the funeral the ruling quorums met to discuss the future of the church and quickly approved the succession of Frederick M. Smith to the prophetic office. They decided that he should not be ordained immediately, but rather should wait until the April 1915 general conference. In the meantime, the administration of the church would be handled without a president but otherwise as it had been in the past. Frederick, although officially president-designate, had exercised basic control over the church's administration since at least 1909 and easily assumed the full duties of his father. Like the world war that raged in Europe, therefore, this act signaled the end of an era and the beginning of a new one.[52]

NOTES

1. Joseph Smith suffered from increasing debilitating illnesses after 1905. His eyesight began to fail; his facial neuralgia, which had first arisen in 1876, became increasingly painful and attacked more often; his obesity weakened his constitution; and seasonal sicknesses such as the flu affected him regularly. See Joseph Smith, "The Memoirs of President Joseph Smith (1832–1914)," *Saints' Herald* 84 (26 June 1937): 818, 84 (3 July 1937): 847; Norma Derry Hiles, "Joseph Smith III: Letters Home," *Saints' Herald* 130 (1 July 1983): 12–13, 21, 30, for discussions of his illnesses.

2. D. Michael Quinn, "The Mormon Succession Crisis of 1844," *Brigham Young University Studies* 16 (Winter 1976): 187–233, points out that as a result of either church law or tradition there were eight legitimate means of succession available to the presidency in 1844, each causing confusion within the church. Quinn asserted that the eight methods included succession: (1) by a counselor in the First Presidency (Sidney Rigdon); (2) by special or secret appointment (James J. Strang, Lyman Wight, Alpheus Cutler, Joseph Smith III); (3) through the office of associate president (the disfellowshipped Oliver Cowdery and the deceased Hyrum Smith); (4) by the presiding patriarch (the deceased Hyrum Smith and William B. Smith); (5) by appointment through the Council of Fifty (Lyman Wight, Alpheus Cutler, Peter Haws, George J. Adams, George Miller, John E. Page); (6) by Quorum of Twelve Apostles (Brigham Young); (7) by the Priesthood Councils of the Seventy, the High Council, and the Twelve Apostles (William Marks); (8) and by a member of the prophet's family (the deceased Hyrum Smith, William B. Smith, and Joseph Smith III).

3. Joseph Smith to A. V. Gibbons, 1 June 1893, Joseph Smith III Letterbook #4, Reorganized Church of Jesus Christ of Latter Day Saints Library–Archives, Independence, Mo.; Joseph Smith, "Pleasant Chat," *True Latter Day Saints' Herald* 14 (October 1868): 105; "Testimony of James Whitehead" in *Complainant's Abstract of Pleading and Evidence*

in the Circuit Court of the United States, Western District of Missouri, Western Division, at Kansas City, Missouri (Lamoni, Iowa: Herald Publishing House, 1893), pp. 27–28, 32; *Autumn Leaves* 1 (May 1888): 202; W. W. Blair, Diary, 17 June 1874, Reorganized Church Library–Archives; Alexander H. Smith, Diary, 14 May 1864, Reorganized Church Library–Archives.

4. *Rules and Resolutions* (Independence, Mo.: Herald Publishing House, 1964), Resolution 386; Book of Doctrine and Covenants (Independence, Mo.: Herald Publishing House, 1970), Section 43.

5. Joseph Smith certainly accepted the doctrine of lineal succession. See Smith, "Memoirs," *Saints' Herald* 82 (5 March 1935): 303, 83 (21 November 1936): 1455, 84 (26 June 1937): 816; Ruth C. Smith, *Concerning the Prophet: Fredrick* [sic] *Madison Smith* (Kansas City: Burton Publishing Co., 1924), pp. 17–18; Charles Cousins, "Impressions of President Frederick M. Smith," *Saints' Herald* 68 (22 November 1921): 1123.

6. There is no adequate biography of Frederick Madison Smith. The most serious analysis concerning this man's life and career has been contributed by Larry E. Hunt. Hunt wrote several articles concerning Frederick M. Smith, notably "Frederick Madison Smith: The Formative Years of an RLDS President," *Journal of Mormon History* 4 (1977): 67–89, which emphasized the subject's natural inclination toward academia and his very gradual acceptance of the church's presidency, and "Frederick Madison Smith: Saint as Reformer," *Courage: A Journal of History, Thought and Action* 3 (Fall 1972): 3–22, which described his social philosophy and attempted to place him in the context of the American reform movement. These articles were the first fruit of Hunt's work on a dissertation about Smith at the University of Missouri, completed in 1978. This dissertation was subsequently published as *Frederick Madison Smith: Saint as Reformer*, 2 vols. (Independence, Mo.: Herald Publishing House, 1982).

7. F. Henry Edwards, *The History of the Reorganized Church of Jesus Christ of Latter Day Saints* (Independence, Mo.: Herald Publishing House, 1973), 5:558. This is a continuation of the series begun by Joseph Smith and Heman C. Smith in 1896.

8. Doctrine and Covenants, Section 124:7.

9. "Conference Minutes, Decatur District," *Saints' Herald* 44 (22 June 1897): 401–2.

10. Smith, "Memoirs," *Saints' Herald* 82 (5 March 1935): 303–4; Smith, *Concerning the Prophet*, p. 130; Edwards, *History of Reorganized Church*, 6:557–59.

11. David H. Smith and W. W. Blair had been called as counselors in the First Presidency in 1873. David, the prophet's brother, had served

only a short time before being committed to the Elgin Hospital for the Insane in 1877. Blair died in office as an old man in 1896. See Doctrine and Covenants, Section 117:3. In 1897 Joseph had appointed his other brother, Presiding Patriarch Alexander H. Smith, and Bishop E. L. Kelley to be informal advisors, but it was understood that their principal duties would lie in other areas. See Doctrine and Covenants, Section 124:7; Edwards, *History of Reorganized Church*, 6:557–58.

12. Doctrine and Covenants, Section 126.

13. R. C. Evans, *Autobiography of R. C. Evans, One of the First Presidency of the Reorganized Church of Jesus Christ of Latter Day Saints* (London, Ontario: Advertiser Printing Co., 1907), pp. 27–198, passim; Roger D. Launius, "R. C. Evans: Boy Orator of the Reorganization," *John Whitmer Historical Association Journal* 3 (1983): 40–50.

14. Joseph Smith to R. C. Evans, 22 May 1896, Joseph Smith III Letterbook #6, Reorganized Church Library–Archives.

15. Launius, "R. C. Evans": 41–44.

16. Joseph Smith to A. R. Smith, 7 June 1903, Joseph Smith III Papers, Reorganized Church Library–Archives; R. C. Evans to E. L. Kelley, 3 July 1903, Edmund L. Kelley Papers, Reorganized Church Library–Archives; "President Smith in England," *Saints' Herald* 50 (5 August 1903): 715, 50 (28 October 1903): 1004; Smith, "Memoirs," *Saints' Herald* 84 (6 February 1937): 178, 84 (13 February 1937): 207–10, 84 (20 February 1937): 241–42, 84 (27 February 1937): 271–74, 84 (6 March 137): 303–6, 84 (13 March 1937): 335–38, 84 (20 March 1937): 369–70, 84 (27 March 1937): 399–402, 84 (3 April 1937): 431–32.

17. Joseph Smith, Journal, 1 January 1903, endpaper, Reorganized Church Library–Archives; R. C. Evans, *Why I Left the Latter Day Saint Church: Reasons by Bishop R. C. Evans* (Toronto, Ontario: n.p., 1918), p. 52; R. C. Evans, *Forty Years in the Mormon Church: Why I Left It* (Shreveport, La.: Lambert Book Co., 1976), p. 137.

18. Joseph Smith to Audentia Smith Anderson, 9 August 1901, 26 November 1906, 4 December 1906, Joseph Smith III Papers; John W. Ruston to Joseph Smith, 29 March 1906, William H. Kelley Papers, Reorganized Church Library–Archives; Smith, Journal, 1 January 1903, endpaper.

19. Smith, "Memoirs," *Saints' Herald* 84 (22 May 1937): 656–57.

20. Joseph Smith to Israel A. Smith, 4 December 1905, Miscellaneous Letters and Papers, Reorganized Church Library–Archives; Deed between Joseph and Ada Smith and Reorganized Church, 15 January 1906, Deed Book S, Recorder's Office, Decatur County Courthouse, Leon, Iowa.

21. Elbert A. Smith, *Brother Elbert: Enlarged Autobiography,* ed. Lynn E. Smith (Independence, Mo.: Herald Publishing House, 1959), pp.

147, 153; Joseph Smith, "Last Will and Testament," 1 February 1906, Miscellaneous Letters and Papers; R. C. Evans to Frederick M. Smith, 20 May 1907, R. C. Evans Papers, Reorganized Church Library–Archives.

22. Doctrine and Covenants, Section 127:8.

23. Evans, *Why I Left the Latter Day Saint Church*, p. 42.

24. R. C. Evans to E. L. Kelley, 21 January 1907, 18 November 1907, 5 January 1908, 6 January 1908, 28 April 1908, 6 June 1908, 19 October 1908, 9 March 1911, R. C. Evans Papers; Joseph Smith to R. C. Evans, 21 April 1908, 26 April 1909, R. C. Evans Papers; "Brother R. C. Evans in Toronto," *Saints' Herald* 53 (28 February 1906): 195–96.

25. On the zionic enterprise and the role in Independence in it during the early twentieth century, see Hunt, *Frederick Madison Smith*, pp. 145–207. See also these basic introductions to the zionic concept: David Premoe, ed., *Zion: the Growing Symbol* (Independence, Mo: Herald Publishing House, 1980); Paul A. Wellington, ed., *Readings on Concepts of Zion* (Independence, Mo.: Herald Publishing House, 1973); Clifford A. Cole and Peter Judd, *Distinctives: Yesterday and Today* (Independence, Mo.: Herald Publishing House, 1984); Miriam Elizabeth Higdon, "Eyes Single to the Glory: The History of the Heavenly City of Zion," in *Restoration Studies I: Sesquicentennial Edition*, ed. Maurice L. Draper and Clare D. Vlahos (Independence, Mo.: Herald Publishing House, 1980), pp. 269–77; Geoffrey F. Spencer, "Symbol and Process: An Exploration into the Concept of Zion," *Restoration Studies I*, pp. 278–86; A. Bruce Lindgren, "Zion as a Doctrine of Providence," *Restoration Studies I*, pp. 287–95; "The Meaning of the Cause of Zion in the Present Age: A Joint Council Seminar, December 4–6, 1974, The Auditorium, Independence, Missouri," and "Zion and the Future of the Church," September 1978, typescripts of important meetings concerning this issue which are available in the Reorganized Church Library–Archives; Diane Dean Peffers, "The Diffusion and Dispersion of the Reorganized Church of Jesus Christ of Latter Day Saints: An Overview" (M.S. thesis, Brigham Young University, 1980).

26. Joseph Smith to Israel A. Smith, 6 May 1906, Miscellaneous Letters and Papers. See also Joseph Smith to Carrie Smith Weld, 11 July 1906, Carrie Smith Weld Collection, Reorganized Church Library–Archives.

27. "Moved to Independence," *Saints' Herald* 53 (8 August 1906): 786; Joseph Smith to Rudolph Etzenhouser, 6 September 1906, Rudolph Etzenhouser Papers, Reorganized Church Library–Archives.

28. Joseph Smith to Audentia Smith Anderson, 15 August 1906, 6 September 1906, 8 October 1906, Joseph Smith III Papers.

29. Frederick M. Smith to V. A. L. Hodges, 27 February 1907, Frederick Madison Smith Papers, Reorganized Church Library–Archives;

Frederick M. Smith to Israel A. Smith, 11 December 1911, Frederick Madison Smith Papers; Smith, *Concerning the Prophet,* p. 140; Joseph Smith to *Herald* Editors, August 1909, Miscellaneous Letters and Papers; Joint Council Minutes, 1906–1938, pp. 97–98, Reorganized Church Library–Archives; Hunt, *Frederick Madison Smith,* pp. 243–53.

30. Heman C. Smith to Joseph Smith, 28 January 1909, Miscellaneous Letters and Papers; Council of Twelve Minutes, 1865–1928, 26 March 1909, Reorganized Church Library–Archives.

31. Evans had been bold enough even to ask directly that he be ordained bishop of Canada. See R. C. Evans to Frederick M. Smith, 22 February 1909, R. C. Evans Papers.

32. Doctrine and Covenants, Section 129:1; Smith, "Memoirs," *Saints' Herald* 84 (26 June 1937): 815–16; R. C. Evans to E. L. Kelley, 4 May 1909, R. C. Evans Papers. Frederick M. Smith's educational background has been discussed in Hunt, *Frederick Madison Smith,* pp. 59–112; Hunt, "Frederick Madison Smith: The Formative Years of an RLDS President," pp. 67–89.

33. Frederick M. Smith, Notes on Joseph Smith, n.d., p. 9, Joseph Smith III Papers.

34. William H. Kelley to Joseph Smith, 27 January 1912, William H. Kelley Papers; Joseph Smith, "A Letter of Instruction," *Saints' Herald* 59 (13 March 1912): 241–48.

35. Joseph Smith III's comments made during his last illness, 29 November 1914, Joseph Smith III Papers.

36. Council of Twelve Minutes, 1865–1928, 12 April 1912.

37. *New York Times,* 30 March 1912; Edwards, *History of Reorganized Church,* 6:576.

38. Smith, "Memoirs," *Saints' Herald* 84 (26 June 1937): 818, 84 (3 July 1937): 847.

39. Edward W. Tullidge, *The Life of Joseph the Prophet* (Plano, Ill.: Herald Publishing House, 1880), passim; Edwards, *History of Reorganized Church,* 5:97–99.

40. Joseph Smith and Heman C. Smith, *The History of the Reorganized Church of Jesus Christ of Latter Day Saints* (Lamoni, Iowa: Herald Publishing House, 1896–1903). Although Joseph Smith is listed as an author, it is clear that this work was principally the result of Heman P. Smith's efforts, with the prophet reviewing and approving the manuscript.

41. Joint Council Minutes, 1905–1926, 9 October 1907, Reorganized Church Library–Archives.

42. Joseph Smith to Israel A. Smith, 31 December 1912, Miscellaneous Letters and Papers.

43. Israel A. Smith, "My Father's Last Years," *Saints' Herald* 81 (6

November 1934): 1409–10, 1426.

44. Audentia Anderson, "Concerning My Father's Memoirs," ibid., 81 (6 November 1934): 1412, 1425–26.

45. Frederick M. Smith, "Concerning Joseph Smith's Memoirs," ibid., 82 (6 August 1935): 995–96; Smith, "Memoirs," *Saints' Herald* 84 (26 June 1937): 817–18.

46. *New York Times,* 27 November 1914; John F. Garver, "President Smith III," *Saints' Herald* 61 (2 December 1914): 1137.

47. "President Smith's Last Message to the Church," ibid., 61 (23 December 1914): 1211.

48. Joseph Smith III's Last Remarks to his Family, 29 November 1914, Joseph Smith III Papers; "Statement of President Joseph Smith to his Son Frederick M. Smith, Sunday, November 29, 1914," *Zion's Ensign* 26 (11 February 1915): 1. Frederick M. Smith's latent authoritarianism has been described in Hunt, *Frederick Madison Smith,* pp. 243–53.

49. *New York Times,* 28 November 1914; Elbert A. Smith, "President Smith's Illness," *Saints' Herald* 61 (9 November 1914): 1161; *Saints' Herald* 61 (23 December 1914): 1209–10.

50. Elbert A. Smith, "Instructions Regarding President Smith's Funeral," *Saints' Herald* 61 (16 December 1914): 1188.

51. Elbert A. Smith, "Death of President Smith," ibid., 61 (16 December 1914): 1185–86.

52. *New York Times,* 24 December 1914; Joint Council Minutes, 1905–1926, 14 December 1914; Edwards, *History of Reorganized Church,* 6:584–87.

Epilogue

Joseph Smith III would have been pleased with the obituaries various newspapers published about his work as president of the Reorganized Church. Invariably they praised his accomplishments as an honorable and upstanding individual of all-around merit and as a moderate and acceptable official of a worthwhile religious institution that stood within the parameters of the American Christian tradition. Throughout his life Smith had sought to make the Reorganized Church into a respected organization that had progressed beyond the revolutionary movement of his father's time, and in large measure he succeeded. He built upon his father's charismatic leadership and the ill-developed institution he inherited, pragmatically assessing the contributions and liabilities of each. He gradually and practically discarded esoteric theological baggage and altered or refined religious traditions to build a viable and acceptable Christian institution. In both goals and methods he was a much different type of leader than his father.

Max Weber, the early twentieth-century German sociologist, developed a theory suggesting that three pure types of leadership existed in any organizational structure based upon the following:

1. Rational grounds—resting on a belief in the "legality" of patterns of normative rules and the right of those elevated to authority under such rules to issue commands (legal authority)
2. Traditional grounds—resting on an established belief in the sanc-

tity of immemorial traditions and the legitimacy of the status of those exercising authority under them (traditional authority)
3. Charismatic grounds—resting on devotion to the specific and exceptional sanctity, heroism, or exemplary character of an individual person and the normative patterns or order revealed or ordained by him (charismatic authority) [1]

While Weber refused to assert that this represented the sum of all leadership types—most leaders were mixtures of at least two of the styles—he suggested that they were useful points of reference for analysis.

Weber also suggested that the charismatic leader most often shakes up the status quo, altering appreciably the manner in which individuals perceive themselves and society in general. Weber specifically placed religious leaders—he often referred to them as prophets—in this category. "We shall understand 'prophet' to mean a purely individual bearer of charisma, who by virtue of his mission proclaims a religious doctrine or divine commitment," he wrote.[2] He asserted explicitly that Joseph Smith, Jr., the founder of Mormonism, could be placed in this category.[3] Through the force of their will, the perception of divine favor, and the religious vision they espoused, these individuals invariably offered their followers an opportunity to radically change their lives and culture. As a result, he added, the movements founded were unusual and outside the realm of acceptance. If they were to survive, their "life forces" had to be subdued and channeled into more common and acceptable expressions. In religious history this has been interpreted as a passage from sect to denomination.[4] Although his conclusions have been altered somewhat since he first developed them, Weber's thesis about charismatic leadership over a movement without much administrative structure and little cohesion beyond the persona of the leader still has validity.[5]

Eric Hoffer built upon Weber's theories about the charismatic leadership type in *The True Believer,* published in 1951. Although it had an overall controversial thesis, this work extended Weber's theories about charismatic leadership. Hoffer noted that charismatic leaders acted as a catalyst that sparked the expression of a deep discontent in certain segments of society. While there could be other ingredients to this catalyst, a dynamic and charismatic leader was a necessary prerequisite. This charismatic leader was able to perceive the discontent of the time; glimpse a vision of a brighter, more rewarding future; articulate the need for change; and drive the vision to its logical conclusion. In some instances there might be more than one type of charismatic leader. The first would be a sort of John the Baptist—a philosopher by nature and a preacher by profession—preparing the way for radical change by espousing the holy goal. This type of leader articulated and justified the resentment and frustrations dammed up in the souls of many people and kindled a vision of a breathtaking future. A second type of charismatic leadership involved an individual who could set the vision on a path toward realization. In essence, this individual carried out the revolution. Once again, just as Weber concluded, Hoffer noted that charismatic leadership tended to be fleeting, and if the movement founded was to survive, it had to be placed on a more stable footing.[6]

The career of Joseph Smith, Jr., fit well into this charismatic model of leadership, for he was a mystic who saw religion as an essential element of everyday life, not as an isolated experience.[7] He enjoyed glimpses of divine truth and spent his life trying to understand and, with varying degrees of success, express it to others. As a charismatic leader in the Weberian sense he gathered around him a group of believers which became known as the Mormon church. This organization was a secular expression of Smith's sacred experience, but it was at best an imperfect attempt to approximate what he had perceived. Paul M. Edwards offered a useful explanation of the dichotomy between Smith's perception of his sacred experience and his secular implementation of it:

> It seems to me we have misinterpreted the role of the institutional church and have studied it as sacred. The Vision may well have been sacred. But the church and the lives of its people are not; they are secular. The study of the church then is not a study of the sources of the sacred event, nor of the sacred event itself, but the story of those who have led their lives in the shadow of the event. The church as an institution is not a confrontation with God, and to study it as such makes the failures of men, God's failures; the inconsistencies of men, God's inconsistencies. . . . To study the church as secular is to study human beings living with the awareness of the sacred as they try to recapture it in symbolic ways.[8]

Edwards suggested that Smith had very little understanding of the requirements of a religious institution operating in an imperfect world. "Joseph was a prophetic voice, but no more the first Mormon than Christ was the first Christian," he commented, adding that he believed that whatever organizational structure the Mormon church developed during the lifetime of Joseph Smith, Jr., may have been accomplished only at the behest of other church leaders, particularly Hyrum Smith. "The loving and sustaining sibling, the cool mind, the natural man; he saw the importance of his brother's mystical experience and the impossibility of translating it into anything but secular events with a sacred mantle. Therefore, he institutionalized it."[9] By making a distinction between the sacred and secular nature of its history, Edwards has made an important stride toward understanding the development of early Mormonism.

In its pure form charismatic leadership has a character specifically foreign to routine organizational structure. Weber suggested that if the type of movement charismatic leaders such as Joseph Smith, Jr., intended had not been altered by others they could not survive: "If this [type of movement] is not to remain a purely transitory phenomenon, but to take on the character of a permanent relationship forming a stable community of disciples or a band of followers or a party organization or any sort of political or hierocratic organization, it is necessary for the character of charismatic authority to become radically changed. Indeed, in its pure form charismatic authority may be said to exist only in the process of originating."[10] The Mormon movement went through some of this "routinization" process, as Weber called it, during the lifetime of its founder; theology and administration were established and made operative, but it was still highly charismatic until the death of the prophet.

Weber noted that the transformation from charismatic leadership to more traditional styles became "conspicuously evident with the disappearance of the personal charismatic leader and with the problem of succession, which inevitably arises."[11] After Joseph Smith, Jr.'s death, the "routinization" process began in earnest, the various factions of the church dealing with it in a variety of ways. Some of them remained essentially charismatic; most of those also were transitory. Others found a way of making succession legitimate through administrative structure and stability. These factions were presided over by what Eric Hoffer termed the practical man of action, such as Joseph Smith III. These individuals were consolidators of revolution. They saved their factions from suicidal dissension, extremely loose organization or intensely tight tyranny, and the recklessness of fanatics. Although this type of leader is absolutely essential to the continued existence of any movement, his rise marks the end of the dynamic phase of the movement, Hoffer noted, for "whereas the life breath of the dynamic phase was protest and a desire for drastic change, the final phase is chiefly preoccupied with administering and perpetuating the power won." Additionally, this type of leader sealed the explosive vigor of the movement in sanctified institutions. They took what they considered the best parts of the earlier phase of the movement—the essence, if you will—placed it into practical application, and built from there.[12]

These more practical leaders were necessarily more calm and less brash. While they might be every bit as committed to the ideals of the movement, they controlled their passions better than did those who started the quest. They were not ideologues; their every action was tempered by practicality and modified by caution. That does not mean that they were without principle, for in every instance within Mormonism they demonstrated their ideological commitment to the vision of the prophet as expounded in his inspired writings and personal attributes.[13]

Joseph Smith III was this type of leader—a pragmatist in the best tradition of American leadership. That is not to say that he had studied and formally applied any of the divergent ideas associated with this philosophy espoused by such original thinkers as Charles S. Pierce, William James, and John Dewey. Rather it was a much more submerged attribute, one which tugged at him in all situations requiring difficult decisions. Translated into his approach to leadership, Smith's pragmatic attitude called for him to make a needed change or decision at the right time. American pragmatism has stressed the necessity of continuous, cooperative experimental reform, but it also has insisted, above all, that while changes are being made the system must be kept running. A proposed change may be morally or theologically right, but it also has to be realizable, based upon past experience and the realities of the situation.[14]

Smith's pragmatism fit well into this mold, placing him squarely in the middle of a great tradition that extended from the very foundation of the nation. This approach informed virtually every action Smith took during his career as president of the Reorganized Church. Smith had a deep commitment to the gospel his father had established. Although he never developed a full theology, Smith accepted what he considered the most important aspects of Mormonism and placed them into practice as best he could. He adhered to the overall concepts of Christianity, appending to them a firm belief in the Book of Mormon, the continuing revelation of God through the prophetic office (his father and himself), and the sacred vision of a zionic society. To those fundamentals he was dedicated, and he allowed no compromise, at least intellectually, in their acceptance. He held these as principles that were inviolate.[15] But the application of these ideals to everyday life was another issue. Smith's public opinions were always restrained by his strong pragmatic sense, by his fine feeling for what, given the fact of human limitations, was realistically possible.

One of the keys to his thinking was his statements that few things in this world were totally one way or the other. Instinctively Smith distrusted doctrinaire thinkers who claimed to know without a doubt what was good or evil and who were prepared to act upon their beliefs regardless of the outcome. "There is no tribunal this side of the judgment seat of God that can determine whether anything is true or not true absolutely," he testified in the Temple Lot case, adding that "we are all liable to be in error, for we recognize that this side of the judgment seat there is no tribunal that can decide that matter."[16] Near the end of his career he made a strikingly similar but more emphatic statement about his belief in taking a middle-of-the-road position. Addressing the church's general conference, he said:

> There is no absolute tribunal this side of the great judgment day that is authorized to determine exactly who is right and who is wrong in a dispute or controversy, such as arises frequently in our midst. Hence it devolves upon us to carry our differences without animosity, without fault finding, without charging evil intent or purpose upon those who may differ from us. I have tried to impress this thought upon you and upon others, and I want now to have you think upon it. . . .
>
> There is no tribunal—I want you to remember this affirmation and I hope these representatives of the press will quote me as I state it

now—there is no tribunal, this side of the great judgment bar, that has the authorized right to sit in judgment upon the faith of men and say whether or not they are heterodox or orthodox. . . .

This makes every man responsible to God. He had a secondary responsibility to those with whom he is associated in labor or work, to observe their rights, while assuming those which he deemed to belong to himself.[17]

By temperament Smith was perhaps more legalistic than tolerant, patient, and noncensorious. But by nature he was also throughout his career practical, moderate, and gradual. He preferred to see changes come slowly, after due deliberation and with the consent of all affected groups. Almost instinctively, Smith inclined to a middle-of-the-road position—a saving attribute for him as Reorganization president. His desire to maintain a relatively harmonious and effective religious movement prompted most of his actions. It fostered his moderate approach on numerous theological issues ranging from baptism of the dead to the nature of the preexistence. To avoid the possibilities of internal dissension and the perception of failure, he consciously advanced the community experiment at Lamoni, Iowa, as a zionic endeavor with less grandiose ambitions than those of early Latter Day Saint communities. The Reorganization's harmony was also important in his struggle with Jason W. Briggs and Zenos H. Gurley, Jr., over the nature of the presidential office and the doctrine of the church. It was critical to the approach he took toward even a religious conception he despised as much as plural marriage, for he pressed his particular views about his father's innocence only when he thought they could be accepted by most of the membership without undue strife. In that instance, perhaps more than any other, Smith demonstrated his principled nature seasoned with pragmatism. He was endlessly opposed to the linkage of his father with the origins of plural marriage; he said as much from the outset of his presidency. However, although I suspect he would have liked to have done so had the membership been willing to accept it—he did not force the church to make any binding, official statements on this subject—in fact, on at least one occasion, at the Joint Council of 1865, he recommended the tabling of such a resolution. But he recognized the volatile nature of the subject and bided his time, gradually making his position the accepted view of the church without destroying church unity.[18]

This pragmatism, which he demonstrated throughout his career as president of the Reorganized Church, was a critical attribute which Smith used successfully first to create a viable religious institution and then to carry forward what he believed should be its programs. Without such an approach Smith might well have presided over an institution which crumbled within a few years of his ordination, for the Reorganized Church was born out of dissident elements of the early Latter Day Saint church. Its intellectual forebearers, if not its actual ones, were the Oliver Cowderys, John Corrills, and the William Laws of the early church. Those individuals could not accept what they considered abuses of authority by the president, abuses which manifested themselves, they believed, in such arenas as church involvement in secular politics and economic activities and in the implementation of esoteric religious practices and theological notions.[19]

The movement that coalesced around Jason W. Briggs and Zenos H. Gurley, Sr., in the 1850s was made up of cautious people who had rejected the more extreme expressions of Mormonism's religious commitment—specifically those theological ideals embraced and furthered by such factional leaders as Brigham Young. Reorganized Church members were repelled by the practice of temple rituals, plural marriage, and the emphasis upon the political kingdom of God that they saw among the Utah Latter-day Saints. They huddled together outside the church's strongholds, operating in branches which were nearly autonomous. The strength of the Reorganization, therefore, was manifested in local branches, and the autonomy they enjoyed in the 1850s has been jealously guarded ever since. Reorganized Latter Day Saints did not accept well any attempts to dictate from above; such had been done before and they had learned that the results were often not what they wanted.[20]

Smith's pragmatic approach was absolutely the right way of dealing with people coming out of this background and perspective. He moved them in directions that he believed would most benefit the church, but he never tried to run roughshod over them. He sought to keep internal conflict to a minimum while building a stable church organization that could accomplish something worthwhile. He recognized that all members of the movement were committed to basically the same ideals, but he understood that there was room for honest and committed individuals to disagree over fundamental questions. The church never adopted anything approaching a universal creed for just such a reason, and Smith tolerated much esoteric thinking on many theological issues because he did not wish to impose his will on others.[21] A more doctrinaire, more forceful, less considerate individual might not have been able to hold together the delicate balance of personalities, ideas, and fears that were primary ingredients for the Reorganized Church of the nineteenth century. Smith's whole approach to this was summarized on his deathbed when he gave a critical piece of advice to his son, Frederick Madison Smith, the man chosen to succeed him. Smith told him that the members and other officials of the Reorganized Church had a persistent habit of becoming "heady and tak[ing] the reins in their hands." He told his son to follow his example and "let it pass, let the church take the consequences and they will after a while grow out of it." Then he added, "It is better that way than to undertake to force them and coerce. That would be bad trouble."[22]

Joseph Smith III was a unique man. He was many things to many Reorganized Church members: friend, prophet, spiritual leader, counselor, administrator, and father figure in later years. I have no wish to deemphasize either his spiritual nature or his religious commitment, and I am mindful of the error of many historians who try to overinterpret their subject, to place fences around their beliefs and pass them off as the whole of the story. Certainly Smith was a man of principles and dedication to the truth as he saw it. But the way in which he approached his tasks, expressed his ideals, and dealt with problems made him an outstanding practical leader. He opposed a right change at the wrong time and supported the same change at the right time. His career represents an important case study in the union of principle and pragmatism in American religious history. Although this may not be the only legitimate interpretation of Joseph Smith III's career, it is fundamental to understanding the individual. A practical man of action, he was able to translate his father's religious dreams into some semblance of reality. Perhaps the full measure of Joseph Smith, Jr.'s sacred vision cannot be placed into a secular framework, but by his tireless efforts to bridge the chasm between ideal and real, Joseph Smith III made the Reorganized Church a practical, viable institution. Thereby, Mormonism as a broad religious tradition benefited immeasurably.

NOTES

1. Max Weber, "The Pure Types of Legitimate Authority," in *Max Weber on Charisma and Institution Building: Selected Papers*, ed. S. N. Eisenstadt (Chicago: University of Chicago Press, 1968), p. 46.

2. Max Weber, "The Prophet," ibid., p. 253.

3. Max Weber, "The Nature of Charismatic Authority and Its Routinization," ibid., p. 49. Weber placed a caveat on his assertion that Joseph Smith, Jr., might fit into this category. He wrote, "Another type is that of Joseph Smith, the founder of Mormonism, who, however, cannot be classified in this way with absolute certainty since there is a possibility that he was a very sophisticated type of deliberate swindler." That was Weber's assessment printed in English in 1947. Since that time significant historical research has suggested that Smith was an absolute believer in his divine mission. See, in this regard, T. L. Brink, "Joseph Smith: The Verdict of Depth Psychology," *Journal of Mormon History* 3 (1976): 74–76; Donna Hill, *Joseph Smith: The First Mormon* (Garden City, N.Y.: Doubleday and Co., 1977); Klaus J. Hansen, *Mormonism and the American Experience* (Chicago: University of Chicago Press, 1981), pp. 13–27. His belief in his own prophetic ministry is very clearly seen in his diaries and correspondence as printed in Dean C. Jessee, *Personal Writings of Joseph Smith* (Salt Lake City, Utah: Deseret Book Co., 1984).

4. For an important discussion of this transition within the Reorganized Church see Maurice L. Draper, "Sect–Denomination–Church Transition and Leadership in the Reorganized Church of Jesus Christ of Latter Day Saints" (M.A. thesis, Kansas University, 1964). For a historiographical framework describing this issue see Alma R. Blair, "Historical Models of the Reorganization," *Commission*, September 1979, pp. 20–24, a publication of the Reorganized Church which traced the development of four major interpretations used by historians to explain the Reorganization's past. The first of these, an obsolete and in large measure defunct interpretation, Blair described as the "true church versus apostasy" approach to history. A second model Blair described as the developing church interpretation; this approach suggested that as time progressed the theology and institutional patterns of the church evolved. In essence, the church changed over time. This approach allowed for explanations of change within the movement without suggesting that it had departed from the pure truths of the gospel. Next Blair described an "interpretation emphasizing the tradition of dissent" within the Reorganization. This approach allowed historians the freedom of analyzing the organization without judging the spirituality of the movement. Instead, they concentrated on explaining the development of the church using as a tool the understanding of the

diverse dissident elements that made up the movement. Finally, as in this instance, Blair described a model in current vogue which he called the "sect-denomination interpretation." This approach accepted as a fundamental basis of interpretation that the Reorganization moved in time from a narrow sect insisting it possessed all religious truth to a denomination recognizing more commonalities rather than differences with other Christian churches.

5. Weber, "The Prophet," pp. 253–67.

6. Eric Hoffer, *The True Believer: Thoughts on the Nature of Mass Movements* (New York: Harper and Row, 1980), pp. xi–xvii, 3–23, 137–55.

7. The suggestion of Joseph Smith, Jr.'s mysticism as well as charismatic nature is not new. See Jan Shipps, "The Prophet Puzzle: Suggestions Leading toward a More Comprehensive Interpretation of Joseph Smith," *Journal of Mormon History* 1 (1974): 3–20; Paul M. Edwards, "The Secular Smiths," *Journal of Mormon History* 4 (1977):3–17; Paul M. Edwards, *Preface to Faith: A Philosophical Inquiry into RLDS Beliefs* (Midvale, Utah: Signature Book, 1984), pp. 31–33.

8. Edwards, "The Secular Smiths," p. 6.

9. Ibid., p. 12.

10. Weber, "Charismatic Authority and Its Routinization," p. 54.

11. Ibid., p. 55.

12. Hoffer, *The True Believer*, pp. 116–23, 156–77. For an excellent discussion of this process among the Utah Latter-day Saints concerning the zionic ideal developed by Joseph Smith, Jr., see Leonard J. Arrington, Feramorz Y. Fox, and Dean L. May, *Building the City of God: Community and Cooperation among the Mormons* (Salt Lake City, Utah: Deseret Book Co., 1976), passim.

13. A case study in the practical nature of leadership, but with an honest attempt to adhere to conceptions developed in an earlier period, can be found in Leonard J. Arrington, *Brigham Young: American Moses* (New York: Alfred A. Knopf, 1985), pp. 402–9. An intellectual discussion of this issue can be found in James McGregor Burns, *Leadership* (New York: Harper and Row, 1978), passim.

14. By the 1890s the philosophy of pragmatism was making avenues into the American consciousness. Pragmatism was the one comprehensive American contribution to Western philosophic thought. As developed by William James and John Dewey, it attacked the fundamental concepts of the nineteenth-century mechanistic world in which humanity was more or less controlled by factors beyond its control, be it Calvinistic predestination, the Hegelian or Marxian dialectic, the process of evolution as developed by Darwin, or the physical universe as described by Newton.

Instead of this determined universe, pragmatism suggested, the world was an open one of constant but uncertain change in which individuals could leave their own marks. Provided the species used its mind creatively and adventurously, was guided by moral sense, and took rational actions, very little was impossible. It might take lengthy periods of time to accomplish reform, but reform was possible; humans controlled their own destinies. Beliefs were all-important in this philosophy, but their real worth were their consequences. Without positive application they held little meaning. Pragmatism was a pluralistic and relativistic concept that led naturally to actions that were both idealistic and rational. It accepted a universe which responded to the actions of humanity. In its more extreme forms it served as a vehicle for the negation of traditional conservatism and creeds of all types.

Joseph Smith III did not carry his pragmatic philosophy to its logical conclusion. He, like most other Americans who embraced certain of its ideas, expressed an imbedded pragmatism that called for reasonable action at the right time. They had no overarching pragmatic scenario for all of life; rather they saw it as representative of their belief that actions should represent the highest form of what was possible to accomplish.

For discussions of formal pragmatic philosophy see Henry Steele Commager, *The American Mind* (New Haven, Conn.: Yale University Press, 1952), pp. 91–98; Philip P. Weiner, *Evolution and the Founders of Pragmatism* (Cambridge, Mass.: Harvard University Press, 1949); Edward Carter Moore, *American Pragmatism: Pierce, James, and Dewey* (New York: Columbia University Press, 1961). For an application of the American pragmatic philosophy to a great politician see T. Harry Williams, "Abraham Lincoln: Pragmatic Democrat," in *The Enduring Lincoln: Lincoln Sesquicentennial Lectures at the University of Illinois*, ed. Norman A. Graebner (Urbana: University of Illinois Press, 1959), pp. 23–46.

15. For a succinct discussion of Smith's theological conceptions see Clare D. Vlahos, "Moderation as a Theological Principle in the Thought of Joseph Smith III," *John Whitmer Historical Association Journal* 1 (1981): 3–11.

16. "Testimony of Joseph Smith," in *Complainant's Abstract of Pleading and Evidence in the Circuit Court of the United States, Western District of Missouri, Western Division, at Kansas City, Missouri* (Lamoni, Iowa: Herald Publishing House, 1893), p. 494.

17. General Conference Minutes, 1910, pp. 1, 937–38, Reorganized Church of Jesus Christ of Latter Day Saints Library–Archives, Independence, Mo.

18. In this regard see Alma R. Blair, "RLDS Views of Polygamy: Some Historiographical Notes," *John Whitmer Historical Association Journal*

5 (1985): 16–28. Blair noted, "In the earliest years of the Reorganization most of the members sorrowfully recognized that Joseph Smith, Jr., was directly responsible for polygamy. They did not suggest any other person was responsible, and they did not give a sophisticated historical analysis of its evolution. It was an error, but they were grateful that the prophet finally came to oppose it. The next generation of members [especially beginning in the mid-1870s], under the tutelage of Joseph Smith III, 'cleared' the martyr's name of any significant connection with the doctrine and found but lust to be the cause of polygamy and Brigham Young to be its originator. This explanation remained unchanged until the 1960s when it was proposed that polygamy was the result of larger social and theological factors" (Blair, "RLDS Views of Polygamy," p. 26).

19. The best discussion of the origins of the Reorganized Church is Alma R. Blair, "The Reorganized Church of Jesus Christ of Latter Day Saints: Moderate Mormons," in *The Restoration Movement: Essays in Mormon History,* ed. F. Mark McKiernan, Alma R. Blair, and Paul M. Edwards (Lawrence, Kan.: Coronado Press, 1973), pp. 207–30. One of the important but largely neglected areas of Mormon historical inquiry is the role of dissent in the development of the Latter Day Saint movement. The one overview dealing with this issue, although it is generally unsympathetic to the dissident elements, is Leonard J. Arrington, "Centrifugal Tendencies in Mormon History," in *To the Glory of God: Mormon Essays on Great Issues,* ed. Truman G. Madsen (Salt Lake City, Utah: Deseret Book Co., 1972), pp. 165–77. One should review the following publications on specific dissenting episodes. On the Kirtland and Far West periods of 1837–1838 see Marvin S. Hill, "Cultural Crisis in the Mormon Kingdom: A Reconsideration," *Church History* 49 (September 1980): 286–97; Max A. Parkin, *Conflict at Kirtland: A Study of the Nature and Causes of External and Internal Conflict of the Mormons in Ohio between 1830 and 1838* (Provo, Utah: Brigham Young University Department of Seminaries and Institutes of Religion, 1967); Richard Lloyd Anderson, *Investigating the Book of Mormon Witnesses* (Salt Lake City, Utah: Deseret Book Co., 1981), passim, on the dissent of the witnesses to the divinity of the Book of Mormon; Stanley R. Gunn, *Oliver Cowdery: Second Elder and Scribe* (Salt Lake City, Utah: Bookcraft, 1962), pp. 141–64; Lyndon W. Cook, "'I Have Sinned Against Heaven, and Am Unworthy of Your Confidence, But I Cannot Live without a Reconciliation:' Thomas B. Marsh Returns to the Church," *Brigham Young University Studies* 20 (Spring 1980): 389–400. On dissent in Nauvoo as expressed by those associating with William Law, see Lyndon W. Cook, "William Law: Nauvoo Dissenter," *Brigham Young University Studies* 22 (Winter 1982): 47–72; Lyndon W. Cook, "'Brother Joseph Is Truly a

Wonderful Man, He Is All Could Wish a Prophet to Be': Pre-1844 Letters of William Law," *Brigham Young University Studies* 20 (Winter 1980): 207–18; Robert Bruce Flanders, *Nauvoo: Kingdom on the Mississippi* (Urbana: University of Illinois Press, 1965), pp. 242–77; Dallin H. Oaks, "The Suppression of the Nauvoo *Expositor*," *Utah Law Review* 9 (Winter 1965): 862–903; John Frederick Glaser, "The Dissaffection of William Law," in *Restoration Studies III*, ed. Maurice L. Draper and Debra Combs (Independence, Mo.: Herald Publishing House, 1986), pp. 163–75. On the continuation and expansion of the dissenting tradition in the Reorganized Church of the nineteenth century, see Alma R. Blair, "The Tradition of Dissent—Jason W. Briggs," in *Restoration Studies I: Sesquicentennial Edition*, ed. Maurice L. Draper and Clare D. Vlahos (Independence, Mo.: Herald Publishing House, 1980), pp. 146–61; Clare D. Vlahos, "The Challenge to Centralized Power: Zenos H. Gurley, Jr., and the Prophetic Office," *Courage: A Journal of History, Thought, and Action* 1 (March 1971): 141–58. For more recent applications of this tradition see Larry E. Hunt, *Frederick Madison Smith: Saint as Reformer*, 2 vols. (Independence, Mo.: Herald Publishing House, 1982), which describes in detail the Supreme Directional Control controversy of the 1910s and 1920s; William J. Knapp, "Professionalizing Religious Education in the Church: The 'New Curriculum' Controversy," *John Whitmer Historical Association Journal* 2 (1982): 47–59. On religious dissent generally see Edwin Scott Gaustead, *Dissent in American Religion* (Chicago: University of Chicago Press, 1973).

20. Autonomy for the Reorganized Church branches has been noted in Douglas D. Alder and Paul M. Edwards, "Common Beginnings, Divergent Beliefs," *Dialogue: A Journal of Mormon Thought* 11 (Spring 1978): 18–28. When Joseph Smith III appeared to be centralizing too much authority in his office, some church leaders rebelled. See Vlahos, "Challenge to Centralized Power," pp. 141–58, and Blair, "The Tradition of Dissent," pp. 146–61.

21. As late as 1 October 1969 the church issued a formal statement of belief, *Exploring the Faith: A Series of Studies in the Faith of the Church Prepared by a Committee on Basic Beliefs* (Independence, Mo.: Herald Publishing House, 1970). Apostle Clifford A. Cole, chairman of the Basic Beliefs Committee, wrote that "we do not present this statement as a final work. Most of all, we do not want people to ever think of it as a creed" (preface).

22. Joseph Smith III's Last Remarks to his Family, 29 November 1914, Joseph Smith III Papers. See also "Statement of President Joseph Smith to His Son Frederick M. Smith, Sunday, November 29, 1914," *Zion's Ensign* 26 (11 February 1915): 1.

Bibliographical Note

No dearth of manuscripts hindered the preparation of this study of the life of Joseph Smith III. The Reorganized Church prophet wrote voluminously, and happily most of his papers appear to have been preserved. The largest and most valuable collection of Joseph Smith III papers is located in the Library–Archives of the Reorganized Church of Jesus Christ of Latter Day Saints, Independence, Missouri. Spanning his mature life, it includes ten letterpress books of correspondence sent, hundreds of original letters received, and an equally impressive set of letters written by other leaders of the Reorganized Church, which cast considerable light on the career of Smith. Joseph Smith III also kept personal diaries for over fifty years, although most appear to have been used for expense information and random notations. The Reorganized Church Library–Archives has forty-one volumes spanning a period from 1859 to 1908. A fine description of this collection of Joseph Smith III's papers can be found in Daniel T. Muir, "Sources for Studies in the Life of Joseph Smith III," *Courage: A Journal of History, Thought, and Action* 1 (December 1970): 93–101. Additionally, papers by his relatives and other Reorganized Church officials and the minutes of meetings of several important administrative bodies within the Reorganization are available at this archive.

There are also many documents bearing upon the life of Joseph Smith III contained in the Historical Department of the Church of Jesus Christ of Latter-day Saints, Salt Lake City, Utah; at the Special Collections section of the Harold B. Lee Library, Brigham Young University, Provo, Utah; and at the Restoration History Manuscript Collection, Frederick Madison Smith Library, Graceland College, Lamoni, Iowa. There are smaller collections, some of which are duplicated materials, relating to Joseph

Smith III at the Chicago Historical Society; the Lovejoy Library, Southern Illinois University, Edwardsville, Illinois; the H. H. Bancroft Library, University of California, Berkeley; the J. Willard Marriott Library, University of Utah, Salt Lake City; the Utah State Historical Society, Salt Lake City; the Bienecke Library, Yale University, New Haven, Connecticut; and the Special Collections department of the Western Illinois University Library, Macomb, Illinois.

Government and official documents were somewhat useful in the preparation of this biography. I consulted federal census returns for the locale of Joseph Smith III from 1850 to 1910, available from the National Archives and Records Administration, Washington, D.C., which provided valuable demographic information about the prophet and his household and surrounding community. Additionally, probate, chancery, marriage, land, claims, and other records from Hancock and Kendall counties, Illinois; Decatur County, Iowa; and Jackson County, Missouri, contained important facts about the Smith family's secular activities. For the course of the antipolygamy crusade I found helpful James D. Richardson, ed., *Messages and Papers of the President of the United States,* 26 vols. (Washington, D.C.: Bureau of National Literature and Art, 1897).

Court documents were also useful in preparing sections dealing with legal actions. The decision on the Kirtland Temple Suit is in Reorganized Church of Jesus Christ of Latter Day Saints vs. Lucius Williams, et al., 23 February 1880, Court of Common Pleas, Book J, Doc. 60, p. 432, in the Lake County Courthouse, Painesville, Ohio. For the Temple Lot Suit several records are available. The unofficial publication, *Complainant's Abstract of Pleading and Evidence in the Circuit Court of the United States, Western District of Missouri, Western Division, at Kansas City, Missouri* (Lamoni, Iowa: Herald Publishing House, 1893), contains considerable testimony presented by the Reorganization to support its claim as the "true successor" of the original Mormon church. Official records of the suit can be found in Reorganized Church of Jesus Christ of Latter Day Saints vs. Church of Christ et al., 60 *Federal Reporter,* 935–48 (1894); Church of Christ vs. Reorganized Church of Jesus Christ of Latter Day Saints et al., 70 *Federal Reporter,* 17–89 (1895); Church of Christ at Independence, Missouri et al., vs. Reorganized Church of Jesus Christ of Latter Day Saints, 71 *Federal Reporter,* 250 (1895); and Church of Christ at Independence, Missouri et al., vs. Reorganized Church of Jesus Christ of Latter Day Saints, 163 *US,* 314 (1896).

Important to any study of the career of Joseph Smith III are the periodicals of the Reorganized Church, for he carefully monitored the church publications. The most important newspaper, without question, was the *True Latter Day Saints' Herald,* shortened to simply the *Saints' Herald* in

1877, of which Smith was the working editor throughout most of his life. This publication began in January 1860 and has continued to the present. Issued first as a monthly, then a semi-monthly, and finally a weekly, the *Saints' Herald* during Smith's lifetime published news of importance to the church as well as official statements of policy and theology. Equally important for this study, between 1934 and 1937 the *Saints' Herald* published serially the "Memoirs of President Joseph Smith (1832–1914)," which proved invaluable. In 1979 Herald Publishing House, Independence, Missouri, collected together this serialization and issued it as a book. Other useful Reorganized Church publications included: *Autumn Leaves* (Lamoni, Iowa) 1888–1928; *Journal of History* (Lamoni, Iowa) 1908–1925; *The Messenger* (Salt Lake City, Utah) 1874–1877; *Saints' Advocate* (Plano, Illinois) 1878–1886; and *Zion's Ensign* (Independence, Missouri) 1891–1932. A useful survey of the movement's serial publications can be found in Sara Hallier, "RLDS Periodicals—Past and Present," *Saints' Herald* 130 (1 January 1983): 20–22.

I found pertinent information on the early Mormon movement in several other church publications: *Latter Day Saints' Messenger and Advocate* (Kirtland, Ohio) 1835–1837; *Latter Day Saints' Elder's Journal* (Far West, Missouri) 1838; and *Times and Seasons* (Nauvoo, Illinois) 1839–1846. Important Utah Latter-day Saint periodicals were: *Latter-day Saints Millennial Star* (Liverpool, England); *Deseret News* (Salt Lake City, Utah); *Improvement Era* (Salt Lake City, Utah); *Journal of Discourses* (Salt Lake City, Utah); and *Latter-day Saints' Historical Record* (Salt Lake City, Utah).

A surprisingly rich source of material about Joseph Smith III and the Reorganized Church was found in the secular newspapers of the era. Particularly helpful were the *New York Herald*, the *New York Times*, the *New York Tribune*, and the *New York World*. For the career of Joseph Smith III in Illinois, I have surveyed the files of the *Amboy* (Illinois) *Times*, the *Carthage* (Illinois) *Republican*, the *Chicago Journal*, the *Kendall County Record* (Yorkville, Illinois), the *Lee County Times* (Amboy, Illinois), the *Plano* (Illinois) *Mirror*, the *Quincy* (Illinois) *Herald*, the *Sangamo Journal* (Springfield, Illinois), the *Springfield* (Illinois) *Weekly Republican*, the *Warsaw* (Illinois) *Message*, the *Warsaw* (Illinois) *Signal*, and the *Weekly Argus* (Sandwich, Illinois). Newspapers most useful for collecting bits of information about the prophet's Iowa and Missouri sojourns were the *Iowa State Register* (Des Moines, Iowa), and the *Kansas City* (Missouri) *Journal*. Finally, several miscellaneous newspapers provided valuable information. These included the *Hancock Eagle* (Nauvoo, Illinois), the *Nauvoo* (Illinois) *Expositor*, the *Northern Islander* (St. James, Michigan), the *Painesville* (Ohio) *Telegraph*, *The Return* (Davis City, Iowa), the *Salt*

Lake (Utah) *Daily Herald,* the *Salt Lake* (Utah) *Tribune,* the *Utah Daily Reporter* (Salt Lake City, Utah), and the *Voree* (Wisconsin) *Herald.*

The writings considered sacred by the Latter Day Saints were fundamental to an understanding of many of the decisions made by Joseph Smith III. The Book of Mormon (Palmyra, N.Y.: E. B. Grandin, 1830) contains valuable insights into such issues as the nature of the zionic ideal, plural marriage, and morality. It has been reissued periodically by both the Latter-day Saint and Reorganized Latter Day Saint churches with chapter and verse notations. I have used in the narrative the 1966 reader's version issued by Herald Publishing House, Independence, Mo., because it contains several carefully made alterations to the text which improve clarity. Throughout his life Joseph Smith, Jr., worked on a revision of the King James version of the Bible, first published in 1867 by the Reorganized Church. The edition used in this study is *Holy Scriptures: Containing the Old and New Testaments, an Inspired Revision of the Authorized Version* (Independence, Mo.: Herald Publishing House, 1944). I have also used throughout this study the Book of Doctrine and Covenants (Independence, Mo.: Herald Publishing House, 1970), which is a modern republishing of revelations dating from before the organization of the Mormon movement in 1830 along with the inspired writings of Joseph Smith III and later presidents of the Reorganized Church. The Utah Latter-day Saint counterpart of this scriptural record is The Doctrine and Covenants of the Church of Jesus Christ of Latter- day Saints (Salt Lake City, Utah: Deseret Book Co., 1968).

Most of the books written by Reorganized Church leaders during the latter nineteenth and early twentieth centuries contain material of varying importance about Joseph Smith III. Only those works which supplied the most valuable information are listed here. For instance, Mary Audentia Anderson, the daughter of Smith, collected several interesting, although noncritical, recollections of the prophet in *Joseph Smith 1832–1914: A Centennial Tribute* (Independence, Mo.: Herald Publishing House, 1932), which had much information about his home life. *The Memoirs of President W. W. Blair,* edited by Frederick W. Blair (Lamoni, Iowa: Herald Publishing House, 1908), contains considerable information about the prophet and the administration of the church by a longtime associate in the First Presidency. R. C. Evans, a member of the First Presidency who eventually left the Reorganized Church, commented on Joseph Smith III in his *Autobiography of R. C. Evans* (London, Ontario: Advertiser Printing Co., 1907) and *Forty Years in the Mormon Church: Why I Left It* (Shreveport, La.: Lambert Book Co., 1976). An equally important source by yet another member of the First Presidency was Elbert A. Smith, *Brother Elbert: Enlarged Autobiography,* ed. Lynn E. Smith (Independence, Mo.: Herald

Publishing House, 1959). Finally, the relationship of Joseph Smith III with his oldest son is illuminated by Ruth C. Smith, *Concerning the Prophet: Fredrick* [sic] *Madison Smith* (Kansas City: Burton Publishing Co., 1924).

I have used many of the secondary materials bearing upon the subject. One of these was the documentary history of the movement, Joseph Smith III and Heman C. Smith, *The History of the Reorganized Church of Jesus Christ of Latter Day Saints,* 4 vols. (Independence, Mo.: Herald Publishing House, 1967–1973), which quotes extensively from the writings of early church leaders to record the church's history through 1890. F. Henry Edwards has added four volumes to this series to bring the story of the Reorganization up to 1948. Additionally, several less ambitious histories of the Reorganized Church have been published. Some of these older works include Edward W. Tullidge, *The Life of Joseph the Prophet* (Plano, Ill.: Herald Publishing House, 1880), which contains not only a lengthy summation of the history of the Reorganization but also a candid autobiography of Joseph Smith III; Vida E. Smith, *The Young People's History of the Church,* 2 vols. (Lamoni, Iowa: Herald Publishing House, 1918); Inez Smith Davis, *The Story of the Church* (Independence, Mo.: Herald Publishing House, 1976), which has gone through ten editions since first appearing in 1934; and Georgia Metcalf Stewart, *How the Church Grew* (Independence, Mo.: Herald Publishing House, 1959).

Since the advent of the "New Mormon History" in the 1960s, literally hundreds of books and articles have appeared that have informed this study in one way or another. I have enumerated many of them in the chapter notes and will refrain from doing so here. Increasingly, publishers of note have been willing to issue book-length studies on Mormon history. The result has been an outpouring of stimulating monographic literature. Moreover, many periodicals—most importantly the *Journal of Mormon History; Dialogue: A Journal of Mormon Thought; Brigham Young University Studies;* the *John Whitmer Historical Association Journal;* the *Utah Historical Quarterly; Sunstone;* the now defunct *Courage: A Journal of History, Thought, and Action; Restoration;* and *Restoration Studies*—have specialized in publishing worthy articles on this subject.

Index